Lecture Notes in Computer Science 5261

Commenced Publication in 1973
Founding and Former Series Editors:
Gerhard Goos, Juris Hartmanis, and Jan van Leeuwen

T0224098

Nigel Thomas   Carlos Juiz (Eds.)

Computer Performance Engineering

5th European Performance Engineering Workshop, EPEW 2008
Palma de Mallorca, Spain, September 24-25, 2008
Proceedings

 Springer

Volume Editors

Nigel Thomas
Newcastle University
School of Computing Science
Newcastle upon Tyne, NE1 7RU, UK
E-mail: nigel.thomas@ncl.ac.uk

Carlos Juiz
Universitat de les Illes Balears
Departament de Ciències Matemàtiques i Informàtica
07122 Palma de Mallorca, Spain
E-mail: cjuiz@uib.es

Library of Congress Control Number: 2008935032

CR Subject Classification (1998): C.4, D.4, H.3.4, D.2

LNCS Sublibrary: SL 2 – Programming and Software Engineering

ISSN 0302-9743
ISBN 978-3-540-87411-9 Springer Berlin Heidelberg New York

Springer is a part of Springer Science+Business Media

springer.com

© Springer-Verlag Berlin Heidelberg 2008

Typesetting: Camera-ready by author, data conversion by Scientific Publishing Services, Chennai, India
Printed on acid-free paper   SPIN: 12522019   06/3180   5 4 3 2 1 0

Preface

This volume of LNCS contains papers presented at the 5th European Performance Engineering Workshop held in Palma de Mallorca during September 24–25, 2008.

The workshop is truly international; the European part of the title refers only to its location. Papers were submitted from Asia, North and South America, although the majority were from Europe. In all, 39 papers were submitted from which 16 were chosen following peer review. Every member of the Programme Committee was responsible for reviewing at least five papers each in a little over two weeks; a degree of dedication without which the workshop could not be a success. The selection criteria were harsh and by necessity several excellent papers were rejected. However, the result is a programme of the highest quality.

The accepted papers reflect the diversity of modern performance engineering. There were a number of papers presented which tackled theoretical modelling issues in stochastic process algebra, stochastic activity networks, queueing theory and the analysis of Markov chains. Other papers addressed practical problems in communications networks, embedded systems and resource allocation. For the first time at EPEW there was a paper concerning the evaluation of trust. There was also a session on software performance engineering, showing the continued importance of this area within the wider performance community.

We were delighted to have keynote presentations from Boudewijn Haverkort of Twente University and Stephen Gilmore of the University of Edinburgh. These talks reflected the state of performance engineering today. Professor Haverkort presented a personal perspective on 20 years of performance engineering. Dr. Gilmore presented an overview of recent developments in fluid modelling using stochastic process algebra; a powerful approach for modelling large-scale problems in computing and biochemistry.

As Programme Co-chairs we would like to thank everyone involved in making EPEW 2008 a success: Springer for their continued support of the workshop series, the local Organizing Committee, the Programme Committee and reviewers, and of course the authors of the papers submitted, without whom there could not be a workshop. We thrust that you, the reader, find the papers in this volume interesting, useful and inspiring, and we hope to see you at future European Performance Engineering Workshops.

July 2008   Nigel Thomas
                                                                                Carlos Juiz

Organization

Organizing Committee

General Chair	Ramón Puigjaner (University of the Balearic Islands, Spain)
Workshop Chairs	Nigel Thomas (Newcastle University, UK)
	Carlos Juiz (University of the Balearic Islands, Spain)
Local Arrangements:	Bartomeu Serra
	Pere P. Sancho
	Isaac Lera
	Carlos Guerrero
	Mehdi Khouja

Programme Committee

Jeremy Bradley	Imperial College London, UK
Mario Bravetti	Università di Bologna, Italy
Lucy Cherkasova	HP Labs, USA
Lucia Cloth	University of Twente, The Netherlands
Michel Cukier	University of Maryland, USA
Tadeusz Czachórski	Polish Academy of Sciences, Gliwice, Poland
Jean-Michel Fourneau	Université de Versailles, France
Stephen Gilmore	University of Edinburgh, UK
Armin Heindl	Universität Erlangen-Nürnberg, Germany
Helmut Hlavacs	University of Vienna, Austria
András Horváth	Università di Torino, Italy
Carlos Juiz	Universitat de les Illes Balears, Spain
Tomáš Kalibera	Purdue University, USA
Helen Karatza	Aristotle University of Thessaloniki, Greece
Leïla Kloul	Université de Versailles, France
Samuel Kounev	Cambridge University, UK
Fernando López Pelayo	University Castilla-La Mancha, Spain
Aad van Moorsel	Newcastle University, UK
Manuel Núñez Garcia	Universidad Complutense de Madrid, Spain
Ramón Puigjaner	Universitat de les Illes Balears, Spain
Marina Ribaudo	University of Genova, Italy
Marco Scarpa	Universitá di Messina, Italy
Markus Siegle	Universität der Bundeswehr München Germany
Mark Squillante	IBM T.J. Watson Research Center, NY, USA

Ann Tai   IA Tech Inc., USA
Miklós Telek   Budapest University of Technology and
                             Economics, Hungary
Nigel Thomas   Newcastle University, UK
Sabine Wittevrongel   Universiteit Gent, Belgium
Katinka Wolter   Humboldt Universität zu Berlin, Germany

Additional Referees

César Andrés	Mercedes Merayo
Fernando Cuartero	Antonio Puliafito
Stijn De Vuyst	Carmelo Ragusa
Gregorio Díaz	Martin Riedl
Katja Gilly	Pere P. Sancho
Carlos Guerrero	Johann Schuster
Richard Hayden	Giuseppe Scionti
Jane Hillston	Michael Smith
Mehdi Khouja	Bart Steyaert
Matthias Kuntz	Maria Vigliotti
Isaac Lera	Joris Walraevens
Francesco Longo	Johannes Zapotoczky

Table of Contents

Performance Query Specification and Measurement

Computer and Communications Networks

Queueing Theory and Markov Chains

Applications

Performance and Dependability Evaluation: Successes, Failures and Challenges

Boudewijn R. Haverkort

University of Twente,
Centre for Telematics and Information Technology,
Faculty for Electrical Engineering, Mathematics and Computer Science,
P.O. Box 217, 7500 AE Enschede, Netherlands
http://dacs.cs.utwente.nl/

Abstract. Over the last 40 years, the field of model-based performance and dependability evaluation has seen important developments, successes and scientific breakthroughs. However, the field has not matured into a key engineering discipline which is heavily called upon by computer system and software engineers, even though it is well-known that already the use of simple analytical models can result in better insight in system performance. In the area of communication system design, performance evaluation has become more of a mainstream activity, albeit almost exclusively using discrete-event simulation techniques.

What circumstances made that almost all of our excellent work on analytical performance and dependability evaluation did not find the acceptance and use we think it deserves?

On the basis of an historical account of the major developments in the area over the last 40 years, I will address probable reasons for the relatively moderate success and acceptance of model-based performance and dependability evaluation. What did we do right, what did we do wrong? Which circumstances led to successes, and where did we fail?

Based on the gathered insights, I will discuss upcoming challenges for the field and recommend research directions for the decade to come.

Keywords: Dependability evaluation, performance evaluation, Markov chains, model checking, scalability, security, verification.

N. Thomas and C. Juiz (Eds.): EPEW 2008, LNCS 5261, p. 1, 2008.

Partial Evaluation of PEPA Models for Fluid-Flow Analysis

Allan Clark, Adam Duguid, Stephen Gilmore, and Mirco Tribastone

LFCS, University of Edinburgh

Abstract. We present an application of *partial evaluation* to performance models expressed in the PEPA stochastic process algebra [1]. We partially evaluate the state-space of a PEPA model in order to remove uses of the cooperation and hiding operators and compile an arbitrary sub-model into a single sequential component. This transformation is applied to PEPA models which are not in the correct form for the application of the fluid-flow analysis for PEPA [2]. The result of the transformation is a PEPA model which is amenable to fluid-flow analysis but which is *strongly equivalent* [1] to the input PEPA model and so, by an application of Hillston's theorem, performance results computed from one model are valid for the other. We apply the method to a Markovian model of a key distribution centre used to facilitate secure distribution of cryptographic session keys between remote principals communicating over an insecure network.

1   Introduction

Fluid-flow approximation of PEPA models [2] enables the numerical analysis of models of vast scale using ordinary differential equations (ODEs). The model sizes which can be analysed using transformation into an ODE representation pass effortlessly beyond the maximum attainable using exact discrete-state representations such as continuous-time Markov chains. However, fluid-flow analysis is applicable to PEPA models in a particular form where the model is structured as the cooperation of replicated copies of sequential components. For example, if P, Q and R are sequential PEPA components available in M, N and O replications and $\mathcal{K}$ and $\mathcal{L}$ are cooperation sets then the model

$$P[M] \underset{\mathcal{K}}{\bowtie} \left(Q[N] \underset{\mathcal{L}}{\bowtie} R[O] \right)$$

is immediately suitable for fluid-flow analysis but the model

$$P[M] \underset{\mathcal{K}}{\bowtie} \left((Q \underset{\mathcal{L}}{\bowtie} R)[N] \right)$$

is not, because of the use of the cooperation operator ($\bowtie$) nested inside the array of N replications. We use partial evaluation to transform the unsuitable model into an equivalent model of the form:

$$P[M] \underset{\mathcal{K}}{\bowtie} QR[N]$$

N. Thomas and C. Juiz (Eds.): EPEW 2008, LNCS 5261, pp. 2–16, 2008.

The new model has a new sequential component QR which exactly respects the interaction between the original Q and R. The new sequential component is generated in such a way that we can recover the states of Q and R from the state of QR. The transformation can be applied compositionally to a model to generate an equivalent which is suitable for fluid-flow analysis without generating the full state-space of the original model. Specifically, the cost of the transformation depends only on the form of the components Q and R and does not depend on the values of M or N.

The original contributions of the present paper are the following.

1. We present a novel application of Hillston's theorem to the partial evaluation of a PEPA model. The theorem [1] guarantees that the strong equivalence relation of PEPA is a congruence for the PEPA process algebra and thus the partially evaluated model is equivalent to the original.
2. We present four styles of analysis of the same model three of which allow the analysis at large scales. The model analysed represents the Needham-Schroeder-Lowe protocol. We compare the performance results obtained using all four analysis methods.

2 Case Study: Key Distribution Centres

Key distribution centres enable secure communication between remote principals across an insecure network. The distribution centre acts as a trusted third party, allowing users to register a key with the centre and use a robust cryptographic protocol to establish a secure communication between two principals who have no previous communication history and no secure shared communications channels.

One possible candidate for the chosen cryptographic protocol is the Needham-Schroeder-Lowe protocol [3] which hardens the Needham-Schroeder protocol [4] against replay attacks. The goal of the protocol is to enable secure communication between Alice and Bob. The protocol has five steps, which we describe informally first.

- Alice sends a message to the server requesting a session with Bob.
- The server generates a new session key K_{AB}, encrypted under Alice's registered key, K_{AS}, together with a copy encrypted for Bob.
- Alice forwards the copy on to Bob, who can decrypt it.
- Bob sends a random number (a *nonce*) to Alice, encrypted under the session key.
- Alice makes a small change to the nonce and sends it back to Bob.

The traditional representation of such a protocol is as a narration, setting out more methodically the information presented above. In the notation used below $X \to Y$ denotes a communication from X to Y, $x_1, \ldots, x_n$ denotes a tuple of n values and $\{x_1, \ldots, x_n\}_K$ denotes a tuple of n values encrypted under the cryptographic key K.

$(request)$ 1. $A \to S : A, B, N_A$
$(response)$ 2. $S \to A : \{N_A, K_{AB}, B, \{K_{AB}, A\}_{K_{BS}}\}_{K_{AS}}$
$(sendBob)$ 3. $A \to B : \{K_{AB}, A\}_{K_{BS}}$
$(sendAlice)$ 4. $B \to A : \{N_{AB}\}_{K_{AB}}$
$(confirm)$ 5. $A \to B : \{N_{AB} - 1\}_{K_{AB}}$

After these five steps are complete Alice and Bob can use the key in a secure session ($usekey$).

A representation of the protocol such as this is adequate for the analysis of the correctness of function of the protocol using a logic such as the BAN logic [5] but it is not suitable for performance analysis. Time is abstracted away in the model above, as it is in classical process algebras. In a *stochastic* process algebra such as PEPA [1] the communication events and the encryption steps have an expected average duration. Performance results such as response time and utilisation can be calculated from a PEPA model of a key distribution centre, as shown in [6] and [7]. Conversely, data is abstracted away in the PEPA model and so it is not suitable for correctness analysis[1].

A PEPA model of a key distribution centre such as the one shown in Figure 1 can be used to produce a finite discrete-state representation of the system with quantified durations associated to each activity.

$$KDC \stackrel{def}{=} (request, r_q).KDC + (response, r_p).KDC$$

$$Alice \stackrel{def}{=} (request, r_q).(response, r_p).Alice_1$$
$$Alice_1 \stackrel{def}{=} (sendBob, r_B).Alice_2$$
$$Alice_2 \stackrel{def}{=} (sendAlice, \infty).(confirm, r_c).Alice_3$$
$$Alice_3 \stackrel{def}{=} (usekey, r_u).Alice$$

$$Bob \stackrel{def}{=} (sendBob, \infty).Bob_1$$
$$Bob_1 \stackrel{def}{=} (sendAlice, r_A).(confirm, \infty).Bob_2$$
$$Bob_2 \stackrel{def}{=} (usekey, \infty).Bob$$

$$System \stackrel{def}{=} KDC \underset{\mathcal{L}}{\bowtie} \Big((Alice \underset{\mathcal{M}}{\bowtie} Bob)[N] \Big)$$

where $\mathcal{L} = \{\ request, response\ \}$
$\mathcal{M} = \{\ sendBob, sendAlice, confirm, usekey\ \}$

Fig. 1. PEPA model of the Key Distribution Centre presented in [6]

The derivation graph underlying this PEPA model can be converted into a Continuous-Time Markov Chain (CTMC) which can be readily solved to find the steady-state distribution over all of the reachable states of the model [8] or analysed to determine transient probability distributions and response-time profiles [9].

---

[1] The original Needham-Schroeder protocol and the modified Needham-Schroeder-Lowe protocol would have the same representation in PEPA.

Exact discrete-state models of complex systems face the well-known problem of state-space explosion where, as the complexity of the system under study increases, there is an exponential growth in the state-space of the underlying model. Out-of-core [10] and disk-based solution methods [11] allow modellers to tolerate very large state-spaces but at the cost of greater and greater numerical solution times.

As the number of paired principals (N) in the PEPA model increases the machine representation of the probability distribution requires more and more storage and longer and longer computation times to calculate. The size of the state space of the Markovian model is 6^N which grows very rapidly with N. Fortunately we have available in the PEPA Eclipse Plug-in an implementation of the state-space aggregation algorithm for PEPA [12] which allows us to better cope with increases in N. The state-space sizes before and after aggregation are shown in Table 1.

Table 1. Full and aggregated statespace sizes as calculated by the PEPA Eclipse Plugin [8]

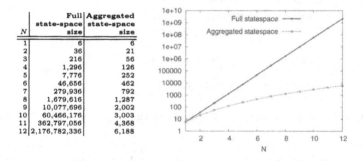

N	Full state-space size	Aggregated state-space size
1	6	6
2	36	21
3	216	56
4	1,296	126
5	7,776	252
6	46,656	462
7	279,936	792
8	1,679,616	1,287
9	10,077,696	2,002
10	60,466,176	3,003
11	362,797,056	4,368
12	2,176,782,336	6,188

Use of the aggregation algorithm allows us to tolerate larger state-spaces but this too will reach a limit and at that point we will need to rely on other techniques to analyse the model. In this paper we make use of three techniques; fluid-flow analysis, stochastic simulation and reduction to a closed queueing network, to allow us to continue to analyse the model past the limit on the number of clients imposed by the state-space explosion problem on the CTMC analysis. For two of the techniques the model must first be partially evaluated and this is discussed in the next section. Following this we detail the analysis by each method.

3 Partial Evaluation

Our model of the key distribution centre shown in Figure 1 exhibits synchronisation nested within an array and is thus in its present form unsuitable for fluid-flow analysis. However we can apply the partial evaluation technique described in the introduction transforming the synchronisation: $(Alice \bowtie_{\mathcal{M}} Bob)$ into an equivalent component: $AliceBob$.

This is achieved by considering this synchronisation as an entire model and deriving the entire state-space of this smaller model. Deriving the entire state-space of this synchronisation transforms multiple (in this case two) synchronised components into a single sequential component. The number of states in the new sequential component depends only on the form and synchronised activies of the involved components and not on any part of the larger model containing the original cooperation. In particular if the synchronisation occurs nested within an array – as is the case with our model – the partial evalation is the same regardless of the size of the array.

$$KDC \stackrel{def}{=} (request, r_q).KDC + (response, r_p).KDC$$

$$AliceBob \stackrel{def}{=} (request, r_q).AliceBob_1$$
$$AliceBob_1 \stackrel{def}{=} (response, r_p).AliceBob_2$$
$$AliceBob_2 \stackrel{def}{=} (sendBob, r_B).AliceBob_3$$
$$AliceBob_3 \stackrel{def}{=} (sendAlice, r_A).AliceBob_4$$
$$AliceBob_4 \stackrel{def}{=} (confirm, r_c).AliceBob_5$$
$$AliceBob_5 \stackrel{def}{=} (usekey, r_u).AliceBob$$

$$System \stackrel{def}{=} KDC \bowtie_{\mathcal{L}} AliceBob[N]$$

$$\text{where } \mathcal{L} = \{\, request, response \,\}$$

Fig. 2. Partially evaluated PEPA model of the Key Distribution Centre

When we apply partial evaluation to the PEPA model shown in Figure 1 we obtain the model in Figure 2. There is a one-to-one correspondence between the states of the original synchronised components $(Alice \bowtie_{\mathcal{M}} Bob)$ and the sequential component $AliceBob$ as indicated in Table 2. In turn there is a one-to-one correspondence between the states of the original PEPA model and the states of the partially-evaluated PEPA model.

Table 2. Bisimilar states in the original and partially-evaluated PEPA models

Original PEPA model		Partially-evaluated PEPA model
$Alice$	Bob	$AliceBob$
$(response, r_p).Alice_1$	Bob	$AliceBob_1$
$Alice_1$	Bob_1	$AliceBob_2$
$Alice_2$	Bob_1	$AliceBob_3$
$(confirm, r_c).Alice_3$	$(confirm, \infty).Bob_2$	$AliceBob_4$
$Alice_3$	Bob_2	$AliceBob_5$

4 Analysis

After the partial evaluation of the key distribution centre PEPA model we have four distinct forms of analysis which we may apply:

1. exact discrete-state analysis by solving the underlying continuous-time Markov chain;
2. manually reduce and approximate the model to a closed queueing system as is done in [6];
3. approximate discrete-state analysis by stochastic simulation of the underlying continuous-time Markov chain; and
4. approximate continuous-state analysis by numerical integration of the underlying fluid-flow differential equations.

We perform each of these in turn on the model of the key distribution centre.

4.1 Markovian Analysis

The first programme of analysis which we undertake is to examine the probability density function (pdf) and cumulative density function (cdf) for a passage through the system behaviour. For this analysis we have used the International PEPA Compiler (ipc) [9] tool suite.

The measurement which we make is from the end of an occurrence of the *request* activity to the end of a *confirm* activity. This measures the time it takes to restart a session and gives us our notion of response time for this system. Note though that in this passage only the *response* activity cooperates with the server the other activities are performed within a single *AliceBob* component and hence the delay from these activities is unaffected by the number of clients in the system. This is an important performance metric since sessions may need to be restarted frequently. This is necessary because after a period of continued use a session key should not be considered safe due to too many ciphertexts being available to an attacker.

We vary the rate r_u (the rate of the *usekey* activity). This essentially varies the duration of a session (*usekey* is the session). We are measuring between the *request* and *confirm* activities as performed by only the *first* Alice/Bob pairing because otherwise we have essentially a meaningless measurement. The ability to isolate and probe a particular Alice/Bob pair is given to us by the use of *location-aware* stochastic probes [13]. The results are shown in Figure 3.

Because we are using the full numerical solution technique we are limited in the number of clients that may participate in the model. Because of the low number of clients the centre is able to cope with demand very well and varying the rate at which keys are used – and therefore the rate at which requests arrive – does not have a significant impact on the passage of interest. This further motivates us to apply large state-space size analysis techniques.

The numerical solution of the underlying Markov chain has allowed us to obtain response-time quantiles. However we can also use the Markov chain to compute the steady-state probability distribution, i.e. the long-term probability

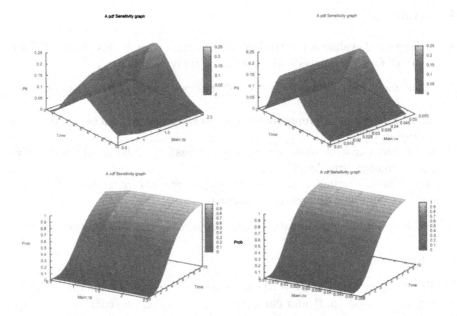

Fig. 3. The top two graphs depict the probability density function (pdf) and the bottom two graphs the cumulative density function (cdf) of the passage from *usekey* to *confirm* for a particular Alice/Bob pair. In the graphs on the left we vary the rate at which the server responds while in the graphs on the right we vary the rate at which session keys are consumed and hence the rate at which requests arrive at the server.

of being in each state. This information allows us to compute throughput and utilisation which for this model will give us the average number of clients waiting to be processed by the server and the average response-time. The results are computed using the PEPA Eclipse Plug-in [8] and are shown together in comparison to the same measures as computed using the other three analysis techniques in Section 4.3.

4.2   Analytical Solution

We have seen that it is possible to transform the original model into one suitable for analysis using ordinary differential equations and stochastic simulation while being certain that we are analysing an equivalent model. Another technique is to continue simplifying the model until we have one which may be solved analytically. We may lose the exact correspondence between the original model and simplified model however if we are careful in our transformations we may still relate the performance measurements obtained from the simplified model to the original model.

In the case of the key distribution centre it is possible to reduce the model to that of a simple closed queueing system. This simpler model has one queue station representing the key distribution centre and each client performing an

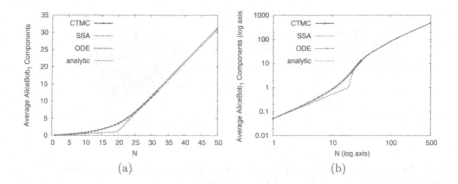

Fig. 4. The average number of AliceBob1 components varied as the number of client pairs (N) is increased, using all of the separate analysis techniques

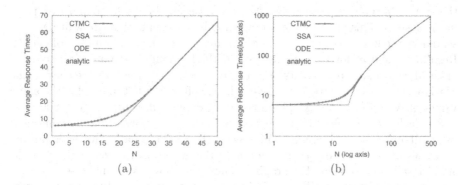

Fig. 5. The average response times measured as the number of clients is increased

exponential delay after being serviced before returning to the queue. This technique is described in detail in [6]. This represents only an approximate solution because in the original model each client pair performs a sequence of activities before returning to the queue. This sequence of (exponentially delayed) activities will give rise to an Erlang distributed delay.

From this closed queueing system we can compute the average number of clients waiting in the queue and from this the average response time. As mentioned above these results are shown for all analysis techniques in Section 4.3.

4.3   Simulation and Fluid-Flow Analysis

The work in the early part of this paper was concerned with transforming the PEPA model of the key distribution centre into a form which was suitable for ODE analysis. We reap the benefits of this work here because we can efficiently compute mean trajectories through the model state space for large-scale models.

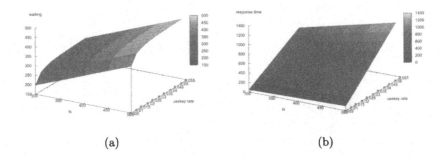

(a)   (b)

Fig. 6. The sensitivity at varying values of N of the rate of key consumption (the rate of the *usekey* activity) as measured by the ODE analysis

In this section we perform those analyses with the partially-evaluated model. The graphs in Figure 4 show the average number of $AliceBob_1$ components in the system varying as we increase N – the total number of Alice and Bob pairs in the system. This gives us the average number of clients that are waiting to be served by the key distribution center as a function of the total number of clients. Results are shown for all four analysis methods though the numerical solution via a Markov chain has results only up to $N = 32$, the limit before solving the Markov chain becomes too expensive. The graph on the left highlights the small values of $N \leq 50$ and the graph on the right depicts all values of $N \leq 500$.

Similarly the graphs in Figure 5 show average response-time as computed using all four analysis methods. Once again the Markov chain solution is limited to values of $N \leq 32$ and correspondingly the graph on the left highlights the smaller values of N while the graph on the right allows N to increase to 500.

Encouragingly we see that as N increases the agreement between the measurements improves. At very small values of N the ODE differs from the other

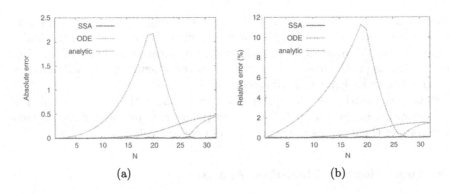

(a)   (b)

Fig. 7. Each graph plots the difference in measured average number of waiting clients for the given analysis method against the Markov chain solution as the number of clients N is increased. The graph on the left (a) depicts the absolute error while the graph on the right (b) depicts the error relative to the number of clients.

methods, whilst the queueing method, stochastic simulation and Markov chain method continue to show good agreement for all measured values of N. This provides us with confidence that the stochastic simulation analysis is providing accurate results and hence we use this to compare how well our ODE analysis is performing at large values of N where it is not possible to compare with the Markov chain solution. We are also pleased to note that the queueing and ODE methods begin to show agreement with the Markov chain solution (and therfore also the simulation results) before the limit of the Markov chain solution. In the following section we give a more detailed comparison of the results.

Sensitivity Analysis. Recall from Section 4.1 that we performed sensitivity analysis for small values of N using the Markovian solution method of analysis. We found that varying the rate at which the server responds affects the response time as one would expect. However varying the rate at which keys are consumed – and therefore the rate at which requests arrive at the server – did not significantly affect the response time. We reasoned that this was because N was so low that whenever a client made a request there was very likely to be no other clients already waiting in the queue even as we increased the rate of key consumption. To achieve any noticable effect the rate that the clients use the key must be set unrealistically high.

We have repeated this sensitivity analysis at higher levels of N in order to understand the influence of varying the rate of key consumption. The graphs in figure Figure 6 show the effect that varying this rate has on the number of clients waiting (left) and the response time (right). Here we can see a significant effect caused by changing the rate at which requests arrive at the server. Having done this we can conclude that although the Markovian solution allows for very accurate results, if the number of clients is unrealistically low, any conclusion obtained from sensitivity analysis of the Markovian method cannot be assumed to apply at larger values of N. Thus our analysis using ordinary differential equations and stochastic simulation is a necessary endeavour.

5   Comparison

In the previous section we compared the results from the four methods of analysis, noting disagreement at low values of N ($N <\approx 25$) between the ODE analysis and other methods. For higher values of N the data indicated better agreement over all four methods. In this section we look closer at the differences between the different analyses.

Taking the Markovian analysis as our yardstick we can compare how well the other three analysis methods perform for values of $N \leq 32$. The graphs in Figure 7 show the error in the measured average number of waiting clients. The graphs in Figure 8 show the error as compared with the Markovian solution in the measured response time. In both sets of graphs we depict in the left graph the absolute error, as the difference between the given analysis method and Markovian solution, while in the right hand graph this value is given relative to

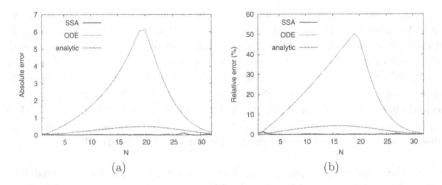

Fig. 8. Each graph plots the difference in measured response time for the given analysis method against the Markov chain solution as the number of clients N is increased. The graph on the left (a) depicts the absolute error while the graph on the right (b) depicts the error relative to the response-time as calculated using the Markov chain solution.

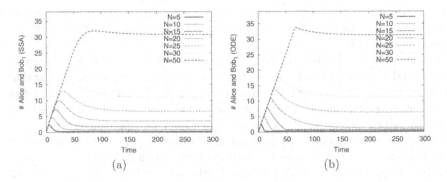

Fig. 9. Time-series data for SSA and ODE, graph (a) and (b) respectively, for various values of N

the number of clients in the system. This is because, particularly in the case of average number of clients waiting, an error of 5 is more significant when there are only 15 clients in the system as when there are over 100. In the case of the response-time error normalising by the number of clients does not make sense so we instead divide the error by the response-time as calculated by the Markov chain solution.

The disagreement seen in Figures 4 and 5 can clearly be seen here, peaking at approximately 12% around $N = 20$ for the ODE analysis. The SSA analysis shows very good agreement with the CTMC, shown by a maximum error of 0.1% for $N = 1 \ldots 32$. What the previous graphs failed to show was the minor, but increasing error between the CTMC and analytical analysis. What is unclear from Figure 7 is whether the error between the CTMC and analytical approaches has peaked or not. If we assume the level of error between CTMC and SSA were to remain constant, as we did in Section 4.3, then we can be confident comparing

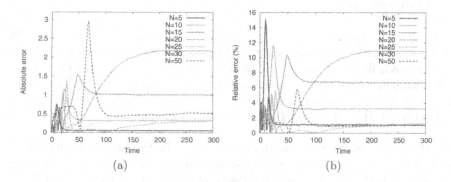

Fig. 10. Graphs for absolute error (a) and relative error (b) for $N = 5 \ldots 50$

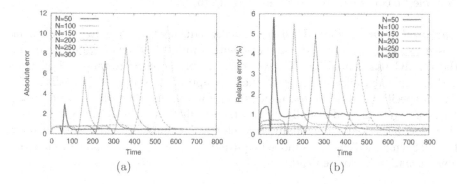

Fig. 11. Graphs for absolute error (a) and relative error (b) for $N = 50 \ldots 300$

the SSA and the analytical method. This comparison shows an error of no more than 1.4% for $N = 1 \ldots 500$. Looking at response times (Figure 8) we see that for lower values of N the error can be as high as 50% and a peak of 4.5% for the analytical method.

So far comparison has been at steady-state; however SSA and ODE analysis both allow comparison for any value of t. Figure 9 shows the time-series data for the number of waiting clients ($AliceBob_1$), and Figure 10 the absolute and relative error for $N = 5 \ldots 50$. Figure 11 shows the absolute and relative error for $N = 50 \ldots 300$.

What is clear from these graphs is that the reported error for the steady-state is not the peak error seen. From Figure 7 we could see an error of approximately 12% when $N \approx 20$, whereas the peak value seen from this sample of N is closer to 15% when $N = 5$. Figure 11 shows that the peak error observed decreases as N increases, showing a peak error of approximately 3.5% for $N = 300$, and a steady-state error of 0.2%. If the graph was extended to show $N = 500$ the peak error seen would be approximately 3% and a steady-state error of less than 0.1%.

6 Conclusions

By applying partial evaluation of the Markovian state-space of a PEPA model we have been able to transform a model unsuitable for fluid-flow analysis into one for which fluid-flow analysis is immediately applicable. Fluid-flow analysis allows us to examine the dynamics of models of large-scale at low computational cost. This has provided us with four possible analysis methods for this model each with a distinct set of advantages and disadvantages:

CTMC. Compiling the model to the CTMC allows for the most detailed analysis of the model. We can obtain passage-time quantiles which none of the other analysis methods yet support. The disadvantage though is clear - the CTMC representation suffers from the well known state-space explosion problem. We can mitigate this to some degree using state-space aggregation. In this particular example we could cope with values of N up to 32.

Analytical Approximation. By first manually reducing the model to an equivalent closed queueing network we can cope with values of N much larger than for the CTMC based analysis. We can comfortably cope with values of N over a thousand. The disadvantage of such an approach is that it is available to only a specific kind of model, namely those which may be reduced to a closed queueing system. Additionally such a transformation is model dependent and therefore must be done manually. In each case the modeller must work to show that the simplified model is indeed equivalent to the original model or that the approximation is close enough.

Simulation. We can use stochastic simulation to analyse our model. This again allows us to cope with larger state space sizes. The drawback in this case is that our results will only ever be an approximation to the true results. As our accuracy requirements increase so do the number of simulations which must be run and thus the computation time.

Fluid-flow. The approach we have used in this paper is to partially-evaluate the model into a form suitable for translation into ordinary differential equations. This has similar advantages to the reduction to a closed queueing network. However the partial evaluation of the parallel sub-components is a well defined transformation which may be automated. Moreover all partially-evaluated models are known to be equivalent to their original models. The disadvantage of this approach is that for the solution to the ODEs to be accurate we require a large number of components. That is the model cannot be used for small values of N. This is in direct contrast to the CTMC method which can be used effectively for small values of N but cannot cope with larger values of N.

We believe that the combination of CTMC analysis for small values of N and ODE analysis – via partial evaluation of parallel sub-components where required – forms an important partnership in the analysis of large scale parallel models. The CTMC analysis can be used not only for analysis for small values of N

where the ODE analysis is inappropriate but also to gain greater insight into the properties of the model since the CTMC analysis permits such analyses as the computation of passage-time quantiles. Meanwhile analysis for large values of N can be obtained through fluid-flow analysis.

In doing such a combination of analyses the modeller will likely look for the crossover point. The crossover point is the value of N at which the ODE analysis agrees with the CTMC analysis. In general we would like this value to be lower than the upper bound on N for the CTMC analysis. Otherwise the modeller must guess at the crossover point though stochastic simulation can be used to provide some assurance. Through our use of aggregation of the state-space of the model we are hopeful that many models fall into the former category.

Acknowledgements: This work has been partially sponsored by the project SEN-SORIA, IST-2005-016004.

References

1. Hillston, J.: A Compositional Approach to Performance Modelling. Cambridge University Press, Cambridge (1996)
2. Hillston, J.: Fluid flow approximation of PEPA models. In: Proceedings of the Second International Conference on the Quantitative Evaluation of Systems, Torino, Italy, September 2005, pp. 33–43. IEEE Computer Society Press, Los Alamitos (2005)
3. Lowe, G.: An attack on the Needham-Schroeder public key authentication protocol. Information Processing Letters 56(3), 131–136 (1995)
4. Needham, R., Schroeder, M.: Using encryption for authentication in large networks of computers. Communications of the ACM 21(12), 993–999 (1978)
5. Burrows, M., Abadi, M., Needham, R.M.: A logic of authentication. ACM Transactions on Computing Systems 8(1), 18–36 (1990)
6. Zhao, Y., Thomas, N.: Approximate solution of a PEPA model of a key distribution centre. In: Kounev, S., Gorton, I., Sachs, K. (eds.) SIPEW 2008. LNCS, vol. 5119, pp. 44–57. Springer, Heidelberg (2008)
7. Zhao, Y., Thomas, N.: Fluid flow analysis of a model of a secure key distribution centre. In: Argent-Katwala, A., Dingle, N.J., Harder, U. (eds.) Proceedings of the 24th UK Performance Engineering Workshop, July 2008, pp. 160–171. Imperial College London (2008)
8. Tribastone, M.: The PEPA Plug-in Project. In: Harchol-Balter, M., Kwiatkowska, M., Telek, M. (eds.) Proceedings of the 4th International Conference on the Quantitative Evaluation of SysTems (QEST), September 2007, pp. 53–54. IEEE, Los Alamitos (2007)
9. Clark, A.: The ipclib PEPA Library. In: Harchol-Balter, M., Kwiatkowska, M., Telek, M. (eds.) Proceedings of the 4th International Conference on the Quantitative Evaluation of SysTems (QEST), September 2007, pp. 55–56. IEEE, Los Alamitos (2007)
10. Kwiatkowska, M., Mehmood, R., Norman, G., Parker, D.: A symbolic out-of-core solution method for Markov models. In: Proc. Workshop on Parallel and Distributed Model Checking (PDMC 2002). Electronic Notes in Theoretical Computer Science, vol. 68.4. Elsevier, Amsterdam (2002)

11. Knottenbelt, W.J., Harrison, P.G.: Distributed disk-based solution techniques for large Markov models. In: Proc. 3rd International Workshop on the Numerical Solution of Markov Chains (NSMC 1999), Zaragoza, Spain, September 1999, pp. 58–75 (1999)
12. Gilmore, S., Hillston, J., Ribaudo, M.: An efficient algorithm for aggregating PEPA models. IEEE Transactions on Software Engineering 27(5), 449–464 (2001)
13. Argent-Katwala, A., Bradley, J., Clark, A., Gilmore, S.: Location-aware quality of service measurements for service-level agreements. In: Barthe, G., Fournet, C. (eds.) TGC 2007. LNCS, vol. 4912, pp. 222–239. Springer, Heidelberg (2008)

An Empirical Investigation of the Applicability of a Component-Based Performance Prediction Method

Anne Martens[1], Steffen Becker[2], Heiko Koziolek[3], and Ralf Reussner[1]

[1] Chair for Software Design and Quality
Am Fasanengarten 5, University of Karlsruhe (TH), 76131 Karlsruhe, Germany
[2] FZI Forschungszentrum Informatik
Haid-und-Neu-Straße 10-14, 76131 Karlsruhe, Germany
[3] ABB Corporate Research, Wallstadter Str. 59, 68526 Ladenburg, Germany
{martens,sbecker,koziolek,reussner}@ipd.uka.de

Abstract. Component-based software performance engineering (CBSPE) methods shall enable software architects to assess the expected response times, throughputs, and resource utilization of their systems already during design. This avoids the violation of performance requirements. Existing approaches for CBSPE either lack tool support or rely on prototypical tools, who have only been applied by their authors. Therefore, industrial applicability of these methods is unknown. On this behalf, we have conducted a controlled experiment involving 19 computer science students, who analysed the performance of two component-based designs using our Palladio performance prediction approach, as an example for a CBSPE method. Our study is the first of its type in this area and shall help to mature CBSPE to industrial applicability. In this paper, we report on results concerning the prediction accuracy achieved by the students and list several lessons learned, which are also relevant for other methods than Palladio.

Keywords: Performance Prediction, Empirical Study, Controlled Experiment.

1   Introduction

A benefit of component-based development is the possibility to reason on properties of the complete systems based on component specifications supplied by individual component developers. With this approach, it is possible for software architects to assess the functional and extra-functional (e.g., performance, reliability) properties of a component-based system during early development stages. To do so, software architects combine component specifications to form architecture specifications. The specifications are design models (e.g. in UML) annotated with performance properties. After modelling the architecture, software architects can check performance predictions from tools analysing the architecture specifications against their requirements. This may avoid implementing designs with poor extra-functional properties and prevent subsequent costs for restructuring an implementation after detecting design-related flaws.

Researchers have developed several methods in this context, which aim at performance (i.e., response times, throughput, resource utilisation) predictions for component-based designs [4]. However, there are few real-life case studies involving

N. Thomas and C. Juiz (Eds.): EPEW 2008, LNCS 5261, pp. 17–31, 2008.

these compo-nent-based methods, which still lack industrial maturity. Several methods (e.g., [8,10,20]) simply lack tool support, while other methods (e.g., [5,6,7,23]) rely on prototypical implementations, which only have been used by their authors and require specialist knowledge. Therefore, their applicability in an industrial setting involving typical developers is unknown. Further methods for component-based performance analysis are outside the scope of this paper as they are measurement-based (i.e. predictions are based on observation of the implemented system's performance) and do not target early design stages, and also do not involve reusable component performance specifications (e.g., [13,15]).

To investigate the applicability, we conducted a controlled experiment with 19 computer science students, who analysed the performance of two different component-based designs using the Palladio method [4] as an example for a CBSPE method. We also let the students apply the well-known SPE method [21], which is not specific for component-based systems, on the same designs and compared the results. The study involved training the students in the methods and the accompanying tools as well as designing several architectural design alternatives for the analysed systems, which the students evaluated for their performance properties.

In a former paper [17], we reported on results concerning the effort needed by the students to model and analyse the system. We found that the effort was less than twice as high as for a method without reusable, component-based performance specifications (i.e., the SPE method). Therefore, the effort of creating a component performance specification could already be justified, if the component and its performance model is reused at least once. For reasons of self-containedness, sections 2, 3.2 - 3.4, 5 and 6 are similar in both papers, as they describe and discuss the common experiment setting.

For this paper, we have analysed the data collected during the experiment further (also see [16]). We focus on the accuracy of the predictions achieved by the students compared to a sample solution. Additionally, we searched for reasons for the achieved prediction accuracy by analysing the models created during the experiment and evaluating questionnaires filled out by the participants after the experiment. While the results have been obtained for a single CBSPE method, they are also interesting for the authors of other CBSPE methods. Therefore, we describe lessons learned during the study.

The contributions of this paper are (i) experimental results about the prediction accuracy achieved by third-party users of a CBSPE method and (ii) a quantitative and qualitative analysis for the reasons that led to the achieved prediction accuracy. Our study is the first of its type in this area, as we are not aware of any other studies on a CBSPE method being applied by third-party users. This may be a result of the novelty of these methods. The study helps to bring CBSPE closer to industrial maturity and is an important prerequisite for large scale industrial case studies.

The paper is organised as follows. Section 2 briefly describes the Palladio performance prediction method, so that the reader can assess the experimental tasks. Section 3 explains the goals, questions, hypotheses, and metrics used in this experiment according to the GQM paradigm [3] and describes the experimental design and conduction. Section 4 first lists the results for the formerly defined metrics collected in this experiment and afterwards discusses lessons learned. Section 5 includes potential threats to the validity of our study to round up the experimental description. Section 6 lists related work to this study, before Section 7 concludes the paper.

2 Palladio Component Model

The Palladio Component Model (PCM) [5,19] is a meta-model for specifying and analysing component-based software architectures with focus on performance prediction.

This meta-model is divided among the separate developer roles of a component-based development process, providing each role with a domain-specific language suited to capture their specific knowledge [5]. The language of component developers targets at producing independent, reusable component specifications, that are parametrised by influence factors whose later values are unknown to the component developer. In particular, these are (i) the performance measures of external service calls, which depend on the actual binding of the component's required interfaces (provided by the software architect in the assembly model), (ii) the actual resource demands which depend on the allocation of the components to hardware resources (provided by the system deployer), and (iii) performance-relevant input/output parameters of service calls (provided by the domain expert in the usage model).

The parametric behavioural specification used in the PCM as part of the software model is the *Resource Demanding Service Effect Specification* (RD-SEFF) which is a control and data flow abstraction of single component services. It specifies control flow constructs like loops or branches if they affect external service calls. Additionally, it abstracts component internal computations in so called *internal actions* which only contain the resource demand of the action but not its concrete behaviour. Calling services and parameter passing are specified using *external call actions*, which only refer to the component's required interfaces to stay independent of the component binding.

Tool support. The PCM is supported by the PCM-Bench (see [19]), which is based on the Eclipse platform and provides UML-like graphical editors for PCM instances. For performance annotations, it uses a textual syntax, providing editors which help entering the expression with auto-completions, type-checking and syntax highlighting. OCL is applied to increase completeness and correctness of PCM model instances. A simulation tool predicts performance measures of the G/G/n queueing system a PCM instance represents. It uses specialised queueing networks as the performance model and is generated from a PCM instance using model transformations.

The resulting prediction metrics are response time distributions of single external service calls as well as for a whole scenario. They are visualised as cumulative distribution functions (CDFs) or histograms. The utilisation of resources is visualised using pie charts.

3 Empirical Investigation

For the empirical investigation, we formulated a goal, two question and derived metrics using the Goal-Question-Metric approach [3] The goal of this work is to *empirically evaluate the applicability of the Palladio approach from a third-party user's point of view.*

The same metrics can also be used when repeating this experiment, also for other approaches. In this paper, we focus on the results for the achieved accuracy when Palladio is applied by third-party users. Details of the concerned two questions, their hypotheses, and their metrics are presented in section 3.1. For comparison, with the same question and metrics, we also investigated the SPE approach [21], which offers no special support for component-based systems. For brevity, we keep the presentation of the SPE results short and focus on the results for Palladio.

We conducted the investigation as a controlled experiment. Section 3.2 presents the experiment's design, section 3.3 describes the preparation of the participants, and section 3.4 presents the systems under study.

3.1 Questions and Metrics

Due to space limitations, only informal explanations of the metrics are given here. The formal definitions can be found in [16, p.35]. Table 1 summarises questions and metrics.

To study the applicability of Palladio, we first carefully created performance models of the systems under study ourselves as sample solutions. These sample solutions are unique for the information provided in the experimental task, as adding any information or omitting any information from the experimental task would not reflect the system properly any more. During the experiment, we gave the students enough information to create performance models for the different design alternatives themselves. Afterwards, we assessed the participants' models by comparing their prediction to predictions from the sample solution. Thus, in the following, *quality of the models* is defined to be the similarity to the sample solution. We measured the applicability in terms of how well the participants understand the approaches and how usable the given tools are, and therefore we asked the following questions and defined the following metrics.

Q1: What is the quality of the created performance prediction models? First, a performance model should enable predictions that are similar to the reference performance model (i.e. the sample solution) when analysed. Here, the predicted response time was an important performance metric. Thus, we defined metric 1.1: *Relative deviation of predicted mean response times of the participants and of the reference model* (percentage).

To assess different design alternatives when designing or changing a system, the relation of the respective response times is also of interest. We let the participants evaluate

Table 1. Summary GQM Questions and Metrics

Question 1	What is the quality of the created performance prediction models?
Metric 1.1	Relative deviation of predicted mean response times of the participants and of the reference model.
Metric 1.2	Percentage of correct design decisions.
Metric 1.3	Normalised deviation in design decision rankings.
Question 2	What are the reasons for potentially deviating predictions?
Metric 2.1	Problems when creating the models and classification

several design alternatives and measured how many participants correctly identified the best design alternative in respect of its response time by stating metric 1.2: *Percentage of correct design decisions*.

As a software architect does not necessarily choose the design alternative with the best performance, but might consider other quality attributes or cost, the results for the performance-wise inferior design alternatives are also important. Thus, next to identifying the best design alternative, the participants had to rank all alternatives. The ranking of design alternatives by the participants was compared to the ranking of the design alternatives of the reference solution in metric 1.3: *Normalised deviation in design decision rankings*. For this metric, we counted how many ranks lie between the position of a design alternative in the ranking of a participant and the correct position of a this design alternative in the ranking for the reference solution. We normalised this metric so that a correct ranking has a deviation of 0% and the reversed ranking a deviation of 100%. Additionally, we recognised very similar response times as virtually equal design alternatives and did not punish rankings that permuted them.

Our hypothesis 1 was that (1) the average deviation as measured with metric 1.1 is not larger than 10%, (2) 80% of the participants can choose the correct design decision and (3) the rankings deviate no more than 10% in average for both Palladio and SPE.

Q2: What are the reasons for potentially deviating predictions? Several factors might influence the quality of a prediction. First of all, the participants need to understand the approaches and their various concepts. Additionally, the tools has to be usable and support an easy creation and maintenance of the models. Problems in both areas could lead to modelling errors and therefore to erroneous predictions. Next to modelling problems, errors in interpreting the prediction results might lead to false conclusions. This depended on the results the approach gave as well as on visualisation of results in the tool.

To measure the problems, we documented questions of the participants and errors in the final models, that appeared during the acceptance test or were found in the final models. Each such question or error is counted as one problem in metric M2.1: *Problems when creating the models and classification*.

Our hypothesis 2 was that most problems arise from a lack of understanding and tool difficulties.

3.2 Experiment Design

The study was conducted as a controlled experiment. The participants of this study were students of a master's level course. In an experiment, it is desirable to trace back the observations to changes of one or more independent variables. Therefore, all other variables influencing the results need to be controlled. The *independent variable* in this study was the prediction approach (i.e. Palladio or SPE). Observed *dependent variables* were the quality of the created models in terms of similarity with a reference model and the problems occurring during the experiments or being detected in the final models.

The experiment was designed as a cross-over trial [12] as depicted in figure 1. The participants were divided into two groups, each applying an approach to a given task. In a second session, the groups applied the other approach to a new task. Thus, each

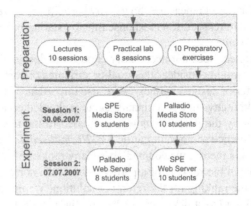

Fig. 1. Experiment design

participant worked on two tasks in the course of the experiment (inter-subject design) and used both approaches. This allowed us to collect more data points and balanced potential differences in individual factors like skill and motivation between the two experiment groups. Additionally, using two tasks lowered the concrete task's influence and increased the generalisability.

We balanced the grouping of the participants based on the results in the preparatory exercises: We divided the better half randomly into the two groups, as well as the less successful half, to ensure that the groups were equally well skilled for the tasks. We chose not to use a counter-balanced experiment design, as we would have needed to further divide the groups. In that case, the groups would have been to small and the individual's performance would have been too much an influence. We expected a higher threat to validity from the individual participant's performance than from sequencing effects (also called carry-over effects, [12]).

Before handing in, the participants' solutions were checked for minimum quality (less than 50% deviation) by comparing the created models to the respective reference model. This acceptance test included the comparison of the predicted response time with the reference model's predicted response time as well as a check for the models' well-formedness.

3.3 Student Teaching

The 19 computer science students participating in the experiment were trained in applying Palladio and SPE in a course covering both theory and practical labs. For the theory part, there was a total of ten lectures, each of them took 1.5h. The first three lectures were dedicated to foundations of performance prediction and CBSE. Then, two lectures introduced SPE followed by five lectures on Palladio. The three additional lectures on Palladio in comparison to SPE were due to its more complex meta-model which allows for reusable prediction models. In parallel to the lectures, eight practical labs took place, again, each taking 1.5h. During these sessions, solutions to the accompanying ten exercises were presented and discussed. Five of these exercises practised SPE and five Palladio.

The exercises had to be solved by the participants between the practical labs. We assigned pairs of students to each exercise and shuffled the pairs frequently to get different combinations of students work together and exchange knowledge. Each exercise took the students 4.75h in average to complete.

Overall, the preparation phase was intended to ensure a certain level of familiarity with the tools and concepts, because participants who failed two preparatory exercises or an intermediate short test were excluded from the experiment.

3.4 Experiment Tasks

To be applicable for both SPE and Palladio, the experiment tasks can only contain aspects that can be realised with both approaches. For example, the tasks did not make use of the separate developer roles of Palladio.

Both experiment tasks had similar set-ups. The task descriptions contained component and sequence diagrams documenting the static and dynamic architecture of a component-based system. The sequence diagrams also contained performance annotations. The resource environment with servers and their performance properties was documented textually. The detailed task description is available on-line in [16]. For each system, two usage scenarios were given, to reflect both a single-user scenario (*UP1*) and a multi-user scenario leading to contention effects (*UP2*). Additionally, they differed in other performance relevant parameters (see below).

In addition to the initial system, several design alternatives were evaluated. Four of them were designed to improve the system's performance, and the participants were asked to evaluate which alternative is the most useful one. Three of these alternatives implied the creation of a new component, one only changed the allocation of the components and the resource environment by introducing a second machine. With the final fifth alternative, the impact of a change of the component container, namely the introduction of a broker for component lookups, on the performance should be evaluated.

The systems in both tasks were prototypical component-based systems. In the first session, a performance prediction for a web-based system called **Media Store** was conducted. This system stores music files in a database. Users can either upload or download sets of files. The size of the music files and the number of files to be downloaded are performance-relevant parameters. The five design alternatives were the introduction of a cache component that kept popular music files in memory (v_1^{MS}), the usage of a thread pool for database connections (v_2^{MS}), the allocation of two of the components to a second machine (v_3^{MS}), the addition of a component that reduces the bit rate of uploaded files to reduce the file sizes (v_4^{MS}) and the aforementioned usage of a broker (v_5^{MS}).

In the second session, a prototypical **Web Server** system was examined. Here, only one use case was given, a request of an HTML page with further requests of potential embedded multimedia content. Performance-relevant parameters were the number of multimedia objects per page, the size of the content and the proportion of static and dynamic content. The five design alternatives were the introduction of a cache component (v_1^{WS}), the aforementioned usage of a broker (v_2^{WS}), the parallelisation of the **Web Server**'s logging (v_3^{WS}), the allocation of two of the components on a second machine (v_4^{WS}) and the usage of a thread pool within the **Web Server** (v_5^{WS}).

The participants who used the Palladio approach were provided with an initial repository of available components and their interfaces, but not their behavioural description (i.e., RD-SEFFs, see section 2). It made the tasks for SPE and Palladio more comparable, because the participants still had to create the RD-SEFFs with the performance annotations, which is similar to the creation of an SPE model.

4 Results

In this section, we interpret the measured data based on the GQM plan. The structure of this section follows the two questions, each being partitioned into the presentation of the metrics. In the paper, we only present the evaluation of the metrics for Palladio. The results for SPE can be found in [16, p.83]. The metrics are evaluated for both tasks. Finally, the hypothesis of each question is checked based on the measured metrics.

4.1 What is the Quality of the Created Performance Prediction Models?

Metric 1.1: Relative deviation of predicted mean response times between the participants and the reference model. Table 2 shows the results of metric 1.1 for Palladio.

We first consider the average deviation for each task. Overall, the deviation is lower using the **Media Store** and for $UP1$. The overall average is low with 6.9%. Interestingly, the deviation varied a lot between the different design alternatives. For the **Media Store** and Palladio, the alternative v_3^{MS} (second server), has a high deviation, and v_0^{MS} for the $UP2$, too. For the **Web Server** and Palladio, the deviations for the v_2^{WS}, the broker alternative, v_0^{WS}, v_1^{WS} (Cache), and v_3^{WS} (Logging) are also high.

For SPE, we measured a slightly higher average deviation of 8.3% and also strong variations for the different design alternatives.

Metric 1.2: Percentage of correct design decisions. For metric 1.2, we compared the results of the reference model (cf. section 3.1) with the participants rankings and assessed the percentage of correct identification of the performance-wise best design alternative. Some participants did not manage to model all alternatives in the given time and thus, their rankings were incomplete and their results cannot be used (see fig. 1 for the total numbers of participants).

As the predicted response time of the best and second-best alternatives of the **Media Store** were close to each other, we made no distinction between these two. Thus, all participants chose right, because all of them identified either the bit rate (v_4^{MS}) or the

Table 2. Metric 1.1: Relative deviation of the predicted response times for Palladio

		v_0^s	v_1^s	v_2^s	v_3^s	v_4^s	v_5^s	Avg
Media Store	$UP1$	1.93%	0.90%	0.49%	20.08%	3.02%	1.69%	4.69%
($s = MS$)	$UP2$	13.21%	2.20%	4.15%	13.23%	4.42%	3.51%	6.79%
Web Server	$UP1$	1.00%	11.07%	1.94%	4.23%	4.55%	9.40%	5.47%
($s = WS$)	$UP2$	15.92%	20.35%	10.87%	10.67%	2.57%	3.64%	10.67%
Overall $propDevMeanResp_{Pal}$								6.90%

cache option (v_1^{MS}) as the best design alternative and ranked the respective other one second-best.

For the **Web Server**, $UP1$ and Palladio, 4 out of 6 participants who ranked all alternatives identified the second server v_4^{WS} as the best alternative. Of the two others, one actually predicted a lower response time for the cache (v_1^{WS}), the other one seemed to have other reasons or could not correctly interpret the CDF, as the second server v_4^{WS} is faster for his model, too. We get $perc_{WS,UP1,Pal} = 0.67$. All eight SPE participants chose the right alternative: $perc_{WS,UP1,SPE} = 1$.

For usage model 2, all five Palladio participants who ranked all alternatives identified the second server v_4^{WS} as the best alternative. For SPE, 7 out of 8 participants who ranked all alternatives did so: $perc_{WS,UP2,SPE} = 0.88$.

Combined[1] we get $perc_{SPE} = 0.97$ and $perc_{Pal} = 0.85$.

Metric 1.3: Normalised deviation in design decision rankings. Not all participants ranked all alternatives, because they did not complete all predictions or missed the time to complete the ranking, even if they completed the predictions. We still used the incomplete rankings for the evaluation of the metrics, but were careful to weight complete rankings stronger (cf. [16, p.86f]).

For Palladio, the ranks were wrong by 6.5% of the maximum possible permutation. For SPE, the ranks were wrong by 7.3% of the maximum possible permutation. Thus, SPE rankings were more permuted by factor 0.12 compared to Palladio rankings.

Hypothesis 1. With both approaches, the mean response time predicted by the participants only deviates in average 6.9% (Palladio) and 8.3% (SPE) from the mean response time predicted for the reference model. Thus, the deviation of the average is within the limit of 10%. However, for single alternatives, the deviation was higher (see table 2). These pose a threat to hypothesis 1.

Most participants also were able to identify the correct design decisions, in particular 85% for Palladio and 97% for SPE, both is within the bounds of 80%. Finally, the deviation of the ranking is also low (not more than 10% in average).

Overall, the results indicate that hypothesis 1 cannot be rejected for the average case. However, the high variation of the deviation of the predicted mean response time between the different design alternatives hampers assessing hypothesis 1. As the alternatives have differing results, it is unclear how the metrics would be evaluated for different design alternatives.

4.2   What Are the Reasons for Potentially Deviating Predictions?

Metric 2.1: Number of problems and classification. Table 3 shows the problems in the different areas for Palladio, first the tools, then the method itself. For the PCM Bench (i.e. the tool), we identified the problem areas of tool usage, of interpreting the error messages and of bugs of the tool. With Palladio, most problems were with the usage of the tool, e.g. participants asked how to create component parameters or a usage model. Interestingly, there were more usage problems with the **Web Server** task than

---

[1] Note that the percentages for the two systems do not equally influence the results, but are weighted by the number of decisions by definition of the metric (cf. [16, p.41])

Table 3. Metric 2.1: Average number of problems per participant for Palladio

| | Tool | | | | Methodology | | | | | | |
	Usage	Error	Bug	Sum	Parameters	Component parameters	Types and units	Assembly	Usage model	Sum	Sum
Media Store	0.57	0.43	0.29	1.29	1.57	1.00	0.71	0.00	0.00	3.29	4.57
Web Server	2.25	0.38	0.63	3.25	0.63	0.38	0.63	0.13	0.13	1.88	5.13
Both systems	1.41	0.40	0.46	2.27	1.10	0.69	0.67	0.06	0.06	2.58	4.85

with the **Media Store** task. Relatively more tool problems occurred with Palladio (in average 2.27 per participant, that is 47% of the problems) than with SPE (in average 0.24 per participant, that is 5% of the problems). Although the number of participants was relatively small, and outliers might strongly have influenced this result, we still give the average values here. No clear outliers were detected, every participant was included in both groups (because of the cross-over plan) and the effect was fairly large, thus, the average values were still meaningful.

For the Palladio method (i.e., separated from the tool), different problem areas were identified: (1) The specification of parameter values (e.g. specifying the number of requested audio files), especially (2) the specification of component parameters (e.g. specifying the size of audio files stored in the database), (3) the handling of data types (e.g. using string and enum values within the model) and annotation units (e.g. confusing seconds with millisecond within one model), (4) the assembly (wiring the components) and (5) the usage model (specifying the user flow). Here, in average most problems concerned the specification of parameter values, followed by the specification of component parameters and of types and units. Interestingly, this relation is very pronounced for the **Media Store**, but less pronounced for the **Web Server**, where there were equally many problems with parameters and types and units, followed by component parameters. The participants using Palladio for the **Web Server** task had more problems with the tool than with the methodology, the opposite applies to the participants using Palladio for the **Media Store** task. Overall, participants using Palladio had 2.58 methodology problems per participant in average (that is 53% of the problems). In comparison, participants using SPE had 4.21 methodology problems per participant in average (that is 95% of the problems). Thus, compared to SPE, participants using Palladio had more problems with the actual tool implementation and less with the methodology itself.

For Palladio, 77% of the problems occurred during the experiment and were captured in the question protocol, 12% in the acceptance test, and 11% were still present in the final models. For SPE, 30% were captured in the question protocol, 26% in the acceptance test, and 44% of the problems were still present in the final model.

Hypothesis 2. Our hypothesis 2 was that most problems arise from a lack of understanding and tool difficulties. The number of problems detected, being in average more than 4 per participant for both approaches, show that there was a significant number of problems. Still, as the quality of the created models was overall satisfactory, they do not invalidate the principle applicability of the approaches.

As expected, problems arose from a lack of understanding of the methodology and tool difficulties. Additionally, problems with the task description were detected (not included in the table 3 above).

4.3 Lessons Learned

Applicability: The participant in this study were able to create models with a good quality (as defined in section 3.1): Their predictions had a low deviation compared to a reference model, they were mostly able to choose the best design alternative and they successfully ranked the design alternatives based on the predicted performance. The results are comparable to the quality of models created with SPE. As SPE is a mature approach also applied in industry, the results suggest that also Palladio can be applied by third-party users.

Tool influence: A large fraction of the problems detected for Palladio concerned the tool, i.e. the current implementation of the approach. This supports our conviction that the tool is an important part of any study of applicability of approaches, and must be taken into account when designing and executing them.

Methodology: The results also show that there were fewer methodology problems for the component-based approach Palladio than for the mature SPE, even though the meta model is much more complex: While the SPE meta model consists of 28 classes, the Palladio meta model has about 100 classes, of which most are needed in every model. The results show that the complexity of the meta model can be hidden in the tool and does not hinder the applicability. In the qualitative questionnaire, most participants even stated to have understood the Palladio concepts better than SPE constructs [16].

Occurrence of problems: Problems occurred early during the experiment for Palladio, whereas for SPE, more problems remained in the final models as errors. This suggests that a tool support with many constraint checks against the meta model helps the user to identify problems. Thus, checks contribute to fewer errors in the final models.

Interpretation of results: We saw that distribution functions as resulting metrics are comprehensible for the users, although they were harder to interpret than the mean value and resulted in more errors. More teaching effort is required to make users familiar with the analysis results, and more effort should be spent to improve the presentation of the prediction results.

Influence of the system under study: Finally, the study detected an influence of the system under study on the applicability. Both the quality of the created models, the number of problems and the needed effort (cf. [17]) depend on the actual design decision under study. In this study, the Web Server system seems to be in general more fitted for Palladio, whereas the Media Store system seems to be more fitted for SPE. This is also supported by qualitative results, because only some partici-pants from the (Palladio, **Media Store**) group and the (SPE, **Web Server**) group stated that the task at hand was too difficult. All participants from the other two groups stated the task difficulty was adequate.

5 Threats to Validity

To enable the reader to assess our study, we list some potential threats to its validity in the following. We look at the internal, construct, and external validity (a more thorough discussion can be found in [16]).

The *internal validity* states whether changes of an experiment independent variables are in fact the cause for changes of the dependent variables [22, p.68]. Controlling po-tential interfering variables ensures a high internal validity. In our experiment, we eval-uated the pre-experiment exercises and assigned the students to equally capable groups based on the results to control the different capabilities of the participants. A learning effect might be an interfering variable in our experiment, as the students finished the second experiment session faster than the first one.

A potential bias towards or against Palladio was threatening the internal validity in our experiment, as the participants knew that the experimenters were involved in creating this method. However, we did not notice a strong bias from the collected data and the filled-out questionnaires, as the participants complained equally often about the tools of both approaches.

The *construct validity* states whether the persons and settings used in an experiment represent the analysed constructs well [22, p.71]. Palladio and SPE are both typical per-formance prediction methods involving UML-like design models. The SPE approach has no special support for component-based systems, and was chosen for the exper-iment due to its higher maturity compared to existing CBSPE approaches. Addition-ally, SPE only supports M/M/n queueing systems and reports only mean values. We designed the experimental tasks so that not all specific features of Palladio (e.g. sepa-ration of developer roles in component-based development, performance requirements using quantiles) were used to ensure a balanced comparison.

While our experiment involved student without long-time industrial experience, we argue that their performance after the training sessions was comparable to the potential performance of practitioners. Most of the students were close to graduating and will become practitioners soon. Due to the training, their knowledge about the methods was more homogeneous than the knowledge of practitioners with different backgrounds. Studies, such as [11], suggest the suitability of students for similar experiments.

The *external validity* states whether the results of an experiment are transferable to other settings than the specific experimental setting [22, p.72]. While we used medium-sized, self-designed systems for the tasks, we modelled these system designs and the design alternatives after typical distributed systems and commonly known performance patterns [21], which are representative for the systems usually analysed in this area.

We tried to increase the external validity of our study by letting the participants analyse two different systems, so that differences in the results could be traced back to the systems, and not the prediction methods. Effects that are observed for both tasks are thus more likely to be generalisable to other settings.

Still, the systems under study were modelled on a high abstraction level due to the time constraints of such an experiment. More complex systems would increase the external validity, but would also involve more interfering variables, thus decreasing the internal validity. Furthermore, the available information at early development stages is usually limited, which would be reflected by our experimental setting.

6   Related Work

Basics about the area of *performance prediction* can be found in [18,21]. Balsamo et al. [1] give an overview of about 20 recent approaches based on queueing networks, stochastic Petri nets, and stochastic process algebra. Becker et al. [4] survey performance prediction methods specifically targeting component-based systems. Examples are CB-SPE [6], ROBOCOP [7], and CBML [23].

Empirical studies and controlled experiments [22] are still under-represented in the field of model-based performance predictions, as hardly any studies comparable to ours can be found. Balsamo et al. [2] compared two complementary prediction methods (one based on SPA, one on simulation) by analysing the performance of a naval communication system. However, in that study, the authors of the methods carried out the predictions themselves. Gorton et al. [9] compared predicted performance metrics to measurements in a study, but only used one method for the predictions.

Koziolek et al. [14] conducted a study similar to the one presented in this paper. They compared three different performance prediction methods, which were not specific for component-based systems. The study also involved the SPE methods and attested it the most maturity and suitability for early performance predictions and influenced our decision to compare Palladio to SPE.

7   Conclusions

We have conducted a controlled experiment with 19 computer science students investigating the applicability of a CBSPE method (our Palladio method) by third parties. After several training sessions, the students modelled and analysed the performance of two different component-based designs and assessed five different design alternatives for each system. We found that the quality of the models and predictions created by the students deviated less than 10 % from the predictions achieved with a reference model created by the experimentators. Furthermore, we learned that more than 80% of students were able to rank the given design alternatives correctly. Reasons for the still existing deviations in the predictions were traced back to problems with the involved tools (47%) and to problems with the methodology (53%).

To the best of our knowledge, our experiment is the first empirical study involving a CBSPE method applied by persons other than their authors. Researchers and practitioners can benefit from this type of study. Researchers can use the lessons learned during our experiment to improve their own CBSPE methods, as these lessons are not specific for the Palladio method. For practitioners, the training material and improved tool support created for this experiment may lower the barrier to learn a CBSPE method and conduct early performance predictions to create better software architectures.

However, our study is still a first step to rigorously assess the applicability of CB-SPE methods. Similar experiments should be conducted once the tools and methodologies mature further. Future experiments should also compare different CBSPE methods against each other to evaluate their specific benefits and deficits. It would be interesting to compare the predictions to measurements of different implementations of the designs, to analyse larger designs, and to also involve practitioners in the study.

Details on the experimental settings and the results can be found in [16], available online at `http://sdq.ipd.uka.de/diploma_theses_study_theses/completed_theses`

Acknowledgements. We would like to thank Walter Tichy, Lutz Prechelt, and Wilhelm Hasselbring for their kind review of the experimental design and fruitful comments. Furthermore, we thank all members of the SDQ Chair for helping prepare and conduct the experiment. Last, but not least, we thank all students who volunteered to participate in our experiment.

References

1. Balsamo, S., Di Marco, A., Inverardi, P., Simeoni, M.: Model-Based Performance Prediction in Software Development: A Survey. IEEE Trans. on Softw. Eng. 30(5), 295–310 (2004)
2. Balsamo, S., Marzolla, M., Di Marco, A., Inverardi, P.: Experimenting different software architectures performance techniques: A case study. In: Proc. of WOSP, pp. 115–119. ACM Press, New York (2004)
3. Basili, V.R., Caldiera, G., Rombach, H.D.: The Goal Question Metric Approach. In: Marciniak, J.J. (ed.) Encyclopedia of Software Engineering - 2 Volume Set, pp. 528–532. John Wiley & Sons, Chichester (1994)
4. Becker, S., Grunske, L., Mirandola, R., Overhage, S.: Performance Prediction of Component-Based Systems: A Survey from an Engineering Perspective. In: Reussner, R., Stafford, J.A., Szyperski, C.A. (eds.) Architecting Systems with Trustworthy Components. LNCS, vol. 3938, pp. 169–192. Springer, Heidelberg (2006)
5. Becker, S., Koziolek, H., Reussner, R.: Model-based Performance Prediction with the Palladio Component Model. In: Proc. of WOSP, February5–8, 2007, pp. 54–65. ACM Sigsoft, New York (2007)
6. Bertolino, A., Mirandola, R.: CB-SPE Tool: Putting Component-Based Performance Engineering into Practice. In: Crnković, I., Stafford, J.A., Schmidt, H.W., Wallnau, K. (eds.) CBSE 2004. LNCS, vol. 3054, pp. 233–248. Springer, Heidelberg (2004)
7. Bondarev, E., Chaudron, M.R.V., de Kock, E.A.: Exploring performance trade-offs of a JPEG decoder using the DeepCompass framework. In: Proc. of WOSP 2007, pp. 153–163. ACM Press, New York (2007)
8. Eskenazi, E., Fioukov, A., Hammer, D.: Performance Prediction for Component Compositions. In: Crnković, I., Stafford, J.A., Schmidt, H.W., Wallnau, K. (eds.) CBSE 2004. LNCS, vol. 3054, pp. 280–293. Springer, Heidelberg (2004)
9. Gorton, I., Liu, A.: Performance Evaluation of Alternative Component Architectures for Enterprise JavaBean Applications. IEEE Internet Computing 7(3), 18–23 (2003)

10. Hamlet, D., Mason, D., Woit, D.: Component-Based Software Development: Case Studies, March 2004. Series on Component-Based Software Development, chapter Properties of Software Systems Synthesized from Components, vol. 1, pp. 129–159. World Scientific, Singapore (2004)

11. Höst, M., Regnell, B., Wohlin, C.: Using students as subjects - A comparative study of students and professionals in lead-time impact assessment. Empirical Software Engineering 5(3), 201–214 (2000)

12. Jones, B., Kenward, M.G.: Design and Analysis of Cross-over Trials, 2nd edn. CRC Press, Boca Raton (2003)

13. Kounev, S.: Performance Modeling and Evaluation of Distributed Component-Based Systems Using Queueing Petri Nets. IEEE Trans. of SE 32(7), 486–502 (2006)

14. Koziolek, H., Firus, V.: Empirical Evaluation of Model-based Performance Predictions Methods in Software Development. In: Reussner, R., Mayer, J., Stafford, J.A., Overhage, S., Becker, S., Schroeder, P.J. (eds.) QoSA 2005. LNCS, vol. 3712, pp. 188–202. Springer, Heidelberg (2005)

15. Liu, Y., Fekete, A., Gorton, I.: Design-Level Performance Prediction of Component-Based Applications. IEEE Transactions on Software Engineering 31(11), 928–941 (2005)

16. Martens, A.: Empirical Validation of the Model-driven Performance Prediction Approach Palladio. Master's thesis, Universität Oldenburg (November 2007),
    http://sdq.ipd.uka.de/diploma_theses_study_theses/
    completed_theses

17. Martens, A., Becker, S., Koziolek, H., Reussner, R.: An empirical investigation of the effort of creating reusable models for performance prediction. In: CBSE 2008, Karlsruhe, Germany (accepted, 2008)

18. Menasce, D., Almeida, V., Dowdy, L.: Performance by Design. Prentice Hall, Englewood Cliffs (2004)

19. The Palladio Component Model, http://palladio-approach.net

20. Sitaraman, M., Kuczycki, G., Krone, J., Ogden, W.F., Reddy, A.L.N.: Performance Specification of Software Components. In: Proceedings of the 2001 symposium on Software reusability: putting software reuse in context, pp. 3–10. ACM Press, New York (2001)

21. Smith, C.U., Williams, L.G.: Performance Solutions: A Practical Guide to Creating Responsive, Scalable Software. Addison-Wesley, Reading (2002)

22. Wohlin, C., Runeson, P., Höst, M., Ohlsson, M.C., Regnell, B., Wesslén, A.: Experimentation in Software Engineering: an Introduction. Kluwer Academic Publishers, Norwell (2000)

23. Wu, X., Woodside, M.: Performance Modeling from Software Components. SIGSOFT SE Notes 29(1), 290–301 (2004)

A Calibration Framework for Capturing and Calibrating Software Performance Models

Xiuping Wu and Murray Woodside

Dept. of Systems & Computer Eng., Carleton University
Ottawa, ON, Canada, K1S 5B6
{xpwu,cmw}@sce.carleton.ca

Abstract. Software performance engineering could benefit from combining modeling and testing techniques, if performance models could be derived more cheaply and more easily. This work investigates how known testing and estimation methodologies can be combined in a calibration framework, to provide and maintain performance models in sync with a developing product or component library. There are two main aspects. The first addresses a major barrier in practice, the calibration of model parameters that represent quantities that cannot easily be measured directly. This work calibrates these "hidden parameters" efficiently using a Kalman Filter. The second is the exploitation of the filter estimator to control the calibration framework, for example to terminate a test when accuracy is sufficient, and to design tests for parameter coverage. The technique is demonstrated on simulated data and on an implemented Voice-over-IP (VoIP) system.

Keywords: Performance modeling, Performance testing, Parameter estimation, Software performance engineering.

1 Introduction

A recent overview of software performance engineering [25] pointed out that

- the field badly needs more effective methods, that can be applied more quickly and with less effort,
- methods based on models and measurements have been developing separately, and could both benefit from being more strongly connected.

A combination of models with measurements can strengthen both. Measurements evaluate a product, while models can extrapolate beyond the test environment and the existing state of the system, e.g. for scalability analysis. This paper creates a bridge between performance testing and modeling, in the form of a *model calibration framework*. It uses tests to calibrate a model, and uses the model to define and manage the tests, in a kind of bootstrap process. We consider:

- the test environment drivers and stubs, instrumentation, and workload
- what tests should be run (how many, how long, under what conditions?) This involves a form of *coverage of the parameters*,

N. Thomas and C. Juiz (Eds.): EPEW 2008, LNCS 5261, pp. 32–47, 2008.

- what variables should be measured, and how long should each test be run?
- what is the accuracy of the calibrated parameters and the model predictions?
- can the model *structure* be determined (as well as its parameters)?

The uses of the model include predictions across deployments, scalability limits, and diagnosis of performance loss (e.g. [22]). Component software offers special opportunities recognized in the PACC (predictable assembly of certified components) initiative (e.g., [12]). Submodels of components are calibrated and composed into product models in several works, e.g. [5] [6] [16] [28].

Representative examples of the extensive prior work on measurement are [17] on capture and interpretation of data, and [2] on testing a system against requirements. Barber [4] considers workloads for testing. Tests may also be applied to components (e.g. [8]). A performance model helped to interpret test results in [1].

Model calibration by tests was described by Liu and Gorton [16], using a synthetic benchmark. A performance model was created by combining this with a behavior description of the application. In the APPEAR method [9] a simulation model and a statistical model are combined to predict performance. Muskens described a compositional prediction method [19] with two parts, service composition and behavior composition. Given a scenario, the method composes the required services, and computes its CPU cost. However, it does not calibrate the CPU demands.

An extended Kalman filter, similar to the estimator used below, was applied successfully in [26] to track the parameters of a time-varying system. It was shown that the filter parameters (which depend on the changing environment) do not have to be precisely known, but do affect the accuracy of tracking. The evaluation of the filter performance is however different in the present case, in which the parameters are not changing. It is also possible to use non-sequential least squares estimation [15], but the sequential filter has some advantages for our purposes.

The present paper defines the concept of a model calibration environment, and methodology for using it (including compensation for drivers and stubs that exploits the performance model, and a concept of model parameter coverage, based on estimation accuracy). Two sets of experiments are described which demonstrate the Kalman filter estimator in action, and show that it is effective with several parameters (e.g., four).

2 A Calibration Environment for Software Performance Models

The calibration environment has the following features:

1) *The workload* to be applied to a system or component is described by a *usage profile,* analogous to a "user operational profile" [18] but adapted to performance and to software which is not necessarily driven by the user directly. The usage profile defines a mixture of request types into the system, and their parameters.
2) *Test configurations* include the system under test, drivers to apply requests, stubs to provide essential additional functionality, and instrumentation.
3) *Instrumentation* concentrates on delays and throughputs of requests measured at accessible interfaces, and device utilizations.

4) *Estimation:* the estimator adjusts the model parameters to match the model predictions to the measured values. The accuracy of the fitted parameters and of the model predictions is also estimated by confidence intervals.

5) *Parameter coverage*: a parameter is *covered* by a set of tests if it is estimated with adequate accuracy. The estimator can analyze coverage.

6) *Stopping:* A sequential estimator is used, which can be stopped when sufficient accuracy is obtained, to avoid excessive measurement effort.

Figure 1 illustrates the calibration methodology including the entities (model, usage profile, test plan, etc.) and some of the flows in the process of testing. The parts of the process which are stressed here are outlined in bold in Fig. 1.

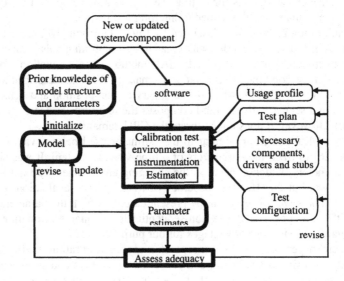

Fig. 1. The process

2.1 Software Performance Models and Layered Queueing

As surveyed by Balsamo et al. [3], the performance model may be a queueing network (QN), a timed Petri net, or an extended QN. This work applies to any kind of performance model, and abstracts it as a vector function h:

$y = h(x, u)$

y = a vector of m performance measures predicted by the model

x = a vector of n parameters which are to be estimated

u = a vector of parameters which are known, called here *configuration parameters*.

This work considers only analytic models, in order to compute the sensitivity of the performance to the parameters using numerical differentiation. The sensitivity is a matrix H:

$$H = \partial h/\partial x, \quad h_{ij} = \partial h_i/\partial x_j \approx [h_i(x+\Delta x_j 1_j; u) - h_i(x; u)]/\Delta x_j \quad (1)$$

in which Δx_j is a small increment in x_j and 1_j is a unit vector in the jth direction. Small elements in H indicate low sensitivity of the measurements to a parameter, and for calibration purposes some measurement must have adequate sensitivity to each parameter.

Examples below use a form of extended QN called a Layered Queueing Network (LQN) [10] [11] in which servers represent processors, software entities and their resources. An LQN resembles a software architecture, as in Figure 2 for a small three-tier web application. Servers are *tasks* (the bold rectangles) or *processors* (the ovals), with multiplicity shown in curly brackets, e.g. {100}. Tasks provide services called *entries* (the light rectangles attached to the tasks), which make *CPU demands* (numbers in brackets, e.g. [3 ms]) and make *requests* to other entries (the arrows, labeled by frequency parameters, e.g. (0.4) for the average requests from QueryPage to ComputePg. The Users also have a pure delay called a *think time* that the user spends between making requests (e.g. {Z=1000 ms}).

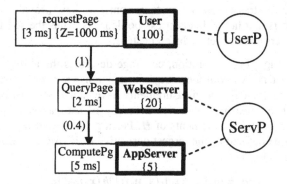

Fig. 2. An LQN model of a Web Application System, showing the notation

Requests may be synchronous (a blocking call-return pattern) indicated by a solid arrowhead, as in Fig. 2, or asynchronous (open arrowhead), or forwarding (dotted arrow, signifying that the responsibility of replying is forwarded with the request).

Tasks and processors have queues and may be "multiple" resources (multithreaded task, multiprocessor). Entries define classes of service at a task, with a service time that includes both the CPU delay, and blocking delays for service from other entries.

3 Calibration Tests

The measurements for calibrating a model to predict mean values are averaged over a sampling period, which we will call a *step*, of length S sec.

A basic requirement is that at least one measurement variable (as represented in the model) should be sensitive to each parameter to be estimated (should have a non-zero entry in the H matrix). This is typically satisfied by mean response times at the interface of operations whose host demands are to be estimated, processor utilizations, and mean request counts (throughputs) for operations.

Tests and Configurations. The test deployment is usually simpler than a full deployment. The drivers simulate the source of requests, and apply requests corresponding to the usage profile. The stubs provide key functionality which is essential to obtain meaningful performance. Stubs may have to be more elaborate than in functional testing, in order to provide accurate performance in the system under test.

Efficient tests require substantial sensitivity of *some* measurements to each parameter, in *some* test step. It may help to apply test steps with different system configurations. The *configuration parameters* are the elements of the model vector u. They may include:

- workload intensity, either as the number of emulated users and their think time, or as the arrival rate of requests
- other variations within the scope of the usage profile, e.g. selection of operations
- deployment parameters like the size of storage or thread pools.
- hardware parameters like processor, storage or network multiplicities and speeds.

By putting different stresses on the system, configurations provide different sensitivites to parameters, e.g heavy loads stress bottlenecks. Thus the sensitivity requirements for parameters can be met in different steps.

Parameter Coverage. For calibration, coverage describes the ability to estimate all the desired parameters. A trivial measure defines parameter x_j as covered, if $H_{ij} \neq 0$ for some measurement (that is, the measurements have non-zero sensitivity to the parameter). A stronger measure relates to accuracy of estimation, which informally depends on the magnitude of elements of H. For a given parameter x_j the magnitude of sensitivity can be defined as the largest derivative in H over all measurements and steps, normalized as follows:

$$sens_i = \max_{jk} [(x_j/h_i(\mathbf{x}, \mathbf{u}_k)) \, |\partial h_i(x, u_k)/\partial x_j|] \qquad (2)$$

An ad hoc measure of coverage magnitude for a set of tests is the smallest $sens_i$:

$$converage \; magnitude = \min_i \max_{jk} [(x_j/h_i(x, u_k)) \, |(H_k)_{ij}|] \qquad (3)$$

Test Plan. A test plan describes a series of steps, numbered $k = 1 ... K$, each with a deployment, request patterns, a configuration specified by u_k and a nominal duration S_k. The request patterns are selected from the usage profile. The same step definition can be repeated multiple times, at some shorter duration for each instance, if desired.

Compensation for Effect of Drivers and Stubs. The loading of resources by drivers and stubs can be compensated by modeling them explicitly, either as precalibrated submodels, or as model elements calibrated during the test. In either case their contribution to measured performance is separated from that of the subsystem under test.

4 Test Interpretation: Model Estimation

An initial performance model structure must be created with preliminary estimates of its parameters. The initial model can be found from a previous version of the system, from expert knowledge as suggested by Smith and Williams [22] or by analysing the software specifications. From UML specifications annotated with the performance profile [20] a performance model can be created using techniques surveyed in [24]. The model structure can also be derived by analyzing traces from running software, (see e.g. [13]).

The estimator requires an initial model that includes this parameter information:

- x_0, the initial parameter vector and
- p_0, a vector of variances of x_0 representing its uncertainty. We can choose:
  - $(p_0)_i = (x_0)_i^2$, showing uncertainty of same order as x (recommended).
  - if uncertainty is stated as a range $x_0 \pm \Delta$, and we interpret $\pm \Delta_i$ as a confidence interval for about 95% confidence, $(p_0)_i = (\Delta_i/2)^2$
  - after a small change in the product, $(p_0)_i$ = the previous variance estimate.

4.1 Maximum-Likelihood Estimation

The likelihood of a set of measured vectors z_k (normally distributed with covariance R), over a sequence of steps with configuration vectors u_k, $k = 1..K$, is maximized by the vector $\hat{x}$ which minimizes the quadratic deviation measure E [27]:

$$\hat{x} = \arg \min E(x), \quad E(x) = \Sigma_k (y_k - z_k)^T R^{-1}(y_k - z_k), \quad y_k = h(x_k; u_k) \quad (4)$$

The well-known Gauss-Newton iterative solution for nonlinear regression 0 solves a sequence of multivariate linear regressions, from some nominal starting parameter x. Each iteration gives an optimal increment Δx:

$$\Delta x = (\Sigma_k H_k^T R^{-1} H_k)^{-1} \Sigma_k H_k^T R^{-1} e_k, \quad e_k = (y_k - z_k) \quad (5)$$

At convergence the covariance matrix of the solution is

$$P = (mse) (\Sigma_k H_k^T R^{-1} H_k)^{-1}, \quad mse = (\Sigma_k e_k^T R^{-1} e_k)/(mK - n) \quad (6)$$

where (mK-n) is the degrees of freedom = (data values) − (fitted parameters).

Assuming normality of z and approximate linearity of $h(x, u)$, the posterior distribution of x is normal with covariance matrix P. Then the confidence interval at level α for the ith parameter (which has sample variance sqrt(P_{ii})) is

$$\hat{x}_i \pm t(1-\alpha/2; mK-n) (sqrt(P_{ii})) \quad (7)$$

where t is the t-statistic with (mK-n) degrees of freedom. By the linearization of h, the deviation Δy due to a deviation Δx in x, is given by $\Delta y = H \Delta x$, so y is also approximately normal with mean $\hat{y} = h(\hat{x}, u)$ and covariance matrix C:

$$C = \text{Cov}(y) = H(\hat{x}, u) P H^T(\hat{x}, u) \quad (8)$$

4.2 Sequential Estimation and the Extended Kalman Filter (EKF)

Sequential estimation gives a new estimate at each timestep, and can be used to decide when to stop a test. One such estimator, the Kalman Filter (see, e.g. [14]) was originally proposed to track a time-varying state vector in a dynamic system. Its extension for nonlinear systems was applied in [26] to tracking time-varying parameters. Its use for calibration is somewhat different because parameters are constant and we are concerned about the transient accuracy of estimation.

The EKF used here considers a vector x_k at discrete time instants numbered by k which drifts according to a random process:

$$x_k = x_{k-1} + w_{k-1} \tag{9}$$

where w_{k-1} is a random increment of covariance Q (we assume negligible drift, so $Q = 0$ or is very small).

The performance measurement vector z_k at time step k is modeled by:

$$z_k = h(x_k, u_k) + v_k \tag{10}$$

where $h(x_k, u_k)$ is the model prediction and v_k is the random measurement error. v_k is assumed to have mean zero and a normal distributions with covariance matrix $\mathbf{R}_k$ assumed to be diagonal and constant over different steps.

The filter is initialized with the values of R and Q (we used a very small diagonal matrix for Q), and with x_0 and $P_0 = \text{diag}(p_0)$. Its operation proceeds as follows:

EKF1: Project the process state ahead: $\qquad \hat{x}^-_k = \hat{x}_{k-1}$ (11)

EKF2: Project the estimate error covariance ahead. P^-_{k-1} represents the covariance matrix of the estimates $\hat{x}^-_{k-1}$: $\qquad P^-_k = P_{k-1} + Q$ (12)

- EKF3: Compute the Kalman Gain $\mathbf{K}$: $K_k = P^-_k H^T_k (H_k P^-_k H^T_k + R)^{-1}$ (13)

- EKF4: Update the estimate of the process state based on the measurement z_k and the prediction error e_k: $\qquad e_k = z_k - h(\hat{x}_{k-1}, u_k)$ (14)

$$\hat{x}_k = \hat{x}^-_k + K_k e_k \tag{15}$$

- EKF5: Update the estimate error covariance: $\qquad P_k = (I - K_k H_k) P^-_k$ (16)

Equations (11) – (16) are applied at each time-step, with the H matrix defined in Eq. (1). They give the feedback structure shown in Fig. 3.

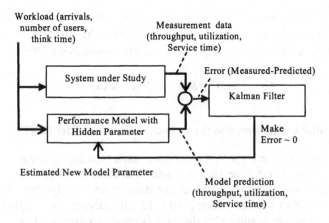

Fig. 3. The Feedback Loop in a Kalman Filter [14]

For the estimator to converge, an identifiability condition must be satisfied. In the present application rank it is $(H_k) \geq n$. This implies there must be at least as manyindependent measured quantities as there are estimated parameters $(m > n)$, and makes the *coverage magnitude* defined in Eq. (3) greater than zero.

5   A Voice-over-IP (VoIP) System

A simple but realistic demonstration of estimation was carried out on a lab deployment of a VoIP system based on the open-source VOCAL (Vovida Open Communication Application Library [7]). The rate of opening new connections and the connection delay are key performance measures. Connection operations were studied, using SIP "request" messages INVITE, REGISTER and BYE messages and "response" messages TRYING and OK. Tests used the call setup scenario in Fig. 4, and a call teardown scenario.

The system elements entering into the setup scenario are user agents for the caller and callee, marshal servers (MS) at both ends, a process redirect server RS which incorporates SIP standard redirect, location and registration services, and a Call Duration Recording server CDR for billing purposes. The Ingress Marshal Server includes user authentication and management of routing the call to the Egress MS, which routes to the callee. More details can be found in [21].

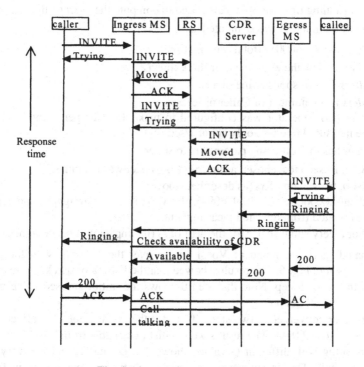

Fig. 4. Message flow in a Call Setup

The marshal server and redirect server are implemented in VOCAL in one process we shall call VocalServer, and this is what will be modeled. The process structure is reflected in the initial model in Fig. 5. VocalServer does marshaling, location discovery, provides routing, and may record billing. After the routing is set up, the call is forwarded to the Callee. The reply to the Caller indicates a successful set up.

The subsystem under test is the VocalServer process, with one parameter to be estimated, the CPU demand per call $s2$. The VOCAL load test driver is the Caller task (multiple tasks), and the VOCAL user agent provided the Callee stub process (one process for each Caller, to simplify delay logging). The execution demands $s1$ and $s3$ were calibrated in advance, however the assigned think time is not provided accurately by the driver, so the actual average think time Z of Caller was estimated along with $s2$. The application was deployed on a Linux network with one processor for multiple Callers, one for VocalServer, and one with a Callee for each Caller. The Callers were configured to make a total of 5000 calls per measurement/estimation step.

5.1 Experiments

The measured variables for each step were:

- the average response time as indicated on Fig. 5,
- the average total delay for a call,
- the total running time for 5000 calls, used to compute the average throughput.

The system throughput (f) was computed as:

f = (total calls = 5000) / (total running time).

Applying Little's law the effective user think time (Z) is:

Z = *Callers* / f - (response time of a call)

where *Callers* is the number of Caller processes.

When the load generator was configured to make 15 calls per second, with five Callers, the measured rate was only about 7/sec.

The estimator has the following parameters to set up.

- x_0 = 8.0 milliseconds, chosen arbitrarily (its impact was examined),
- P_0 = 64.0, the square of x_0 (as described above),
  R = diag(0.000003697, 11.5976094), the variances of throughput and response time, estimated from repeated measurements.
- Q = 0 or a very small scalar for the drift of s_2 (its impact will be examined)

The estimated service demand of Vocal Server over the 12 steps with the data in Table 1 is shown in Fig. 6. The results showed that the Estimator quickly converged starting at the second step. Note that step 0 shows the initial guessed value of CPU demand of the Vocal Server.

The estimator converged in two steps. To test if the initial value of s_1 affects the results, it was set to = 2.0 ms. The results were indistinguishable from Fig. 6.

Experimenting with different Q values shows that Q must be zero or very small, for the best result. This is entirely reasonable when the parameters are in fact not

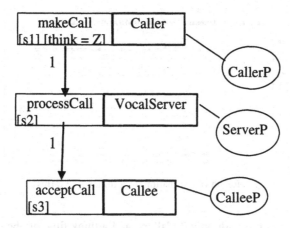

Fig. 5. The Initial LQN Model for Call Setup in VOCAL

Table 1. Measurement Data for VOCAL

Step	Throughput (calls/ms)	Response time (ms)	Think time (ms)
0	0.0357	92.8	47.1
1	0.0393	90.8	40.3
2	0.0380	88.0	44.3
3	0.0354	97.9	45.2
4	0.0390	88.3	42.3
5	0.0420	84.8	40.0
6	0.0373	91.7	44.0
7	0.0353	94.9	46.8
8	0.0365	94.7	44.5
9	0.0371	91.1	44.7
10	0.0365	94.2	45.0
11	0.0396	87.2	42.6

changing, but it contrasts with results found when tracking parameters which vary, in which case a too-large value of Q had little penalty [29].

5.2 Model Validation

The model was used to predict the performance of two different configurations:

1) the load generator was configured to have a lower call rate, and thus a longer think time (about 267 milliseconds). There are still 5 concurrent load generators each making 1000 calls for each measurement step. The measurement data was collected and averaged over 24 steps. The average measured system throughput was 0.0144 calls per millisecond, compared to the predicted throughput of 0.01618 calls per millisecond. The relative error is about 12%.

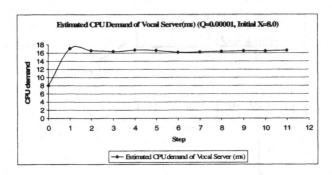

Fig. 6. Result of Estimation with Initial s_1=8.0 (ms)

2)   the system was run with only 3 Callers, and a think time of about 27 milliseconds. The measurement data was collected for 12 steps with 5000 calls from
each Caller, per step. The measured throughput was 0.0336 calls/ms, and the
model predicted 0.0349 calls/ms., a relative error of 3.9% which is much
smaller than case 1).

The prediction errors in these two cases were considered satisfactory.

6 Simulation Study

A deeper inquiry into estimator capability was carried out on simulated data for the
system shown in Fig. 7, representing an online bookstore. The CPU demand parameters labeled $x1$ to $x4$ in Fig. 7 were estimated from data generated using the values
shown (e.g., the simulation had $x1$= 12 ms, and then $x1$ was estimated).

6.1 Experiments

The simulated system was configured with N = 15 concurrent users and single-
threaded servers. The first experiment was set up to run each step for 15000 s, which
included about 10,000 responses. The measured variables for each step were:

- C = user cycle time, which includes the thinking time
- service time of CheckOutService
- service time of ShoppingCart
- service time of BookOrder
- service time of Inventory

Each service time measurement includes the CPU time spent by the entry and the time
the entry blocks and waits for replies from its lower layers.

The simulation was run for 10 steps, which gives 95% confidence intervals less
than 4% of the mean performance measures. These intervals were used to set R, in the
filter, Q was set to 0, and the initial estimates were all set to 5 ms.

The results in Fig. 8 show that the estimator converges quickly, by the second step.
The estimation error was almost zero, except that $x1$ was underestimated by about

5%, perhaps to compensate for an approximation error. The CheckOut service time has high variance, which may cause its waiting time approximation to be low, and the user cycle time prediction includes the sum of x1 and this waiting time.

The parameters fitted to data from a simulation with 15 users were used to predict system performance over a range of users from 5 to 50, with the results:

Table 2. Results for varying loads, and parameters calibrated for $N = 15$

Users N	5	10	**15**	20	25	30	35	40	45	50
Measured C	1133.7	1264.9	**1472.6**	1762.9	2137.2	2539.9	2948.1	3331.9	3794.3	4232.4
Predicted C	1139.9	1264.5	**1496.8**	1840.7	2232.7	2640.4	3054.1	3470.5	3888.8	4308.1

These results show that the model predictions can be used for conditions that are quire different from the test conditions. The relative errors are less than 4.5%.

Some variations were introduced into this study:

1. Different initial values. The starting value of 5 for all parameters was replaced by 10, 15 and 20. The estimation results were identical after the first two steps.
2. The measurement step length was reduced from 15000 s to 100 s, and **R** was adjusted to reflect the (poor) accuracy of the shorter experiment. Estimates over 10 steps did not converge, showing that there must be sufficient data in the total

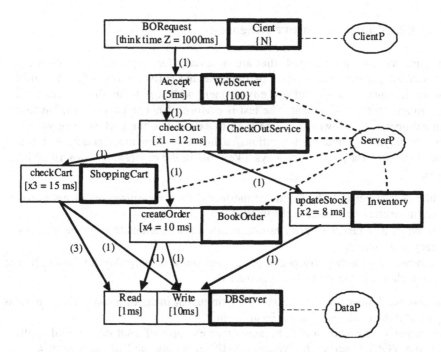

Fig. 7. LQN for simulated bookstore system

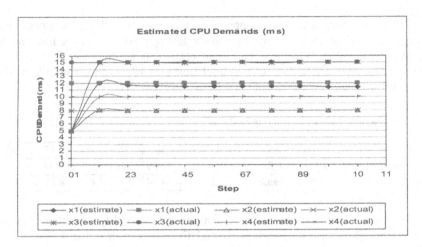

Fig. 8. Estimated vs. real CPU demands for bookstore system (Initial $x_0 = 5$)

experiment. Application of stopping rules based on filter accuracy can control this efficiently.

3. The system was simulated and modeled with multithreaded servers. The results were similar to Fig. 8, but with larger final errors.

7 Conclusions and Future Research

Concepts have been presented, that are necessary for a general calibration environment for performance models of implemented software systems. The calibration environment is a kind of test environment with significant differences from a performance test environment. The test is performed not to pass or fail, but to obtain parameter values which can be used to extrapolate the performance values to other deployments and configurations, using a performance model. A Kalman Filter estimator for parameters plays a key role in the environment described here, because it

- allows parameters to be estimated indirectly, from measurements of performance quantities that are visible at the interfaces of the system,
- provides a sequence of error estimates that allows the test to continue until accuracy is sufficient,
- compensates for the influence of drivers and stubs, if submodels for their influence are included in the model being estimated.

The process defined for the calibration environment includes a test revision process triggered if the model accuracy is insufficient.

Parameter estimation was illustrated by an example of a substantial real application, the VOCAL server for voice-over-IP telephony, and on data from a more complex simulated system with more processes. In the former case the test driver was modeled to compensate for its influence, not because it loaded the system up,but because the load generator was strongly influenced by pushback from the server.

In both cases the resulting model gave response time predictions for conditions different from the test, accurate within a few percent.

The practical value of this approach lies in using the performance model to explore performance properties, to predict performance for a range of deployments (e.g. for scalability analysis), and to optimizing the configurations for different customers. Future research can examine the impact of usage profiles on parameter accuracy (especially with several classes of workload and many parameters), models that apply across multiple alternative usage profiles, the best choice of model structure when there are several candidates, and the choice of measurements when there are many parameters.

The use of the accuracy estimates derived from the P matrix in Eq (16), to determine the coverage magnitude or to control the duration of a measurement trial, requires more extensive experiments and will be reported separately.

The general framework could be used with other estimators, and with other functional forms besides a performance model. However a performance model should in principle provide a superior fit to the data and superior extrapolation capability, because its structure is derived from the underlying phenomena of resource usage and resource saturation, which for instance do not give the usual polynomial or exponential functions used in regression.

Acknowledgments. The tracking filter was originally developed by Tao Zheng. This research was supported by the Natural Sciences and Engineering Research Council of Canada (NSERC).

References

[1] Avritzer, A., Weyuker, E.J.: The Role of Modeling in the Performance Testing of E-Commerce Applications. IEEE Trans. Software Eng. 30(12) (December 2004)

[2] Avritzer, A., Kondek, J., Liu, D., Weyuker, E.J.: Software performance testing based on workload characterization. In: Proc. 3rd Int. Workshop on Software and Performance (WOSP 2002), Rome, pp. 17–24 (2002)

[3] Balsamo, S., DiMarco, A., Inverardi, P., Simeoni, M.: Model-based Performance Prediction in Software Development. IEEE Trans. Software Eng. 30, 295–310 (2004)

[4] Barber, S.: Creating Effective Load Models for Performance Testing with Incomplete Empirical Data. In: Proc. Sixth IEEE International Workshop on Web Site Evolution (WSE 2004) (2004)

[5] Bertolino, A., Mirandola, R.: CB-SPE Tool: Putting Component-Based Performance Engineering into Practice. In: Proc. 7th Int. Symposium on Component-Based Software Engineering, Edinburgh (2004)

[6] Bondarev, E., Muskens, J., de With, P., Chaudron, M., Lukkien, J.: Predicting Real-Time Properties of Component Assemblies. In: Proc. 30th Euro. Micro. Conf. IEEE, Los Alamitos (2004)

[7] Dang, L., Jennings, C., Kelly, D.: Practical VoIP Using VOCAL. O'Reilly Media, Sebastopol (2002)

[8] Denaro, A.P.G., Emmerich, W.: Early Performance Testing of Distributed Software Applications. In: Proc. 4th Int. Workshop on Software and Performance, Redwood Shores, California, January 2004, pp. 94–103 (2004)

[9] Eskenazi, E., Fioukov, A.V., Hammer, D.K., Obbink, H.: Performance prediction for industrial software with the APPEAR method. In: Proc. 4th Progess Symp. on Embedded Systems (2003)

[10] Franks, R.G., et al.: Performance Analysis of Distributed Server Systems. In: Proc. 6th Int. Conf. on Software Quality, Ottawa, October 28-30, 1996, pp. 15–26 (1996)

[11] Franks, R.G., et al.: Layered Queueing Network Solver and Simulator User Manual, Dept. of Systems and Computer Engineering, Carleton University (December 2005)

[12] Hissam, S.A., et al.: Packaging Predictable Assembly. In: Bishop, J.M. (ed.) CD 2002. LNCS, vol. 2370, pp. 108–124. Springer, Heidelberg (2002)

[13] Israr, T., Woodside, M., Franks, R.G.: Interaction tree algorithms to extract effective architecture and layered performance models from traces. J. Systems and Software 80(4), 474–492 (2007)

[14] Jazwinski, A.H.: Stochastic Processes and Filtering Theory. Academic Press, London (1970)

[15] Kutner, M.H., Nachtsheim, C.J., Neter, J., Li, W.: Applied Linear Statistical Models, 5th edn. McGraw-Hill, New York (2005)

[16] Liu, Y., Fekete, A., Gorton, I.: Design-Level Performance Prediction of Component-Based Applications. IEEE Trans. on Software Eng. 31(11) (November 2005)

[17] Miller, B.P., Callaghan, M.D., Cargille, J.M., Hollingsworth, J.K., Irvin, R.B., Karavanic, K.L., Kunchithapadam, K., Newhall, T.: The Paradyn Parallel Performance Measurement Tool. IEEE Computer 28(11) (November 1995)

[18] Musa, J.D.: The Operational Profile in Software Reliability Engineering: An Overview. IEEE Software 10, 14–32 (1993)

[19] Muskens, J., Chaudron, M.: Prediction of Run-Time Resource Consumption in Multi-task Component-Based Software Systems. In: Proc. 7th Int. Symp. on Component-Based Software Engineering, Edinburgh, May 24-25 (2004)

[20] Object Management Group, UML Profile for Schedulability, Performance, and Time Specification, Version 1.1, OMG document formal/05-01-02 (January 2005)

[21] Rosenberg, J., et al.: The Session Initiation Protocol (SIP), IETF RFC 3261 (June 2002), http://www.ietf.org/rfc/rfc3261.txt

[22] Smith, C.U., Williams, L.G.: Performance Solutions. Addison-Wesley, Reading (2002)

[23] Woodside, C.M., Neilson, J.E., Petriu, D.C., Majumdar, S.: The Stochastic Rendezvous Network Model for Performance of Synchronous Client-Server-Like Distributed Software. IEEE Trans. on Computers 44(1), 20–34 (1995)

[24] Woodside, M., Petriu, D.C., Petriu, D.B., Shen, H., Israr, T., Merseguer, J.: Performance by Unified Model Analysis (PUMA). In: Proc. 5th Int. Workshop on Software and Performance, Palma de Mallorca, pp. 1–12 (2005)

[25] Woodside, M., Franks, R.G., Petriu, D.C.: The Future of Software Performance Engineering. In: Briand, L., Wolf, A. (eds.) Proc. Future of Software Engineering 2007, May 2007, vol. P2829, pp. 171–187. IEEE Computer Society, Los Alamitos (2007)

[26] Woodside, M., Zheng, T., Litoiu, M.: Service system resource management based on a tracked layered performance model. In: Proc. 3rd Int. Conf. on Autonomic Computing (ICAC 2006), pp. 123–133 (2006)

[27] Woodside, M.: The Relationship of Performance Models to Data. In: Proc. SPEC Int. Performance Evaluation Workshop (SIPEW 2008). LNCS, vol. 5119, Darmstadt. Springer, Heidelberg (2008)
[28] Wu, X., Woodside, M.: Performance Modeling from Software Components. In: Proc. 4th Int. Workshop on Software and Performance, Redwood Shores, CA, pp. 290–301 (2004)
[29] Zheng, T., Woodside, M., Litoiu, M.: Performance Model Estimation and Tracking using Optimal Filters. IEEE Trans. on Software Eng. (June 2008)

Performance Evaluation of Embedded ECA Rule Engines: A Case Study

Pablo E. Guerrero*, Kai Sachs, Stephan Butterweck, and Alejandro Buchmann

Dept. of Computer Science, Technische Universität Darmstadt
D-64283 Darmstadt, Germany
{guerrero, sachs, butterweck, buchmann}@dvs.tu-darmstadt.de

Abstract. Embedded systems operating on high data workloads are becoming pervasive. ECA rule engines provide a flexible environment to support the management, reconfiguration and execution of business rules. However, modeling the performance of a rule engine is challenging because of its reactive nature. In this work we present the performance analysis of an ECA rule engine in the context of a supply chain scenario. We compare the performance predictions against the measured results obtained from our performance tool set, and show that despite its simplicity the performance prediction model is reasonably accurate.

Keywords: Performance Evaluation and Prediction, Embedded Systems, ECA Rule Engines, Active Functionality Systems.

1 Introduction and Motivation

As software and hardware are becoming more complex, system engineers look more at architectures that help them cope with the speed at which the *business logic* changes. In architectures centered on *rule engines* [1], developers describe the business logic in terms of *rules* composed by *events*, *conditions* and *actions* (hereafter called ECA rules). These ECA rules are precise statements that describe, constrain and control the structure, operations and strategy of a business.

Business logic executes on multiple platforms with different capabilities ranging from clusters, through workstations all the way down to small embedded devices. To relieve developers from knowing in advance on which environment rules will execute, it is convenient to offer a uniform ECA abstraction for all of them. We have developed a complete ECA rule engine middleware [2] which supports a uniform rule definition language across platforms. Our implemented ECA rule engine offers a high level programming abstraction and thus achieves a fast change of re-utilizable business logic.

This flexibility comes at a performance cost. Therefore, the study of this tradeoff is crucial before migrating to an ECA middleware architecture. To avoid overload and unexpected errors, it is important to know the processing limits

---

* Supported by the DFG Graduiertenkolleg 492, *Enabling Technologies for Electronic Commerce*.

N. Thomas and C. Juiz (Eds.): EPEW 2008, LNCS 5261, pp. 48–63, 2008.

and possible bottlenecks of a rule engine. However, evaluating reactive behavior is not trivial, especially for embedded devices where resources such as processing power, memory and bandwidth are scarce.

The main contribution of this work is an analytical performance model for ECA rule engines. We discuss the difficulties in building a performance model of an ECA rule engine and present one that, despite its simplicity, accurately predicts overall system utilization. The measurement and monitoring of the ECA rule engine and its individual services are supported by our performance evaluation tool set. The model is validated against a case study based on SAP's intention to move business processing towards the periphery [2].

2 Background

2.1 ECA Rule Engines

An ECA rule engine is a software system that executes Event-Condition-Action (ECA) rules [3]. ECA rules contain a) a description of the events on which they should be triggered; b) an optional condition, typically referring to external system aspects; and c) a list of actions to be executed in response. In general, the structure of an ECA rule is ON <event> IF <condition> THEN <action>. Events are relevant changes of state of the environment that are communicated to the ECA rule engine via messages, possibly originated at heterogeneous sources.

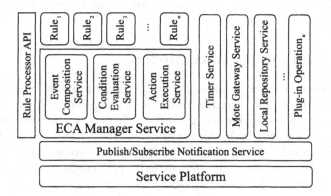

Fig. 1. ECA Rule Manager architecture

Our rule engine, depicted in Figure 1, was designed as a set of independent services, or *bundles*, managed by a service platform. For the embedded implementation we have chosen the Open Services Gateway initiative (OSGi) Service Platform, because of its minimalist approach to service life-cycle management and dependency checking. The services are decoupled from each other via a *Publish/Subscribe* notification service, for which we use a REBECA [4] event broker wrapped as a service. The *ECA Manager* service exposes a *Rule Processor API* over which rules can be (un)registered and (de)activated. The rule execution is split and delegated to elementary services, namely *Event Composition, Condition Evaluation* and *Action Execution*. Conditions and actions invoke high level functions exposed by other services such as the *Local Repository* service. This plug-in mechanism allows to dynamically extend the set of operations.

2.2 Performance Analysis

Performance has been studied in the context of Active Database Management Systems (aDBMS) [5,6,7,8]. These are complete "passive" DBMS extended with the possibility to specify reactive behavior beyond that of triggers. ECA rule engines, which stem from aDBMS, are more flexible in that they can interact with any arbitrary system, but do not necessarily provide full database functionality.

The work in [9] identified requirements for aDBMS benchmarks. Important aspects were the *response times* of event detection and rule firing, as well as the *memory management* of semi-composed events. The BEAST micro-benchmark [10,11] reported on the performance of various aDBMS available at the time, such as ACOOD, Ode, REACH and SAMOS. BEAST does not propose a typical application to test its performance. Konana et al. [12], in contrast, focus on a specific E-Broker application which allowed the evaluation of latency with respect to event arrival rate, among others. The experiments in [13] evaluate the effects of execution semantics (e.g., immediate vs. deferred execution) by means of simulation.

Previous work has focused on evaluating the performance of systems or prototypes, rather than predicting it. This is due to the complex nature of ECA rule engines and rule interactions.

3   Analytical Performance Model

In order to understand how a rule engine performs, we begin by defining relevant performance metrics. These metrics, mostly stemming from [14], aim at a statistical analysis of the rule engine and are not specific to ours, thus they can be used for an objective comparison. In this paper we employ *service time R, throughput μ, CPU utilization U* and *queue length* to model the system performance.

Building a performance model for an ECA rule engine requires an understanding of its rules and their relationships. An initial, straightforward attempt to come up with an analytic performance model is to consider the entire *rule engine* as a single black box. However, this approach is not convenient for our purposes because it leads to inaccurate results.

At a finer granularity, the model could be unbundled into the *event broker* and its individual *rules* as black boxes, each with a separate queue as depicted in Figure 2. For the time being, we consider that rules are independent of each other, i.e. each event can cause the triggering of only one rule. We are aware that this condition is not the general case, and will be later relaxed. The first step consists in obtaining the service time R_{broker}, associated with the event broker, and R_i (with $i = 1, ..., n$), associated with the n deployed rules. From these service times, the average throughput μ can be obtained as follows:

$$\mu_{broker} = 1/R_{broker}; \; \mu_i = 1/R_i \text{ with } i = 1, ..., n$$

To calculate the CPU utilization U, the workload λ as well as the probability for a certain event to occur p_i (and thus the probability for a certain rule to be executed) have to be specified:

$$U = U_{broker} + \sum_{i=1}^{n} U_i = \lambda/\mu_{broker} + \sum_{i=1}^{n} p_i * \frac{\lambda}{\mu_i} \text{ (where } \sum_{i=1}^{n} p_i = 1)$$

In addition to the assumption of rule independence, this model presents the problem that it does not allow loops, i.e., cases in which a condition or action statement feeds an event to the broker and thus a service is visited twice (cf. the lower dotted line in Figure 2 for rule R_n). In the worst case, under a constant load, the number of events that *revisit* these services would grow infinitely. Next, we present our approach to solve the preceding issues.

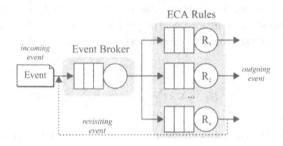

Fig. 2. Performance model with rules as black-boxes

3.1 A Simplified Model: Event Paths

The idea of the model is to consider all the possible *paths* that events may cause and assign a queue to each (see Figure 3.a). A *path* is defined as the sequence of ECA services an event goes through, possibly of different rules. The simplest paths to be identified are those initiated by events (whether they are simple or composite) that directly trigger a single rule and then exit the system. These paths must be then distinguished if, depending on the event values, the execution may conclude at the Condition Evaluation service or it may proceed until the Action Execution service. Moreover, the path must be split if it involves condition or action statements that differ in their service time under certain situations (first-time invocations, warm-up, caching, etc.). Finally, if a statement may generate another event which in turn triggers another rule, an extra path is included with the additional services. This avoids having loops between queues in the model (i.e., services are never visited twice).

In this approach, the service time R_i of each event path i starts at the time of the entrance of the event at the rule engine, during its stay at all the involved services, and stops at its final departure (this is exemplified in the interaction diagram of Figure 3.b). Measuring each event path's service time might require

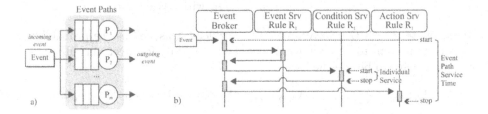

Fig. 3. a) event paths model, b) an actual event path for rule R_1

a major effort. However, and as it is shown in Section 4.2, it is acceptable to use the sum of the service times of the particular services an event path involves.

From the service time of each event path, their average throughput μ_i can be obtained, as before, from $\mu_i = 1/R_i$. To calculate the CPU utilization U for an event path model, the service times of the event paths need to be measured. The workload λ also must be defined, i.e., the probability p_i for each path to occur is needed. The CPU utilization for a model with m event paths can be calculated as follows:

$$U = \sum_{i=1}^{m} U_i = \lambda \times \sum_{i=1}^{m} \frac{p_i}{\mu_i}, \text{ with } \sum_{i=1}^{m} p_i = 1 \tag{1}$$

The simplicity of this model is counterbalanced by the fact that the more rules exist, the more complex the determination of all event paths gets. Note that this is not an operational problem but needed for the proper performance analysis. When the system must manage 100's or 1000's of rules, the number of paths can grow large, thus the usefulness of the model can be restrictive. This is not a major threat in embedded systems, since given their limited resources, the rule sets are small. Lastly, the model assumes an understanding of the rules and their relations.

3.2   Queueing Behavior

To calculate the length of a queue over time, both its service time R_i and the workload at time t, λ_t, are needed. The queue size behavior is quite intuitive: a queue grows (or shrinks) at a rate equal to the difference between the incoming events per time unit (λ_t) and the processed events per time unit (μ). Mathematically, the queue length Q is recursively constructed with the formula:

$$Q(t) = \begin{cases} 0 & \text{if } t = 0; \\ \max\{0; Q(t-1) + \lambda_t - \mu\} & \text{otherwise.} \end{cases} \tag{2}$$

3.3   Performance Evaluation Tool Set

The goal of the tool set is to support the testing phase of the software development process by helping measure and monitor different performance metrics of a rule engine. The system supports the creation of test data, generation of events, and different time measurements. Its architecture, depicted in Figure 4 on the greyed area on the top left, is divided in two parts: one running on a server side, and the other running on the embedded, target system, as OSGi bundles.

The *Data Generator* runs on the server side. Its function is to generate the necessary test data for the performance evaluation. This includes the generation of *domain-specific data*, as well as *event properties*, i.e., metadata describing events. The user needs to describe each of the event types and provide the probability of their occurence.

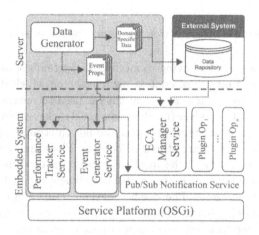

Fig. 4. Performance Evaluation Tool Set architecture

The *Event Generator* is concerned with generating and publishing at the correct points in time the necessary events the rule engine needs for a performance evaluation. The workload parameters such as which events to generate, at which time, with which frequency and the total run time, are obtained from the Data Generator. Event generation can take two forms (illustrated in Figure 5). In the *constant* mode, events are published following a constant rate ρ, during a specified interval width ϖ. The rate can be incrementally scaled by a Δ factor, which is typically used to increase the event workload and stress the system. In the *impulse* mode, events are published following a Gaussian function, which better suits real world situations of bursty event sequences. This mode must be parameterized with an interval width ϖ and a peak a. Finally, both modes can be configured to have a *gap* after each interval.

The *Performance Tracker* service is responsible for tracing service times and queue lengths. There are two mechanisms to measure service times. The first consists of adding code that starts and stops a timer in the particular component methods that are to be measured, and then send the time observations to the tracker. This mode is used when a measurement starts and stops in the same component. The second alternative consists in starting a timer, let the tracker initiate the process to be measured, and then stop it when the process

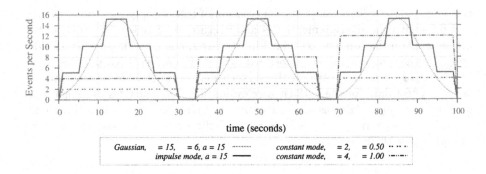

Fig. 5. Different event generation patterns with $\varpi = 30$ seconds and $gap = 5$ seconds

is finished. This mode avoids having to modify the system's source code, but includes method invocation times, context switches, etc., which don't necessarily relate to the service to be measured, and thus is used to measure service times of event paths. For both modes, the Performance Tracker attempts to measure the average service time over multiple runs, and not the time an individual event took. The time observations are stored in *buckets*. The granularity of the buckets determines the accuracy of the measurements, but also affects the memory requirement. With each new run, the buckets are flushed to disk for later analysis, which enables their reuse. The queue lengths can also be traced over time, normally in conjunction with the Event Generator in impulse mode. Since tracing queue length over time requires large amounts of memory, the traces are restarted with every new impulse.

Additionally, we have implemented a set of scripts which measure, monitor and collect other metrics, e.g. CPU, which are provided by the OS.

4 Case Study

The selected scenario is part of a supply chain environment, where a supplier ships goods stacked in pallets to a retail distribution center. These pallets have RFID tags and wireless sensors attached to them. The supplier's system sends an *Advance Shipping Notice* (ASN) to the retailer. An ASN can be seen as a document consisting of a list of *Electronic Product Codes* (EPCs) and optional constraints about the good's conditions, which imply the usage of sensors. On the other end of the supply chain, the retailer's enterprise application receives the ASN. Once the shipment arrives at the destination, a comparison between the delivered goods and the received ASN needs to be carried out.

The retailer's system is organized in 4 layers (columns in Figure 6). The inbound process is initiated at the destination when the retailer's enterprise application (1st column) receives an ASN {a}. The document is stored in an ASN Repository for later use {b}. When a truck arrives at the distribution center, a dock is assigned for unloading and the pallets are scanned while entering the warehouse. When an EPC is obtained from a scanned RFID tag on a pallet

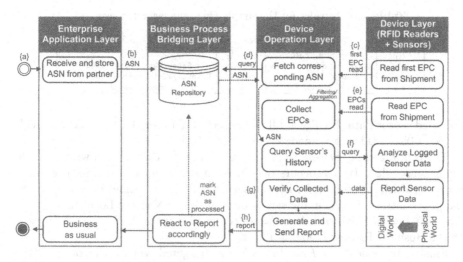

Fig. 6. Advance Shipping Notice inbound process

{c}, the corresponding ASN is fetched from the ASN Repository {d} while (in parallel) other tags are being aggregated {e}. Additionally, the Device Operation Layer can initiate sensor data validation of the attached sensor to check the logged transport conditions {f} (e.g., in case of perishable goods, temperature and humidity values are relevant, while for other goods shock, acceleration and pressure values are of interest). Based on the fetched ASN, the accuracy verification is carried out {g}. The result of the complete verification is sent to the Business Process Bridging Layer {h}, where further business logic is applied.

The rule engine implements the functionality of the Device Operation Layer, running on a Crossbow Stargate hardware platform. This is based on an Intel X-Scale processor and offers multiple network connectivity options. The system is bundled with Embedded Linux BSP, on top of which IBM's J9 Java VM for the ARM processor runs. The rule engine's services run on Oscar, an open source OSGi implementation. The sensor nodes used are Crossbow's Mica2s. We implemented a logging component in TinyOS that is able to be wirelessly queried, analyze its data and answer with the required information. For this prototype we also experimented with the Skyetek M1 Mini RFID reader attached to a Mica2's sensor board, which fed the rule engine with EPCs stored in ISO 15693 tags.

The business logic of the scenario was split into four ECA rules, which are summarized in Table 1. The rule *Incoming EPC* (R_1) listens for EPC events. Its condition part C_1 uses the Local Repository service to search for an ASN containing the received EPC. If there is no local cached copy, the Local Repository tries to fetch it from the remote ASN Repository. If no matching ASN is found, an UnexpectedEPC event is published and the action part of the rule is not executed. If a matching ASN does exist, the action part of the rule, A_1, is executed. First, the EPC is checked as 'seen'. Then, if the pallet carries a sensor node, it is queried for its

Table 1. ECA rules for the supply chain management scenario

Rule ID	Rule Name	Services	Reacts to
R_1	Incoming EPC	C_1, A_1	EPC
R_2	Incoming Sensor Data	E_2, A_2	SensorData | MoteTimeOut
R_3	End of Shipment	E_3, A_3	DataCollectionReady | ASNTimeOut
R_4	EPC Exception	A_4	UnexpectedEPC

collected sensor data. Finally, if all the expected data for the ASN has been collected, a `DataCollectionReady` event is published.

The rule *Incoming Sensor Data* (R_2) is triggered either when a wireless node sends sensor data (which occurs only when a sensor node is queried) or when a timer (which is associated with the sensor node query) times out. The action part A_2 registers this incoming sensor data in the ASN at the Local Repository. The rule *End of Shipment* (R_3) reports the results of the ASN comparison back to the Business Process Bridging Layer.

Finally, the rule *EPC Exception* (R_4) is triggered when an incoming EPC does not belong to any ASN. Its action A_4 consists in reporting the EPC back to the Business Process Bridging Layer, together with contextual information such as date, time, and dock where it was read. Note that rules R_1 and R_4 react to simple events, and thus don't require the Event Composition service, while in contrast, rules R_2 and R_3 react to composite events, in this case a disjunction with a timeout.

4.1   Identification of Event Paths

In this section we analyze the ECA rules of the ASN scenario in order to identify the event paths. The first step in modeling the ASN scenario with event paths was to write down all sequences of ECA services that an event can take. Concerning the execution of the rule *Incoming EPC*, it was very important whether the corresponding ASN already exists in the Local Repository, or it had to be fetched from the ASN Repository, since this distinction affected the service time. For that reason, event paths containing C_1 were split into two paths. The event paths were:

1. **Event Path I**: $C_1 \rightarrow A_1$
   Triggered by an EPC event, with no associated sensor data, where the corresponding ASN document still has unchecked EPCs besides the one recently read.
   - **I.1**: The ASN document already existed in the Local Repository.
   - **I.2**: The ASN document had to be fetched from the ASN Repository.
2. **Event Path II**: $C_1 \rightarrow A_1 \rightarrow E_3 \rightarrow A_3$
   Triggered by an EPC event, with no associated sensor data, where the corresponding ASN document is now completed. A `DataCollectionReady` event follows, which reports the ASN comparison results to the Business Process Bridging Layer.
   - **II.1**: The ASN document already existed in the Local Repository.
   - **II.2**: The ASN document had to be fetched from the ASN Repository.

3. **Event Path III**: $C_1 \to A_4$

   This path starts with an EPC event for which no ASN is found, thus is chained with an UnexpectedEPC event which triggers the report to the server.

4. **Event Path IV**: $C_1 \to A_1 \to E_2 \to A_2$

   This path is similar to path I, except that the EPC has sensor data associated. The respective sensor node is queried, to which a SensorData event is answered. This data is finally registered in the ASN document.

   - **IV.1**: The ASN document already existed in the Local Repository.
   - **IV.2**: The ASN document had to be fetched from the ASN Repository.

5. **Event Path V**: $C_1 \to A_1 \to E_2 \to A_2 \to E_3 \to A_3$

   This event path is similar to event path IV, aside from the fact that the ASN does not have unchecked EPCs anymore, hence the ASN is reported back to the ASN Repository.

   - **V.1**: The ASN document already existed in the Local Repository.
   - **V.2**: The ASN document had to be fetched from the ASN Repository.

4.2 Measured Service Times

This subsection summarizes the results on service times. For these experiments, the Event Generator was used in *constant* mode, with $\rho = 20$ events / minute. This low frequency ensured that events were not influenced by each other. The experiments ran for 80 minutes, the first 30 being ignored as warm-up phase.

The service times of individual services and the event paths are summarized in Table 2 and 3, respectively. We compare both approaches to measure service times in Figure 7. The absolute (i.e., concrete) min., max. and avg. values for both the sum of individual service times and event paths is shown in 7(a). Figure 7(b) contrasts the relative service time difference between the event path average service time (middle greyed area, 100%) against the min., max. and avg. sum of individual service times. The average deviation for these event paths was 9.25%.

4.3 Queueing Behavior

In this section we present the results about the queueing behavior. To study this, it is necessary to have event bursts such that queues form, followed by periods without events. For this purpose, the Event Generator was used in impulse mode, with intervals of $\varpi = 30$ seconds and a *gap* $= 4.5$ minutes (where no events were sent). During the peak, the Event Generator published events with a peak

Table 2. Service times for the Event, Condition and Action services

ID	Rule	Note	Event	Condition	Action
R_1	Incoming EPC	fetch ASN	—	241.75ms	87.78ms
		do not fetch ASN	—	29.22ms	104.41ms
		no ASN available	—	192.05ms	—
R_2	Incoming Sensor Data		6.36ms	—	41.47ms
R_3	End of Shipment		6.50ms	—	253.15ms
R_4	Unknown EPC		—	—	53.83ms

Table 3. Service times for event paths

EVENT PATH	DESCRIPTION	SERVICE TIME
I	$C_1 \rightarrow A_1$	
I.1	do not fetch the ASN	174.15ms
I.2	fetch the ASN	383.59ms
II	$C_1 \rightarrow A_1 \rightarrow E_3 \rightarrow A_3$	
II.1	do not fetch the ASN	352.93ms
II.2	fetch the ASN	575.87ms
III	$C_1 \rightarrow A_4$	
	fetch the ASN	239.99ms
IV	$C_1 \rightarrow A_1 \rightarrow E_2 \rightarrow A_2$	
IV.1	do not fetch the ASN	197.50ms
IV.2	fetch the ASN	449.46ms
V	$C_1 \rightarrow A_1 \rightarrow E_2 \rightarrow A_2 \rightarrow E_3 \rightarrow A_3$	
V.1	do not fetch the ASN	420.61ms
V.2	fetch the ASN	632.64ms

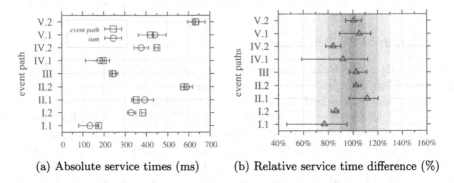

(a) Absolute service times (ms)   (b) Relative service time difference (%)

Fig. 7. Service time measurements: absolute values (a) and relative difference (b)

$a = 15$ events/s. Once this 5-minute process finished, it was repeated again. For the measurement of the queue length, the Performance Tracker service was used. Each time the Event Generator started sending events for the 30 seconds period, it also started the queue trace at the tracker, hence queue lengths of all observed queues were recorded at every second. The queues to be observed were selected by the Event Generator in the initialization phase.

Now we present the queueing behavior of the Condition Evaluation service for the rule R_1, i.e., C_1. For this purpose, a test was carried out where the ASN Repository stores 200 ASNs, each containing one EPC with no sensor data. The queue length predictions were based on the service times for C_1 from Table 2. The Condition Evaluation service does not have its own queue. Indeed, events were queued in the Event Broker service, waiting for being serviced by C_1. The Event Broker can be seen as the queue of the Condition Service because its service time is negligible. The Event Generator split the ϖ interval in five stages. The event arrival rate at the Broker varied at these stages according to the workload λ_t as defined in Equation 3.

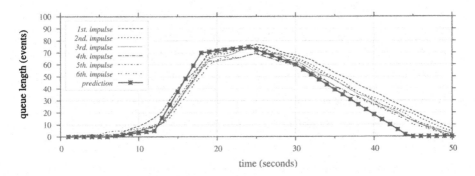

Fig. 8. Measured and predicted queue length for service C_1

$$\lambda_t = \begin{cases} 1\frac{2}{3} \text{ events/s if } 1 \leq t \leq 6 \text{ or } 25 \leq t \leq 30 \\ 5 \text{ events/s if } 7 \leq t \leq 12 \text{ or } 19 \leq t \leq 24 \\ 15 \text{ events/s if } 13 \leq t \leq 18 \end{cases} \tag{3}$$

From C_1's service time (where the ASN must be fetched), we obtained $\mu = 1/0.24175$ events/s $= 4.13$ events/s. By using Equation 2, the queue length can be calculated. For the measurement, the Event Generator ran for a period of 30 minutes, thus 6 queue traces were obtained. The comparison between the predicted values and each of the 6 runs, presented in Figure 8, shows that the calculations were considerably accurate.

Next, we discuss the more general case where multiple interacting services operated sequentially on incoming events. For space reasons, we consider here only the event path II.1, which involved the sequence of services $C_1 \rightarrow A_1 \rightarrow E_3 \rightarrow A_3$. The ECA rule engine was designed with a single real queue for all the incoming events. The resulting behavior is difficult to calculate analytically. Therefore, we wrote a small script that simulated it. On the measurements side, the Event Generator was configured to run over a 40 minutes period. We compare the simulated and empirical measurements in Figure 9 (a) and (b), respectively.

These two plots are considerably similar, except at $t \geq t_d$. This difference revealed a relation between the rules R_1 and R_3 which was unforeseen at the time we designed the queue length simulator. The issue arises when an EPC event for a particular ASN must wait too long in the Broker queue. When this wait exceeds a predefined timer, an `ASNTimeOut` event is triggered, which sends the (incomplete) ASN document back to the repository and thus has to be re-fetched. This also explains the higher amount of events on the queues of R_3.

4.4 CPU Utilization

We now present the results on CPU utilization. In this supply chain scenario, the workload is distributed across 5 EPC types, to which we assigned a percentage in Table 4(a). This selection covered the four rules of the scenario.

In order to calculate the CPU utilization using Equation 1, however, the probabilities of each *event path* (and not the EPC types) are needed. For this purpose, we fixed the number of EPCs per ASN for this experiments to 100 EPCs. With

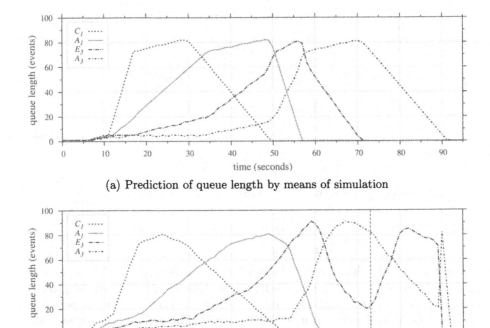

(a) Prediction of queue length by means of simulation

(b) Measured queue length

Fig. 9. Predicted (a) and measured (b) queue lengths for event path II.1

this consideration, the probabilities of each event path were shaped. First, the 25% assigned to Checked EPCs were mapped to event path I.1, I.2, II.1 and II.2, because a Checked EPC always causes the triggering of R_1, followed (sometimes) by R_3 if the ASN document is completed. Second, the 10% of Unexpected EPCs were mapped to event path III. Finally, the remaining EPC types (which accounts for 65%) were mapped to event paths IV.1, IV.2, V.1 and V.2. These probabilities are shown in Table 4(b).

The average service time can be calculated using the information from Table 3 and the formula: $\mu = \sum_{i \in paths} p_i * \mu_i = 222.63$ ms, with $\sum_{i \in paths} p_i = 1$. The CPU utilization, in turn, is calculated from: $U_t = \lambda_t / \mu$. The CPU utilization was monitored using the standard Linux top command; a script piped it to a file for later analysis. Both for the calculations and measurements, the average number of incoming events started with $\rho = 40$ events/minute, and it was incremented by a factor $\Delta = 0.5$ every $\varpi = 10$ minutes. The prediction and the measurement were executed over a total of 65 minutes.

In Figure 10 we show a plot of the published events over time (right y axis), together with the measured and predicted results (left y axis). It is easy to notice that the utilization remained constant for 10 minutes and then increased slightly. However, the measured utilization drifted significantly from the predicted one.

Table 4. Settings for CPU utilization prediction and measurement

(a) Workload characterized according
to event types

EPC TYPE:	ASSIGNED %
Checked EPC	25%
Checked EPC with sensor data	25%
Checked EPC with missing sensor data	20%
Checked EPC with infringing sensor data	20%
Unexpected EPC	10%

(b) Event path probabilities

EVENT PATH	%
I.1	⇐ 23%
I.2	⇐ 1%
II.1	⇐ 0%
II.2	⇐ 1%
III	⇐ 10%
IV.1	⇐ 59%
IV.2	⇐ 3%
V.1	⇐ 0%
V.1	⇐ 3%

At higher λ rates, the difference was about 15%, which turned the prediction unacceptable. The reason for this was that the ECA rules executed several actions that were I/O bound, particularly blocking invocations with large roundtrips. For instance, the fetching of ASN objects (i.e., XML documents) was implemented by an RMI call which took about 160ms. Equation 1, though, relies on the assumption that the CPU is kept busy all the time. Given this consideration, we adjusted the service times by subtracting pure I/O operation times associated to each event path, and recalculated the average throughput. As a result, the (adjusted) CPU utilization prediction, also plotted in Figure 10, resulted a reasonable approximation of the observed one.

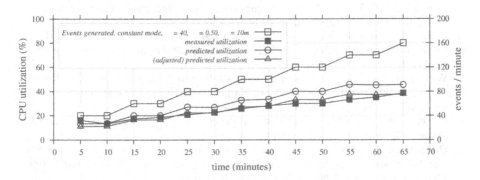

Fig. 10. Measured and predicted CPU utilization using the event path model

5 Conclusions and Future Work

We presented a performance evaluation of an ECA rule engine on an embedded device. This area has not been well explored because it deals with two complex domains: the resource constraints of embedded devices and the complex reactive nature of ECA systems.

The model we developed eliminates, to a certain extent, the problems of rule independence and revisiting events. The proposed solution, based on identifying *event paths*, has shown to be reasonably accurate in predicting performance. Furthermore, the presented work helped understand the entire system more deeply and enhance it in different ways. Queueing behavior analysis exposed timing dependencies between rules that were not evident before.

The model's simplicity can be offset by the effort required to find manually all event paths and obtain their probabilities. It might be useful to integrate a tool that, by statically analyzing the ECA rules, automatically identifies the paths that the events may take. By dynamically tracing incoming events, the relevant paths could be identified and their probability determined by the frequency with which the path was traced. Finally, we are working on developing a comprehensive methodology for performance evaluation of ECA rule engines, independently of the underlying platform under test. This requires the application of the steps described in this paper to further projects to confirm the validity of the method based on event paths.

References

1. Bornhövd, C., Lin, T., Haller, S., Schaper, J.: Integrating Automatic Data Acquisition with Business Processes - Experiences with SAP's Auto-ID Infrastructure. In: 30th VLDB, Toronto, Canada (2004)
2. Guerrero, P.E., Sachs, K., Cilia, M., Bornhövd, C., Buchmann, A.: Pushing Business Data Processing Towards the Periphery. In: 23rd ICDE, Istanbul, Turkey, pp. 1485–1486. IEEE Computer Society, Los Alamitos (2007)
3. Cilia, M.: An Active Functionality Service for Open Distributed Heterogeneous Environments. PhD thesis, Dept. of Computer Science, Technische Universität Darmstadt, Germany (August 2002)
4. Mühl, G.: Large-Scale Content-Based Publish/Subscribe Systems. PhD thesis, Dept. of Computer Science, Technische Universität Darmstadt, Germany (September 2002)
5. Widom, J., Ceri, S. (eds.): Active Database Systems: Triggers and Rules for Advanced Database Processing. Morgan Kaufmann Series in Data Management Systems, vol. 77. Morgan Kaufmann, San Francisco (1996)
6. Paton, N.W. (ed.): Active Rules in Database Systems. Monographs in Computer Science. Springer, New York (1999)
7. Dittrich, K.R., Gatziu, S., Geppert, A.: The Active Database Management System Manifesto: A Rulebase of ADBMS Features. In: Sellis, T.K. (ed.) RIDS 1995. LNCS, vol. 985, pp. 3–20. Springer, Heidelberg (1995)
8. Cilia, M.: Active Database Management Systems. In: Rivero, L.C., Doorn, J.H., Ferraggine, V.E. (eds.) Encyclopedia of Database Technologies and Applications, pp. 1–4. Idea Group (2005)
9. Zimmermann, J., Buchmann, A.P.: Benchmarking Active Database Systems: A Requirements Analysis. In: OOPSLA 1995 Workshop on Object Database Behavior, Benchmarks, and Performance, pp. 1–5 (1995)
10. Geppert, A., Gatziu, S., Dittrich, K.: A Designer's Benchmark for Active Database Management Systems: 007 Meets the BEAST. In: Sellis, T.K. (ed.) RIDS 1995. LNCS, vol. 985, pp. 309–326. Springer, Heidelberg (1995)
11. Geppert, A., Berndtsson, M., Lieuwen, D., Zimmermann, J.: Performance Evaluation of Active Database Management Systems Using the BEAST Benchmark. TR IFI-96.01, Dept. of Computer Science, University of Zurich (1996)

12. Konana, P., Mok, A.K., Lee, C.G., Woo, H., Liu, G.: Implementation and Performance Evaluation of a Real-Time E-Brokerage System. In: 21st IEEE Real-Time Systems Symposium, pp. 109–118 (2000)
13. Baralis, E., Bianco, A.: Performance Evaluation of Rule Execution Semantics in Active Databases. In: 13th ICDE, pp. 365–374. IEEE Computer Society, Los Alamitos (1997)
14. Menasce, D.A., Almeida, V.A.F.: Capacity Planning for Web Services: Metrics, Models, and Methods. Prentice Hall PTR, NJ (2001)

Towards State Space Reduction Based on T-Lumpability-Consistent Relations

Marco Bernardo

Università di Urbino "Carlo Bo" – Italy
Istituto di Scienze e Tecnologie dell'Informazione

Abstract. Markovian behavioral equivalences can be exploited for state space reduction before performance evaluation takes place. It is known that Markovian bisimilarity corresponds to ordinary lumpability and that Markovian testing and trace equivalences correspond to a coarser exact relation we call T-lumpability. While there exists an ordinary-lumpability-consistent aggregation algorithm, this is not the case with T-lumpability. Based on the axiomatization of Markovian testing and trace equivalences, we provide a sufficient condition for T-lumpability that can easily be embedded in the aggregation algorithm for ordinary lumpability, thus enhancing the potential for exact state space reduction. We also identify a class of systems – those providing incremental services – for which the resulting aggregation algorithm turns out to be useful.

1 Introduction

Markovian behavioral equivalences [2] are a formal means to establish whether different models represent systems that behave the same from the functional and performance point of view. For instance, Markovian bisimilarity [6] considers two models to be equivalent whenever they are able to mimic each other's functional and performance behavior step by step. Instead, Markovian testing equivalence [1] considers two models to be equivalent whenever an external observer interacting with them by means of tests is not able to distinguish between them from the functional or performance viewpoint. Finally, Markovian trace equivalence [8] considers two models to be equivalent whenever they are able to execute computations with the same functional and performance characteristics.

These equivalences can be exploited in practice for reducing the state space underlying a model before functional verification and performance evaluation take place. In our Markovian framework, the state space underlying a model represents a continuous-time Markov chain (CTMC). Useful CTMC-level aggregations are those that are exact. Given two CTMCs such that the second one is an exact aggregation of the first one, the transient/stationary probability of being in a macrostate of the second CTMC is the sum of the transient/stationary probabilities of being in one of the constituent microstates of the first CTMC. This means that, when going from the first CTMC to the second CTMC, all the performance characteristics are preserved.

N. Thomas and C. Juiz (Eds.): EPEW 2008, LNCS 5261, pp. 64–78, 2008.
© Springer-Verlag Berlin Heidelberg 2008

Markovian bisimilarity is consistent with an exact CTMC-level relation that is known under the name of ordinary lumpability [6,3], whereas Markovian testing and trace equivalences induce a coarser exact CTMC-level relation that we call T-lumpability [1]. Therefore, all the three Markovian behavioral equivalences are equally useful in principle for state space reduction purposes.

However, while there exists a polynomial-time aggregation algorithm for ordinary-lumpability [5], this is not the case with T-lumpability. In fact, while in the case of ordinary-lumpability-based state space reduction the states that can be aggregated are precisely those equivalent to each other, two T-lumpable states that are not ordinarily lumpable cannot be aggregated. This can be seen by looking at the axiomatization of Markovian testing and trace equivalences on a typical Markovian process calculus. Their characterizing laws show that the states that can be aggregated are not the two we are considering, but the ones reachable from them in one transition [1].

The contribution of this paper is to derive a sufficient condition for T-lumpability from the characterizing laws of Markovian testing and trace equivalences, which can be smoothly embedded as a state space preprocessing step in the aggregation algorithm for ordinary lumpability. Besides enhancing the potential for exact state space reduction in practice, we also identify a class of systems for which the resulting aggregation algorithm turns out to be useful. This is the class of systems providing incremental services, i.e. services consisting of sequences of phases such that each service is an extension of another.

This paper is organized as follows. In Sect. 2 we present a motivating example for our work, in which we introduce incremental services. In Sect. 3 we recall the definitions of Markovian bisimilarity, Markovian testing equivalence, and Markovian trace equivalence in a process algebraic framework, so that we can later on exhibit their characterizing equational laws. In Sect. 4 we recall the corresponding exact CTMC-level relations, i.e. ordinary lumpability and T-lumpability. In Sect. 5 we discuss the state space reduction issue by illustrating the characterizing laws of the three Markovian behavioral equivalences. In Sect. 6 we show how to modify the aggregation algorithm for ordinary lumpability in a way that takes into account the characterizing laws of the T-lumpability-consistent Markovian behavioral equivalences. Finally, Sect. 7 contains some concluding remarks.

2   Motivating Example: Incremental Services

Consider a set of services, each of which can be described as a sequence of phases. Then we can define the length of each of those services as the number of its phases and we can say that one of them is a prefix of another one if the phases of the former occur at the beginning of the latter exactly in the same order. We call those services incremental if each of them is a prefix of another one, except for the longest one.

We can distinguish between two ways of using incremental services, which we call eager and lazy, respectively. In the eager case, the client preselects the entire sequence of phases, hence the server knows in advance the specific service to be provided. By contrast, in the lazy case, the client decides what to do after each phase, so the specific service to be delivered is known only at the end. Whether the behavior of the client is eager or lazy has a remarkable impact on the size of the state space of the incremental service model.

In order to formalize this behavior, we can use a Markovian process calculus consisting of a set $\mathcal{P}$ of process terms built from a set $Name \times \mathbf{R}_{>0}$ of exponentially timed actions and a set of typical operators like the inactive process $\underline{0}$, the action prefix operator $<a, \lambda>.P$, the alternative composition operator governed by the race policy $P_1 + P_2$, the parallel composition operator $P_1 \parallel_S P_2$, and possibly recursive defining equations of the form $B \stackrel{\Delta}{=} P$. The semantics of each process term P is constructed by applying operational rules that yield a state-transition graph $[\![P]\!]$ called labeled multitransition system, whose states correspond to process terms derivable from P and whose transitions are labeled with actions.

As an example of incremental services, consider an Italian restaurant. What can be served is an appetizer, or an appetizer followed by the first course (typically pasta), or an appetizer followed by the first course and the second course (typically meat or fish with some vegetables), or an appetizer followed by the two main courses and some cheese, or an appetizer followed by the two main courses, some cheese and a dessert, or an appetizer followed by the two main courses, some cheese, a dessert and some fruit, or a complete Italian meal (appetizer, first course, second course, cheese, dessert, fruit, and espresso).

Suppose that a client takes $1/\lambda$ time units on average to read the menu, that course i is prepared and served in $1/\mu_i$ time units on average for $1 \leq i \leq 7$, and that subsequence i of the complete meal is selected with probability p_i for $1 \leq i \leq 7$.

An eager client preselects the desired subsequence of the complete meal, hence the related behavior can be described as follows:

$Eager \stackrel{\Delta}{=} <read, \lambda \cdot p_1>.<appetizer, \mu_1>.\underline{0} +$
$\qquad <read, \lambda \cdot p_2>.<appetizer, \mu_1>.<first\_course, \mu_2>.\underline{0} +$
$\qquad <read, \lambda \cdot p_3>.<appetizer, \mu_1>.<first\_course, \mu_2>.$
$\qquad\qquad\qquad <second\_course, \mu_3>.\underline{0} +$
$\qquad <read, \lambda \cdot p_4>.<appetizer, \mu_1>.<first\_course, \mu_2>.$
$\qquad\qquad\qquad <second\_course, \mu_3>.<cheese, \mu_4>.\underline{0} +$
$\qquad <read, \lambda \cdot p_5>.<appetizer, \mu_1>.<first\_course, \mu_2>.$
$\qquad\qquad\qquad <second\_course, \mu_3>.<cheese, \mu_4>.$
$\qquad\qquad\qquad <dessert, \mu_5>.\underline{0} +$
$\qquad <read, \lambda \cdot p_6>.<appetizer, \mu_1>.<first\_course, \mu_2>.$
$\qquad\qquad\qquad <second\_course, \mu_3>.<cheese, \mu_4>.$
$\qquad\qquad\qquad <dessert, \mu_5>.<fruit, \mu_6>.\underline{0} +$
$\qquad <read, \lambda \cdot p_7>.<appetizer, \mu_1>.<first\_course, \mu_2>.$
$\qquad\qquad\qquad <second\_course, \mu_3>.<cheese, \mu_4>.$
$\qquad\qquad\qquad <dessert, \mu_5>.<fruit, \mu_6>.<espresso, \mu_7>.\underline{0}$

A lazy client instead decides after each course whether to stop or to proceed with the next course, hence the related behavior can be described as follows where p_{l-r} stands for $\sum_{l \leq i \leq r} p_i$ with $1 \leq l \leq r \leq 7$:

$Lazy \overset{\Delta}{=} <read, \lambda>.Lazy_1$

$Lazy_1 \overset{\Delta}{=} <appetizer, \mu_1 \cdot p_1>.\underline{0} + <appetizer, \mu_1 \cdot p_{2-7}>.Lazy_2$

$Lazy_2 \overset{\Delta}{=} <first\_course, \mu_2 \cdot \frac{p_2}{p_{2-7}}>.\underline{0} + <first\_course, \mu_2 \cdot \frac{p_{3-7}}{p_{2-7}}>.Lazy_3$

$Lazy_3 \overset{\Delta}{=} <second\_course, \mu_3 \cdot \frac{p_3}{p_{3-7}}>.\underline{0} + <second\_course, \mu_3 \cdot \frac{p_{4-7}}{p_{3-7}}>.Lazy_4$

$Lazy_4 \overset{\Delta}{=} <cheese, \mu_4 \cdot \frac{p_4}{p_{4-7}}>.\underline{0} + <cheese, \mu_4 \cdot \frac{p_{5-7}}{p_{4-7}}>.Lazy_5$

$Lazy_5 \overset{\Delta}{=} <dessert, \mu_5 \cdot \frac{p_5}{p_{5-7}}>.\underline{0} + <dessert, \mu_5 \cdot \frac{p_{6-7}}{p_{5-7}}>.Lazy_6$

$Lazy_6 \overset{\Delta}{=} <fruit, \mu_6 \cdot \frac{p_6}{p_{6-7}}>.\underline{0} + <fruit, \mu_6 \cdot \frac{p_7}{p_{6-7}}>.Lazy_7$

$Lazy_7 \overset{\Delta}{=} <espresso, \mu_7>.\underline{0}$

The labeled multitransition systems $[\![Eager]\!]$ and $[\![Lazy]\!]$ are shown below, where every action name is represented through its initials:

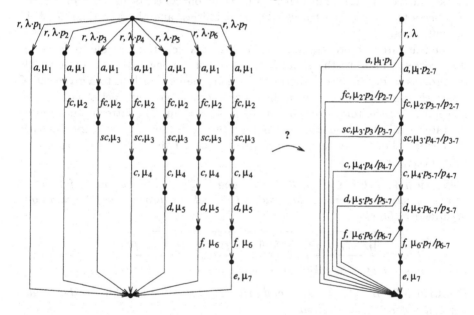

As can be noted, $[\![Eager]\!]$ has 30 states and 35 transitions, whereas $[\![Lazy]\!]$ has only 9 states and 14 transitions. It can also be observed that the time taken by the client to consume a meal follows a phase-type distribution in both cases.

While the eager behavior occurs more frequently in practice, the lazy behavior is more convenient when analyzing incremental services due to its reduced state space. In general, if we consider a set of $k \geq 2$ incremental services, its eager description will have $\sum_{1 \leq i \leq k} i = \frac{k \cdot (k+1)}{2} = O(k^2)$ states, whereas its lazy description will have only $O(k)$ states.

Switching from one description to the other – and hence from one phase-type distribution to the other – is feasible only if they are equivalent. If we use a behavioral equivalence like Markovian bisimilarity, which is highly sensitive to branching points, there is no hope to relate the two descriptions. What we need is thus a less discriminating equivalence. It can be easily shown that the two descriptions are Markovian testing equivalent. But, unfortunately, there is no aggregation algorithm that, consistently with Markovian testing equivalence, would allow us to transform the labeled multitransition system for the eager description into the labeled multitransition system for the lazy description.

3 Markovian Behavioral Equivalences

In this section we recall the definitions of Markovian bisimilarity, Markovian testing equivalence, and Markovian trace equivalence in our process algebraic framework.

3.1 Exit Rates and Computations

Markovian behavioral equivalences are based on concepts like the exit rates of process terms and the traces, the probabilities, and the durations of their computations.

The exit rate of a process term is the rate at which it is possible to leave the state corresponding to the term. We distinguish among (a) the rate at which the process term can execute actions of a given name that lead to a given set of terms, (b) the total rate at which the process term can execute actions of a given name, and (c) the total exit rate of the process term. The latter is the sum of the rates of all the actions that the process term can execute, and coincides with the reciprocal of the average sojourn time in the CTMC state corresponding to the process term.

Definition 1. *Let $P \in \mathcal{P}$, $a \in Name$, and $C \subseteq \mathcal{P}$. The exit rate of P when executing actions of name a that lead to C is defined through the following non-negative real function:*

$$rate(P, a, C) = \sum \{\!\!| \lambda \mid \exists P' \in C. P \xrightarrow{a, \lambda} P' |\!\!\}$$

where the summation is taken to be zero whenever the multiset is empty. ∎

Definition 2. *Let $P \in \mathcal{P}$. The total exit rate of P is defined through the following non-negative real function:*

$$rate_t(P) = \sum_{a \in Name} rate(P, a, \mathcal{P})$$

where $rate(P, a, \mathcal{P})$ is the total exit rate of P with respect to a. ∎

A computation of a process term is a sequence of transitions that can be executed starting from the state corresponding to the term. The length of a computation is given by the number of transitions occurring in it. We say that two computations are independent of each other if neither is a proper prefix of the other one. In the following, we denote by $\mathcal{C}_f(P)$ and $\mathcal{I}_f(P)$ the multisets of finite-length computations and of finite-length independent computations of $P \in \mathcal{P}$, respectively. Below we inductively define the trace, the execution probability, and the stepwise average duration of an element of $\mathcal{C}_f(P)$, using symbol "∘" to denote the sequence concatenation operator.

Definition 3. *Let $P \in \mathcal{P}$ and $c \in \mathcal{C}_f(P)$. The trace associated with the execution of c is the sequence of action names labeling the transitions of c, which is defined by induction on the length of c through the following $Name^*$-valued function:*

$$trace(c) = \begin{cases} \varepsilon & \text{if } length(c) = 0 \\ a \circ trace(c') & \text{if } c \equiv P \xrightarrow{a,\lambda} c' \end{cases}$$

where ε is the empty trace. ∎

Definition 4. *Let $P \in \mathcal{P}$ and $c \in \mathcal{C}_f(P)$. The probability of executing c is the product of the execution probabilities of the transitions of c, which is defined by induction on the length of c through the following $\mathbf{R}_{]0,1]}$-valued function:*

$$prob(c) = \begin{cases} 1 & \text{if } length(c) = 0 \\ \frac{\lambda}{rate_t(P)} \cdot prob(c') & \text{if } c \equiv P \xrightarrow{a,\lambda} c' \end{cases}$$

We also define the probability of executing a computation of C as:

$$prob(C) = \sum_{c \in C} prob(c)$$

for all $C \subseteq \mathcal{I}_f(P)$. ∎

Note that $prob(C)$ would not be well defined if set C contained computations that are not indepedent of each other.

Definition 5. *Let $P \in \mathcal{P}$ and $c \in \mathcal{C}_f(P)$. The stepwise average duration of c is the sequence of the average sojourn times in the states traversed by c, which is defined by induction on the length of c through the following $(\mathbf{R}_{>0})^*$-valued function:*

$$time(c) = \begin{cases} \varepsilon & \text{if } length(c) = 0 \\ \frac{1}{rate_t(P)} \circ time(c') & \text{if } c \equiv P \xrightarrow{a,\lambda} c' \end{cases}$$

where ε is the empty stepwise average duration. We also define the multiset of computations of C whose stepwise average duration is not greater than θ as:

$$C_{\leq \theta} = \{\!\! | \, c \in C \mid length(c) \leq length(\theta) \land \\ \forall i = 1, \ldots, length(c). \, time(c)[i] \leq \theta[i] \, |\!\!\}$$

for all $C \subseteq \mathcal{C}_f(P)$ and $\theta \in (\mathbf{R}_{>0})^*$. ∎

The reason why we consider the stepwise average duration instead of the standard average duration (intended as the sum of the average sojourn times in the traversed states) is explained in [1].

3.2 Markovian Bisimilarity

Markovian bisimilarity [6] considers two process terms to be equivalent whenever they are able to mimic each other's functional and performance behavior step by step.

Whenever a process term can perform actions with a certain name that reach a certain set of terms at a certain speed, then any process term equivalent to the given one has to be able to respond with actions with the same name that reach an equivalent set of terms at the same speed. This can be formalized through the comparison of the process term exit rates.

Definition 6. *An equivalence relation $\mathcal{B} \subseteq \mathcal{P} \times \mathcal{P}$ is a Markovian bisimulation iff, whenever $(P_1, P_2) \in \mathcal{B}$, then for all action names $a \in Name$ and equivalence classes $C \in \mathcal{P}/\mathcal{B}$:*

$$rate(P_1, a, C) = rate(P_2, a, C)$$
■

Since the union of all the Markovian bisimulations can be proved to be the largest Markovian bisimulation, the definition below follows.

Definition 7. *Markovian bisimilarity, denoted by $\sim_{\mathrm{MB}}$, is the union of all the Markovian bisimulations.*
■

3.3 Markovian Testing Equivalence

Markovian testing equivalence [1] considers two process terms to be equivalent whenever an external observer interacting with them by means of tests is not able to distinguish between them from the functional or performance viewpoint.

A test can be represented through another process term, which interacts with the term to be tested by means of a parallel composition operator that enforces synchronization on all action names. Since a test should be conducted in a finite amount of time, for the test formalization we restrict ourselves to non-recursive, finite-state process terms. In our Markovian framework, tests are made out of passive actions, each equipped with a weight $w \in \mathbf{R}_{>0}$. The idea is that, in any of its states, a process term to be tested probabilistically generates the proposal of an action to be executed among those enabled in that state, then the test reacts by probabilistically selecting a passive action (if any) with the same name as the proposed action.

Definition 8. *The set $\mathcal{T}$ of tests is generated by the following syntax:*

$$
\begin{array}{l}
T ::= \mathrm{s} \mid T' \\
T' ::= <a, *_w>.T \mid T' + T'
\end{array}
$$

where $a \in Name$, $w \in \mathbf{R}_{>0}$, and s stands for success.
■

Let us denote by $\longrightarrow_T$ the transition relation for tests. The following operational rule defines the interaction of $P \in \mathcal{P}$ and $T \in \mathcal{T}$:

$$\frac{P \xrightarrow{a,\lambda} P' \quad T \xrightarrow{a,*w}_{\mathrm{T}} T'}{P \parallel T \xrightarrow{a,\lambda \cdot \frac{w}{weight(T,a)}} P' \parallel T'}$$

where $weight(T,a) = \sum \{\!| w \mid \exists T'. T \xrightarrow{a,*w}_{\mathrm{T}} T' |\!\}$ is the weight of T with respect to a.

Definition 9. *Let $P \in \mathcal{P}$ and $T \in \mathcal{T}$. The interaction system of P and T is process term $P \parallel T$, where we say that:*

- *A configuration is a state of the labeled multitransition system underlying $P \parallel T$.*
- *A configuration is successful iff its test component is s.*
- *A computation is successful iff so is the last configuration it reaches.*

We denote by $\mathcal{SC}(P,T)$ the multiset of successful computations of $\mathcal{C}_\mathrm{f}(P \parallel T)$. ∎

Note that $\mathcal{SC}(P,T) \subseteq \mathcal{I}_\mathrm{f}(P \parallel T)$, because of the maximality of the successful test-driven computations, and that $\mathcal{SC}(P,T)$ is finite, because of the finitely-branching structure of the considered terms.

Markovian testing equivalence relies on comparing the process term probabilities of performing a successful test-driven computation within a given sequence of average amounts of time.

Definition 10. *Let $P_1, P_2 \in \mathcal{P}$. We say that P_1 is Markovian testing equivalent to P_2, written $P_1 \sim_{\mathrm{MT}} P_2$, iff for all tests $T \in \mathcal{T}$ and sequences $\theta \in (\mathbf{R}_{>0})^*$ of average amounts of time:*
$$prob(\mathcal{SC}_{\leq\theta}(P_1,T)) = prob(\mathcal{SC}_{\leq\theta}(P_2,T))$$
∎

3.4 Markovian Trace Equivalence

Markovian trace equivalence [8] considers two process terms to be equivalent whenever they are able to execute computations with the same functional and performance characteristics.

It relies on comparing the process term probabilities of performing a computation within a given sequence of average amounts of time.

Definition 11. *Let $P \in \mathcal{P}$, $c \in \mathcal{C}_\mathrm{f}(P)$, and $\alpha \in Name^*$. We say that c is compatible with α iff:*
$$trace(c) = \alpha$$
We denote by $\mathcal{CC}(P,\alpha)$ the multiset of finite-length computations of P that are compatible with α. ∎

Note that $\mathcal{CC}(P,\alpha) \subseteq \mathcal{I}_\mathrm{f}(P)$, because of the compatibility of the computations with the same trace α, and that $\mathcal{CC}(P,\alpha)$ is finite, because of the finitely-branching structure of the considered terms.

Definition 12. *Let $P_1, P_2 \in \mathcal{P}$. We say that P_1 is Markovian trace equivalent to P_2, written $P_1 \sim_{\mathrm{MTr}} P_2$, iff for all traces $\alpha \in Name^*$ and sequences $\theta \in (\mathbf{R}_{>0})^*$ of average amounts of time:*
$$prob(\mathcal{CC}_{\leq\theta}(P_1, \alpha)) = prob(\mathcal{CC}_{\leq\theta}(P_2, \alpha))$$
∎

4   Induced CTMC-Level Relations

All of the three Markovian behavioral equivalences recalled in the previous section induce CTMC-level relations. In order to ease the formalization of these relations, we take an arbitrary CTMC with state space S, whose transitions are labeled not only with rates but also with the same action name a. In other words, a CTMC is viewed as a labeled transition system in which the label set is $\{a\} \times \mathbf{R}_{>0}$. This allows us to define the induced CTMC-level relations as special cases of the considered Markovian behavioral equivalences.

Markovian bisimilarity is consistent with a CTMC-level relation known under the name of ordinary lumpability [6,3].

Definition 13. *Let $s_1, s_2 \in S$. We say that s_1 and s_2 are ordinarily lumpable iff there exists a partition $\mathcal{O}$ of S such that s_1 and s_2 belong to the same equivalence class and, whenever $z_1, z_2 \in O$ for some $O \in \mathcal{O}$, then for all $O' \in \mathcal{O}$:*
$$\sum_{z' \in O'} \{\!| \lambda \mid z_1 \xrightarrow{a,\lambda} z' |\!\} = \sum_{z' \in O'} \{\!| \lambda \mid z_2 \xrightarrow{a,\lambda} z' |\!\}$$
∎

Markovian testing and trace equivalences induce a coarser CTMC-level relation that we call T-lumpability [1].

Definition 14. *Let $s_1, s_2 \in S$. We say that s_1 and s_2 are T-lumpable iff for all tests $T \in \mathcal{T}$ and sequences $\theta \in (\mathbf{R}_{>0})^*$ of average amounts of time:*
$$prob(\mathcal{SC}_{\leq\theta}(s_1, T)) = prob(\mathcal{SC}_{\leq\theta}(s_2, T))$$
∎

Since the transitions of the CTMC are all labeled with the same action name, the branching structure of tests adds no distinguishing power with respect to traces. Thus, the definition above is equivalent to the one below.

Definition 15. *Let $s_1, s_2 \in S$. We say that s_1 and s_2 are T-lumpable iff for all traces $\alpha \in Name^*$ and sequences $\theta \in (\mathbf{R}_{>0})^*$ of average amounts of time:*
$$prob(\mathcal{CC}_{\leq\theta}(s_1, \alpha)) = prob(\mathcal{CC}_{\leq\theta}(s_2, \alpha))$$
∎

5   An Axiom-Based View of State Space Reduction

According to Markovian bisimilarity (resp. ordinary lumpability), two equivalent states can reach sets of equivalent states by performing transitions with the same names and the same total rates. This causes equivalent states of a labeled multitransition system (resp. CTMC) to be precisely the states that can be aggregated. In other words, the partition induced by the equivalence relation, whose elements correspond to equivalence classes, can be directly exploited for state space reduction purposes. This can easily be seen through the equational law characterizing $\sim_{MB}$, which establishes that:

$$\boxed{<a,\lambda_1>.P_1 + <a,\lambda_2>.P_2 \sim_{MB} <a,\lambda_1+\lambda_2>.P}$$

whenever:

$$\boxed{P_1 \sim_{MB} P \sim_{MB} P_2}$$

Its effect at the state space reduction level is shown below:

From $\sim_{MB}\subset\sim_{MT}\subset\sim_{MTr}$ we derive that more states can be related to each other when using Markovian testing and trace equivalences (resp. T-lumpability). However, these additional equivalent states must be carefully treated at state space reduction time. The reason is that they cannot be aggregated. What turns out is that the states they reach – which are not necessarily equivalent to each other – can be sometimes aggregated. This is clearly shown by the characterizing law for $\sim_{MT}$ – which subsumes the one for $\sim_{MB}$ – and the characterizing law for $\sim_{MTr}$ – which subsumes the one for $\sim_{MT}$ [1].

The first characterizing law establishes that $\sim_{MT}$ allows choices to be deferred as long as they are related to branches starting with actions having the same name – as in the $\sim_{MB}$ case – that are immediately followed by actions having the same names and the same total rates in all the branches. Formally:

$$\boxed{\begin{array}{l}\sum_{i\in I} <a,\lambda_i>.\sum_{j\in J_i} <b_{i,j},\mu_{i,j}>.P_{i,j} \sim_{MT} \\ <a,\sum_{k\in I}\lambda_k>.\sum_{i\in I}\sum_{j\in J_i} <b_{i,j},\frac{\lambda_i}{\Sigma_{k\in I}\lambda_k}\cdot\mu_{i,j}>.P_{i,j}\end{array}}$$

whenever:

- I is a finite index set with $|I| \geq 2$.
- J_i is a finite index set for all $i \in I$, with the related summation being $\underline{0}$ whenever $J_i = \emptyset$.
- For all $i_1, i_2 \in I$ and $b \in Name$:

$$\boxed{\sum_{j\in J_{i_1},b_{i_1,j}=b}\mu_{i_1,j} = \sum_{j\in J_{i_2},b_{i_2,j}=b}\mu_{i_2,j}}$$

with each summation being zero whenever its index set is empty.

The effect at the state space reduction level of the simplest instance of the law above is shown below:

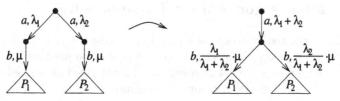

where the two initial states are related by $\sim_{MT}$ but not by $\sim_{MB}$ (unless $P_1 \sim_{MB} P_2$), while the two states reached by the initial state on the left are aggregated on the right although they are not necessarily equivalent in any sense.

The second characterizing law establishes that $\sim_{MTr}$ allows choices to be deferred as long as they are related to branches starting with actions having the same name – as in the $\sim_{MB}$ and $\sim_{MT}$ cases – that are followed by terms having the same total exit rate. Note that – unlike the $\sim_{MT}$ case – the names and the total rates of the initial actions of such derivative terms can be different in the various branches. Formally:

$$\boxed{\begin{array}{c} \sum_{i \in I} <a, \lambda_i>. \sum_{j \in J_i} <b_{i,j}, \mu_{i,j}>.P_{i,j} \quad \sim_{MTr} \\[2mm] <a, \sum_{k \in I} \lambda_k>. \sum_{i \in I} \sum_{j \in J_i} <b_{i,j}, \frac{\lambda_i}{\Sigma_{k \in I} \lambda_k} \cdot \mu_{i,j}>.P_{i,j} \end{array}}$$

whenever:

- I is a finite index set with $|I| \geq 2$.
- J_i is a finite index set for all $i \in I$, with the related summation being $\underline{0}$ whenever $J_i = \emptyset$.
- For all $i_1, i_2 \in I$:

$$\boxed{\sum_{j \in J_{i_1}} \mu_{i_1,j} = \sum_{j \in J_{i_2}} \mu_{i_2,j}}$$

with each summation being zero whenever its index set is empty.

The effect at the state space reduction level of the simplest instance of the law above is shown below:

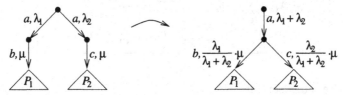

where the two initial states are related by $\sim_{MTr}$ but not by $\sim_{MT}$ (unless $b = c$). As before, the two states reached by the initial state on the left are aggregated on the right although they are not necessarily equivalent in any sense.

It is worth observing that the two laws characterizing $\sim_{MT}$ and $\sim_{MTr}$, respectively, differ only for functional details, whereas they are identical from the performance point of view – consistently with the fact that both $\sim_{MT}$ and $\sim_{MTr}$ rely on the same CTMC-level relation.

6   Aggregation Algorithm for T-Lumpability

For Markovian bisimilarity (resp. ordinary lumpability) it is well known that a partition refinement algorithm in the style of [7] can be used, which exploits the fact that the equivalence relation can be characterized as a fixed point of successively finer relations. In fact, for $\sim_{MB}$ we have:

$$\sim_{MB} = \bigcap_{i \in \mathbf{N}} \sim_{MB,i}$$

where $\sim_{MB,0} = \mathcal{P} \times \mathcal{P}$ and $\sim_{MB,i}$ is defined as follows for $i \geq 1$: whenever $(P_1, P_2) \in \sim_{MB,i}$, then for all $a \in$ *Name* and $C \in \mathcal{P}/\sim_{MB,i-1}$:

$$rate(P_1, a, C) = rate(P_2, a, C)$$

In other words, $\sim_{MB,0}$ induces a trivial partition with a single equivalence class that coincides with $\mathcal{P}$, $\sim_{MB,1}$ refines the previous partition by creating an equivalence class for each set of terms that possess the same total exit rates with respect to the same action names, and so on.

The minimization algorithm for $\sim_{MB}$ (resp. ordinary lumpability) proceeds as follows:

1. Build the initial partition with a single class including all the states, then initialize a list of splitters with this class.
2. Refine the current partition by splitting each of its classes according to the exit rates towards one of the splitters, then remove this splitter from the list.
3. For each split class, insert into the list of splitters all the resulting subclasses except for the largest one.
4. If the list of splitters is not empty, go back to the refinement step.

The time complexity is $O(m \cdot \log n)$, where n is the number of states and m is the number of transitions. In order to achieve this complexity, it is necessary to resort to a splay tree when representing the subclasses arising from the splitting of a class [5].

Since $\sim_{MT}$ and $\sim_{MTr}$ (resp. T-lumpability) are coarser than $\sim_{MB}$ (resp. ordinary lumpability), the algorithm above can be used as a basis to construct an aggregation algorithm for T-lumpability-based relations. The idea is to include a preprocessing step at the beginning of the algorithm, which rewrites the state space in a way that the additional states that can be aggregated as discussed in Sect. 5 are actually aggregated before the partition refinement process starts:

0. Preprocess the state space by aggregating the states reachable by a state that satisfies the conditions associated with the law characterizing $\sim_{MT}$ or $\sim_{MTr}$.

More precisely, two states s_1, s_2 can be aggregated in the above preprocessing step if the following four constraints are satisfied:

(*i*) There exists at least one state z with outgoing transitions reaching both s_1 and s_2 that are labeled with the same action name.
(*ii*) s_1 and s_2 have the same total exit rate (in the $\sim_{MT}$ case, this constraint must hold with respect to individual action names).
(*iii*) There is no state z' with outgoing transitions reaching only one between s_1 and s_2.

(*iv*) Given any two states z_1, z_2 with outgoing transitions reaching both s_1 and s_2, for $i = 1, 2$ the probability with which z_1 reaches s_i is equal to the probability with which z_2 reaches s_i (in the $\sim_{MT}$ case, this constraint must hold with respect to individual action names).

Constraints (*i*) and (*ii*) are straightforward consequences of the characterizing laws, whereas constraints (*iii*) and (*iv*) describe the context in which T-lumpability-consistent aggregations can safely take place.

Constraint (*iii*) avoids aggregations like the following:

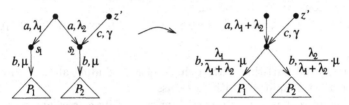

where z' would be enabled to reach P_1. We observe that in this scenario a correct aggregation would be the following:

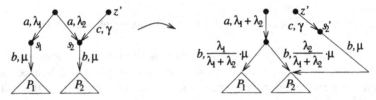

This requires a duplicate s_2' of s_2 – which in process algebraic terms could be formalized as $s_2 + \underline{0}$ – hence it may be in contrast with our objective of reducing the state space. In general, the suitability of duplicating states depends on the difference between the numbers of states before and after the duplication/aggregation process, which is zero in the example above.

Constraint (*iv*) avoids aggregations in situations like the following:

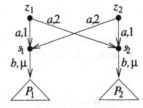

Here the problem is that the new state resulting from the aggregation of s_1 and s_2 should reach P_1 with probability $1/3$ and P_2 with probability $2/3$ when coming from z_1, while it should reach P_1 with probability $2/3$ and P_2 with probability $1/3$ when coming from z_2. This is not possible in a memoryless stochastic model like a CTMC. It could only be achieved by duplicating both s_1 and s_2 in such a way that z_1 reaches $s_{1,1}$ and $s_{1,2}$ while z_2 reaches $s_{2,1}$ and $s_{2,2}$. At that point $s_{1,1}$ and $s_{1,2}$ could be aggregated into s_1' and $s_{2,1}$ and $s_{2,2}$ could be aggregated into s_2', as shown below:

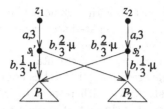

Also in this case duplication may be in contrast with our objective of reducing the state space, hence the same remark as for the previous constraint applies.

From the point of view of singling out states that can be aggregated according to T-lumpability but not according to ordinary lumpability, constraints (i) and (ii) are strictly necessary as they are connected to the characterizing laws. Likewise, constraint (iv) is strictly necessary as it guarantees that the stochastic model obtained after the aggregation process is still a CTMC. By contrast, constraint (iii) expresses a sufficient but not necessary condition. Consider for instance the following scenario:

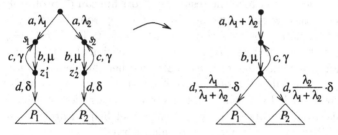

Constraint (iii) is violated because there is a state (z_1') reaching only s_1 and another state (z_2') reaching only s_2. Nevertheless, the aggregation shown above is consistent with T-lumpability.

The preprocessing step to be applied before the refinement process of the minimization algorithm for $\sim_{MB}$ (resp. ordinary lumpability) can be implemented through a depth-first visit of the state space, provided that both the reachability relation and its inverse relation are represented in the labeled multitransition system to be reduced. In other words, every state has to encode not only its outgoing transitions, but also its incoming transitions. During the visit, for each state we check whether some of its derivative states satisfy constraints (i) and (ii). If this is the case, we check whether constraints (iii) and (iv) are satisfied as well by those derivative states (here inverse reachability is needed). If so, those derivative states are aggregated into a new state according to the characterizing law for the equivalence relation of interest ($\sim_{MT}$ or $\sim_{MTr}$). The time complexity of the visit is $O(n + m)$, where n is the number of states and m is the number of transitions of the labeled multitransition system.

If we go back to the incremental service example of Sect. 2, we see that the preprocessing step trasforms $[Eager]$ into $[Lazy]$, thus achieving a quadratic reduction of the state space size. As usual, the other steps of the resulting aggregation algorithm come into play in case of symmetries. Suppose that at the Italian restaurants there are $h \geq 2$ independent clients, each identical to the eager client. Then the description of the whole set of clients will have $O(\alpha^h)$ states for some $\alpha > 1$, while the aggregated state space will have $O(h)$ states at the end of the partition refinement process.

In the case of identical clients using incremental services, we observe that the T-lumpability-consistent aggregation algorithm has not only the effect of further reducing the size of the state space with respect to the ordinary-lumpability-consistent minimization algorithm. In fact, if applied to each client individually before composing the clients in parallel, it speeds up the execution of the last application of the algorithm itself to the whole system.

7 Conclusion

We have exploited the characterizing laws of Markovian testing and trace equivalences to enhance the potential for exact state space reduction of ordinary lumpability. Moreover, we have singled out a class of systems – those providing incremental services – to which the resulting algorithm can be profitably applied.

Concerning future work, we would like to develop some heuristics that help deciding whether and when it is convenient to perform local state duplications in order to satisfy constraints (*iii*) and (*iv*) in situations like those in Sect. 6.

Furthermore, we would like to investigate whether the algorithm for verifying classical testing equivalence proposed in [4] – which reduces testing equivalence verification over labeled transition systems to the verification of a generalization of bisimilarity over acceptance graphs – can be of help in order to strengthen our T-lumpability-consistent aggregation algorithm.

References

1. Bernardo, M.: "Non-Bisimulation-Based Markovian Behavioral Equivalences". Journal of Logic and Algebraic Programming 72, 3–49 (2007)
2. Bernardo, M.: A Survey of Markovian Behavioral Equivalences. In: Bernardo, M., Hillston, J. (eds.) SFM 2007. LNCS, vol. 4486, pp. 180–219. Springer, Heidelberg (2007)
3. Buchholz, P.: Exact and Ordinary Lumpability in Finite Markov Chains. Journal of Applied Probability 31, 59–75 (1994)
4. Cleaveland, R., Hennessy, M.: Testing Equivalence as a Bisimulation Equivalence. Formal Aspects of Computing 5, 1–20 (1993)
5. Derisavi, S., Hermanns, H., Sanders, W.H.: Optimal State-Space Lumping in Markov Chains. Information Processing Letters 87, 309–315 (2003)
6. Hillston, J.: A Compositional Approach to Performance Modelling. Cambridge University Press, Cambridge (1996)
7. Paige, R., Tarjan, R.E.: Three Partition Refinement Algorithms. SIAM Journal on Computing 16, 973–989 (1987)
8. Wolf, V., Baier, C., Majster-Cederbaum, M.: Trace Machines for Observing Continuous-Time Markov Chains. In: Proc.of the 3rd Int. Workshop on Quantitative Aspects of Programming Languages (QAPL 2005), Edinburgh, UK. ENTCS, vol. 153(2), pp. 259–277 (2005)

A Ticking Clock: Performance Analysis of a Circadian Rhythm with Stochastic Process Algebra

Jeremy T. Bradley

Department of Computing, Imperial College London
180 Queen's Gate, London SW7 2BZ, United Kingdom
jb@doc.ic.ac.uk

Abstract. We apply performance analysis techniques to a biological modelling problem, that of capturing and reproducing the Circadian rhythm. A Circadian rhythm provides cells with a clock by which to regulate their behaviour. We consider two distinct stochastic models of the Circadian rhythm – one unbounded and the other bounded. We consider a fluid approximation of the models, and, by conversion to a set of ordinary differential equations, we are able to reproduce the correct rhythm. We show that with a bounded model, the clock phase can be affected by modifying the ability to manufacture some proteins.

1 Introduction

Many biological systems make use of a Circadian clock to keep track of the passage of time. The Circadian clock has evolved to create periodic concentrations of chemicals, in such a way that cells can regulate their behaviour according to the time of day or season of the year [1,2].

The basic Circadian mechanism uses a two gene-regulated positive and negative feedback mechanism to achieve regular periodic fluctuations in the concentration of a protein within the cell. The exact concentration of protein provides the cell with a means of determining the time of day.

We compare modelling techniques from different modelling paradigms, stochastic π-calculus [3] and PEPA [4], to generate two distinct Circadian clock models. The stochastic π-calculus model has an unbounded state-space and we suggest a systematic approach for generating an equivalent but bounded PEPA model. A bounded process model has the advantage of generating a finite continuous-time Markov chain which can be analysed using standard CTMC techniques. Although in this case, we do not use this aspect of the finite model, we make use of a further feature of the finite PEPA model that allows us to restrict the total amount of fluctuating protein that is capable of being made. This allows us to simulate resource starvation and observe its effect on the Circadian rhythm.

Recent innovations in the analysis of stochastic process algebras allow massive stochastic state spaces to be analysed. We take advantage of a fluid approximation for both stochastic π-calculus [3] and PEPA [5,6] to generate sets of ordinary

N. Thomas and C. Juiz (Eds.): EPEW 2008, LNCS 5261, pp. 79–94, 2008.

differential equations which capture the time-varying concentrations of chemicals in the system.

In this paper, we introduce the versions of PEPA and stochastic π-calculus being used. We describe the mechanism behind the Circadian clock in Section 2 and present the process models in Section 3. We discuss solutions of the resulting ODEs from the process models in Section 4.

2   Circadian Clock

Figure 1 (as used in [1]) shows a biological graphical description of a Circadian clock with two DNA molecules for proteins A and R interacting through their respective mRNA molecules.

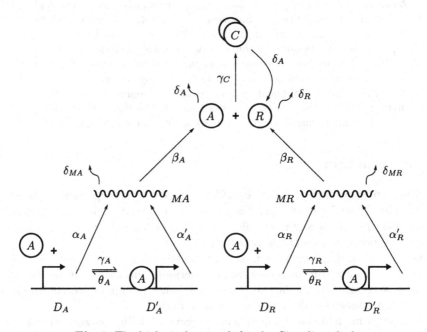

Fig. 1. The biological network for the Circadian clock

In the diagram, there are two DNA molecules, D_A and D_R, which describe proteins A and R. These DNA molecules generate mRNA molecules which in turn generate their respective proteins. High concentrations of the R protein absorb the A molecules and therefore R acts as a repressor for A. In the absence of A, R will degrade naturally.

A also acts as an activator for the generation of mRNA for both A and R molecules. An A protein can bind with either DNA strand to enable generation of mRNA for A or R at a much accelerated rate, compared to the DNA being unbound. Thus, we have several opportunities for constructive and destructive

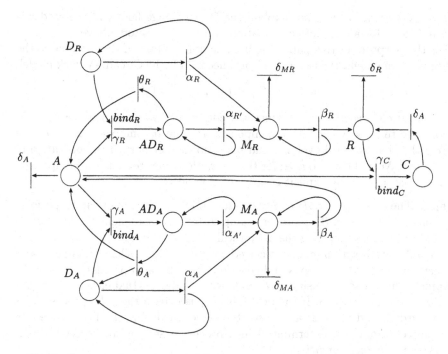

Fig. 2. An equivalent unbounded Petri net model of the gene/protein network

feedback within the system. The result is that the concentration of A should oscillate in anti-phase to the concentration of R. The spikes in the concentration of A act as the ticks of a clock for an organism.

For computer science audience, we derive a stochastic Petri net equivalent system for Figure 1, shown in Figure 2. We use Figure 2 to create both stochastic π-calculus and PEPA models of the gene network.

3   Stochastic Process Models

3.1   Stochastic π-Calculus

π-calculus [7] was designed to be a data-oriented extension of CCS [8] and stochastic π-calculus was, in turn, a timed extension of that. The original stochastic π-calculus, as defined by Priami [3], has the following syntax:

$$P ::= \mathbf{0} \mid (\pi, r).P \mid (\nu x)P \mid [x = y]P \mid P + P \mid (P \mid P) \mid P(y_1, \ldots, y_n)$$

where π may be either $x(y)$ representing data y being input on channel x or $\bar{x}(y)$ which represents data y being output on channel x or τ representing a silent action.

In this system, P denotes a system component, which can send data (or names) along channels. That data can be compared and conditional execution can be expressed. We will not explain the full language here and the reader is directed to [3] for a complete explanation of all the operators above.

For the purposes of this paper, we use a simpler subset of the calculus as the full breadth of stochastic π-calculus is not needed for the Circadian clock model.

$$P ::= \mathbf{0} \mid \pi_r.P \mid P + P \mid (P \mid P) \mid A$$

The central construction $\pi_r.P$ denotes a component which can undertake a π action at rate r to evolve into a component P. The $\mathbf{0}$ component represents a system that has stopped evolving and plays no further part in the operation of the system. We will have no need for the restriction operator, νx, the comparison operator, $[x = y]$ or the explicit concept of channels.

Prefix. The operation $\pi_r.P$ expresses the ability of a component to perform π-action at rate r. The rate, r, samples from an exponential distribution and determines how long the action will take. The action π above can either be an emitted action, a, or a received coaction, $\bar{a}$, or a silent τ action. Silent actions occur when actions and coactions from parallel processes cooperate.

Choice. This is encoded using by $P_1 + P_2$, which indicates that either the process P_1 or P_2 can proceed. If the possibility P_1 is chosen then the process P_2 is discarded, and vice-versa. In the stochastic π-calculus the first process to complete its action determines which process is selected to proceed; this is known as a *race condition*.

Parallel process. A parallel process, $P_1 \mid P_2$, runs two processes P_1 and P_2 in parallel. Actions and coactions in P_1 and P_2 cooperate to produce silent actions. In the original paper of stochastic π-calculus Priami also dictates that the rate of a cooperating action should inherit a function of the rates of the constituent action and coaction. In subsequent versions, the rate of the resulting cooperating τ directly inherits the rate of the constituent actions.

Constant. We assign names to behaviour associated with components. Constants are components whose meaning is given by a defining equation. The notation for this is $X \stackrel{def}{=} E$. The name X is in scope in the expression on the right hand side meaning that, for example, $X \stackrel{def}{=} \pi_r.X$ performs π at rate r forever.

3.2 PEPA

PEPA [4] as a performance modelling formalism has been used to study a wide variety of systems: multimedia applications [9], mobile phone usage [10], GRID scheduling [11], production cell efficiency [12] and web-server clusters [13] amongst others. The definitive reference for the language is [4].

As in all process algebras, systems are represented in PEPA as the composition of *components* which undertake *actions*. In PEPA the actions are assumed to have a duration, or delay. Thus the expression $(\alpha, r).P$ denotes a component which can undertake an α action at rate r to evolve into a component P. Here $\alpha \in \mathcal{A}$ where $\mathcal{A}$ is the set of action types. The rate r is interpreted as a random delay which samples from an exponential random variable with parameter, r.

PEPA has a small set of combinators, allowing system descriptions to be built up as the concurrent execution and interaction of simple sequential components. The syntax of the type of PEPA model considered in this paper may be formally specified using the following grammar:

$$S ::= (\alpha, r).S \mid S + S \mid C_S$$
$$P ::= P \bowtie_L P \mid P/L \mid C$$

where S denotes a *sequential component* and P denotes a *model component* which executes in parallel. C stands for a constant which denotes either a sequential component or a model component as introduced by a definition. C_S stands for constants which denote sequential components. The effect of this syntactic separation between these types of constants is to constrain legal PEPA components to be cooperations of sequential processes.

More information and structured operational semantics on PEPA can be found in [4]. A brief discussion of the basic PEPA operators is given below:

Prefix. The basic mechanism for describing the behaviour of a system with a PEPA model is to give a component a designated first action using the prefix combinator, denoted by a full stop, which was introduced above. As explained, $(\alpha, r).P$ carries out an α action with rate r, and it subsequently behaves as P.

Choice. The component $P + Q$ represents a system which may behave either as P or as Q. The activities of both P and Q are enabled. The first activity to complete distinguishes one of them: the other is discarded. The system will behave as the derivative resulting from the evolution of the chosen component.

Constant. It is convenient to be able to assign names to patterns of behaviour associated with components. Constants are components whose meaning is given by a defining equation. The notation for this is $X \stackrel{def}{=} E$. The name X is in scope in the expression on the right hand side meaning that, for example, $X \stackrel{def}{=} (\alpha, r).X$ performs α at rate r forever.

Hiding. The possibility to abstract away some aspects of a component's behaviour is provided by the hiding operator, denoted P/L. Here, the set L identifies those activities which are to be considered internal or private to the component and which will appear as the unknown type τ.

Cooperation. We write $P \bowtie_L Q$ to denote cooperation between P and Q over L. The set which is used as the subscript to the cooperation symbol, the *cooperation set* L, determines those activities on which the components are forced to synchronise. For action types not in L, the components proceed independently and concurrently with their enabled activities. We write $P \parallel Q$ as an abbreviation for $P \bowtie_L Q$ when L is empty. Further, particularly useful in fluid analysis is, $P[n]$ which is shorthand for the parallel cooperation of n P-components, $\underbrace{P \parallel \cdots \parallel P}_{n}$.

In process cooperation, if a component enables an activity whose action type is in the cooperation set it will not be able to proceed with that activity until the other component also enables an activity of that type. The two components then proceed together to complete the *shared activity*. Once enabled, the rate of a shared activity has to be altered to reflect the slower component in a cooperation.

In some cases, when a shared activity is known to be completely dependent only on one component in the cooperation, then the other component will be made *passive* with respect to that activity. This means that the rate of the activity is left unspecified (denoted $\top$) and is determined upon cooperation, by the rate of the activity in the other component. All passive actions must be synchronised in the final model.

Within the cooperation framework, PEPA respects the definition of *bounded capacity*: that is, a component cannot be made to perform an activity faster by cooperation, so the rate of a shared activity is the minimum of the apparent rates of the activity in the cooperating components.

The definition of the derivative set of a component will be needed later in the paper. The derivative set, $ds(C)$, is the set of states that can be reached from a the state C. In the case, where C is a state in a strongly connected sequential component, $ds(C)$ represents the state space of that component.

Overview of ODE Generation. In this section, we give a brief summary of how differential equations are generated for PEPA in particular. Further details can be found in [5,6]. Consider a PEPA model made up of component types C_i, such that the system equation has the form:

$$C_1[n_1] \underset{L}{\bowtie} C_2[n_2] \underset{L}{\bowtie} \cdots \underset{L}{\bowtie} C_m[n_m] \tag{1}$$

where $C[n]$ is the parallel composition of n C-components. Take C_{ij} to be the jth derivative state of component C_i. The cooperation set L is made up of common actions to C_i for $1 \leq i \leq m$.

Fluid analysis approximates the number of derivatives of each component that are present in the system at a time t with a set of differential equations. Now a numerical vector form for such a model would consist of $(v_{ij} \ : \ 1 \leq i \leq m, 1 \leq j \leq |ds(C_i)|)$ where v_{ij} is the number of C_{ij} components in the system at a given time. A set of coupled differential equations can be created to describe the time-variation of v_{ij} as follows:

$$\frac{\mathrm{d}v_{ij}(t)}{\mathrm{d}t} = - \sum_{k \,:\, C_{ij} \xrightarrow{(a,\cdot)} C_{ik}} \text{rate of } a\text{-action leaving } C_{ij}$$
$$+ \sum_{k \,:\, C_{ik} \xrightarrow{(b,\cdot)} C_{ij}} \text{rate of } b\text{-action leaving } C_{ik} \tag{2}$$

A very similar technique exists for creating fluid models of stochastic π-calculus and details can be found in [14].

3.3   Modelling Differences

CCS versus CSP Communication. The distinction between the communication formalisms in stochastic π-calculus and PEPA is inherited from CCS [8] and CSP [15] respectively, and gives rise to an important difference in the way biological models are created in many cases (although, not as it happens, this one).

Stochastic π-Calculus has a binary communication model and, if no restriction is used, can initiate communication between any two processes in a system arbitrarily, if they enable the appropriate action–coaction pair. By contrast, PEPA uses an n-way communication model which requires all processes producing an a-action to synchronise, if specified in the appropriate cooperation set. This will often mean that PEPA models would need a mediator component to act as conduit or network for the communication between a group of components in a stochastic π-calculus style.

$$(P \parallel \cdots \parallel P) \bowtie_L Mediator$$

In the event, there is no communication within groups of proteins, mRNA or DNA so no such extra network components are required here.

Parallel Components. An equally important distinction between stochastic π-calculus and PEPA is that stochastic π-calculus allows dynamic component generation whereas PEPA has a static cooperation specification. This means that a stochastic π-calculus model can spawn and kill processes to increase or reduce a population. Conversely, PEPA models have to have a predefined population in a cooperation structure that is going to be appropriate for the duration on the model's lifecycle.

In the Circadian clock model, the major difference between modelling in stochastic π-calculus and PEPA is the way in which new molecules are generated. In stochastic π-calculus, it is succinct to have new molecules spontaneously appear in parallel out of individual molecule descriptions, as in:

$$D_A \stackrel{def}{=} \tau_{\alpha_A}.(D_A \mid M_A) \tag{3}$$

Here, after an exponential delay at rate α_A, a D_A molecule becomes a D_A and an M_A molecule. In effect, this means that the D_A molecule remains intact and an M_A molecule is spontaneously created.

In contrast, PEPA has a notion of a *static cooperation structure* which encourages the creation of independent molecule lifecycles which capture an individual molecule's state, even if one of those states is just the potential to create the molecule. The PEPA equivalent of Equation (3) is given by:

$$D_A \stackrel{def}{=} (trans_A, \alpha_A).D_A$$
$$M'_A \stackrel{def}{=} (trans_A, \top).M_A \tag{4}$$

Here the state M'_A represents the concept of there being sufficient resources in the system that, when driven by a $trans_A$ action from the DNA molecule D_A, an M_A molecule is instantiated.

This single modelling difference between the formalisms has large implications. To start with the stochastic π-calculus model can grow unboundedly, generating an indefinite number of M_A molecules, in this example. Whereas in the PEPA model, we would have to pre-specify the number of M_A molecules that the system was capable of creating using the following system equation:

$$D_A \underset{\{trans_A\}}{\bowtie} \underbrace{(M'_A \parallel \cdots \parallel M'_A)}_{n}$$

Such a system would have the capacity to generate n molecules of M_A and no more.

As to which approach is appropriate, that will depend on the modelling situation and the facets of the system that the modeller is trying to capture.

The unbounded nature of the stochastic π-calculus model generates an infinite stochastic state space, which would make probabilistic model checking, in all but the most fortunate of cases, impossible. So if tools such as PRISM, PEPA Workbench or ETMCC are to be employed to perform probabilistic analysis on biological systems, it would seem that the PEPA style of modelling is more appropriate.

It should be noted though that if explicit state-space representation techniques are used by the tool, then even if a bounded and finite model is generated, only a very small version will be capable of being analysed as the state space quickly becomes unmanageable.

The only practical way to analyse such large models is through continuous state-space representation via numerical ODE solution or stochastic simulation. As yet there is no model checking framework in which these techniques can be used.

Predefined Synchronisation Rate. Again comparing the same snippets of process model from Equation (3) and (4), we note that the rate of delay prior to molecule generation is defined as α_A. As discussed earlier this process is a succinct way of representing a synchronisation between the environment (the amino acids that are the building blocks of proteins and mRNA) and the DNA molecule. It could be said that as there was no explicit definition of how the individual processes participated in the synchronisation, that this does not produce a composable model. However, a counter argument would quite reasonably suggest that the action was τ-action anyway and not observable by other processes and that the above example was an abstraction of underlying cooperation.

3.4   Stochastic π-Calculus Model

Based on our description of Section 2, we construct a stochastic π-calculus model of the Circadian clock. In the system below, D_A and D_R represent the DNA molecules for the proteins A and R. Similarly, M_A and M_R represent the mRNA molecules for the proteins A and R.

$$D_A \stackrel{def}{=} bind_{A_{\gamma_A}}.D_{A'} + \tau_{\alpha_A}.(D_A \mid M_A)$$
$$D_{A'} \stackrel{def}{=} \tau_{\theta_A}.(D_A \mid A) + \tau_{\alpha_{A'}}.(D_{A'} \mid M_A)$$
$$D_R \stackrel{def}{=} bind_{R_{\gamma_R}}.D_{R'} + \tau_{\alpha_R}.(D_R \mid M_R)$$
$$D_{R'} \stackrel{def}{=} \tau_{\theta_R}.(D_R \mid A) + \tau_{\alpha_{R'}}.(D_{R'} \mid M_R)$$
$$M_A \stackrel{def}{=} \tau_{\delta_{M_A}}.0 + \tau_{\beta_A}.(M_A \mid A)$$
$$M_R \stackrel{def}{=} \tau_{\delta_{M_R}}.0 + \tau_{\beta_R}.(M_R \mid R)$$
$$A \stackrel{def}{=} \overline{bind_{A_{\gamma_A}}}.0 + \overline{bind_{R_{\gamma_R}}}.0 + \overline{bind_{C_{\gamma_C}}}.0 + \tau_{\delta_A}.0$$
$$R \stackrel{def}{=} bind_{C_{\gamma_C}}.C + \tau_{\delta_R}.0$$
$$C \stackrel{def}{=} \tau_{\delta_A}.R$$

Below are the ODEs as generated by applying the systematic transformation of [14] to the stochastic π-calculus model of the Circadian clock, above. The term $[X]$ represents the time-varying concentration of element X.

$$\frac{d}{dt}[D_A] = \theta_A[D_{A'}] - \gamma_A[D_A][A]$$

$$\frac{d}{dt}[D_{A'}] = -\theta_A[D_{A'}] + \gamma_A[D_A][A]$$

$$\frac{d}{dt}[D_R] = \theta_R[D_{R'}] - \gamma_R[D_R][A]$$

$$\frac{d}{dt}[D_{R'}] = -\theta_R[D_{R'}] + \gamma_R[D_R][A]$$

$$\frac{d}{dt}[M_A] = -\delta_{MA}[M_A] + \alpha_A[D_A] + \alpha_{A'}[D_{A'}]$$

$$\frac{d}{dt}[M_R] = -\delta_{MR}[M_R] + \alpha_R[D_R] + \alpha_{R'}[D_{R'}]$$

$$\frac{d}{dt}[A] = \beta_A[M_A] + \theta_A[D_{A'}] + \theta_R[D_{R'}]$$
$$- \gamma_A[D_A][A] - \gamma_R[D_R][A] - \gamma_C[A][R] - \delta_A[A]$$

$$\frac{d}{dt}[R] = \beta_R[M_R] + \delta_A[C] - \gamma_C[A][R] - \delta_R[R]$$

$$\frac{d}{dt}[C] = -\delta_A[C] + \gamma_C[A][R]$$

3.5 PEPA Model

The following is the PEPA model of the Circadian clock. A distinct model from the stochastic π-calculus version and a larger model description, necessary to capture a bounded model. Where complex molecules are created, for instance between the DNA molecule D_A and the protein A, we create explicit versions of each AD_A and A_{D_A}, since we cannot have a single component representing the complex as we do in the stochastic π-calculus model.

$$D_A \stackrel{def}{=} (bind_{AD_A}, \gamma_A).AD_A + (mk_{MA}, \alpha_A).D_A$$
$$AD_A \stackrel{def}{=} (unbind_{AD_A}, \theta_A).D_A + (mk_{MA}, \alpha_{A'}).AD_A$$
$$D_R \stackrel{def}{=} (bind_{AD_R}, \gamma_R).AD_R + (mk_{MR}, \alpha_R).D_R$$
$$AD_R \stackrel{def}{=} (unbind_{AD_R}, \theta_R).D_R + (mk_{MR}, \alpha_{R'}).AD_R$$
$$M'_A \stackrel{def}{=} (mk_{MA}, \top).M_A$$
$$M_A \stackrel{def}{=} (decay_{MA}, \delta_{MA}).M'_A + (mk_A, \beta_A).M_A$$
$$M'_R \stackrel{def}{=} (mk_{MR}, \top).M_R$$
$$M_R \stackrel{def}{=} (decay_{MR}, \delta_{MR}).M'_R + (mk_R, \beta_R).M_R$$
$$A' \stackrel{def}{=} (mk_A, \top).A$$
$$A \stackrel{def}{=} (bind_{AD_A}, \gamma_A).AD_A + (bind_{AD_R}, \gamma_R).AD_R + (bind_{AR}, \gamma_C).A_C$$
$$\qquad + (decay_A, \delta_A).A'$$
$$A_{D_A} \stackrel{def}{=} (unbind_{AD_A}, \top).A$$
$$A_{D_R} \stackrel{def}{=} (unbind_{AD_R}, \top).A$$
$$A_C \stackrel{def}{=} (unbind_{AR}, \top).A'$$
$$R' \stackrel{def}{=} (mk_R, \top).R$$
$$R \stackrel{def}{=} (bind_{AR}, \gamma_C).C + (decay_R, \delta_R).R'$$
$$C \stackrel{def}{=} (unbind_{AR}, \delta_A).R$$

The different process definitions represent the different states of the molecules in the system. The states M'_A, M'_R, A' and R' represent potential to create the molecules M_A, M_R, A and R. The system would start in the state with the potential to create n_X molecules of X for $X \in \{M_A, M_R, A, R\}$.

$$Circadian \stackrel{def}{=} (D_A \parallel D_R) \underset{\mathcal{L}}{\bowtie} ((M'_A[n_{M_A}] \parallel M'_R[n_{M_R}]) \underset{\mathcal{M}}{\bowtie} (A'[n_A] \underset{\mathcal{N}}{\bowtie} R'[n_R]))$$
$$\mathcal{L} = \{bind_{AD_A}, unbind_{AD_A}, bind_{AD_R}, unbind_{AD_R}, mk_{MA}, mk_{MR}\}$$
$$\mathcal{M} = \{mk_A, mk_R\}$$
$$\mathcal{N} = \{bind_{AR}, unbind_{AR}\}$$

In the stochastic π-calculus model, molecules of A, R as well as mRNA degraded and disappeared from the system. There is a closed-system assumption in the PEPA model, that degrading proteins break down into their constituent amino acids, which can then be used to form new molecules of A, R and mRNA.

Note that in the differential equations below, we deliberately translated active cooperation between pairs of components using a mass-action semantics, which is physically appropriate for the model. This should technically involve using a different PEPA cooperation operator, or a user-defined rate function; this issue has been addressed in subsequent biologically oriented versions of PEPA [16]. The passive cooperation is translated using the methodology from [6] where, as a feature of the model, the passive molecule is always assumed to be present. This prevents numerical difficulties with indicator functions.

$$\frac{d}{dt}[D_A] = \theta_A[D_A] - \gamma_A[D_A][A]$$

$$\frac{d}{dt}[AD_A] = -\theta_A[D_A] + \gamma_A[D_A][A]$$

$$\frac{d}{dt}[D_R] = \theta_R[D_R] - \gamma_R[D_R][A]$$

$$\frac{d}{dt}[AD_R] = -\theta_R[D_R] + \gamma_R[D_R][A]$$

$$\frac{d}{dt}[M'_A] = \delta_{MA}[M_A] - \alpha_A[D_A] - \alpha_{A'}[AD_A]$$

$$\frac{d}{dt}[M_A] = -\delta_{MA}[M_A] + \alpha_A[D_A] + \alpha_{A'}[D_{A'}]$$

$$\frac{d}{dt}[M'_R] = \delta_{MR}[M_R] - \alpha_R[D_R] - \alpha_{R'}[AD_R]$$

$$\frac{d}{dt}[M_R] = -\delta_{MR}[M_R] + \alpha_R[D_R] + \alpha_{R'}[D_{R'}]$$

$$\frac{d}{dt}[A'] = \delta_A[C] - \beta_A[M_A]$$

$$\frac{d}{dt}[A] = \beta_A[M_A] + \theta_A[AD_A] + \theta_R[AD_R]$$
$$- \gamma_A[D_A][A] - \gamma_R[D_R][A] - \gamma_C[A][R] - \delta_A[A]$$

$$\frac{d}{dt}[A_{D_A}] = -\theta_A[AD_A] + \gamma_A[D_A][A]$$

$$\frac{d}{dt}[A_{D_R}] = -\theta_R[AD_R] + \gamma_R[D_R][A]$$

$$\frac{d}{dt}[A_C] = -\delta_A[C] + \gamma_C[A][R]$$

$$\frac{d}{dt}[R'] = -\beta_R[M_R] + \delta_R[R]$$

$$\frac{d}{dt}[R] = \beta_R[M_R] + \delta_A[C] - \gamma_C[A][R] - \delta_R[R]$$

$$\frac{d}{dt}[C] = -\delta_A[C] + \gamma_C[A][R]$$

3.6   Parameters

The initial conditions and parameter values for the Circadian clock models are taken directly from [1]: $D_A = D_R = 1$ *mol*, $D'_A = D'_R = M_A = M_R = A = R = C = 0$, which require that the cell has a single copy of the activator and repressor genes: $D_A + D'_A = 1$ *mol* and $D_R + D'_R = 1$ *mol*.

$$\alpha_A = 50h^{-1}$$
$$\alpha_{A'} = 500h^{-1}$$
$$\alpha_R = 0.01h^{-1}$$
$$\alpha_{R'} = 50h^{-1}$$
$$\beta_A = 50h^{-1}$$
$$\beta_R = 5h^{-1}$$
$$\delta_{MA} = 10h^{-1}$$
$$\delta_{MR} = 0.5h^{-1}$$

$$\delta_A = 1h^{-1}$$
$$\delta_R = 0.2h^{-1}$$
$$\gamma_A = 1mol^{-1}hr^{-1}$$
$$\gamma_R = 1mol^{-1}hr^{-1}$$
$$\gamma_C = 2mol^{-1}hr^{-1}$$
$$\theta_A = 50h^{-1}$$
$$\theta_R = 100h^{-1}$$

4   Evaluation

In this section we evaluate the results of analysing the stochastic π-calculus and PEPA models against the differential equations from [1] and also against each other. To generate the differential equation models from the process algebra descriptions we use the automated techniques for PEPA [5,6] and stochastic π-calculus [14], outlined in Section 3.2.

In Figure 3, we see the solutions of the differential equations for the original Circadian clock model as reproduced from Vilar *et al.* [1]. We note that their is an initial surge of A to about 1700 *mol* followed by periodic peeks at 1400 *mol* every 24 hours.

In Figure 4, we show both the concentration on A and of the repressor R as extracted from the stochastic π-calculus model. The basic features of the activator protein as identified from Figure 3 are present, and indeed we know this to be identical to the results of Figure 3 as the ODEs generated for Equation (5) are identical to the model ODEs that appeared in [1]. We note that the R repressor acts almost completely out of phase with the A protein as would be expected.

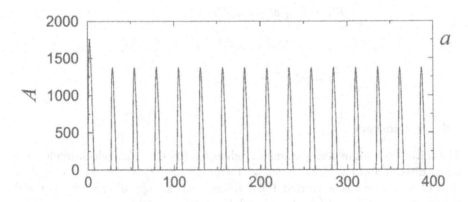

Fig. 3. Concentration of A protein varying against time from the original model [1]

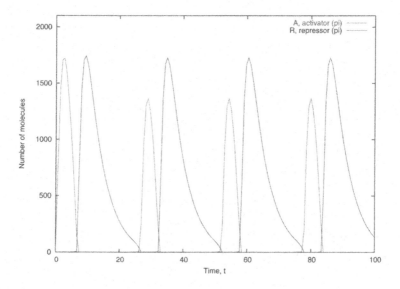

Fig. 4. Concentration of A activator (peaks 1,3,5,7) and R repressor varying against time from the stochastic π-calculus model

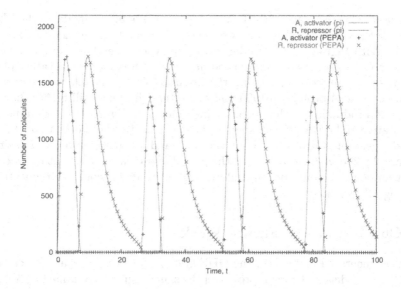

Fig. 5. Concentration of A activator and R repressor varying against time from the stochastic π-calculus (lines) and PEPA (points) model

Figure 4 shows the results of the PEPA solution superposed on the results from the stochastic π-calculus model. The solutions overlay each other, despite the fact that the models differ and the sets of differential equations differ.

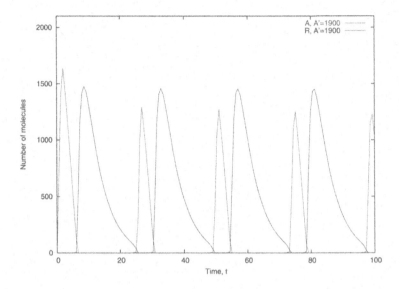

Fig. 6. Concentration of A activator (peaks 1,3,5,7) and R repressor varying against time from the PEPA model with restricted A and R facility

We now take advantage of the fact that we have a bounded model in the PEPA version of the Circadian clock that we have checked numerically against the other models. With Figure 4, we consider a scenario where the ability to construct A activator was in some way limited, perhaps through resource starvation of the building-block amino acids. Using the bounded PEPA model, we restrict the ability to make A protein to 1900 mol and although this is still higher than the peak of A production in the unconstrained model of Figure 4, we see a distinct quantitative and qualitative change in the concentrations of both A and R. The periodic peak of A drops by about 400 mol, and the periodic peak of R drops similarly by 200 mol. Additionally, the period of oscillation of A has dropped by about an hour. It would be very interesting to see if this could be replicated in a biological scenario.

5   Conclusion and Future Work

We have generated and solved the ODE systems for both stochastic π-calculus and PEPA models and have reproduced the same results as obtained by Vilar *et al.* [1], in both cases. Despite bounding the state space of the PEPA model and generating distinct sets of differential equations, we obtained identical results for both stochastic π-calculus and PEPA models. We aim to show that this corresponds to the state-space truncation proposed by Degasperi and Gilmore [17] and that the probability of reaching the *truncated states* during a normal execution of the system is negligible. This would provide a quantitative justification for the truncation.

We showed that truncating the model not only provides a finite state-space (as expected) but also gives us the capacity to test the system in a restricted resource scenario. We note that restricting the capacity of the PEPA model to make key proteins upsets the phase of the Circadian rhythm, but does not destroy it altogether.

We also intend to study further how newer modelling formalisms, designed specifically for biological applications, such as Bio-PEPA [16] could express such a model and capture resource restriction as examined here.

Acknowledgements

The author would like to acknowledge the help of Thomas Thorne whose MSc report contributed valuable work to previous versions of this paper. The author would also like to thank Stephen Gilmore for providing significant insight into state-space truncation approximation techniques.

References

1. Vilar, J.M.G., Kueh, H.Y., Barkai, N., Leibler, S.: Mechanisms of noise-resistance in genetic oscillators. PNAS 99, 5988–5992 (2002)
2. Barkai, N., Leibler, S.: Biological rhythms: Circadian clocks limited by noise. Nature 403, 267–268 (2000)
3. Priami, C.: A stochastic π-calculus. In: Gilmore, S., Hillston, J. (eds.) Process Algebra and Performance Modelling Workshop, June 1995. The Computer Journal, vol. 38(7), pp. 578–589. CEPIS, Edinburgh (1995)
4. Hillston, J.: A Compositional Approach to Performance Modelling. Distinguished Dissertations in Computer Science, vol. 12. Cambridge University Press, Cambridge (1996)
5. Hillston, J.: Fluid flow approximation of PEPA models. In: QEST 2005, Proceedings of the 2nd International Conference on Quantitative Evaluation of Systems, Torino, September 2005, pp. 33–42. IEEE Computer Society Press, Los Alamitos (2005)
6. Bradley, J.T., Gilmore, S.T., Hillston, J.: Analysing distributed internet worm attacks using continuous state-space approximation of process algebra models. Journal of Computer and System Sciences (in press, July 2007)
7. Milner, R., Parrow, J., Walker, D.: A calculus of mobile processes. Information and Computation 100, 1–40 (1992)
8. Milner, R. (ed.): A Calculus of Communication Systems. LNCS, vol. 92. Springer, Heidelberg (1980)
9. Bowman, H., Bryans, J.W., Derrick, J.: Analysis of a multimedia stream using stochastic process algebras. The Computer Journal 44(4), 230–245 (2001)
10. Fourneau, J.M., Kloul, L., Valois, F.: Performance modelling of hierarchical cellular networks using PEPA. Performance Evaluation 50, 83–99 (2002)
11. Thomas, N., Bradley, J.T., Knottenbelt, W.J.: Stochastic analysis of scheduling strategies in a GRID-based resource model. IEE Software Engineering 151, 232–239 (2004)

12. Holton, D.R.W.: A PEPA specification of an industrial production cell. In: Gilmore, S., Hillston, J. (eds.) PAPM 1995, Proceedings of the 3rd International Workshop on Process Algebra and Performance Modelling, Edinburgh, June 1995. The Computer Journal, vol. 38(7), pp. 542–551. OUP (1995)
13. Bradley, J.T., Dingle, N.J., Gilmore, S.T., Knottenbelt, W.J.: Derivation of passage-time densities in PEPA models using ipc: the Imperial PEPA Compiler. In: Kotsis, G. (ed.) MASCOTS 2003, Proceedings of the 11th IEEE/ACM International Symposium on Modeling, Analysis and Simulation of Computer and Telecommunications Systems, pp. 344–351. IEEE Computer Society Press, Los Alamitos (2003)
14. Cardelli, L.: On process rate semantics. Theoretical Computer Science 391, 190–215 (2008)
15. Hoare, C.A.R.: Communicating sequential processes. Communications of the ACM 21, 666–677 (1978)
16. Ciocchetta, F., Hillston, J.: Bio-PEPA: An extension of the process algebra PEPA for biochemical networks. In: Cannata, N., Merelli, E. (eds.) FBTC 2007, Proc. of the From Biology To Concurrency and Back, July 2008. Electronic Notes in Theoretical Computer Science, vol. 194(3), pp. 103–117. Elsevier, Amsterdam (2008)
17. Degasperi, A., Gilmore, S.T.: Sensitivity analysis of stochastic models of bistable biochemical reactions. In: Bernardo, M., et al. (eds.) SFM 2008. LNCS, vol. 5016, pp. 1–20. Springer, Heidelberg (2008)

Assembly Code Analysis Using Stochastic Process Algebra

Lamia Djoudi and Leïla Kloul

PRiSM, Université de Versailles, 45, Av. des Etats-Unis, 78000 Versailles
{ladj,kle}@prism.uvsq.fr

Abstract. Currently compilers contain a large number of optimisations which are based on a set of heuristics that are not guaranteed to be effective to improve the performance metrics. In this paper, we propose a strategy which allows us the analysis and the choice of the best optimisation, by focusing on the hot part of an assembly code. In our approach, for each optimisation applied, the code of the hot loop is extracted and its dependency graph generated. Finally, and in order to select the best optimisation, the generated graphs are analytically analysed using stochastic process algebra.

Keywords: Assembly code, Code optimisation, Data dependencies graph, Stochastic process algebra, Performance analysis.

1 Introduction

Due to complex interactions between hardware mechanisms and software dynamic behaviours, scientific code optimisation at compile time is an extremely difficult task. State-of-the-art compilers are still challenged to achieve high performance independently from runtime or micro-architectural parameters. As regard the application, the knowledge of its behaviour implies a serious effort and a high degree of expertise.

Currently compilers contain a large number of optimisations which are based on a set of heuristics that are not guaranteed to be effective to improve the performance metrics. Achieving high performance relies heavily on the ability of the compiler to exploit the underlying architecture and the quality of the code it produces. This requires a full understanding and a full control of the application behaviour the compiler has when compiling the application to provide a precise diagnostic about the success or failure of an optimisation if applied. It also requires the ability to transmit to the compiler certain architecture characteristics to make it choose the right optimisation to apply.

Before starting to optimise an application, the programmer must identify the main factors limiting the performances of its application. For that, two types of code analysis techniques can be used: static and dynamic techniques.

Static techniques extract opportune information from the program analysis (source, assembly or binary code). These techniques are usually faster than dynamic analysis but less precise.

N. Thomas and C. Juiz (Eds.): EPEW 2008, LNCS 5261, pp. 95–109, 2008.

Dynamic techniques require a dynamic execution of the program (real execution or simulation). Profiling a program consists in collecting opportune information during its execution in order to guide efficient optimisations (dead code elimination, prefetching, instruction scheduling, memory layout transformation, ...). These optimisations can be applied either by transforming the initial source code or the assembly code, or by re-compiling it guided by the collected information. Several dynamic techniques can be used, among which we have instrumentation and sampling.

- Instrumentation inserts instructions to collect information. Several instrumentation methods exist: source modification, compiler injected instrumentation, binary rewriting to get an instrumented version of an executable, and binary translation at runtime. Instrumentation adds code to increment counters at entry/exit function, reading hardware performance counters, or even simulate hardware to get synthetic event counts. The instrumentation runtime can dramatically increase the execution time such that time measurements become useless. It may also result in a huge code. Moreover it does not help in finding the bottlenecks if there are any. MAQAO[4] and EEL[10] are examples of tools which are based on the instrumentation.
- Sampling consists in taking measuring points during short time intervals. The validity of the results depends on the choice of the measures and their duration. Prof [11] and GProf [7] are examples of sampling-based tools.

Obtaining dynamic information on the behaviour of a program is relatively complex. In one hand the application size is increased and on the other hand the number, the complexity and the interactions of the transformations (optimisations) to apply are important. Moreover the validity of these information depends on the input parameters of the program.

However certain information like the execution time or the iteration number can be obtained only dynamically and they have an impact on the effectiveness of the optimisations. As a large application may execute for hours and sometimes even days, if a developer is focusing on the implementation or the tuning of a key computation, it will be far more efficient and less cumbersome to run just the key computation, isolated from the rest of the program.

In this paper, we propose a strategy which allows the analysis and the choice of the best transformation, by focusing on the hot part of a code. It is well known that loop optimisation is a critical part in the compiler optimisation chain. A routinely stated rule is that 90% of the execution time is spent in 10% of the code. The main characteristic of our strategy is the assembly code isolation. We isolate the hot loop from a large application for the purpose of performance tuning. We are interested in the assembly code because it is the natural place to observe performance. It is close enough to the hardware and it is possible to check the job done by the compiler.

Our approach is based on: (1) a static analysis of the code to predict the data dependency, (2) a dynamic analysis to select the hot loop in code, (3) a code isolation to extract the hot loop from a large application in order to apply different transformations with different input data and finally (4) an analytical modelling to select the best transformation.

While we use the MAQAO tool for code analysis, we have chosen to use PEPA [8] as the performance modelling technique. Our objective is the investigation of the impact of each of the transformations on the execution time of the code. The results obtained are compared to those obtained when executing the code and it is shown that our approach based on PEPA achieves comparable results, but at a much lower cost.

Structure of the paper: in Section 2, we give a brief overview of the tool MAQAO and the formalism PEPA before describing our approach. In Section 3, we present a case study and show how to apply our approach. Section 4 is dedicated to the numerical results. We finally conclude, in Section 5, with a discussion about the possible extensions of our work.

2 The Approach

The approach we propose allows bridging the gap between the code analysis provided by MAQAO and the PEPA-based analytical modelling for a formal analysis of the code performances. Before developing this approach, we present the main characteristics of MAQAO and give a brief overview of PEPA.

2.1 MAQAO

MAQAO [4] stands for Modular Assembly Quality Analyzer and Optimizer. The concept behind this tool is to centralise all low level performance information and build correlations. As a result, MAQAO produces more and better results than the sum of the existing individual methods. Additionally, being based after the compilation phase allows a precise diagnostic of compiler optimisation successes and/or failures. MAQAO provides several options among which we have:

- MAQAOPROFILE[5] is an option which allows us to give a precise weight to all executed loops, therefore underscoring hotspots. Correlating this information provides the relevant metrics:

  (i) the hotpath at run-time which passes through the whole program and where the application spends the most of its time.

  (ii) the monitoring trip count is very rewarding. By default most of compiler optimisations target asymptotic performance. Knowing that a loop is subjected to a limited number of iterations allows us to choose the optimisations characterised by a cold-start cost.

- Static Analyser: MAQAO's static module extracts the entire code structure and expresses it using a set of graphs: Call Graphs (CGs), Control Flow Graphs (CFGs) and Data Dependencies Graphs (DDGs). Computing the DDGs is a key issue to determine critical path latency in a basic block and perform instructions re-scheduling or any code manipulation technique. It also allows an accurate understanding of dynamic performance hazards

and determines the shortest dependency that corresponds to the overlapping bottleneck.
- MAQAOADVISOR proposes different transformations to apply on the hot loops, at the code source level, to improve the performances of the code. The program is then compiled again and the new assembly code is resubmitted to MAQAO for a new analysis of the code.

2.2 PEPA

In PEPA a system is described as an interaction of *components* which engage, either singly or multiply, in *activities*. These basic elements of PEPA, components and activities, correspond to *states* and *transitions* in the underlying Markov process. Each activity has an *action type*. Activities which are private to the component in which they occur are represented by the distinguished action type, τ. The duration of each activity is represented by the parameter of the associated exponential distribution: the *activity rate*. This parameter may be any positive real number, or the distinguished symbol $\top$ (read as *unspecified*). Thus each activity, a, is a pair (α, r) consisting of the action type and the activity rate respectively. We assume a countable set of components, denoted $\mathcal{C}$, and a countable set, $\mathcal{A}$, of all possible action types. We denote by $Act \subseteq \mathcal{A} \times \mathbb{R}^+$, the set of activities, where $\mathbb{R}^+$ is the set of positive real numbers together with the symbol $\top$.

PEPA provides a small set of combinators which allow expressions to be constructed defining the behaviour of components, via the activities they undertake and the interactions between them.

Prefix $(\alpha, r).P$: This is the basic mechanism for constructing component behaviours. The component carries out activity (α, r) and subsequently behaves as component P.

Choice $P + Q$: This component may behave either as P or as Q: all the current activities of both components are enabled. The first activity to complete, determined by a *race condition*, distinguishes one component, the other is discarded.

Cooperation $P \bowtie_L Q$: Components proceed independently with any activities whose types do not occur in the *cooperation set L* (*individual activities*). However, activities with action types in the set L require the simultaneous involvement of both components (*shared activities*). When the set L is empty, we use the more concise notation $P \parallel Q$ to represent $P \bowtie_\emptyset Q$.

The published stochastic process algebras differ on how the rate of shared activities are defined. In PEPA the shared activity occurs at the rate of the slowest participant. If an activity has an unspecified rate, denoted $\top$, the component is *passive* with respect to that action type. This means that the component does not influence the rate at which any shared activity occurs.

Hiding P/L: This behaves as P except that any activities of types within the set L are *hidden*, i.e. they exhibit the unknown type τ and can be regarded as an internal delay by the component. These activities cannot be carried out in cooperation with another component.

Constant $A \stackrel{def}{=} P$: Constants are components whose meaning is given by a defining equation. $A \stackrel{def}{=} P$ gives the constant A the behaviour of the component P. This is how we assign names to components (behaviours).

The evolution of a model is governed by the structured operational semantics rules of the language. This gives rise to a continuous-time Markov chain which can be solved to obtain a steady-state probability distribution from which performance measures can be derived.

2.3   The Proposed Approach

When the assembly code of an application is submitted to MAQAO for instrumentation, the hot loops of the program are selected and the corresponding Data Dependencies Graphs (DDGs) are generated, one for each hot loop. These graphs are computed with intra and inter iteration dependencies and are enriched with static cycles estimated by compiler.

In our approach, and in order to investigate the impact of each transformation on the code performances, we propose to extract, after each transformation applied, the hot loops of an application using the DDGs. Based on these graphs which provide only static information on the transformation applied, we build a PEPA model for each new version of a selected loop.

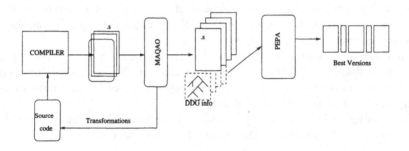

Fig. 1. Building PEPA models from the DDGs of a selected loop

In this paper, three code transformations are investigated. Each time the DDG of the selected loop is extracted and the corresponding PEPA model built. The first transformation, called *noUnroll* transformation, consists in adding to the hot loop, at the source level, a command which forces the compiler to not unroll the code. The second transformation consists in reducing the definition interval of the loop index. We call it the *index inversion* transformation. Finally the last transformation investigated consists in breaking the data dependencies of the code. In this case, an instruction of the hot loop is decomposed in several instructions to execute several iterations separately.

In the following, using a case study we show how we apply each of the transformations on the original code of a selected loop, the corresponding generated DDG and the PEPA model.

3   Case Study

To investigate the impact of the selected transformations on the execution time of the code, we consider the CX3D application. CX3D is an MPI application used to simulate Czochralski crystal growth [2], a method applied in the silicon-wafer production to obtain a single crystal from semiconductors, metals, ... It covers the convection processes occurring in a rotating cylindrical crucible filled with liquid melt.

The program of the C3XD application contains several hot loops. The one we select and extract is the inner loop of the following code where $Imax = 31$, $Kmax = 91$ and $Nmax = 41$.

DO I = 2, Imax
  DO K = 2, Kmax
    DO N = 2, Nmax
      Pnew = Max(Pnew, DP(I, K, N))
      CONTINUE

In the following we apply each of the three transformations described above on the inner loop of this code. In each case, we present the generated DDG of this loop and for each graph, we describe its corresponding PEPA model.

3.1   The Original Code

To start, we consider the original version of the loop and generate its corresponding DDG using MAQAO (Figure 2). Each node of the graph contains the assembly instruction to be executed and a number.

Three types of instructions are used: *add*, *ldfd* and *fmax*. Instruction *ldfd* represents a floating point memory access instruction. It is an $8-byte$ float point load instruction. Instruction *fmax* determines the maximum numeric value of its arguments (floating-point maximum) [9].

The numbering in the graph specifies the order in which the instructions have to be executed. According to this numbering, several instructions have to be

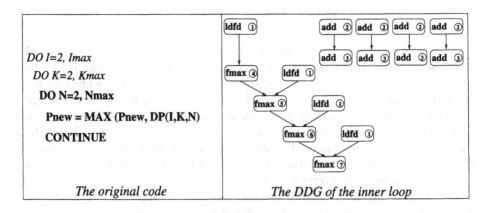

Fig. 2. The original code and the DD Graph of selected loop

executed at the same time. For example, all loading instructions $ldfd$ have to be executed at the same time, at stage 1 of the execution process. Similarly, four add instructions are to be executed simultaneously at stage 2 and stage 3. Unlike the loading instructions, instructions $fmax$ have to be executed sequentially.

In the following, we present the PEPA model of the graph of the selected loop.

The PEPA Model. This model consists of five components types. These components are built such that their activities match the instructions in the graph and their ordering. Note that because some instructions appear several times in the graph and to avoid any ambiguity in the PEPA model, we number the corresponding activities.

- Component $Register$ plays the role of an instruction register which specifies the next instruction to execute. It allows us to respect the instruction order given by the graph as well as the simultaneous execution of certain instructions. Action type $load$ models the loading instruction $ldfd$ and action $fmax_4$ models the first $fmax$ instruction to be executed at stage 4 of the graph. Actions add_i, $i = 2, 3$, model the instructions add to be executed at stages 2 and 3 respectively.

$$Register \stackrel{def}{=} (load, r).Register_1 \qquad Register_2 \stackrel{def}{=} (add_3, \top).Register_3$$
$$Register_1 \stackrel{def}{=} (add_2, \top).Register_2 \qquad Register_3 \stackrel{def}{=} (fmax_4, s_4).Register$$

- Component $Maxi$ models the left path of the graph, from $(ldfd, 1)$ to $(fmax, 7)$. Action types $fmax_i$, $i = 5, 6, 7$ model the three last $fmax$ in the path.

$$Maxi \stackrel{def}{=} (load, \top).Maxi_1 \qquad Maxi_3 \stackrel{def}{=} (fmax_6, s_6).Maxi_4$$
$$Maxi_1 \stackrel{def}{=} (fmax_4, \top).Maxi_2 \qquad Maxi_4 \stackrel{def}{=} (fmax_7, s_7).Maxi$$
$$Maxi_2 \stackrel{def}{=} (fmax_5, s_5).Maxi_3$$

- Components $Comp_i$, $i = 5, 6$, each of these components models a branch, $Comp_1$ for branch $(ldfd, 1)$ to $(fmax, 5)$ and $Comp_2$ for $(ldfd, 1)$ to $(fmax, 6)$.

$$Comp_i \stackrel{def}{=} (load, \top).Comp'_i \qquad Comp'_i \stackrel{def}{=} (fmax_i, \top).Comp_i$$

- Component $Comp_{j,k}$, $j = 1, \ldots, Nmax$ and $k = 1, 2$ models the last branch of the main part of the graph, that is from $(ldfd, 1)$ to $(fmax, 7)$. As this $fmax$ is the last instruction to be executed in the whole graph, $Comp_{j,k}$ allows us to model also the iteration process of the inner loop in the code. If $1 \le j \le Nmax - 1$, we have:

$$Comp_{j,1} \stackrel{def}{=} (load, \top).Comp_{j,2} \qquad Comp_{j,2} \stackrel{def}{=} (fmax_7, \top).Comp_{j+1,1}$$

Finally when $j = Nmax$, we have:

$$Comp_{Nmax,1} \stackrel{def}{=} (load, \top).Comp_{Nmax,2}$$
$$Comp_{Nmax,2} \stackrel{def}{=} (fmax_7, \top).Comp_{1,1}$$

102   L. Djoudi and L. Kloul

– Component *Adder* models the behaviour of a sequence $(add, 2)$ to $(add, 3)$ in the graph. The four sequences of this type in the graph have to synchronise on both instructions. Therefore, these sequences are aggregated in the PEPA model to a single component with the same activities and the same rate.

$$Adder \stackrel{def}{=} (add_2, a_2).Adder' \qquad\qquad Adder' \stackrel{def}{=} (add_3, a_3).Adder$$

The whole model equation is:

$$CodeO \stackrel{def}{=} (Adder \underset{K_1}{\bowtie} (Register \underset{K_2}{\bowtie} (Maxi \underset{K_3}{\bowtie} (Comp_1 \underset{K_4}{\bowtie} (Comp_2 \underset{K_4}{\bowtie} Comp_{1,1})))))$$

where the cooperation sets are defined as $K_1 = \{add_2, add_3\}$, $K_2 = \{load, fmax_4\}$, $K_3 = \{load, fmax_5, fmax_6, fmax_7\}$ and $K_4 = \{load\}$.

3.2 The noUnroll Transformation

The *noUnroll* transformation consists in introducing a command to force the compiler to not unroll the program. We use command *"Cdir\$ nounroll"* as shown in Figure 3. The consequence of such a command is the generation of a much smaller dependency graph. Like in the previous graph, each node consists of the assembly instruction and a number specifying its position in the execution process. This graph specifies that two instructions, *add* and *ldfd*, must be executed simultaneously at stage 2.

The PEPA Model. As the DDG of the selected loop is simpler in this case, the corresponding PEPA model is also simpler. It consists of three components.

– Component $Register_i$ $1 \leq i \leq Nmax$: as in the previous model, this component plays the role of an instruction register. However, it also allows modelling the $Nmax$ iterations of the modelled loop. For $1 \leq i < Nmax$, we have:

$$Register_i \stackrel{def}{=} (add, \top).Register_i' \qquad Register_i' \stackrel{def}{=} (fmax, \top).Register_{i+1}$$

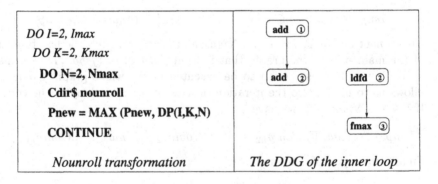

Fig. 3. The code with no unroll and the DD Graph of selected loop

The last iteration of the loop is given by $i = Nmax$, such that:

$$Register_{Nmax} \stackrel{def}{=} (add, \top).Register'_{Nmax}$$
$$Register'_{Nmax} \stackrel{def}{=} (fmax, \top).Register_1$$

- Component $Process_1$ models the sequence of add instructions. However, as the second add in the sequence has to be executed at the same time as $ldfd$, both are modelled using activity add_load.

$$Process_1 \stackrel{def}{=} (add, a).Process'_1 \qquad Process'_1 \stackrel{def}{=} (add\_load, l).Process_1$$

- Component $Process_2$ models the $ldfd$ and $fmax$ sequence of instructions.

$$Process_2 \stackrel{def}{=} (add\_load, \top).Process'_2 \qquad Process'_2 \stackrel{def}{=} (fmax, f).Process_2$$

The whole model equation is given by:

$$CodeN \stackrel{def}{=} (process_1 \underset{\{add\_load\}}{\bowtie} process_2) \underset{\{add,fmax\}}{\bowtie} Register$$

3.3 Index Inversion Transformation

This transformation consists in exchanging the inner loop index with the outer loop index which is smaller. Thus the number of iterations of the inner loop becomes smaller (31 instead of 41). Consequently, the generated graph is a simple two node graph. This dramatic reduction in the graph size, compared to the one of the original code, is due to the fact that as $Nmax$ is now smaller, the CPU does not need to use the $L3$ memory cache, it uses the $L2$ memory cache only.

The PEPA Model. For this version of the program, the PEPA model consists of two components $Process$ and $Register_i$, $1 \leq i \leq Nmax$.

- Component $Process$ models the behaviour described by the graph. That is loading the data before executing instruction $fmax$.

$$Process \stackrel{def}{=} (load, l).Process_1 \qquad Process_1 \stackrel{def}{=} (fmax, f).Process$$

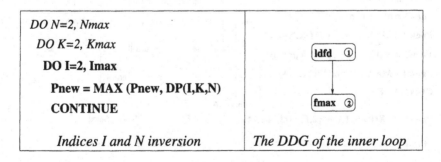

DO N=2, Nmax
DO K=2, Kmax
DO I=2, Imax
Pnew = MAX (Pnew, DP(I,K,N)
CONTINUE

Fig. 4. Code with index inversion and the DD Graph of selected loop

– Component $Register_i$ models the iteration process.

$$Register_i \overset{def}{=} (fmax, \top).Register_{i+1} \quad if \ 1 \leq i < Nmax$$
$$Register_i \overset{def}{=} (fmax, \top).Register_1 \quad if \ i = Nmax$$

The model equation consists of the cooperation of the two components of the model over activity $fmax$.

$$CodeI \overset{def}{=} Process \underset{\{fmax\}}{\bowtie} Register_1$$

3.4   Breaking the Dependencies

The last transformation investigated consists in breaking the data dependencies of the code. In this case, the instruction of the inner loop is decomposed in four instructions in order to execute four iterations in one (see Figure 5).

Note that $lfetch$ instruction is used to explicitly prefetch data into the L1, L2, or L3 caches [9].

The PEPA Model. As the DDG generated after this transformation is bigger than the previous one, the PEPA model is also bigger. It consists of eleven components in which a combined name for an activity implies the simultaneous execution of the instructions behind this name.

– Component $Register$ plays the role of the instruction register which states the next instruction to be executed in a program. Following the numbering used in the graph, the order of instructions is the following.

$$Register \ \overset{def}{=} (ldfd\_add_1, l).Register_1$$
$$Register_1 \overset{def}{=} (lfetch\_add_2, d_2).Register_2$$
$$Register_2 \overset{def}{=} (lfetch\_add_3, d_3).Register_3$$
$$Register_3 \overset{def}{=} (lfetch\_add_4, d_4).Register_4$$
$$Register_4 \overset{def}{=} (lfetch\_add_5, d_5).Register_5$$

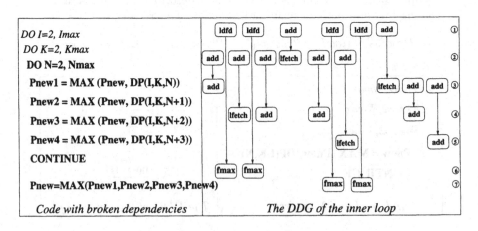

Fig. 5. The code with broken dependencies

$$Register_5 \stackrel{def}{=} (fmax_6, f_6).Register_6$$
$$Register_6 \stackrel{def}{=} (fmax_7, f_7).Register$$

Note that the index of an activity refers to the execution stage number.
- Component $Process_1$ models sequence $(ldfd, 1)$ to $(fmax, 6)$ which appears twice in the graph. As both sequences must synchronise on both instructions, a single component models both sequences.

$$Process_1 \stackrel{def}{=} (ldfd\_add_1, \top).Process_1' \qquad Process_1' \stackrel{def}{=} (fmax\_6, \top).Process_1$$

- Component $Process_2$ models sequence $(add, 1)$ to $(lfetch, 2)$.

$$Process_2 \stackrel{def}{=} (ldfd\_add_1, \top).Process_2' \qquad Process_2' \stackrel{def}{=} (lfetch\_add_2, \top).Process_2$$

- Component $Process_3$ models sequence $(ldfd, 1)$ to $(fmax, 7)$ which appears twice in the graph. As both sequences must synchronise on both instructions, a single component models both sequences.

$$Process_3 \stackrel{def}{=} (ldfd\_add_1, \top).Process_3' \qquad Process_3' \stackrel{def}{=} (fmax_7, \top).Process_3$$

- Component $Process_4$ models sequence $(add, 1)$ to $(lfetch, 3)$.

$$Process_4 \stackrel{def}{=} (ldfd\_add_1, \top).Process_4' \qquad Process_4' \stackrel{def}{=} (lfetch\_add_3, \top).Process_4$$

- Component $Process_5$ models sequence $(add, 2)$ to $(add, 3)$.

$$Process_5 \stackrel{def}{=} (lfetch\_add_2, \top).Process_5' \qquad Process_5' \stackrel{def}{=} (lfetch\_add_3, \top).Process_5$$

- Component $Process_6$ models sequences starting with $(add, 2)$ and finishing with add or $lfetch$ at stage 4. The three sequences can be modelled using a single component.

$$Process_6 \stackrel{def}{=} (lfetch\_add_2, \top).Process_6' \qquad Process_6' \stackrel{def}{=} (lfetch\_add_4, \top).Process_6$$

- Component $Process_7$ models sequence $(add, 2)$ to $(lfetch, 5)$.

$$Process_7 \stackrel{def}{=} (lfetch\_add_2, \top).Process_7' \qquad Process_7' \stackrel{def}{=} (lfetch\_add_5, \top).Process_7$$

- Component $Process_8$ models sequence $(add, 3)$ to $(lfetch, 4)$.

$$Process_8 \stackrel{def}{=} (lfetch\_add_3, \top).Process_8' \qquad Process_8' \stackrel{def}{=} (lfetch\_add_4, \top).Process_8$$

- Component $Process_9$ models sequence $(add, 3)$ to $(add, 5)$.

$$Process_9 \stackrel{def}{=} (lfetch\_add_3, \top).Process_9' \qquad Process_9' \stackrel{def}{=} (lfetch\_add_5, \top).Process_9$$

- Component $Iteration_i$, $1 \leq i \leq Nmax$: it models the iteration process of the loop. If $1 \leq i < Nmax$, we have:

$$Iteration_i \stackrel{def}{=} (ldfd\_add_1, \top).Iteration_{i,1} \qquad Iteration_{i,1} \stackrel{def}{=} (fmax_7, \top).Iteration_i$$

When $i = Nmax$, we have

$$Iteration_{Nmax} \stackrel{def}{=} (ldfd\_add_1, \top).Iteration_{Nmax,k}$$
$$Iteration_{Nmax,1} \stackrel{def}{=} (fmax_7, \top).Iteration_1$$

The complete model equation is:

$$CodeC \stackrel{def}{=} Iteration_1 \underset{M_1}{\bowtie} (Register \underset{M_2}{\bowtie} (Process_1 \underset{M_3}{\bowtie} (Process_2 \underset{M_4}{\bowtie} (Process_3$$
$$\underset{M_3}{\bowtie} (Process_4 \underset{M_3}{\bowtie} (Process_5 \underset{M_6}{\bowtie} (Process_6 \underset{M_7}{\bowtie} (Process_7$$
$$\underset{M_8}{\bowtie} (Process_8 \underset{M_5}{\bowtie} Process_9)))))))))$$

where the cooperation sets are defined as $M_1 = \{ldfd\_add_1, fmax_7\}$, $M_2 = \{ldfd\_add_1, lfetch\_add_2, lfetch\_add_3, lfetch\_add_4, lfetch\_add_5, fmax_6, fmax_7\}$, $M_3 = \{ldfd\_add_1\}$, $M_4 = \{ldfd\_add_1, lfetch\_add_2\}$, $M_5 = \{lfetch\_add_3\}$, $M_6 = \{lfetch\_add_2, lfetch\_add_3\}$, $M_7 = \{lfetch\_add_2, lfetch\_add_4\}$ and $M_8 = \{lfetch\_add_5\}$.

4   Numerical Results

As one of the sensitive performance measures for our application is the time required to complete the execution of the selected loop, we have used the HYDRA analyser [3] to compute the cumulative passage-time distribution function for completing a hot loop. To translate the PEPA model into an HYDRA input file, we have used Imperial PEPA Compiler (IPC) [1].

The parameters values we have used in our experiments are reported in Table 6. For these values, the cumulative passage-time distribution function for completing the execution of the selected loop is given in Figures 7 and 8.

Original		NoUnroll		Inversion		Breaking Dep.	
Rates	Values	Rates	Values	Rates	Values	Rates	Values
s_1, s_2, s	3	l	1.25	f	7.5	d_1, d_2, d_3, f_1, l	7.5
s_3	2.143	f	15	l	1.25	d_4	1.667
a_1, r	7.5	a	7.5			f_2	3
a_2	1.5						

Fig. 6. The parameters values $(nanoseconds^{-1})$

Figures 7 and 8 show that, on the three transformations investigated, only the *index inversion* transformation has a positive impact on the execution time of the selected loop. For all values of the iteration number $Nmax$, the time required to complete the execution is smaller when applying this transformation. Thus, when $Nmax = 12$ (Figure 7 left), we can see that, in the worst case, with the original code the loop will be completed in 10 *nanoseconds* while when using the *index inversion*, the completion time is only 5 *nanoseconds*.

Similarly, when $Nmax = 40$ (Figure 8 right), it will require about 30.10^{-9} *seconds* to complete the loop in the the worst, instead of 10 *nanoseconds* with the *index inversion*.

These figures show also that it is far much better to keep the loop in its original version than using any other transformation as both the *noUnroll* and *breaking dependencies* transformations may increase the execution time, the worst being the *breaking dependencies* transformation.

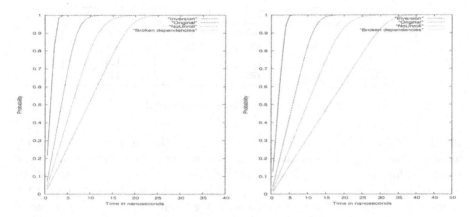

Fig. 7. Cumulative passage-time distribution function for $Nmax = 12$ and $Nmax = 20$

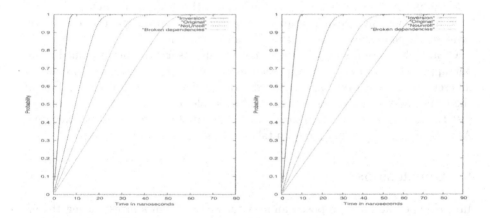

Fig. 8. Cumulative passage-time distribution function for $Nmax = 32$ and $Nmax = 40$

In the following we compare these results of the analytical model to the execution times of the loop on a BULL Itanium 2 Novascale system, 1.6GHz, 3MB of L3. The codes were compiled using Intel ICC/IFORT 9.1.

As specified by the DDGs seen in Section 3, some instructions have to be executed at the same time. This is possible on a non parallel machine like Itanium 2 because its processor is built around the EPIC (Explicitly Parallel Instruction Computing) architecture which main feature is the coupling between software and hardware. In this case the compiler is given the task of arranging the code in a certain way to benefit from the parallelism in order to simplify the hardware architecture of the processor.

Table 9 summarises the execution times obtained for our loop. The results are given for different values of the iteration number $Nmax$ and the three transformations. The times reported in this table are higher than the ones obtained with

Loop trip	Original	NoUnroll	Inversion	Breaking Dep.
12	134	135	61	309
20	404	405	132	689
32	787	788	265	1279
40	938	1052	372	1739

Fig. 9. Execution times (*nanoseconds*)

the analytical model. The main reason is related to the rates used in the PEPA models. These rates are computed using the number of cycles the compiler has estimated for each assembly instruction before the code execution. During the execution these estimated numbers may not be the ones used, and be higher because of the processor speed, its availability, the inputs/outputs, or the memory size.

However, like the results of the analytical model, the results in Table 9 show that the *index inversion* transformation leads to the best execution times. Moreover, like previously, they show that it is better to use the original code than the *breaking dependencies* or the *noUnroll* transformation.

Clearly these results lead to the same conclusions as the ones obtained using our approach. However, our approach allows us to investigate the impact of different transformations on a selected loop quicker than a direct execution of the code. Indeed, if the results reported in Table 9 are the execution times of just the loop, the whole program of the CX3D application had to be executed. And the execution of this program takes several minutes using MAQAO.

5   Conclusions

In this paper we have proposed an approach which allows investigating the effectiveness of several optimisations on the execution time of the code.

The stem of our work is the diagnostic that in scientific computing a consequent fraction of the execution time is the time spent in loops with a limited number of iterations. We come out with a novel method for quickly evaluating different transformations in order to select the best one. The technique is faster than simulation and instrumentation because we isolate and evaluate just the hot loops.

In the future, we plan to extend our approach in two important ways. First, we are interested in developing an interface between MAQAO and PEPA, in order to provide the user with an automatic formal approach. We also plan to propose an infrastructure to cooperate with dynamic analysis when we have large input data that lead to cache misses. Indeed, while our approach is fairly straightforward, it does rely on a host of program analysis available in Itanium 2 compiler. In the case of large input data, performance may be unpredictable even if only two parameters are taken into account. In the future, we propose to combine analytical modelling with the tracing of cache behaviour.

References

1. Bradley, J.T., Dingle, N.J., Gilmore, S.T., Knottenbelt, W.J.: Extracting passage times from PEPA models with the HYDRA tool: A case study. In: Proceedings of the Nineteenth annual UK Performance Engineering Workshop, pp. 79–90 (2003)
2. Czochralski, J.: Z. Phys. Chem. 92 (1918)
3. Dingle, N.J.: Parallel Computation of Response Time Densities and Quantiles in Large Markov and Semi-Markov Models, PhD. Thesis, Imperial College, London (2004)
4. Djoudi, L., Barthou, D., Carribault, P., Lemuet, C., Acquaviva, J.-T., Jalby, W.: MAQAO: Modular Assembler Quality Analyzer and Optimizer for Itanium 2. In: The 4th Workshop on EPIC architectures and compiler technology, San Jose (2005)
5. Djoudi, L., Barthou, D., Tomaz, O., Charif-Rubial, A., Acquaviva, J., Jalby, W.: The Design and Architecture of MAQAOPROFILE: an Instrumentation MAQAO Module. In: The 6th Workshop on architectures and compiler technology, San Jose (2007)
6. Djoudi, L., Noudohouenou, J., Jalby, W.: MAQAOAdvisor: A MAQAO Module For Detecting Analyzing And Fixing Performance Problem. In: The 1st International Workshop on Tools Infrastructures and Methodologies for the Evaluation of Research Systems, Austin (2008)
7. Graham, S.L., Kessler, P.B., Mckusick, M.K.: Gprof: A call graph execution profiler. SIGPLAN Not. 17(6), 120–126 (1982)
8. Hillston, J.: A Compositional Approach to Performance Modelling, PhD. Thesis, University of Edinburgh (1994)
9. Intel Itanium 2 Processor Reference Manual For Software Development and Optimization, 251110-002 (April 2003)
10. Larus, J.R., Schnaar, E.: EEL: Machine-Independent Executable Editing. In: PLDI 1995: Proceedings of the ACM SIGPLAN conference on Programming language design and implementation, La Jolla, California (June 1995)
11. Hill, M.: "prof", Unix Programmer's Manual, Section 1. Bell Laboratories, NJ (January 1979)

Product Form Steady-State Distribution for Stochastic Automata Networks with Domino Synchronizations

J.M. Fourneau

[1] PRiSM, Université de Versailles-Saint-Quentin, CNRS, UniverSud,
Versailles, France
[2] INRIA Projet Mescal, LIG, CNRS, Montbonnot, France

Abstract. We present a new kind of synchronization which allows Continuous Time Stochastic Automata Networks (SAN) to have a product form steady-state distribution. Unlike previous models on SAN with product form solutions, our model allows synchronization between three automata but functional rates are not allowed. The synchronization is not the usual "Rendez-Vous" but an ordered list of transitions. Each transition may fail. When a transition fails, the synchronization ends but all the transitions already executed are kept. This synchronization is related to the triggered customer movement between queues in a network and this class of SAN is a generalization of Gelenbe's networks with triggered customer movement.

1 Introduction

Since they have been introduced by B. Plateau [19] to evaluate the performance of distributed algorithms, Stochastic Automata Networks (SAN for short) have been associated to new research on numerical solvers. The key idea is to take into account the tensor decomposition of the transition matrix of a SAN to improve the storage of the model and the complexity of the vector-matrix product [7]. An automaton consists of states and transitions which represent the effects of events. These events are classified into two types: local events or synchronizing events. A local event affects a single automaton and is modeled by some local transitions. On the opposite, a synchronizing event modifies the state of more than one automaton (but loops are considered as valid transitions). Transitions rates may be fixed or functions of the states of the whole set of automata. For a continuous-time SAN, it is proved that the generator matrix of the associated Markov chain can be written as:

$$Q = \overset{n}{\underset{i=1}{\otimes_g}} L_i + \sum_{r=1}^{s} \overset{n}{\underset{i=1}{\otimes_g}} M_i^r + N, \tag{1}$$

where n is the number of automata, s is the number of synchronizations, L^i and M_i^r are matrices which describe respectively the local transitions and the effect

N. Thomas and C. Juiz (Eds.): EPEW 2008, LNCS 5261, pp. 110–124, 2008.

of synchronization r on automaton i. $\otimes_g$ and $\oplus_g$ denote the generalized tensor product and generalized tensor sum. N is a diagonal matrix used to normalize the generator. These operators have been generalized to handle functional rates and probabilities in the definition of the SAN. As we consider here models without functions, we only have to use a simpler version of this equation with ordinary tensor sum and product. We do not present here the general theory which now can be found in many publications [7,10,19,20,23]. The first algorithm proposed was a numerical resolution of steady-state distribution of the Markov chain associated to a SAN [20] using the power method. Since then, several numerical methods have been investigated [3,4,5,7,12,23]. As a SAN is a modular decomposition into automata which are connected by synchronized transitions, SAN are closely related to Stochastic Process Algebra. Therefore, new results on SAN may be easily translated into other models based on composition such as process algebra, for instance PEPA ([16]). The tensor decomposition of the generator has been generalized for Stochastic Petri Nets (see for instance [6]) and other modular specification methods as well [18].

Recently, some analytical results for SAN have been presented. First, B. Plateau et al. [21] have considered SAN without synchronization. They proved that a product form steady-state distribution exists as soon as some local balance conditions are satisfied. Even without synchronization, the transitions of the automata are still dependent because of functional rates and the generator matrix has in this case a very simple expression:

$$Q = \overset{n}{\underset{i=1}{\otimes_g}} L_i. \tag{2}$$

Plateau's result is closely related to Boucherie's result on Markov chains in competition [1] and Robertazzi's theorems on Petri nets [22]. This theory has been generalized in [9,10] to find a very simple algebraic sufficient condition for product form of steady-state solution of continuous-time SAN. Similarly a more complex sufficient condition has been proved in [11] for discrete-time SAN. These conditions are based on the existence of a common vector in the kernel of all the matrices obtained when the functional rates change.

In [2], we have considered SANs with a special case of synchronization denoted as a limited synchronization. In a limited synchronization, only two automata are active. We have also restricted ourself to SAN without functional rates. Let I be the identity matrix. The generator of a SAN with limited synchronization is:

$$Q = \otimes_{i=1}^n L_i + \sum_{r=1}^s \otimes_{i=1}^n M_i^r + N, \tag{3}$$

with for all r, $M_i^r = I$ for all i except two distinct indices. For a synchronization r, these are denoted as the master and the slave. We note the indices as $msr(r)$ and $sl(r)$. Note that as functional terms are not allowed, the former expression is based on usual tensor sum $\oplus$ and product $\otimes$. We proved a sufficient condition to have a product form steady-state distribution which is based on the existence of a solution for a fixed-point system between the instantaneous arrival rate and the steady-state distributions of the automata in isolation. Some typical queueing networks such as Jackson's networks or Gelenbe's networks of positive and negative customers [13] had been shown to be examples of this type of SAN. For both networks, the fixed-point system is equivalent to the well-known flow equation. Our proof was based on global balance equation. Indeed, there is no local balance (in the usual sense) for Gelenbe's networks.

Here we extend this result for synchronizations between three automata. However we have to change the description of synchronizations. The assumption on synchronization used to define the SAN methodology was the "Rendez-Vous". Here, we consider a completely different kind of synchronization: the Domino synchronization that we will introduce more formally in the next section. Briefly, a Domino synchronization is an ordered list of tuples (automaton number, list of transitions inside this automaton). The synchronization takes place according to the order of the list. The synchronization may completely succeed or be only partial if some conditions are not satisfied. The main idea comes from the networks of queues with triggered customer movement presented by Gelenbe [14]. We also generalize a previous approach [8] where a similar result based on the global balance equation and a fixed point system had been published. Here we present a more general framework, more examples of product form results, and show some links with the algebraic theory presented in [9,10] where the assumptions are also based on some properties of the eigenvalues of the automata in isolation.

The rest of the paper is organized as follows: in section 2, we describe Domino synchronization. In section 3, we state the main theorem of the paper. Section 4 is devoted to examples and links with previous results on other product form for component based models such as PEPA. Finally, we give some conclusions and some perspectives to extend our results to more general synchronizations.

2   Domino Synchronization

In this paper, we restrict ourself to continuous-time SAN without functions. The generator is based on the tensor sum and product local components. Recall that with

$$A = \begin{pmatrix} a_{11} & a_{12} \\ a_{21} & a_{22} \end{pmatrix} \quad \text{and} \quad B = \begin{pmatrix} b_{11} & b_{12} & b_{13} \\ b_{21} & b_{22} & b_{23} \\ b_{31} & b_{32} & b_{33} \end{pmatrix},$$

the tensor sum $A \oplus B$ is given by:

$$\left(\begin{array}{ccc|ccc} a_{11}+b_{11} & b_{12} & b_{13} & a_{12} & 0 & 0 \\ b_{21} & a_{11}+b_{22} & b_{23} & 0 & a_{12} & 0 \\ b_{31} & b_{32} & a_{11}+b_{33} & 0 & 0 & a_{12} \\ \hline a_{21} & 0 & 0 & a_{22}+b_{11} & b_{12} & b_{13} \\ 0 & a_{21} & 0 & b_{21} & a_{22}+b_{22} & b_{23} \\ 0 & 0 & a_{21} & b_{31} & b_{32} & a_{22}+b_{33} \end{array} \right),$$

and the tensor product $A \otimes B$ is:

$$\begin{pmatrix} a_{11}b_{11} & a_{11}b_{12} & a_{11}b_{13} & a_{12}b_{11} & a_{12}b_{12} & a_{12}b_{13} \\ a_{11}b_{21} & a_{11}b_{22} & a_{11}b_{23} & a_{12}b_{21} & a_{12}b_{22} & a_{12}b_{23} \\ a_{11}b_{31} & a_{11}b_{32} & a_{11}b_{33} & a_{12}b_{31} & a_{12}b_{32} & a_{12}b_{33} \\ \hline a_{21}b_{11} & a_{21}b_{12} & a_{21}b_{13} & a_{22}b_{11} & a_{22}b_{12} & a_{22}b_{13} \\ a_{21}b_{21} & a_{21}b_{22} & a_{21}b_{23} & a_{22}b_{21} & a_{22}b_{22} & a_{22}b_{23} \\ a_{21}b_{31} & a_{21}b_{32} & a_{21}b_{33} & a_{22}b_{31} & a_{22}b_{32} & a_{22}b_{33} \end{pmatrix}.$$

The state space of the system is the cartesian product of the states of the automata which are combined in the network. The effective state space is in general only a subset of this product. The synchronization formerly used for SAN are defined as "Rendez-Vous". This simply says that a synchronized transition is possible, if and only if, all automata are ready for this synchronized transition. We have to consider a completely different type of synchronization: the Domino of three automata. The name comes from a group of Domino tiles which fall one after the other. Of course, if one tile does not fall, the Domino effect stops but the tiles already fallen stay down. As we synchronize three automata and we do not allow functional rates, the generator is given by:

$$Q = \otimes_{i=1}^{n} L_i + \sum_{r=1}^{s} \otimes_{i=1}^{n} M_i^r + N, \tag{4}$$

with for all r, $M_i^r = I$ for all i except three distinct indices. Let us now more precisely define a Domino synchronization.

Definition 1. *Let r be a synchronization number or label. The Domino synchronization consists of an ordered list of three automata called the master $msr(r)$, the slave $sl(r)$ and the relay $rl(r)$. The synchronization is performed according to the list order. The master of synchronization r is the initiator of the synchronization. It performs its transition. The slave may obey or not to the request of the master. If it does not follow the master, it makes a loop and the synchronization stops without any interaction with the third automaton (i.e. the relay). But the transition of the master is kept. If the slave obeys, it performs a real transition (i.e. not a loop) and the third automaton (i.e. the relay) now has to make a transition. This transition is either a loop (the relay refuses to follow) or a real transition (the relay obeys). In both cases, the master and the slave perform their transitions. The relay and the slave follow the master according to their local state and the list of transitions marked by label r.*

Remark 1. Note that this definition of synchronization implies that the master is never blocked by the slave or the relay (it is not a rendez-vous). This implies that every state of the automata $sl(r)$ and $rl(r)$ is the origin of at least one synchronized transition marked by synchronization label r.

The automata are defined by the following matrices which may be either finite or infinite:

- n transition rate matrices denoted as L_l for automaton l. L_l models the rates of local transitions. The matrices are normalized, i.e.

$$L_l[k,i] \geq 0 \ if \ i \neq k \ and \ \sum_i L_l[k,i] = 0.$$

- s tuples of three matrices (D^r, E^r, T^r). In the tensor product associated to Domino synchronization $r \otimes_{i=1}^n M_i^r$ all matrices except (D^r, E^r, T^r) are equal to Identity. In the usual description of a SAN [19] the master of a synchronization is a transition rate matrix and the other matrices used in the tensor product are transition probability matrices. We use the same formulation here. In D^r we find the transitions due to synchronization r on the master automaton. It is assumed that the synchronizations always have an effect on the master (i.e. its transition is not a loop).

  The effect of synchronization r on the slave (i.e. automaton $sl(r)$) is specified by matrix E^r. E^r is a transition probability matrix. For a Domino synchronization and for any state k we assume the following: either $E^r[k,k] = 0$, or $E^r[k,k] = 1$. If $E^r[k,k]$ is 1, synchronization r has no effect on the slave when it is in state k It is said that synchronization r fails during the second step. The synchronized transition takes place on the master but there is no effect on the slave and the synchronization is stopped at this step. Thus, the relay does not synchronize.

  Otherwise (i.e. $E^r[k,k] = 0$), row k of matrix E^r gives the transition probability out of state k for the slave. And the synchronization tries now to trigger a transition of the automaton $rl(r)$. T^r is a transition probability matrix with the same assumptions already presented for E^r. Similarly, the synchronization may have an effect on the relay (a real transition and a probability in matrix T^r) or it may fail in state k ($T^r[k,k] = 1$). All matrices are normalized, i.e. for all k we have:

$$D^r[k,i] \geq 0 \ if \ i \neq k \ and \ \sum_i D^r[k,i] = 0,$$
$$E^r[k,i] \geq 0 \ and \ \sum_i E^r[k,i] = 1,$$
$$T^r[k,i] \geq 0 \ and \ \sum_i T^r[k,i] = 1.$$

- Due to the assumptions on E^r it is useful to decompose the matrix into two non negative matrices E_1^r and E_2^r such that $E^r = E_1^r + E_2^r$, and for all i and j we have: $E_1^r[i,j] = E^r[i,j]1_{E^r[i,i]=0}$ and $E_2^r[i,j] = E^r[i,j]1_{E^r[i,i]=1}$. Thus E_1^r describes the slave transitions when it obeys to the master request while E_2^r models the loops made by the slave when it does not accept the request.

To complete the description of the generator of the SAN, one must give the description of the normalization associated to synchronization r. Let N^r be this matrix. N^r is a negative diagonal matrix and the total normalization (denoted as N in Equation 1) is $N = \sum_{r=1}^s N^r$.

Definition 2. *Let M be a matrix, $\sigma(M)$ is a diagonal matrix with the size of M such that for all index i, $\sigma(M)[i,i] = \sum_j M[i,j]$. As usual $diag(M)$ is a diagonal matrix whose elements are the diagonal elements of M.*

For the sake of readability, we assume that the SAN is suitably reordered such that the automata involved in synchronization r are the first three ones. The description of the other automata is simply an Identity which is denoted here as I_1 to avoid the confusion. The SAN description associated to Domino synchronization r consists in 4 terms:

1. $(D^r - diag(D^r)) \otimes E_1^\tau \otimes T^r \otimes I_1$: the slave accepts the synchronization.
2. $(D^r - diag(D^r)) \otimes E_2^\tau \otimes I \otimes I_1$: the slave does not accept the synchronization.
3. $diag(D^r) \otimes \sigma(E_1^r) \otimes \sigma(T^r) \otimes I_1$: normalization of term 1.
4. $diag(D^r) \otimes \sigma(E_2^r) \otimes I \otimes I_1$: normalization of term 2.

3   Product Form Solution

We now establish a sufficient condition for a SAN with Domino synchronization to have steady-state distribution which is obtained as the product of the steady-state distributions of the automata in isolation.

Remark 2. Let us introduce some notation:

- To keep the proofs as clear as possible, we use in the following indices i, j, k and m for states, l for an automaton, r for a synchronization.
- Finally, we denote by $((k_1, k_2, \cdots, k_n) \Diamond (list\ (automaton, state)))$ the state where all automata are in the state defined by $(k_1, k_2, \cdots, k_n)$, except the ones in the list. So, $((k_1, k_2, \cdots, k_n) \Diamond ((l, i)))$ represents the state where for all m, automaton m is in state k_m except automaton l which is in state i.

Theorem 1. *Consider a SAN with n automata and s with Domino synchronizations. Consider matrices $\overline{D^r} = D^r - diag(D^r)$ and E^r associated to the description of synchronization r. Assume that E^r and $\overline{D^r}$ share a positive eigenvector. Let g_l be such an eigenvector. Let Ω_r (resp. Γ_r) be the eigenvalue for matrix E^r (resp. $\overline{D^r}$) associated to g_l. If g_l is in the kernel of matrix $\left[L_l + \sum_{r=1}^s \left(D^r 1_{msr(r)=l} + \Gamma_r (E^r - \sigma(E^r)) 1_{sl(r)=l} + \Gamma_r \Omega_r (T^r - \sigma(T^r)) 1_{rl(r)=l} \right) \right]$, then the steady-state distribution has a product form solution:*

$$Pr(X_1, X_2, \cdots, X_n) = C \prod_{l=1}^n g_l(X_l), \qquad (5)$$

and C is a normalization constant.

The proof is based on some properties of tensor products which are presented at the end of this section. Let us first present below the global balance equation. Here, we just explain the various terms which appear in this equation.

$$Pr(\boldsymbol{k})(\sum_{l=1}^n \sum_{i \neq k_l} L_l[k_l, i] + \sum_{r=1}^s \sum_{i \neq k_{msr(r)}} D^r[k_{msr(r)}, i]) \qquad (6)$$

$$= \sum_{l=1}^{n} \sum_{i \neq k_l} L_l[i, k_l] Pr(\boldsymbol{k} \Diamond((l, i)))$$

$$+ \sum_{r=1}^{s} \sum_{i \neq k_{msr(r)}} D^r[i, k_{msr(r)}] \sum_{j \neq k_{sl(r)}} E^r[(j, k_{sl(r)})] \sum_{m \neq k_{rl(r)}} T^r[m, k_{rl(r)}] \times$$
$$Pr(\boldsymbol{k} \Diamond((msr(r), i), (sl(r), j), (rl(r), m)))$$

$$+ \sum_{r=1}^{s} \sum_{i \neq k_{msr(r)}} D^r[i, k_{msr(r)}] \sum_{j \neq k_{sl(r)}} E^r(j, k_{sl(r)}) 1_{T^r[k_{rl(r)}, k_{rl(r)}]=0} \times$$
$$Pr(\boldsymbol{k} \Diamond((msr(r), i), (sl(r), j)))$$

$$+ \sum_{r=1}^{s} \sum_{i \neq k_{msr(r)}} D^r[i, k_{msr(r)}] 1_{E^r[k_{sl(r)}, k_{sl(r)}]=0} Pr(\boldsymbol{k} \Diamond((msr(r), i)))$$

$$(7)$$

- On the left-hand-side, $L_l[k_l, i]$ is the rate for local transition out of state k_l for automaton l and $D^r[k_l, i]$ is the transition rate of a synchronization which jumps out of state k_l.
- On the right-hand-side, the first term describes local transitions into state k_l . The second term is associated to a complete synchronization of the three automata. In the third term, we consider a synchronization which fails at the third step (i.e. the relay), and finally, the last term describes a synchronization which fails at the second step. The slave does not accept the transition.

Let us rewrite the conditions of the theorem: there exists a solution $(g_l)_l$, $(\Gamma_r, \Omega_r)_r$ to the fixed point system:

$$\begin{cases} \Gamma_r \, g_l = g_l \, \overline{D^r} & if \quad msr(r) = l, \\ \Omega_r \, g_l = g_l \, E^r & if \quad sl(r) = l, \\ g_l \left[L_l + \sum_{r=1}^{s} \left(D^r 1_{msr(r)=l} \right. \right. \\ \quad + \Gamma_r (E^r - \sigma(E^r)) 1_{sl(r)=l} \\ \quad \left. \left. + \, \Gamma_r \Omega_r (T^r - \sigma(T^r)) 1_{rl(r)=l} \right) \right] = 0, \end{cases} \tag{8}$$

These equations look quite complex, but a simple interpretation may be given to all of them. The third equation defines g_l as the invariant distribution (up to a normalization constant) of a continuous-time Markov chain which models the automaton in isolation (i.e. $g_l M_l = 0$), with:

$$M_l = L_l + \sum_{r=1}^{s} \left(D^r 1_{msr(r)=l} + \Gamma_r (E^r - \sigma(E^r)) 1_{sl(r)=l} + \Gamma_r \Omega_r (T^r - \sigma(T^r)) 1_{rl(r)=l} \right).$$

$$(9)$$

Remember that E^r and T^r are transition probability matrices. Thus $E^r - \sigma(E^r)$ and $T^r - \sigma(T^r)$ are generators. As L_l and D^r are generators, and Γ_r and Ω_r are positive, matrix M_l is the generator of a continuous-time Markov chain. Of course, this construction does not prove in general that the chain is ergodic.

However, if the chain is finite and if matrix L_l is irreducible, then matrix M_l is irreducible and the chain of the automaton in isolation is ergodic. Furthermore, the four terms of the summation have an intuitive interpretation. The first term corresponds to the local transitions. The last three terms represent the effects of the synchronization on the automata involved in a Domino. The effect on the master are explicitly represented by the transition matrix D^r while the effect on the slave and the relay are represented by the matrices $E^r - \sigma(E^r)$ and $T^r - \sigma(T^r)$ multiplied by appropriate rates. These rates are defined by the first two equations of the fixed point system. Consider the first one: $\Gamma_r\ g_l = g_l\ \overline{D^r}$. This equation states that Γ_r is the left-eigenvalue associated to eigenvector g_l for an operator obtained from matrix D^r by zeroing the diagonal elements. The examples presented in the next section show that this equation is a generalization of queueing networks flow equation. Similarly, Ω_r is defined as the eigenvalue of E^r. Note that, like in product form queueing network, the existence of these flows (Γ_r, Ω_r) does not imply that the whole network send a Poisson streams of synchronization on automaton l. Similarly, the product form holds even if the underlying Markov chain is not reversible.

It is worthy to remark that the conditions of the theorem are based on the same kind of properties used in [9,10,11] to prove product form steady-state distributions for other types of SAN. We present in the next section some examples where the product form holds. Before let us proceed with the proof of the theorem using relations between tensor products and product form distributions we have already used in [9,10,11].

3.1   Proof of the Theorem

The tensor product and sums have many algebraic properties (see [7] for proofs). We give some of them in the following for the sake of completeness.

Property 1 (Basic properties of Tensor Product). Let A, B and C, $A1$, $A2$, $B1$, $B2$ be arbitrary matrices, the following properties hold:

- Associativity: $(A \otimes B) \otimes C = A \otimes (B \otimes C)$.
- Distributivity over Addition:

$$(A_1 + A_2) \otimes (B_1 + B_2) = A_1 \otimes B_1 + A_1 \otimes B_2 + A_2 \otimes B_1 + A_1 \otimes B_2.$$

- Compatibility with matrix multiplication: For all vectors π_A and π_B whose sizes are consistent we have:

$$(\pi_A \otimes \pi_B)(A \otimes B) = (\pi_A A) \otimes (\pi_B B).$$

Before proceeding with the proof it is worthy to remark that a product form solution of n distributions $(\pi_l)_{l=1..n}$ can be written as $C\pi_1 \otimes \pi_2 \otimes \ldots \otimes \pi_n$. Consider the generator or the SAN:

$$Q = \otimes_{i=1}^{n} L_i + \sum_{r=1}^{s} \otimes_{i=1}^{n} M_i^r + \sum_{r=1}^{s} N^r, \tag{10}$$

with for all r, $M_i^r = I$ for all i except for the master, the slave and the relay of synchronization r. A steady-state distribution of the SAN is a probability vector π which satisfies $\pi Q = 0$. Assume that π has product form $Cg_1 \otimes g_2 \otimes \ldots \otimes g_n$. Thus one must check that:

$$(g_1 \otimes g_2 \otimes \ldots \otimes g_n)(\otimes_{i=1}^n L_i) + \sum_{r=1}^s (g_1 \otimes g_2 \otimes \ldots \otimes g_n)((\otimes_{i=1}^n M_i^r) + N^r) = 0. \quad (11)$$

First let us remember that $A \oplus B = A \otimes I + I \otimes B$. Therefore the tensor sum becomes the sum of n tensor products of n matrices ($n-1$ of which are equal to Identity). We then apply the compatibility with ordinary product and we remark that $g_l I = g_l$ to simplify the tensor product.

We have $n + 2s$ products of n terms. The key idea is to factorize into n terms such that each term is a tensor product of n vectors. Furthermore each of these product is equal to zero because one of the vectors is zero. More precisely, each of these terms is equal to: $(g_1 W_1 \otimes g_2 W_2 \otimes \ldots \otimes g_n W_n)$ and all matrices W_i are equal to Identity except one which is equal to M_l (defined in Equation 9). As $g_l M_l = 0$, the tensor product is zero.

For the sake of readability we first present the proof for the first synchronization and the three automata involved in this synchronization. We also assume that the SAN has been reordered such that these automata are the first three ones. More precisely, the master is the first automaton, the slave the second and the relay is the third. We only consider the local terms associated to these automata and the first synchronization. The description of $(g_1 \otimes g_2 \otimes \ldots \otimes g_n)Q$ consists in 7 terms (three coming from the tensor sum, two for the Domino and two for the normalization of the Domino):

$$
\begin{aligned}
&(g_1 F_1 \otimes g_2 \otimes g_3 \otimes \ldots \otimes g_n) \\
+ &(g_1 \otimes g_2 F_2 \otimes g_3 \otimes \ldots \otimes g_n) \\
+ &(g_1 \otimes g_2 \otimes g_3 F_3 \otimes \ldots \otimes g_n) \\
+ &(g_1(D^r - diag(D^r)) \otimes g_2 E_1^r \otimes g_3 T^r \otimes \ldots \otimes g_n) \\
+ &(g_1(D^r - diag(D^r)) \otimes g_2 E_2^r \otimes g_3 \otimes \ldots \otimes g_n) \\
+ &(g_1 diag(D^r) \otimes g_2 \sigma(E_1^r) \otimes g_3 \sigma(T^r) \otimes \ldots \otimes g_n) \\
+ &(g_1 diag(D^r) \otimes g_2 \sigma(E_2^r) \otimes g_3 \otimes \ldots \otimes g_n)
\end{aligned}
$$

Now remember that $g_1(D^r - diag(D^r)) = g_1 \Gamma_r$. Furthermore due to the definition of the Domino, we have: $\sigma(T^r) = I$ and we simplify the sixth term. Furthermore $\sigma(E_1^r) + \sigma(E_2^r) = I$ and we can combine the sixth and seventh terms to obtain after simplification:

$$
\begin{aligned}
&(g_1 F_1 \otimes g_2 \otimes g_3 \otimes \ldots \otimes g_n) \\
+ &(g_1 \otimes g_2 F_2 \otimes g_3 \otimes \ldots \otimes g_n) \\
+ &(g_1 \otimes g_2 \otimes g_3 F_3 \otimes \ldots \otimes g_n) \\
+ &(g_1 \Gamma_r \otimes g_2 E_1^r \otimes g_3 T^r \otimes \ldots \otimes g_n) \\
+ &(g_1 \Gamma_r \otimes g_2 E_2^r \otimes g_3 \otimes \ldots \otimes g_n) \\
+ &(g_1 diag(D^r) \otimes g_2 \otimes g_3 \otimes \ldots \otimes g_n)
\end{aligned}
$$

Now we factorize the first and the last terms. Furthermore we add and subtract the following term: $(g_1(D^r - diag(D^r)) \otimes g_2 \otimes g_3 \otimes \ldots \otimes g_n)$.

$$(g_1(F_1 + diag(D^r)) \otimes g_2 \otimes g_3 \otimes \ldots \otimes g_n)$$
$$+ (g_1 \otimes g_2 F_2 \otimes g_3 \otimes \ldots \otimes g_n)$$
$$+ (g_1 \otimes g_2 \otimes g_3 F_3 \otimes \ldots \otimes g_n)$$
$$+ (g_1 \Gamma_r \otimes g_2 E_1^r \otimes g_3 T^r \otimes \ldots \otimes g_n)$$
$$+ (g_1 \Gamma_r \otimes g_2 E_2^r \otimes g_3 \otimes \ldots \otimes g_n)$$
$$- (g_1(D^r - diag(D^r)) \otimes g_2 \otimes g_3 \otimes \ldots \otimes g_n)$$
$$+ (g_1(D^r - diag(D^r)) \otimes g_2 \otimes g_3 \otimes \ldots \otimes g_n)$$

We factorize the first and the last term and we note that $g_1(D^r - diag(D^r)) = g_1 \Gamma_r$ to simplify the sixth term:

$$(g_1(F_1 + D^r) \otimes g_2 \otimes g_3 \otimes \ldots \otimes g_n)$$
$$+ (g_1 \otimes g_2 F_2 \otimes g_3 \otimes \ldots \otimes g_n)$$
$$+ (g_1 \otimes g_2 \otimes g_3 F_3 \otimes \ldots \otimes g_n)$$
$$+ (g_1 \Gamma_r \otimes g_2 E_1^r \otimes g_3 T^r \otimes \ldots \otimes g_n)$$
$$+ (g_1 \Gamma_r \otimes g_2 E_2^r \otimes g_3 \otimes \ldots \otimes g_n)$$
$$- (g_1 \Gamma_r \otimes g_2 \otimes g_3 \otimes \ldots \otimes g_n)$$

Note that the ordinary product is compatible with the tensor product (i.e. $(\lambda A) \otimes B = A \otimes (\lambda B)$). We also remark that due to the definition of Domino synchronization $\sigma(E_2^r) = E_2^r$ and $\sigma(E_1^r) + \sigma(E_2^r) = I$. Using the distributivity, after cancellation we get:

$$(g_1(F_1 + D^r) \otimes g_2 \otimes g_3 \otimes \ldots \otimes g_n)$$
$$+ (g_1 \otimes g_2(F_2 - \Gamma_r \sigma(E_1^r)) \otimes g_3 \otimes \ldots \otimes g_n)$$
$$+ (g_1 \otimes g_2 \otimes g_3 F_3 \otimes \ldots \otimes g_n)$$
$$+ (g_1 \Gamma_r \otimes g_2 E_1^r \otimes g_3 T^r \otimes \ldots \otimes g_n)$$

We add and we subtract $(g_1 \Gamma_r \otimes g_2 E_1^r \otimes g_3 \otimes \ldots \otimes g_n)$. We factorize the second term:

$$(g_1(F_1 + D^r) \otimes g_2 \otimes g_3 \otimes \ldots \otimes g_n)$$
$$+ (g_1 \otimes g_2(F_2 + \Gamma_r(E_1^r - \sigma(E_1^r))) \otimes g_3 \otimes \ldots \otimes g_n)$$
$$+ (g_1 \otimes g_2 \otimes g_3 F_3 \otimes \ldots \otimes g_n)$$
$$+ (g_1 \Gamma_r \otimes g_2 E_1^r \otimes g_3 T^r \otimes \ldots \otimes g_n)$$
$$- (g_1 \Gamma_r \otimes g_2 E_1^r \otimes g_3 \otimes \ldots \otimes g_n)$$

We apply the assumption on the eigenvalue of E_1^r. We remark that $E_1^r - \sigma(E_1^r) = E^r - \sigma(E^r)$ and that $\sigma(T^r) = I$. After substitution we finally get the decomposition we need:

$$(g_1(F_1 + D^r) \otimes g_2 \otimes g_3 \otimes \ldots \otimes g_n)$$
$$+ (g_1 \otimes g_2(F_2 + \Gamma_r(E^r - \sigma(Er))) \otimes g_3 \otimes \ldots \otimes g_n)$$
$$+ (g_1 \otimes g_2 \otimes g_3(F_3 + \Gamma_r \Omega_r(T^r - \sigma(T^r))) \otimes \ldots \otimes g_n)$$

Now we can continue with the second Domino synchronization and factorize the terms to obtain n tensor products. Each of them contains a product by vector $g_l M_l$ which is zero due to the assumptions of the theorem. Therefore $(g_1 \otimes \ldots \otimes g_n)Q = 0$ and the SAN has a product form steady state distribution.

4 Examples

We define some notation for the various matrices used to describe the SAN:

- I: the identity matrix,
- Upp: the matrix full of 0 except the main upper diagonal which is 1,
- Low: the matrix full of 0 except the main lower diagonal which is 1,
- I^0: the identity matrix except the first diagonal element which is 0.
- $C1$: the null matrix except the first column whose elements are equal to 1.

4.1 Gelenbe's Networks with Customer Triggered Movement

The concept of Generalized networks (G-networks for short) have been introduced by Gelenbe in [13]. These networks contain customers and signals. In the first papers on this topic, signals were also denoted as negative customers. Signals are not queued in the network. They are sent into a queue, and disappear instantaneously. But before they disappear they may act upon some customers present in the queue. As customers may, at the completion of their service, become signals and be routed into another queue, G-networks exhibit some synchronized transitions which are not modeled by Jackson networks. Usually the signal implies the deletion of at least one customer. These networks have a steady-state product form solution under usual Markovian assumptions. Then the effects have been extended to include the synchronization between three queues : a signal originated from queue i and which arrives into queue j triggers a customer movement into queue k, if queue j is not empty. Gelenbe has proved that these networks still have a product form solution under the same assumptions [14]. For the sake of simplicity, we assume that there is no arrival of signals from the outside. We also restrict ourselves to networks where at the completion of their services, the customers become signals to join the queue associated to the slave automaton or leave the network.

We consider an infinite state space. Each automaton models the number of positive customers in a queue. The signal are not represented in the states as they vanish instantaneously. The local transitions are the external arrivals (rate λ_l) and the departures to the outside (rate μ_l multiplied by probability d_l). The synchronization describes the departure of a customer on the master (the end of service with rate μ_l and probability $(1 - d_l)$), the departure of a customer on the slave (a customer movement, if there is any), the arrival of a customer on the relay (always accepted). More formally:

$$L_l = \lambda_l(Upp - I) + \mu_l d_l(Low - I^0),$$
$$D^r = \mu_l(1 - d_l)(Low - I^0), \tag{12}$$
$$E^r = Low \quad and \quad T^r = Upp.$$

After substitution in the system considered in theorem 1, it must be clear that matrix M_l is tridiagonal with constant diagonals. Thus, g_l has a geometric distribution with rate ρ_l:

$$\rho_l = \frac{\lambda_l + \sum_{r=1}^s \Omega_r \Gamma_r 1_{rl(r)=l}}{\mu_l + \sum_{r=1}^s \Gamma_r 1_{sl(r)=l}}.$$

Of course, one must check that for all l, ρ_l is smaller than 1. Because of its geometric distribution, g_l is an eigenvector of operators $\overline{D^r}$ and E^r. Finally, we obtain: $\Omega_r = \rho_{sl(r)}$ and $\Gamma_r = \rho_{msr(r)}\mu_{msr(r)}(1 - d_{msr(r)})$, which is roughly the generalized flow equation which has been found in [14] when the routing matrix only contains one non zero entry.

4.2   Three Deletions

Consider the following model:

$$
\begin{aligned}
L_l &= \lambda_l(Upp - I) + \mu_l d_l(Low - I^0), \\
D^r &= \mu_l(1 - d_l)(Low - I^0), \\
E^r &= T^r = Low.
\end{aligned}
\tag{13}
$$

This SAN describes a network of queues where the three queues involved in the synchronization delete one customer if there is any in the queue. However the deletions of customer are ordered. The deletion in the relay only occurs if the deletion in the slave was successful. Matrix M_l is tridiagonal with constant diagonals. g_l has a geometric distribution with rate ρ_l:

$$
\rho_l = \frac{\lambda_l}{\mu_l + + \sum_{r=1}^{s} \Omega_r \Gamma_r 1_{rl(r)=l} + \sum_{r=1}^{s} \Gamma_r 1_{sl(r)=l}}.
$$

and $\Omega_r = \rho_{sl(r)}$ and $\Gamma_r = \rho_{msr(r)}\mu_{msr(r)}(1 - d_{msr(r)})$.

4.3   Jackson and Gelenbe's Network

Of course it is possible to describe a Jackson network of queues as follows:

$$
\begin{aligned}
L_l &= \lambda_l(Upp - I) + \mu_l d_l(Low - I^0), \\
D^r &= \mu_l(1 - d_l)(Low - I^0), \\
E^r &= Upp \quad and \quad T^r = I.
\end{aligned}
\tag{14}
$$

Similarly a Gelenbe's network with negative customers is described by:

$$
\begin{aligned}
L_l &= \lambda_l(Upp - I) + \mu_l d_l(Low - I^0), \\
D^r &= \mu_l(1 - d_l)(Low - I^0), \\
E^r &= Low \quad and \quad T^r = I.
\end{aligned}
\tag{15}
$$

And we can find easily the flow equations.

4.4   The Relay Jumps to Zero

Consider the following model:

$$
\begin{aligned}
L_l &= \lambda_l(Upp - I) + \mu_l d_l(Low - I^0), \\
D^r &= \mu_l(1 - d_l)(Low - I^0), \\
E^r &= Low \quad and \quad T^r = C1.
\end{aligned}
\tag{16}
$$

This SAN describes a network of queues. Each automaton models the number of positive customers in a queue. The synchronization delete one customer in the master and the slave and flushes out the relay. Matrix M_l is not tridiagonal anymore but g_l is still geometric and we have a product form result.

4.5   Networks with More Complex Effect

It is worthy to remark that matrices T^r and L_l only appear in one equation. Therefore, it is possible to find new results if we keep the geometric distribution for g_l and the matrices $\overline{D^r}$ and E^r unchanged. Indeed, the first two equations of the fixed point system are still verified for the eigenvector. And this gives two relations between the eigenvalues Γ_r and Ω_r and the rate of the geometric distribution of g_l.

Theorem 2. *Assume that $\overline{D^r} = \alpha Low$ and $E^r = Low$, then for every matrices L_l and T^r which imply a geometric distribution for g_l with rate ρ_l, the SAN has a product form distribution if the flow equation in ρ_l has a solution whose components are smaller than 1.*

4.6   Product Form for PEPA Models

As SAN are closely related to Stochastic Process Algebra, the results we have obtained here can be applied on PEPA models. Similarly, as some papers have been published on PEPA models with product form steady state solution [15,17], one may compare the approaches and the results even if it is not possible here to define PEPA specifications.

Hillston and Thomas considered in [17] PEPA models which belongs to the class of continuous-time Markov chains in competition studied by Boucherie [1]. The PEPA models are based on guarded transitions and the conditions established by Boucherie can be algorithmically detected at the syntactic level while the assumptions made by Boucherie need some modeling expertise. Boucherie's condition has been extended for SAN in [9,10] and are not related to the model presented here. The conditions in [10] like the condition of Theorem 1 are mostly numerical: they require to compute eigenvalues for some matrices and compare them. However it may be possible that one can generalize the approach in [17] to take into account this numerical approach at a high level.

Harrison and Hillston have also proved product form results for PEPA models using reversibility theory [15]. To the best of our knowledge, the comparison between this approach and results presented in [9,10] and in our paper remains to be done.

5   Conclusions

Domino synchronization limited to three modules allow SAN to have a product form steady-state distribution. This result is based on the synchronization description and some properties of the tensor sum and product. Our result holds even if the underlying Markov chain is not reversible. Similarly, local balances do not hold (at least for Gelenbe's networks which are included in our model). However, Domino synchronization are far less powerful for specification than the usual "Rendez-Vous". For instance, they do not allow the blocking of the master by the slave. More theoretically, the Domino synchronization with product form is much more general than the three automata case we have presented here. It remains to generalize to arbitrary size Domino synchronization and to explain why they allow product form. Finally, one must consider functional transitions (such as in [9,10,11]) and combine both approaches.

Acknowledgement. this work is partially supported by ANR grant SMS (ANR-05-BLAN-0009-02).

References

1. Boucherie, R.: A Characterization of independence for competing Markov chains with applications to stochastic Petri nets. IEEE Trans. Software Eng. 20(7), 536–544 (1994)
2. Boujdaine, F., Fourneau, J.M., Mikou, N.: Product Form Solution for Stochastic Automata Networks with synchronization. In: 5th Process Algebra and Performance Modeling Workshop, Twente, Netherlands (1997)
3. Buchholz, P., Dayar, T.: Comparison of Multilevel Methods for Kronecker-based Markovian Representations. Computing Journal 73(4), 349–371 (2004)
4. Dayar, T., Gusak, O., Fourneau, J.M.: Stochastic Automata Networks and Near Complete Decomposability. SIAM Journal and Applications 23, 581–599 (2002)
5. Dayar, T., Gusak, O., Fourneau, J.M.: Iterative disaggregation for a class of lumpable discrete-time SAN. Performance Evaluation, 2003 53(1), 43–69 (2003)
6. Donnatelli, S.: Superposed stochastic automata: a class of stochastic Petri nets with parallel solution and distributed state space. Performance Evaluation 18, 21–36 (1993)
7. Fernandes, P., Plateau, B., Stewart, W.J.: Efficient Descriptor-Vector Multiplications in Stochastic Automata Networks. JACM, 381–414 (1998)
8. Fourneau, J.M.: Domino Synchronization: product form solution for SANs. Studia Informatica 23, 4(51), 173–190
9. Fourneau, J.M., Plateau, B., Stewart, W.: Product form for Stochastic Automata Networks. In: Proc. of ValueTools 2007, Nantes, France (2007)
10. Fourneau, J.M., Plateau, B., Stewart, W.: An Algebraic Condition for Product Form in Stochastic Automata Networks without Synchronizations. Performance Evaluation (to appear, 2008)
11. Fourneau, J.M.: Discrete Time Markov chains competing over resources: product form steady-state distribution. In: QEST 2008 (to appear, 2008)
12. Fourneau, J.M., Quessette, F.: Graphs and Stochastic Automata Networks. In: Proc. of the 2nd International Workshop on the Numerical Solution of Markov Chains, Raleigh, USA (1995)
13. Gelenbe, E.: Product form queueing networks with negative and positive customers. Journal of Applied Probability 28, 656–663 (1991)
14. Gelenbe, E.: G-networks with triggered customer movement. Journal of Applied Probability 30, 742–748 (1993)
15. Harrison, P., Hillston, J.: Exploiting Quasi-reversible Structures in Markovian Process Algebra Models. Computer Journal 38(7), 510–520 (1995)
16. Hillston, J.: A compositional approach to Performance Modeling, Ph.D Thesis, University of Edinburgh (1994)
17. Hillston, J., Thomas, N.: Product Form Solution for a Class of PEPA Models. Performance Evaluation 35(3-4), 171–192 (1999)

18. Kloul, L., Hillston, J.: An efficient Kronecker representation for PEPA models. In: de Alfaro, L., Gilmore, S. (eds.) PROBMIV 2001, PAPM-PROBMIV 2001, and PAPM 2001. LNCS, vol. 2165. Springer, Heidelberg (2001)
19. Plateau, B.: On the Stochastic Structure of Parallelism and Synchronization Models for Distributed Algorithms. In: Proc. ACM Sigmetrics Conference on Measurement and Modeling of Computer Systems, Austin, Texas (August 1985)
20. Plateau, B., Fourneau, J.M., Lee, K.H.: PEPS: A Package for Solving Complex Markov Models of Parallel Systems. In: Proceedings of the 4th Int. Conf. on Modeling Techniques and Tools for Computer Performance Evaluation, Majorca, Spain (September 1988)
21. Plateau, B., Stewart, W.J.: Stochastic Automata Networks: Product Forms and Iterative Solutions, Inria Report 2939, France
22. Lazar, A., Robertazzi, T.: Markovian Petri Net Protocols with Product Form Solution. Performance Evaluation 12, 66–77 (1991)
23. Stewart, W.J., Atif, K., Plateau, B.: The numerical solution of Stochastic Automata Networks. European Journal of Operation Research 86(3), 503–525 (1995)

State-Aware Performance Analysis with eXtended Stochastic Probes

Allan Clark and Stephen Gilmore

University of Edinburgh, Scotland

Abstract. We define a mechanism for specifying performance queries which combine instantaneous observations of model states and finite sequences of observations of model activities. We realise these queries by composing the state-aware observers (called *eXtended Stochastic Probes* (XSP)) with a model expressed in a stochastically-timed process algebra. Our work has been conceived in the context of the process algebra PEPA. However the ideas involved are relevant to all timed process algebras with an underlying discrete-state representation such as a continuous-time Markov chain.

1 Introduction

When modelling complex systems we generally wish to make queries and therefore must describe the set of states in which we are interested. The analysis in question may be a steady-state query asking a question such as: "In the long-run what percentage of its time does the server spend idle?" The set of states in which we are interested is then the *steady-set*. Passage-time queries are often concerned with events, however the query must still be specified as a set of states, which we will call the *passage-set*. To perform a passage-time analysis the solver can extract the set of source states and the set of target states from the passage-set. The set of source states is taken to be all of those states in the passage-set which are the target of some transition whose source lies outside the passage-set. Conversely the set of target states is taken to be the set of states outside the passage-set which are the target of some transition whose source lies in the passage-set.

More generally whether we are performing a steady-state or passage-time analysis we will be interested in specifying the *query-set*. There are currently two kinds of mechanism for specifying query-sets: *state-specifications* and *activity-specifications*.

We are interested in the robustness and portability of our query specifications. For robustness we would like to ensure that our query specification remains correct whenever we make unrelated changes to our model. For portability we would like one query specification to be used over several differing models. Additionally it is important that we are able to make many different queries without needing to alter the model. We have found that the above two query specification techniques alone are insufficient for our aims. Additionally allowing the user to specify their queries using either is still not sufficiently expressive. We have found it necessary to combine the two into one specification language which allows state-specifications to be intermixed within an activity probe specification. This language we have called *eXtended Stochastic Probes* (XSP).

N. Thomas and C. Juiz (Eds.): EPEW 2008, LNCS 5261, pp. 125–140, 2008.

Structure of this paper. The rest of this paper is structured as follows: section 2 discusses related work and section 3 formally introduces the two separate specification techniques; state specifications and activity probes as well as formally introducing our extension which allows the combination of both approaches. Section 4 provides details of the conversion of extended probe specifications into our target language PEPA as implemented in our PEPA compiler. A detailed example is provided in sections 5 and 6. Finally conclusions are presented in section 7.

2 Related Work

The use of a regular expression-like language to describe a probe component which is automatically added to a PEPA model was studied by Katwala, Bradley and Dingle [1]. The addition of probe components has been a feature of the Imperial PEPA Compiler [2] (now the International PEPA Compiler) since it was first developed and remains so in the derivative work ipclib [3].

Stochastic probes describe activity-observations. We have previously extended this formalism to locate activities within structured models [4]. We introduced immediate actions into communicating local probes to convey state information without perturbing the performance analysis which was being made. In the present work we add state-observations to the existing stochastic probes language which specifies location-aware activity-observations.

A widely-used language for describing logical properties of continuous-time Markov chains is CSL (Continuous Stochastic Logic), introduced by Aziz, Sanwal, Singhal and Brayton [5]. An application of CSL to a process algebra must first translate the higher-level state information exposed to the user to the states of the Markov chain. The well-formed formulae of CSL are made up of *state formulae* ϕ and *path formulae* ψ. The syntax of CSL is below.

$$\phi ::= true \mid false \mid a \mid \phi \wedge \phi \mid \phi \vee \phi \mid \neg \phi \mid$$
$$\mathcal{P}_{\bowtie p}[\psi] \mid \mathcal{S}_{\bowtie p}[\phi]$$
$$\psi ::= X \phi \mid \phi \, U^I \, \phi \mid \phi \, U \, \phi$$

Here a is an atomic proposition, $\bowtie \in \{<, \leq, >, \geq\}$ is a relational parameter, $p \in [0, 1]$ is a probability, and I is an interval of $\mathbb{R}$. Derived logical operators such as implication ($\Rightarrow$) can be encoded in the usual way.

The implementation of the CSL logic in the model-checker PRISM [6] is extended with additional state-specifications called *filters*. An example is shown in the following formula where

$$\mathcal{P}_{>0.97}[true \, U^I \, \phi_2\{\phi_1\}]$$

determines whether the probability of, from a state satisfying the filter ϕ_1, reaching a state satisfying ϕ_2 within interval I is greater than 0.97.

Because CSL can only describe states and not the events which cause state transitions – namely actions – CSL (without filters) was extended with activity-specifications by Baier, Cloth, Haverkort, Kuntz and Siegle [7] to provide the language asCSL. In that work the authors added activity observations to a state-aware logic. This has recently been further extended to provide the language CSL^{TA} [8] by Donatelli, Haddad and Sproston. This language allows properties referring to the probability of a finite sequence of timed activities through the use of a timed automaton.

The XSP language presented here is close to the language which would be obtained by extending asCSL with the state-filters used in PRISM. However it would extend the language of asCSL+filters with observations of activities at locations within a hierarchically-structured performance model. All prior activity-aware variants of CSL (including asCSL and CSL^{TA}) make observations of a Markov chain model without hierarchical component structure. This entails that they cannot be used (say) to distinguish arrivals to server 1 from arrivals to server 2 in the example below

$$Client \underset{\{arrive\}}{\bowtie} \Big((Server1 \underset{\mathcal{L}}{\bowtie} Network) \parallel (Server2 \underset{M}{\bowtie} Raid) \Big)$$

but this distinction can be expressed in the language XSP.

3 State and Probe Specifications

The models which we consider consist of compositions of multiple copies of sequential components cooperating on shared activities. A state-specification is a predicate involving expressions over the multiplicities of the sequential components in a system. The expressions in the predicate may compare a multiplicity to a constant or to the multiplicity of another component. Typical predicates test for the presence, absence or abundance of a particular component but more complex arrangements are possible. For example *ClientWait* > 2 × *ServerReady* specifies those states in which the number of clients waiting is more than twice the number of ready servers. The full syntax for state-specification equations is given in Figure 1(left).

An activity-specification is a labelled regular expression describing the sequence of activities which lead into and out of the query-set. The labels start and stop are used to indicate the activities which enter and exit the query-set respectively. Activity-specifications are realised as *stochastic probes* which are automatically translated into a component which is then attached to the model.

Probes may be attached *globally* to the entire model (thereby observing all of the model behaviour) or *locally* to a specific component (therefore observing from the perspective of this component). The probe cooperates with the component to which it is attached over all of the activities in its alphabet. It is important that the probe is always willing to perform all of these activities in each of its local states in order that it does not alter the behaviour of the model.

A very simple probe may specify the set of states between a *begin* and an *end* activity: *begin*:start, *end*:stop. More complex queries are possible such as:

$$((pass, pass, pass) / send):\text{start}, send:\text{stop}$$

This specifies that if we observe three *pass* activities without observing a *send* activity then the model has entered the query-set. When a *send* activity has been observed then the model has left the query-set. The full syntax for activity-probe specifications is given in Figure 1(right).

$$name := ident \qquad\qquad \text{process name}$$
$$pred := \neg pred \qquad\qquad\qquad \text{not}$$
$$\quad\ \mid true \mid false \qquad\qquad \text{boolean}$$
$$\quad\ \mid if\ pred$$
$$\qquad then\ pred$$
$$\qquad else\ pred \qquad\qquad \text{conditional}$$
$$\quad\ \mid pred \lor pred \qquad\qquad \text{disjunction}$$
$$\quad\ \mid pred \land pred \qquad\qquad \text{conjunction}$$
$$\quad\ \mid expr \qquad\qquad\quad \text{expression}$$
$$expr := name \qquad\qquad \text{multiplicity}$$
$$\quad\ \mid int \qquad\qquad\qquad \text{constant}$$
$$\quad\ \mid expr\ relop\ expr \qquad \text{comparison}$$
$$\quad\ \mid expr\ binop\ expr \qquad \text{arithmetic}$$
$$relop := =\ \mid\ \neq\ \mid\ >\ \mid\ <$$
$$\quad\ \mid\ \geq\ \mid\ \leq \qquad \text{relational operators}$$
$$binop := +\ \mid\ -\ \mid\ \times\ \mid\ \div \qquad \text{binary operators}$$

$$P_{def} := name :: R \quad \text{locally attached probe}$$
$$\quad\ \mid R \qquad\qquad \text{globally attached probe}$$
$$R := activity \qquad\qquad \text{observe action}$$
$$\quad\ \mid R_1, R_2 \qquad\qquad \text{sequence}$$
$$\quad\ \mid R_1 \mid R_2 \qquad\qquad \text{choice}$$
$$\quad\ \mid R{:}label \qquad\qquad \text{labelled}$$
$$\quad\ \mid R\ n \qquad\qquad\quad \text{iterate}$$
$$\quad\ \mid R\{m, n\} \qquad\qquad \text{iterate}$$
$$\quad\ \mid R^+ \qquad\qquad \text{one or more}$$
$$\quad\ \mid R^* \qquad\qquad \text{zero or more}$$
$$\quad\ \mid R^? \qquad\qquad \text{zero or one}$$
$$\quad\ \mid R/activity \qquad\qquad \text{resetting}$$
$$\quad\ \mid (R) \qquad\qquad\quad \text{bracketed}$$

$$R := \ldots \mid \{pred\}R \quad \text{guarded}$$

Fig. 1. The grammar on the left defines the syntax for state-specifications while the grammar on the right defines the syntax for activity-probe-specifications. The grammar extension at the bottom defines the additional syntax for eXtended Probe Specifications.

Activity probes have two abstract states, *running* and *stopped*. An *abstract* state of a (component of a) model, is a set of states with a common property. When the probe is in between the two labels start and stop the probe is said to be in the running state and otherwise in the stopped state.

Probes are stateful components which advance to a successor state whenever an activity is observed which is in the *first-set* of the probe. The first-set of a probe is the set of activities which are enabled at the current position of the probe specification. For example the probe $(a|b), R$ can advance to a state represented by the probe R on observing the activities a or b and its first-set is $\{a, b\}$. A given probe will *self-loop* on any activity which is in the alphabet of the full probe but is not in the current first-set. This means that the probe observes the occurrence of the activity and hence does not prevent the model from performing it, but does not advance.

The novelty in the present paper is the combination of state-specifications, activity-specifications and both local and global observations.

We do this by allowing a sub-probe of an activity-probe specification to be *guarded* by a state-specification. Having already done the work of describing states earlier, the additional syntax—shown in Figure 1(bottom)—is very light.

The meaning of the probe $\{p\}R$ is that any activity which begins the probe R must occur when the state of the model satisfies the state-specification predicate p. If this predicate is not satisfied then the probe self-loops on the given activity. For example the extended probe: $\{Server\_broken > 0\}request :$ start, $response :$ stop is similar to a common query which analyses the response time between the two activities *request* and *response*. Here though the initial observation of the *request* activity is guarded by the state specification $Server\_broken > 0$ and hence all occurences of *request* will be ignored by this probe unless there is at least one process in the *Server_broken* state. This could be used to analyse the response time in the specific case that at least one server is down.

In this paper we will express models in the stochastic process algebra PEPA [9] extended with *functional rates* [10] (known as "marking-dependent rates" in Petri nets). The definition $P \stackrel{def}{=} (\alpha, f).P'$ denotes a component P which performs an activity α at an exponentially-distributed rate determined by evaluating the function f in the current model state. After completing activity α, P behaves as P'.

Another model component $Q \stackrel{def}{=} (\alpha, \top).Q'$ could *cooperate* with P on activity α thus:

$$P \underset{\{\alpha\}}{\bowtie} Q$$

We write $P \parallel Q$ when the cooperation set is empty and $P[3]$ as an abbreviation for $P \parallel P \parallel P$. The component $R \stackrel{def}{=} (\alpha, r_\alpha).R' + (\beta, r_\beta).R''$ chooses to perform activity α with rate r_α with probability $r_\alpha/(r_\alpha + r_\beta)$, and β similarly. The process $a.P$ performs an immediate action a and evolves to P.

4 Implementation

The XSP language is implemented in the International PEPA Compiler (ipc), a stand-alone modelling tool for steady-state and transient analysis of PEPA models. When presented with a PEPA model and an XSP probe, ipc first translates the probe specification into a PEPA component. This translated component is then attached to the model to form a new model. It is this subsequent model which ipc then translates into a Markov chain representing the augmented model and solves the resulting Markov chain for the stationary probability distribution. In the case of a passage-time analysis uniformisation [11,12] is then used to compute the probability density and cumulative distribution functions for the passage across the XSP probe.

Translating probe specifications into valid PEPA components and attaching them to the model before any compilation of the model is performed has several advantages. The user may provide several probe specifications which are translated and added to the model in turn resulting in subsequent augmented models. Thus additional probes may refer not only to activities (and immediate actions) performed by the original model but also those performed by other probes. In this way probes may use immediate actions to perform immediate communication between probe components. Furthermore, although in this paper we have focussed on translating the model augmented with the translated probe using ipc via its Markov Chain representation, we could also analyse the augmented model using other techniques developed for analysing PEPA models, notably stochastic simulation and translation to ordinary differential equations[13] allowing us to cope with models with much larger state spaces. Finally the static analysis used to reject (or warn about) suspect PEPA models can now be run over the entire augmented model including the translated probe components providing further assurance that we have not made a mistake with our specification. This is in addition to some sanity checking over the probe specification itself.

The implementation of XSP follows a tradition of translating regular-expression languages to finite-state automata. We first translate the probe specification into a non-deterministic finite-state automaton. This cannot itself be translated directly into a PEPA component so we next translate this into a deterministic finite automaton. Having done this the self-loops may then be added to each state (recall from section 3 that self-loops must be added to each state of the probe to avoid the probe affecting the behaviour of the model).

Although for some probe specifications it is unavoidable that we increase the state space of the model we wish to keep the cost of this as low as possible. With this in mind the translated deterministic finite automata is minimised. It is the minimised DFA with the addition of the self-loops which can be translated directly into a PEPA model. This final step is a trivial re-formatting stage – we must only take into account whether or not the model performs each observed action as a timed activity or an immediate action. In the case of the former the probe component must passively observe the activity at rate ⊤ and in the case of the latter it is simply added itself as an immediate action.

Probe definitions, and in particular local probe definitions, may use labels to communicate important events to a master probe which the user provides. The :start and :stop labels are special cases of this communication whereby the event is the transition of the probe into the abstract running or stopped states. All communication labels are implemented as immediate actions so as not to distort the behaviour of the model. Care must be taken not to add self-loops to a state in which immediate communication is possible in case the observed action on which the self-loop is performed is itself immediate, which would lead to non-determinism.

The guards on the activities of a probe in an extended probe specification are implemented as guards on the activities of the translated probe component. These in turn may be implemented as functional rates in which the rate is zero if the predicate is false. Care must be taken when adding the self-loops. Previously a self-loop on activity x in the alphabet of the probe was added to a given state if activity x could not currently be performed to advance the state of the probe. Now whenever it is possible for a guarded activity x to advance the state of the probe we must add a self-loop for the case in which the guard is false. However it must not self-loop whenever the guard is true hence the self-loop is itself guarded by the negation of the guard predicate.

To attach the translated probe component to the model we synchronise over the alphabet of the probe. For a global probe it is trivial to attach since we cooperate with the whole model. For the global probe, if *Probe* is the name given to the translated PEPA component in the initial state of the probe and *System* is the original system equation then the augmented model's system equation is given by:

$$Probe \bowtie_{\mathcal{L}} System$$

where $\mathcal{L}$ is the alphabet of the probe. A local probe $P :: R$ is attached by descending through the cooperations (and hiding operators) which make up the *System* component. We attach the probe to the leftmost occurrence of P splitting an array if required. Therefore if *System* is represented by the cooperation $(L \bowtie_{M} P[4]) \bowtie_{N} Q$ then the system equation of our augmented model becomes:

$$(L \bowtie_{M} ((Probe \bowtie_{\mathcal{L}} P) \| P[3])) \bowtie_{N} Q$$

5   An Example Scenario

Our example scenario involves the arbitration of many processes accessing a shared resource. Here we are considering a symmetric multi-processing architecture in which there are several processors which must be allowed access to a shared memory. However the models and query specifications can be applied to similar scenarios involving access by many clients to a shared resource, for example a wireless network in which the clients must compete to send or receive over a shared channel.

With our models we wish to compare choices for arbitration. Here we will compare a round-robin scheme with a first-come, first-served queueing system. In the round-robin scheme each client is given the chance to use the shared resource in turn, at each such turn the client may choose to pass up the opportunity or it may use the resource. In a first-come, first-served queue a client continues to work without the shared resource until it is required and then signals its interest in access to the shared resource. At this point the client is put to the end of the queue of clients and must wait until all the clients ahead of it in the queue have finished with their turn at the resource before being granted access.

We will be concerned with the time it takes from after a specific client has performed some internal *work* (indicating that it is now ready to use the shared resource) until after it has completed a *send*. Here the send activity is used as the name for accessing the shared resource and can be thought of as either sending data to the shared memory in a symmetric multi-processor environment or using the shared channel to send data in a wireless network.

5.1   The Round-Robin Model

For the round-robin scheme we model the resource as a token which may be in one of several places where each place represents a slot in which exactly one client may use the resource. A client is able to perform the *work* activity before being able to use the resource. It must cooperate with the resource and can of course only do this if the token of the resource is in the correct place. In addition to being able to perform a *work* activity the client may pass up the opportunity to use its slot. The *Client* component then is modelled as:

$$Client \stackrel{def}{=} (work, work\_rate).Wait$$
$$+ (pass, \top).Client$$
$$Wait \stackrel{def}{=} (send, send\_rate).Client$$

The resource is modelled by the *Token* process. The *Token* when in position zero may cooperate with the client over the *send* or the *pass* activity. To model each of the other places for the token we could model more clients. Instead we assume that the token moves on from each place at a given rate which encompasses both the possibilities that the respective client sends or passes. In position i the token is modelled by:

$$Token_i \stackrel{def}{=} (delay, delay\_rate).Token_{i-1}$$

When the token is in position zero it is defined as:

$$Token_0 \stackrel{def}{=} (send, \top).Token_M$$
$$+ (pass, pass\_rate).Token_M$$

where M is the number of other places/clients on the network. The main system equation is defined to be:

$Client \bowtie_{\mathcal{L}} Token0$ where $\mathcal{L} = \{send, pass\}$

Figure 2 depicts the entire state space of the model where M is set to four.

0	$Client \bowtie_{\mathcal{L}} Token0$
1	$Wait \bowtie_{\mathcal{L}} Token1$
2	$Wait \bowtie_{\mathcal{L}} Token2$
3	$Wait \bowtie_{\mathcal{L}} Token3$
4	$Wait \bowtie_{\mathcal{L}} Token4$
5	$Wait \bowtie_{\mathcal{L}} Token0$
6	$Client \bowtie_{\mathcal{L}} Token1$
7	$Client \bowtie_{\mathcal{L}} Token2$
8	$Client \bowtie_{\mathcal{L}} Token3$
9	$Client \bowtie_{\mathcal{L}} Token4$

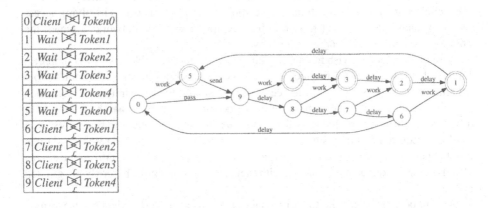

Fig. 2. States of the round-robin model with a passage-time analysis states marked

5.2 The Queue Model

The queue model is a little more complex since the client we are analysing may join the queue at any time but must only be served when it is at the head of the queue. The queue is modelled in a similar fashion to the *Token* process. It may be in one of M states $Queue_i$ where i is the current length of the queue.

The client is now modelled as being in a state of working or in one of a set of M states $Client_i$ each of which corresponds to a position in the queue. When the client performs the *work* activity and is ready to use the shared resource it cooperates with the *Queue* process over an action which indicates into which state the client should proceed. Only once the client is in state $Client_0$ can it perform the *send* activity which will end our passage of interest. Again the other clients in the model may be modelled explicitly but here we allow the queue to move from state $Queue_i$ to state $Queue_{i+1}$ at the (functional) rate $(M - i - Client) \times work\_rate$ since when there are i clients in the queue there will be $M - i$ clients which may join the queue. We subtract one from that if the queried client is not in the queue since this performs its own *work* activity to join the queue. The full model is shown in the appendix.

5.3 The Random Model

The random model is used for comparison. The random scheme operates in a similar fashion to the queue scheme, except that there are a number of clients in the queue and the client which is given access to the shared resource is entirely random. It may be the client that was the first to enter the queue but it may be the client that was last to enter the queue.

In this model we do model the other clients. The client is defined as for the round-robin model except that it need not perform a *pass* activity.

$$Client \stackrel{def}{=} (work, work\_rate).Wait$$

$$Wait \stackrel{def}{=} (send, \top).Client$$

The queue as before may be in one of i states representing how many clients are in the queue. The queue now cooperates with a random waiting client to perform the *send* activity or a random working client to perform a *work* activity. The queue with i waiting clients is defined as:

$$Queue_i \stackrel{def}{=} (work, \top).Queue_{i+1}$$
$$+ (send, send\_rate).Queue_{i-1}$$

In position zero the queue cannot perform a *send* activity and cannot perform a *work* activity when the queue is full. Finally the system definition is given by:

$$Client[5] \underset{\{work, send\}}{\bowtie} Queue0$$

5.4   The Passage-Time Analysis

With these models we wish to analyse the expected time it takes for the resource to be granted to the client once the client is ready. For this we wish to analyse from after a *work* activity has been performed until after a *send* activity has been performed. We therefore must identify the passage-set. That is, the set of states which lie between those two events.

In Figure 2 the states in the passage-set for this particular query are identified using double circles.

To specify this set using a state-specification we must use our knowledge of the system to identify the conditions which hold at all of the states in the passage-set.

For the round-robin model this is simply when the client is in the *Wait* state.

Wait = 1

A similar specification also works for the random model with the caveat that we must specify which *Client* we consider. For the queue model it is whenever the client is in any of the queue states.

$Client1 = 1 \lor Client2 = 1 \lor Client3 = 1 \lor Client4 = 1 \lor Client5 = 1$

To specify this query using an activity probe we use the two activities themselves as the begin and end events for the probe. The probe definition is given as:

Client :: *work*:start, *send*:stop

Note that this same probe works for all three models. For the round-robin and queue models it is not strictly necessary for us to attach the probe to the *Client* component since there is only one client component which may perform the observed activities. However doing so leads to a more robust probe as evidenced by the fact that the same probe can be used for the random model in which there are additional client processes.

Having performed this analysis for all three models we can compare the speed with which each arbitration method allows a waiting client to use the shared resource. Figure 3 shows a comparison of both the cumulative distribution function and the probability density function for the passage-time queries on the three models representing the three arbitration schemes. These functions have been evaluated by applying the uniformisation procedure [11,12] to the CTMC which is generated from the PEPA model.

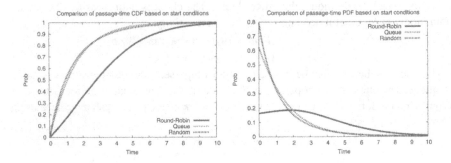

Fig. 3. Comparison between the passage-time results for the three models

From the results we can see that the queue and random models perform very similarly and both outperform that of the round-robin scheme.

The robustness of the query specification in general depends on what the modeller is likely to modify. In our example above the state-specification is vulnerable to any change in the model which increases the number of states in which the client may be in either the abstract state of 'waiting' or the abstract state of 'working'. The abstract state of 'waiting' in our model corresponds to exactly one state of the client, namely: *Wait*. Similarly the abstract state of 'working', which is used to specify that the *send* activity has completed, maps to exactly one component state, namely: *Client*. If the model is modified such that either of these two mappings from abstract state to a concrete set of states is disturbed then the state specification will be invalid and must be revised.

In contrast the activity probe need not be modified since there could for example be any number of unobserved activities and associated intermediate states between the *work* and the *send* activities. However if we modify the set of activities which may cause the model to transition between the abstract states then we must revise our probe specification. For example above there were only two activities which the *Token0* component may perform to become a *Token4* component, namely : *pass* and *send*. However if this were to change then our probe specification would be invalid and would require updating.

5.5 Splitting the Analysis

We may wish to partition the passage-time results we have obtained for our three models to enable us to report the expected time the client has to wait depending on the state of the model at the time at which the client becomes ready to use the shared resource. So for example in the round-robin model above we may wish to ask the question: "What is the expected time between the client performing a *work* activity and the client performing a *send* activity given that the *work* activity occurs when the token process is in state *Token4*?" This question may be of particular interest because it represents the worst case scenario. We have shown that the overall performance in the general case of the round-robin scheme is worse than that of the queue and random schemes. However it may be that the round-robin scheme has less erratic performance in that it matters less at what time the client becomes ready to use the shared resource. It may be that the worst case performance for the round-robin scheme is better than that for both the queue and random schemes. This may be of particular interest in say a network, where traffic can become congested at particular times and hence the worst case performance is of more interest than the average case performance.

To write this exact query as a state-specification we must resort to specifying the source set and the target set explicitly. This is because if we specify the states as a passage-set it will include the states where the token is in places $1 \ldots 3$, while the client is still waiting. Clearly these states are reachable by a transition from a state outside the passage-set. In fact specifying the passage-set in this manner would give identical results to analysing the time the client must wait regardless of when the *work* activity was completed. With this in mind our source and target sets for the round-robin model worst case scenario are specified respectively by:

$$source : Wait = 1 \land Token4 = 1$$
$$target : Client = 1$$

Note however that it is a little unsatisfactory that we had to know so much about the behaviour of the model. Even if one considers this a good thing – modellers should know about the behaviour of their models – the query specification is very fragile in that if we modify our model it is likely that this query specification must also be updated. In addition the target set is larger than necessary. This will not affect the results of the analysis but may cause the analysis time to increase. Again a very similar state-specification can be used for the random model.

For the queue model worst case scenario analysis we can use our knowledge of the system to make our state specification simpler than in the average case, this is because there are fewer source states. Our state query is written as:

$$source : Client5 = 1$$
$$target : Client = 1$$

To write this query as an activity probe we must identify a sequence of activities which will place the model in the source-set and the sequence of activities which will complete the passage (from a source state). Specifying this using an activity probe means that the query need not be split up. This is because the probe is in the abstract running state only when it has passed through a source state. This means that we need not split our specification into two separate ones however the drawback is that the state space is increased. Our query for the round-robin model is specified by:

$$Client :: ((pass|send), work)/delay{:}start, send{:}stop$$

The *(pass|send)* component ensures that the token has moved to state *Token4* before we observe the *work* activity. By restricting the *delay* activity (with */delay*) we assert that the probe will not move past the start label unless the sequence ending with the *work* occurrence does not contain a *delay* activity. This in turn ensures that the token is in the state *Token4* when the probe transitions to running. If a *delay* is observed this resets the probe which must then wait to observe a *pass* or *send* once again.

The state space is increased because there are states in the passage which must be duplicated. For example the state in which the token is in state *Token3* and the client is in state *Wait* is duplicated since the probe component may be in either the running or the stopped state depending on whether the given state was reached via a source-state.

For both the random model and the queue model specifying this condition as an activity probe is particularly difficult. In the following section we detail a far more portable and robust method of obtaining these analysis results, namely the use of eXtended Stochastic Probes (the XSP language).

6   Using eXtended Stochastic Probes

In the previous section we discussed the two main methods for specifying a query-set. Both have advantages and disadvantages and can be used in different circumstances. We used these to obtain a passage-time analysis and then proceeded to split this into distinct queries depending on the state of the model when the passage is begun. We have shown that either of the two methods alone are sometimes unsatisfactory. In this section we provide the same split queries using the combined approach, eXtended Stochastic Probes. The following probe can be used on the round-robin model to analyse the passage in the worst case when the token is as far away as possible.

$$Client :: \{Token4 = 1\}work{:}\text{start}, send{:}\text{stop}$$

This probe will only be started by an observation of the *Client* performing a *work* activity if the token is currently in the state *Token*4. All other occurrences of the *work* activity will be ignored.

To specify the same worst case scenario query for the queue we can specify the extended probe:

$$Client :: \{Queue4 = 1\}work{:}\text{start}, send{:}\text{stop}$$

This specification works in exactly the same way. The only difference is the name of the state of the resource in the worst case scenario. For the random model the probe is exactly the same.

Without changing the models we can make additional queries corresponding to all of the different possible states of the resource at the time at which the client becomes ready to make use of the shared resource. In the case of the round-robin scheme this is the different places that the token may be in. In the case of queue and random models this is the length of the queue. We provide the probes:

$$Client :: \{TokenN = 1\}work{:}\text{start}, send{:}\text{stop}$$
$$Client :: \{QueueN = 1\}work{:}\text{start}, send{:}\text{stop}$$

The graphs in Figure 4 show the cumulative distribution and probability density functions of the passage-time responses given by restricting the probe to the conditions of the shared resource.

6.1   Discussion of Results

With the basic analyses we determined that the average case response-time was worst for the round-robin scheme and very similar for the queue and random schemes. The results for the individual circumstances for the round-robin and the queue models are identical. This is because in both cases the number and rates of the timed activities that we must observe between the source and target are identical for each equivalent circumstance. For example when the queue is empty and the token is in the correct place both models are only measuring one activity, namely the *send* activity. This tells

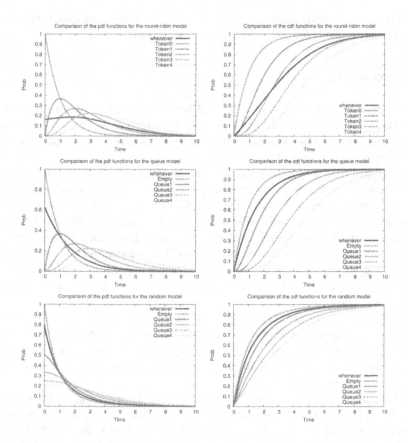

Fig. 4. Graphs of the PDF and CDF functions for the split passage-time results for the three models

us that the reason the average case is worse for the round-robin model is because the unfavourable cases happen more frequently than for the queue model. This may only be the case because of the particular rate values which we have chosen and we may wish to change those rates to see if we could make the round-robin model outperform the queue model (in the average case). Indeed one should perform these experiments with varying rates for both models as we have previously done using a distributed computing platform to analyse the separate instances of each model [14].

In the case of the random model we can see that although the average case performance is very similar to that of the first-come, first-served queue the performance is actually much less varied. This is because for each state of the queue at the time of the client becoming ready to use the resource there are still more paths to the target states over which to average out the performance. For example if the client becomes ready when the queue is empty this is no guarantee that our client will be the next client to use the resource. Similarly if the queue is full we may still be the next client to use the resource. The random queue may have some other less desirable properties, for example a client may wait in the queue while arbitrarily many other clients are processed ahead of it. However our results show that – at least for the parameters we have specified – a client is highly unlikely to spend a long time in the queue.

7   Conclusions

We have described an extension – eXtended Stochastic Probes – to the language of stochastic probes. Our extension allows the modeller to refer to the states of components which are located in a hierarchically-structured performance model expressed in the stochastic process algebra PEPA.

We consider state-specifications alone to be insufficient since they cannot be used to distinguish states based on the activities which have been performed to reach that state. Sometimes to perform the desired analysis we must increase the state-space of the model and state-specifications offer no way to do this automatically. Activity probe specifications are also insufficient for all purposes and in particular are poor at describing states which represent a balancing of activities. This is a frequent kind of query such as "how likely is the server to be operational?" which may be the result of a balance of 'break' and 'repair' activities. Finally allowing *either* state specifications *or* activity probes is still not an acceptable solution. Situations which call for a combination of the two approaches arise when the modeller wishes to combine observations with state descriptions. A common example of such a combination is to ask about the response time when the request is made at a time when a particular system component is in a particular (abstract) state. A standard query is: "What is the response time when at least one of the servers is broken".

We have shown an example consisting of three models describing similar scenarios but each using different modelling techniques. In the round-robin and queue models we have represented only the client component that we wish to analyse while in the random model all of the clients in the system were represented explicitly. The queue model makes use of immediate actions and functional rates. Despite this the extended probe specifications we used to split-up our passage-time analyses were portable across the three models.

Our language of extended probe specifications has been fully implemented in the ipclib library used and distributed with the International PEPA Compiler. This is available for download as open source software from http://www.dcs.ed.ac.uk/pepa/tools/ipc.

Acknowledgements. The authors are supported by the EU FET-IST Global Computing 2 project SENSORIA ("Software Engineering for Service-Oriented Overlay Computers" (IST-3-016004-IP-09)).

References

1. Argent-Katwala, A., Bradley, J., Dingle, N.: Expressing performance requirements using regular expressions to specify stochastic probes over process algebra models. In: Proceedings of the Fourth International Workshop on Software and Performance, Redwood Shores, California, USA, pp. 49–58. ACM Press, New York (2004)

2. Bradley, J., Dingle, N., Gilmore, S., Knottenbelt, W.: Derivation of passage-time densities in PEPA models using IPC: The Imperial PEPA Compiler. In: Kotsis, G. (ed.) Proceedings of the 11th IEEE/ACM International Symposium on Modeling, Analysis and Simulation of Computer and Telecommunications Systems, University of Central Florida, pp. 344–351. IEEE Computer Society Press, Los Alamitos (2003)

3. Clark, A.: The ipclib PEPA Library. In: Harchol-Balter, M., Kwiatkowska, M., Telek, M. (eds.) Proceedings of the 4th International Conference on the Quantitative Evaluation of SysTems (QEST), pp. 55–56. IEEE, Los Alamitos (2007)

4. Argent-Katwala, A., Bradley, J., Clark, A., Gilmore, S.: Location-aware quality of service measurements for service-level agreements. In: Barthe, G., Fournet, C. (eds.) TGC 2007. LNCS, vol. 4912, pp. 222–239. Springer, Heidelberg (2008)

5. Aziz, A., Sanwal, K., Singhal, V., Brayton, R.: Model-checking continuous-time Markov chains. ACM Trans. Comput. Logic 1, 162–170 (2000)

6. Hinton, A., Kwiatkowska, M., Norman, G., Parker, D.: PRISM: A tool for automatic verification of probabilistic systems. In: Hermanns, H., Palsberg, J. (eds.) TACAS 2006. LNCS, vol. 3920, pp. 441–444. Springer, Heidelberg (2006)

7. Baier, C., Cloth, L., Haverkort, B., Kuntz, M., Siegle, M.: Model checking action- and state-labelled Markov chains. In: DSN '04: Proceedings of the 2004 International Conference on Dependable Systems and Networks, Washington, DC, USA, p. 701. IEEE Computer Society, Los Alamitos (2004)

8. Donatelli, S., Haddad, S., Sproston, J.: CSL^{TA}: an Expressive Logic for Continuous-Time Markov Chains. In: QEST 2007: Proceedings of the Fourth Interational Conference on Quantitative Evaluation of Systems, Washington, DC, USA, pp. 31–40. IEEE Computer Society, Los Alamitos (2007)

9. Hillston, J.: A Compositional Approach to Performance Modelling. Cambridge University Press, Cambridge (1996)

10. Hillston, J., Kloul, L.: An efficient Kronecker representation for PEPA models. In: de Alfaro, L., Gilmore, S. (eds.) PAPM-PROBMIV 2001. LNCS, vol. 2165, pp. 120–135. Springer, Heidelberg (2001)

11. Grassmann, W.: Transient solutions in Markovian queueing systems. Computers and Operations Research 4, 47–53 (1977)

12. Gross, D., Miller, D.: The randomization technique as a modelling tool and solution procedure for transient Markov processes. Operations Research 32, 343–361 (1984)

13. Hillston, J.: Fluid flow approximation of PEPA models. In: Proceedings of the Second International Conference on the Quantitative Evaluation of Systems, Torino, Italy, pp. 33–43. IEEE Computer Society Press, Los Alamitos (2005)

14. Clark, A., Gilmore, S.: Evaluating quality of service for service level agreements. In: Brim, L., Leucker, M. (eds.) Proceedings of the 11th International Workshop on Formal Methods for Industrial Critical Systems, Bonn, Germany, pp. 172–185 (2006)

A. The Full Queue Model

A.1. The Client Behaviour

This component represents the system workload.

$$Client \stackrel{def}{=} (work, work\_rate).ClientQ$$
$$+ (delay, \top).Client$$
$$ClientQ \stackrel{def}{=} place0.Client1 + place1.Client2 + place2.Client3$$
$$+ place3.Client4 + place4.Client5$$
$$Client1 \stackrel{def}{=} (delay, \top).send.Client$$
$$Client2 \stackrel{def}{=} (delay, \top).Client1$$
$$Client3 \stackrel{def}{=} (delay, \top).Client2$$
$$Client4 \stackrel{def}{=} (delay, \top).Client3$$
$$Client5 \stackrel{def}{=} (delay, \top).Client4$$

A.2. The Queue Component

This model component has the responsibility of correctly implementing the intended first-in first-out behaviour of the queue. It ensures that the functional rates are correctly evaluated by counting the number (either 0 or 1) of components in the *Client* state.

$$Queue0 \stackrel{def}{=} (join, work\_rate \times 4).Queue1$$
$$+ place0.Queue1$$
$$Queue1 \stackrel{def}{=} (join, work\_rate \times (4 - Client)).Queue2$$
$$+ place1.Queue2$$
$$+ (delay, send\_rate).Queue0$$
$$Queue2 \stackrel{def}{=} (join, work\_rate \times (3 - Client)).Queue3$$
$$+ place2.Queue3$$
$$+ (delay, send\_rate).Queue1$$
$$Queue3 \stackrel{def}{=} (join, work\_rate \times (2 - Client)).Queue4$$
$$+ place3.Queue4$$
$$+ (delay, send\_rate).Queue2$$
$$Queue4 \stackrel{def}{=} (join, work\_rate \times (1 - Client)).Queue5$$
$$+ place4.Queue5$$
$$+ (delay, send\_rate).Queue3$$
$$Queue5 \stackrel{def}{=} (delay, send\_rate).Queue4$$

A.3. The System Equation

Finally, the model components are composed and required to cooperate over the activities in the cooperation set.

$$Client \underset{\mathcal{L}}{\bowtie} Queue0$$

where $\mathcal{L} = \{delay, place\{0..4\}\}$

Natural Language Specification of Performance Trees

Lei Wang, Nicholas J. Dingle, and William J. Knottenbelt

Department of Computing, Imperial College London,
180 Queen's Gate, London SW7 2BZ, United Kingdom
{lw205,njd200,wjk}@doc.ic.ac.uk

Abstract. The accessible specification of performance queries is a key challenge in performance analysis. To this end, we seek to combine the intuitive aspects of natural language query specification with the expressive power and flexibility of the Performance Tree formalism. Specifically, we present a structured English grammar for Performance Trees, and use it to implement a Natural Language Query Builder (NLQB) for the Platform Independent Petri net Editor (PIPE). The NLQB guides users in the construction of performance queries in an iterative fashion, presenting at each step a range of natural language alternatives that are appropriate in the query context. We demonstrate our technique in the specification of performance queries on a model of a hospital's Accident and Emergency department.

Keywords: Performance requirements specification; Natural language; Performance Trees; Performance analysis.

1 Introduction

Performance is a vital consideration for system designers and engineers. Indeed, a system which fails to meet its performance requirements can be as ineffectual as one which fails to meet its correctness requirements. Ideally, it should be possible to determine whether or not this will be the case at design time. This can be achieved through the construction and analysis of a performance model of the system in question, using formalisms such as queueing networks, stochastic Petri nets and stochastic process algebras.

One of the key challenges in performance analysis is to provide system designers with an accessible yet expressive way to specify a range of performance-related queries. These include *performance measures*, which are directed at numerical performance metrics (e.g. *"In a hospital, what is the utilisation of the operating theatre?"*), and *performance requirements*, which indicate conformity to a QoS constraint (e.g. *"In a mobile communications network, is the time taken to send an SMS message between two handsets less than 5 seconds with more than 95% probability?"*).

Formalisms such as Continuous Stochastic Logic (CSL) [3,4] provide a concise and rigorous way to pose performance questions and allow for the composition

N. Thomas and C. Juiz (Eds.): EPEW 2008, LNCS 5261, pp. 141–151, 2008.

of simple queries into more complex ones. Such logics can be somewhat daunting for non-expert users; indeed, a study by Grunkse [9] found that industrial users attempting to specify requirements sometimes put forward formulae that were syntactically incorrect. Even for those comfortable with their use, there still remains the problem of correctly converting informally-specified requirements into logical formulae. Further, CSL is limited in its expressiveness, since it is unable to reason about certain concepts such as higher moments of response time.

Performance Trees [14,15] were recently proposed as a means to overcome these problems. These are an intuitive graphical formalism for expressing performance properties. The concepts expressible in Performance Tree queries are intended to be familiar to engineers and include steady-state measures, passage time distributions and densities, their moments, action frequencies, convolutions and arithmetic operations. An important concern during the development of Performance Trees was ease of use, resulting in a formalism that can be straightforwardly visualised and manipulated as hierarchical tree structures.

Another approach for the accessible specification of performance queries is the use of natural language, whereby users specify their queries textually before they are automatically translated into logical formulae. This allows users to exploit the power of logical formalisms without requiring in-depth familiarity and also minimises the chances of misspecification. Prior work has focused on both unstructured [10] and structured [8,9,12,13] natural language query specification, albeit mostly in the context of correctness – rather than performance – analysis.

Unstructured natural language specification allows a user to freely enter sentences which must then be parsed and checked before being converted into a corresponding performance property. Although this is perhaps the most intuitive query specification mechanism, it must incorporate strategies for resolving ambiguities and context-specific expressions. The conversion process is therefore often iterative, with the user refining their natural language expression in response to the checking until it can be successfully converted into a property.

By contrast, structured natural language specification presents users with a set of expressions which can be composed together in accordance with a predefined structured grammar. If the same grammar is also defined for the logic into which the query will be converted (e.g. as in [9]), the conversion process is relatively straightforward. The main advantage of such structured specification is therefore that there is less "trial and error" involved in forming a query: the user's choices are limited to those provided by the grammar and so they can only construct a natural language query which will always convert directly into a logical formula.

In this paper, we present a structured natural language query specification mechanism for Performance Trees to further improve their accessibility. The grammar of this structured mechanism is provided by the syntax of Performance Trees, which enables a structured natural language query to be converted into a Performance Tree and then evaluated using the existing Performance Tree evaluation architecture [6]. Furthermore, taken together, the natural language and Performance Tree representations provide mutual validation, allowing the user to ensure that their queries capture exactly the performance properties of interest.

The rest of this paper is organised as follows. Section 2 provides a brief overview of Performance Trees and the tool support for their evaluation. Section 3 then presents our structured grammar for the natural language representation of Performance Trees and describes its implementation within the Natural Language Query Builder (NLQB), a module for the Platform Independent Petri net Editor (PIPE) [1,5]. Section 4 demonstrates the use of the NLQB in a case study of a hospital's Accident and Emergency unit. Section 5 concludes and discusses future work.

2 Performance Trees

Performance Trees [14,15] are a formalism for the representation of performance-related queries. They combine the ability to specify performance requirements – i.e. queries aiming to determine whether particular properties hold on system models – with the ability to extract performance measures – i.e. quantifiable performance metrics of interest.

A Performance Tree query is represented as a tree structure consisting of nodes and interconnecting arcs. Nodes can have two kinds of roles: *operation* nodes represent performance-related functions, such as the calculation of a passage time density, while *value* nodes represent basic concepts such as a set of states, an action, or simply numerical or Boolean constants.

Complex queries can be easily constructed by connecting operation and value nodes together. The formalism also supports macros, which allow new concepts to be created with the use of existing operators, and an abstract state-set specification mechanism to enable the user to specify groups of states relevant to a performance measure in terms of the corresponding high-level model (whether this be a stochastic Petri net, queueing network, stochastic process algebra etc.)

Performance Trees have been fully integrated into the Platform Independent Petri net Editor (PIPE), thus allowing users to design Generalised Stochastic Petri Net (GSPN) [2] models and to specify relevant performance queries within a unified environment. PIPE communicates with an Analysis Server which employs a number of (potentially parallel and distributed) analysis tools [7,11] to calculate performance measures. These include steady-state measures, passage time densities and quantiles, and transient state distributions.

3 Structured Grammar for Performance Tree Specification

The current Performance Query Editor incorporated into PIPE requires users to be familiar with Performance Tree nodes (including their graphical representations and semantics). Because of this, a "drag and drop" graphical approach to

Table 1. Structured grammar for Performance Trees

Performance Tree Node	Natural Language Representation	Arguments	Output
RESULT	"is it true that"	*InInterval* | *Subset* | ¬ | ∧ / ∨ | ≥, >, ==, <, ≤	N/A
	"what is the"	*PTD* | *Dist* | *Conv* | *Moment* | *SS:P* | *SS:S* | *FR* | *ProbInInterval* | *ProbInStates* | *StatesAtTime* | ⊕	N/A
PTD	"the passage time density defined by start states" **states** "and target states" **states**	**states, states**	*PTD*
Dist	"the cumulative distribution function calculated from" *PTD*	*PTD*	*Dist*
Conv	"the convolution of" *PTD* "and" *PTD*	*PTD, PTD*	*PTD*
SS:P	"the steady-state probability distribution of" **statefunc** "applied over" **states**	**statefunc, states**	**num**
Perctl	"the" **num** "percentile of" *PTD* | *Dist*	**num,** *PTD* | **num,** *Dist*	**num**
StatesAtTime	"the set of states that the system can be in at the time instant" **num** "within probability bound" *Range*	**num,** *Range*	**states**
ProbInStates	"the transient probability of the system having started in" **states** "and being in" **states** "at the time instant given by" **num**	**states, states, num**	**num**
Moment	"the" **num** " raw moment of" *PTD* | *Dist*	**num,** *PTD* | **num,** *Dist*	**num**
FR	"the frequency of" **action**	**action**	**num**
ProbInInterval	"the probability with which a value sampled from" *PTD* "lies within" *Range*	*PTD, Range*	**num**
InInterval	**num** "lies within" *Range*	**num,** *Range*	**bool**
Subset	**states** "is a subset of" **states**	**states, states**	**bool**
∧ / ∨	**bool** "and/or" **bool** "holds"	**bool, bool**	**bool**
¬	"the negation of" **bool** "holds"	**bool**	**bool**
≥, >, ==, <, ≤	**num** "greater than or equal to/greater than/equal to/less than/less than or equal to" **num**	**num, num**	**bool**
⊕	**num** "plus/minus/raised to the power of/ multiplied by/divided by" **num**	**num, num**	**num**
Range	"the range" **num** "to" **num**	**num, num**	**num**

Table 2. Description of user-specified value nodes

Node	Description
action	The name of an action (transition in GSPN context)
bool	True or False
num	A real number
states	A specification of a subset of reachable states
statefunc	A function applied to a state that returns a real number

building a Performance Tree query can be quite time-consuming. We have therefore developed an alternative approach based on structured natural language and implemented this in the Natural Language Query Builder (NLQB). The NLQB enables users to build performance queries in an iterative manner by selecting natural language fragments from a constantly-updated pull-down menu.

As shown in Table 1, the foundation of the NLQB is a structured natural language grammar derived from the syntax of Performance Trees. Following

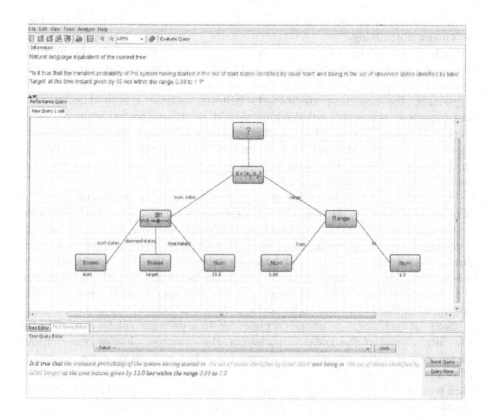

Fig. 1. Screenshot of the Natural Language Query Builder, showing a natural language query specification and the corresponding Performance Tree

the convention introduced in [9], non-terminals (operation nodes) are shown in *italics*, literal terminals (the natural language representation) are given in quotation marks (" ") and non-literal terminals are given in **bold**. These non-literal terminals are user-supplied value nodes and can only be of type **num**, **bool**, **states**, **statefunc** and **action**. A description of the permitted values for these nodes is given in Table 2.

3.1 Using the Natural Language Query Builder

Fig. 1 shows the NLQB in use. The user selects the appropriate phrases from the drop-down menu underneath the main graphical display and at the same time the corresponding Performance Tree is automatically constructed. When a selection has been made, the selected phrase is inserted in the natural language query in the text area and, at the same time, a corresponding Performance Tree node is plotted in an appropriate position. An automatic positioning mechanism calculates the coordinates of the recently created node and its outgoing arcs according to the position of its parent node and its level in the tree. The position of nodes and arcs can be adjusted manually if the user is not satisfied with the automatic positioning.

Each option in the drop-down menu consist of two elements – the natural language representation and the expected arguments. The natural language representation explains the operation that the node carries out, and the expected arguments (displayed in square brackets) indicate the type of its child nodes. The first expected argument is coloured in red, and all other expected arguments are coloured in blue. The user then specifies arguments in turn via the drop-down menu. As an argument is specified, its natural language representation is added to the query. When a value node is required, a dialog is presented to allow the user to make the required assignment.

For example, the *InInterval* node is expressed as *"num* lies within *Range"*. When it is selected by the user, the first expected argument, *num*, indicates that a numerical value is required as input, so the NLQB uses the structured natural language grammar (given in Table 1) to find all nodes that produce numerical output and inserts their natural language representation into the drop-down menu. The other expected argument is a *Range* node; the NLQB only displays the corresponding phrase "the range *num* to *num*" in the menu after the first argument to the *InInterval* node has been supplied.

Each natural language phrase is presented in a different colour according to the output type of the node it represents. For example, phrases representing nodes with Boolean output are coloured black but phrases representing a set of states are in cyan. This aids readability by helping users to easily categorise each part of the natural language representation of their query. The NLQB also provides an undo mechanism to allow users to correct their query.

4   Case Study

We demonstrate how to design queries and calculate the relevant results using the NLQB for two examples based on the Accident and Emergency (A&E) department GSPN model of [6] shown in Fig. 2. There is an initial group of healthy people who fall ill and go to a hospital – arriving either by walking in or by ambulance. Walk-in patients wait in the waiting room for assessment until a nurse becomes available, while ambulance patients wait on a trolley to be assessed by a nurse. Patients are subsequently either seen by a doctor for treatment, sent for lab tests or sent for surgery. The model is parameterised by P, N and D, which denote the number of tokens on the places *healthy* (people), *nurses* and *doctors*, respectively. In the following examples, we set $P = 10$, $N = 4$ and $D = 4$, yielding an underlying Markov chain with 313 986 states.

Example 1. We wish to answer the performance query:

What is the cumulative distribution function of the time taken for all patients in the system to fall ill, complete treatment and be discharged from the hospital?

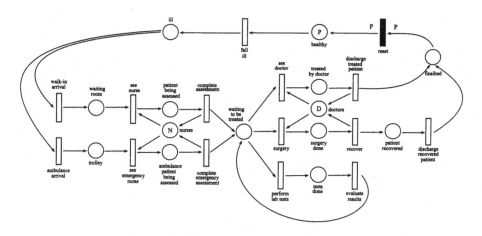

Fig. 2. GSPN model of a Hospital A&E Department [6]

The first thing the NLQB needs to know is whether this query expects a truth value or a quantitative measure as its result. Therefore, the only two available options in the drop-down menu are "Is it true that [bool]?" and "What is the [quantitative measure]?" In this case, we select the second option.

As we have selected the quantitative measure option, the NLQB interrogates the structured grammar table, extracts all operations that produce quantitative values and places their natural language representations into the drop-down menu. We are interested in computing a passage time distribution and so we choose the "cumulative distribution function calculated from [PTD]" as our next input. This is incorporated into the natural language representation of the query and at the same time a *Dist* node is created in the Performance Tree and connected to the *RESULT* node.

The next argument to be specified is "[PTD]", which is displayed in red. This requires two sets of states as arguments which are assigned manually when "Assign States" is selected from the menu (using PIPE's state assignment tool). The specification of the start states in this query (in this case a single start state) is given as:

$$\text{all patients healthy} := (\#(\text{healthy}) = 10) \wedge (\#(\text{nurses}) = 4) \wedge (\#(\text{doctors}) = 4)$$

Similarly, the specification of the target states is:

$$\text{all patients treated} := (\#(\text{finished}) = 10)$$

where $\#(p)$ returns the number of tokens on place p in the model.

The completed query is shown in Fig. 3. The resulting natural language specification is:

What is the cumulative distribution function calculated from the passage time density defined by the set of start states 'all patients healthy' and the set of target states 'all patients treated'?

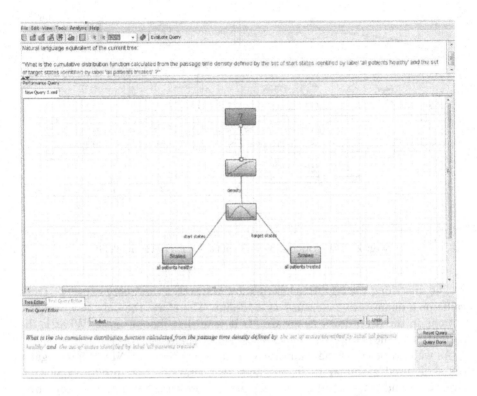

Fig. 3. The expression of Example 1 in the NLQB

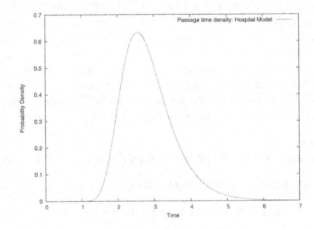

Fig. 4. Probability density function of the time taken to process all patients in the hospital model

Fig. 4 shows the result of evaluating the PTD (passage time density) node sub-query, while Fig. 5 shows the cumulative distribution function resulting from the evaluation of the overall query.

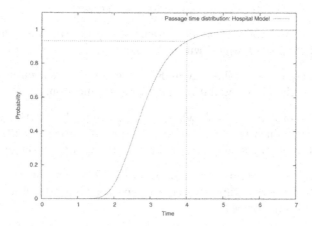

Fig. 5. Cumulative distribution function of the time taken to process all patients in the hospital model. The probability at time $t = 4$ is also marked.

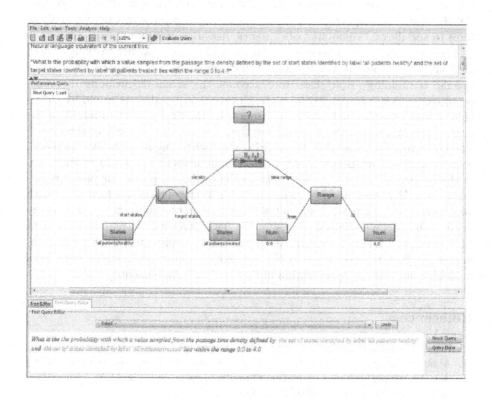

Fig. 6. The expression of Example 2 in the NLQB

Example 2. We wish to answer the performance query:

What is the probability that all patients complete treatment and are discharged from the hospital within 4 time units?

This is constructed in a similar way as Example 1 and, as shown in Fig. 6, the NLQB produces the following natural language specification:

What is the probability with which a value sampled from the passage time density defined by the set of start states 'all patients healthy' and the set of target states 'all patients treated' lies within the range 0 to 4?

From the cumulative distribution function in Fig. 5, we can see that the probability that all patients complete their treatment within 4 time units is 0.933 (rounded to 3 decimal places).

5 Conclusion

In this paper, we have presented a structured natural language query specification mechanism for Performance Trees. We have implemented this in PIPE as the Natural Language Query Builder which can be used with existing analysis tools to specify and calculate performance measures of interest.

There are a number of avenues for future work. Firstly, we are working to provide support for queries tailored to specific user models, i.e. support for model-specific terminology that takes into account the semantic meaning of model components. For example, in the context of the A&E model, we would like to be able to input queries such as "Is the time from the first patient to fall ill to the time of discharge from the hospital less than 4 hours at least 98% of the time?" We intend to accomplish this by requiring the user to augment the system model with information relating abstract model components to real world entities (e.g. in the context of a Petri model, what do the tokens on particular places represent?) Secondly, we would like to augment the Performance Tree formalism with an experimental framework so that we can pose questions such as "How many doctors should be employed to ensure the 98th percentile of patient treatment time is below 4 hours?" Finally, we would like to apply natural language techniques for Performance Trees in the context of important domains outside of modelling such as the specification of Service Level Agreements.

References

1. PIPE: Platform-Independent Petri net Editor, http://pipe2.sourceforge.net
2. Ajmone-Marsan, M., Conte, G., Balbo, G.: A class of Generalised Stochastic Petri Nets for the performance evaluation of multiprocessor systems. ACM Transactions on Computer Systems 2, 93–122 (1984)
3. Aziz, A., Sanwal, K., Singhal, V., Brayton, R.: Verifying continuous-time Markov chains. In: Alur, R., Henzinger, T.A. (eds.) CAV 1996. LNCS, vol. 1102, pp. 269–276. Springer, Heidelberg (1996)

4. Aziz, A., Sanwal, K., Singhal, V., Brayton, R.: Model checking continuous-time Markov chains. ACM Transactions on Computational Logic 1(1), 162–170 (2000)
5. Bonet, P., Llado, C.M., Puijaner, R., Knottenbelt, W.J.: PIPE v2.5: A Petri net tool for performance modelling. In: Proceedings of the 23rd Latin American Conference on Informatics (CLEI 2007), San Jose, Costa Rica (October 2007)
6. Brien, D.K., Dingle, N.J., Knottenbelt, W.J., Kulatunga, H., Suto, T.: Performance Trees: Implementation And Distributed Evaluation. In: Proc. 7th Intl. Workshop on Parallel and Distributed Methods in Verification (PDMC 2008), Budapest, Hungary, March 2008. Elsevier, Amsterdam (2008)
7. Dingle, N.J.: Parallel Computation of Response Time Densities and Quantiles in Large Markov and Semi-Markov Models. PhD thesis, Imperial College, London, United Kingdom (2004)
8. Flake, S., Müller, W., Ruf, J.: Structured English for model checking specification. In: Methoden und Beschreibungssprachen zur Modellierung und Verifikation von Schaltungen und Systemen, Frankfurt, February 2000, pp. 99–108 (2000)
9. Grunske, L.: Specification patterns for probabilistic quality properties. In: Proc. 30th International Conference on Software Engineering (ICSE 2008), Leipzig, Germany, pp. 31–40 (2008)
10. Holt, A., Klein, E.: A semantically-derived subset of English for hardware verification. In: Proc. 37th Annual Meeting of the Association for Computational Linguistics, Maryland VA, USA, pp. 451–456 (1999)
11. Knottenbelt, W.J.: Generalised Markovian analysis of timed transition systems. Master's thesis, University of Cape Town, Cape Town, South Africa (July 1996)
12. Konrad, S., Cheng, B.H.C.: Real-time specification patterns. In: Inverardi, P., Jazayeri, M. (eds.) ICSE 2005. LNCS, vol. 4309, pp. 372–381. Springer, Heidelberg (2006)
13. Smith, R.L., Avrunin, G.S., Clarke, L.A., Osterweil, L.J.: PROPEL: An approach supporting property elucidation. In: Proc. 24th International Conference on Software Engineering (ICSE 2002), Orlando FL, USA, pp. 11–21 (2002)
14. Suto, T., Bradley, J.T., Knottenbelt, W.J.: Performance Trees: A New Approach to Quantitative Performance Specification. In: Proc. 14th IEEE/ACM Intl. Symposium on Modeling, Analysis and Simulation of Computer and Telecommunications Systems (MASCOTS 2006), Monterey, CA, USA, September 2006, pp. 303–313 (2006)
15. Suto, T., Bradley, J.T., Knottenbelt, W.J.: Performance trees: Expressiveness and quantitative semantics. In: Proceedings of the 4th International Conference on the Quantitave Evaluation of Systems (QEST 2007), September 2007, pp. 41–50. IEEE Computer Society Press, Los Alamitos (2007)

Recurrent Method
for Blocking Probability Calculation
in Multi-service Switching Networks
with BPP Traffic

Mariusz Głąbowski

Chair of Communication and Computer Networks, Poznan University of Technology
ul. Polanka 3, 60-965 Poznan, Poland
mariusz.glabowski@et.put.poznan.pl

Abstract. This paper presents a new approximate analytical recurrent calculation method of the occupancy distribution and the blocking probability in switching networks which are offered multi-service traffic streams generated by Binomial (Engset) & Poisson (Erlang) & Pascal traffic sources (BPP traffic). The method is based on the concept of *effective availability*. The proposed calculation algorithm is based on the recurrent calculation of blocking probability in subsequent subsystems of the switching network. These calculations involve determination of occupancy distributions in interstage links as well as in the outgoing links. These distributions are calculated by means of the full-availability group model and the limited-availability group model. The results of analytical calculations of the blocking probabilities are compared with the simulation results of 3-stage and 5-stage switching networks.

Keywords: BPP traffic, switching networks, blocking probability.

1 Introduction

Determining traffic characteristics of multi-service multi-stage switching networks is a complex problem, both in optical and electronic networks [1]. Basic problems associated with the description of such systems arise from a necessity of servicing various types of traffic sources by the network [2]. In principle, the classification of traffic sources is reduced to distinguishing the CBR (Constant Bit Rate) and the VBR (Variable Bit Rate) sources. To define loads introduced into networks by the VBR sources, it is proposed to determine the so-called *equivalent bandwidth* for particular classes of traffic streams generated by the sources [2]. The assignment of several constant bit rates to the VBR sources enables the evaluation of traffic characteristics of switching systems in the virtual-circuit switching networks by means of multi-rate models worked out for the multi-rate circuit switching [2,3,4]. In multi-rate models resources required for the connections of particular classes are the multiplicity of a certain value of bandwidth, the so-called BBU (Basic Bandwidth Unit). While constructing multi-rate models

N. Thomas and C. Juiz (Eds.): EPEW 2008, LNCS 5261, pp. 152–167, 2008.
© Springer-Verlag Berlin Heidelberg 2008

for broadband systems, it is assumed that BBU is the greatest common divisor of the equivalent bandwidths of all call streams offered to the system [2].

Multi-service switching networks were the subject of many analyses [5,6,7,8]. The analytical methods of determination of traffic characteristics of such systems can be classified into two groups. In the first one time-effective algorithms of solving statistical equilibrium equations in a multi-dimensional Markov process are searched for. However, in spite of its great accuracy, this method cannot be used for calculations of larger systems which have practical meaning. The reason for this is an excessive number of states[1] in which a multi-dimensional Markov process occurring within the system can take place [5]. Methods of the other group consist in approximating a multi-dimensional service process by the appropriately constructed one-dimensional Markov chain, which is characterised by a product form solution [9,10,11,12]. Within the latter group, the most effective methods of switching networks calculations are the well-proven methods of the so-called effective availability [7,13,14]. The effective availability is defined as the availability in a multi-stage switching network in which the blocking probability is equal to the blocking probability of a single-stage network (grading) with the same capacity of the outgoing group and with analogous parameters of the traffic stream offered. The modern methods of calculating the effective availability are based on works [13,14] and [15], where all the components of this parameter have been defined. In [7], the practical and universal formulae for calculating the effective availability have been derived for arbitrary multi-stage switching networks carrying a mixture of different multi-rate traffic streams. On the basis of such formulae, the methods for multi-service switching networks with point-to-point, point-to-group and point-to-group with several attempts of setting up a connection have been proposed, firstly for the systems with Poisson traffic streams [7,8], and then with Engset and Pascal traffic streams [16,17,18].

This group of methods, based on the work [7], requires a quite complex process of determination of the effective availability parameter. For each switching network it is necessary to calculate its channel graph and then the so-called *probability of non-availability of last-stage switch* for particular traffic classes. The process of determination of channel graphs is particularly complex in multi-stage networks. Consequently, in [19], a method of determination of the effective availability in multi-rate switching networks in subsequent subsystems (stages) of the switching network was proposed, what reduced significantly the complexity of the method of blocking probability calculation in multi-service switching networks. This method is limited for switching networks with Poisson call streams. However, recently we can notice increasing interest in elaborating effective methods of analysis of multi-service systems in which traffic streams of each class are generated by a finite number of sources. This is due to the fact that in modern networks (e.g. Universal Mobile Telecommunications System) the ratio of source population and capacity of a system is often limited and the value of traffic load offered by calls of particular classes is dependent on the number of occupied

---

[1] A state of a system in the multi-dimensional state space is explicitly described by the number of calls of particular classes carried by the system.

bandwidth units in the group, i.e. on the number of in-service/idle traffic sources. In such systems the arrival process is modeled by Binomial process [20]. On the other hand, the Pascal arrival process is used to model overflow traffic with a given variance and a mean traffic [21]. Consequently, on the basis [22,23,24], in this paper the new recurrent method of blocking probability calculation in the switching networks which are offered multi-service traffic streams generated by Binomial (Engset)–Poisson (Erlang)–Pascal traffic sources has been proposed.

The remaining part of this paper is organised as follows. Section 2 is devoted to the elaboration of the method for blocking probability calculation in multi-stage multi-service switching networks with BPP traffic. In Section 3, the calculation and simulation results for selected switching networks have been compared. Section 4 concludes the paper.

2   Switching Networks Calculations

2.1   Basic Assumptions

Let us consider a switching network with multi-rate BPP (Binomial-Poisson-Pascal) traffic (Fig. 1). Let us assume that each of inter-stage links has the capacity equal to f BBUs and that outgoing transmission links create link groups called directions. The outgoing links can be wired to the directions in different ways. In Figure 1, the outgoing directions in the switching network have been created as follows: each first link of each last-stage switch belongs to the first direction and, analogously, each link n of each last-stage switch belongs to the same direction with a serial number equal to n.

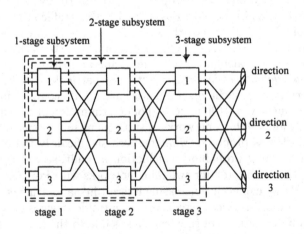

Fig. 1. 3-stage switching network

In general, switching networks can operate with a point-to-group or point-to-point selection. Let us consider first the switching network with a point-to-group selection. Following the control algorithm of this kind of selection [7], the control device of the switching network determines the first-stage switch, on the incoming link of which a class-c call appears (switch α). Then, the control system finds the last-stage switch (switch β) having a free outgoing link (i.e. the link comprising of at least t_c free BBUs) in a required direction. Next, the control device tries to find a connection path between switches α and β. If such a path does not exist, the control system begins the second attempt to set up a connection, i.e. the control system determines another switch β and tries to find a new connection path between switches α and β. The number of attempts is limited to the number of the last-stage switches having at least t_c idle BBUs in the considered direction. If the connection cannot be set up during the last possible attempt, a class-c call is lost as a result of internal blocking. When none of the outgoing links of the demanded direction of the switching network can service the class-c call (i.e. does not have t_c free BBUs) a call is lost due to the phenomenon of external blocking. In the case of a switching network with point-to-point selection, the number of attempts of setting up a new connection is limited to one.

In the paper we have assumed that an interstage link can be modelled by the full-availability group model and a direction can be modelled by the limited-availability group model, described in Sect. 2.2.

2.2   Link Models in Switching Networks

Limited-Availability Group Model. Let us consider the limited-availability group (LAG) model, i.e. the system composed of ν separate transmission links, presented in Fig. 2. Additionally, each of the links of the group has the capacity equal to f BBUs. Thus, the total capacity of the system is equal to $V = \nu f$. The system services a call – only when this call can be entirely carried by the resources of an arbitrary single link. It is therefore an example of a system with a state-dependent service process, in which the "state-dependence" results from the structure of the group.

The group is offered three types of traffic streams: M_I Erlang (Poisson) traffic streams, M_J Engset (Binomial) traffic streams and M_Q Pascal traffic streams. The mean arrival rate of a class-i Erlang traffic stream does not depend on the state of the system and is equal to λ_i, while the mean arrival rate $\lambda_j(n)$ of a class-j Engset traffic stream and the mean arrival rate $\lambda_q(n)$ of a class-q Pascal traffic stream depend on the number of calls being serviced (the system with state-dependent arrival process) in the following way:

$$\lambda_j(n) = (N_j - n_j(n))\gamma_j \ , \tag{1}$$

$$\lambda_q(n) = (S_q + n_q(n))\gamma_q \ , \tag{2}$$

where:

- N_j – the number of sources of Engset class j requiring t_j BBUs,
- $n_j(n)$ – the number of in-service sources of Engset class j in state n,
- γ_j – the mean arrival rate generated by an idle source of Engset class j,

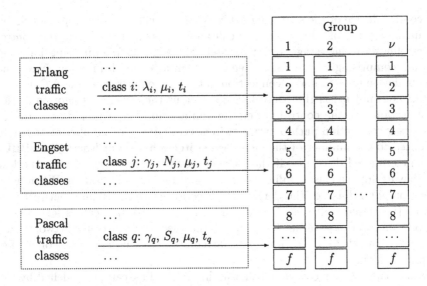

Fig. 2. Exemplary limited-availability group

- S_q – the number of sources of Pascal class q requiring t_q BBUs,
- γ_q – the mean arrival rate generated by an idle source of Pascal class q,
- $n_q(n)$ is the number of in-service sources of Pascal class q in state n.

The mean traffic offered to the system in the state of n BBUs being busy by class-j and -q traffic sources is equal to:

$$A_i(n) = A_i = \lambda_i/\mu_i \ , \tag{3}$$

$$A_j(n) = (N_j - n_j(n))\alpha_j \ , \tag{4}$$

$$A_q(n) = (S_q + n_q(n))\beta_q \ , \tag{5}$$

where $\alpha_j = \gamma_j/\mu_j$ and $\beta_q = \gamma_q/\mu_q$ are the mean traffic offered by an idle source of class j and q, respectively. In the model considered we assume that the holding time for calls of particular BPP traffic classes have an exponential distribution with intensity μ_i, μ_j and μ_q, respectively.

As we can notice in (4) and (5), interrelation between the offered traffic and the number of in-service sources in Engset and Pascal streams makes the direct application of the Kaufman-Roberts recursion (KRR) [11,12] (elaborated for systems with Poisson traffic streams) for determining the occupancy distribution in the considered system impossible. Consequently, in [24] an approximate method has been proposed, which enables us to make the mean value of traffic offered by class j and q dependent on the occupancy state (the number of occupied BBUs) of the group, and thereby to determine the system with a finite population of sources by the KRR. Assuming that the average number $n_j(n)$ of calls currently in service of class j and the average number $n_q(n)$ of calls currently in service of class q in state n is known, KRR can be rewritten in the form that includes characteristics of BPP traffic streams, namely:

$$n\,[Q_n]_V = \sum_{i=1}^{M_I} A_i t_i \sigma_i (n - t_i)\,[Q_{n-t_i}]_V +$$
$$+ \sum_{j=1}^{M_J} (N_j - n_j(n - t_j))\alpha_j \sigma_j(n - t_j)t_j\,[Q_{n-t_j}]_V +$$
$$+ \sum_{q=1}^{M_Q} (S_q + n_q(n - t_q))\beta_q \sigma_q(n - t_q)t_q\,[Q_{n-t_q}]_V \ , \quad (6)$$

where $[Q_n]_V$ is the probability of an event in which there are n busy BBUs in the system and $\sigma_i(n)$, $\sigma_j(n)$, $\sigma_q(n)$ are the so-called conditional state-passage probabilities, i.e. the probability of admission of a class-i, -j and -q call to the service when the system is found in the state n.

According to the considerations presented in [11,22,23], the parameter $n_c(n)^2$ is equal to the reverse transition rate and can be calculated on the basis of the local equations of equilibrium [22,11]:

$$n_c(n) = \begin{cases} \frac{A_c(n-t_c)\sigma_c(n-t_c)[Q_{n-t_c}]_V}{[Q_n]_V} & \text{for } 0 \leq n \leq V \ , \\ 0 & \text{otherwise} \ . \end{cases} \quad (7)$$

Let us notice that in order to determine the parameter $n_c(n)$ the knowledge of the occupancy distribution $[Q]_V$ is necessary. In order to determine the distribution $[Q]_V$ in turn, it is necessary to know the value $n_c(n)$. Equations (7) and (6) form then a set of confounding equations that can be solved with the application of iterative methods.

Let us assume that the distribution $[Q]_V^{(l)}$ is the occupancy distribution for a system with a state-dependent service process and a state-dependent arrival process determined in the l-th iteration, while $n_c^{(l)}(n)$ determines the mean number of calls currently in service of class c determined in the l-th iteration. Thus:

$$n_c^{(l+1)}(n) = \begin{cases} \frac{A_c^{(l+1)}(n-t_c)\sigma_c(n-t_c)\left[Q_{n-t_c}^{(l)}\right]_V}{\left[Q_n^{(l)}\right]_V} & \text{for } 0 \leq n \leq V \ , \\ 0 & \text{otherwise} \ . \end{cases} \quad (8)$$

In line with [24], in the first iteration the parameters $\forall_{j \in M_J} \forall_{0 \leq n \leq V}\ n_j^{(0)}(n) = 0$ and $\forall_{q \in M_Q} \forall_{0 \leq n \leq V}\ n_q^{(0)}(n) = 0$. The adopted assumption means that the Engset and Pascal streams – in the first iteration – can be treated as an equivalent Erlang stream generating the offered traffic with the intensity:

$$A_j^{(0)}(n) = A_j = N_j\alpha_j \ , \qquad A_q^{(0)}(n) = A_q = S_k\beta_q \ , \quad (9)$$

---

[2] In the present paper, the letter "i" denotes an Erlang traffic class, the letter "j" - an Engset traffic class, the letter "q" - a Pascal traffic class, and the letter "c" - an arbitrary traffic class.

which is equal in value to the traffic offered by all free sources of class-j Engset stream and class-q Pascal stream. The state probabilities, obtained on the basis of (6), constitute the input data for the next iteration, where the parameters $n_j(n)$, $n_q(n)$ are designated. The iterative process ends when the assumed accuracy of the iterative process is obtained.

In order to determine the occupancy distribution in the considered system on the basis of (6), it is first necessary to define the state transition coefficients σ_c. These coefficients take into account the dependence between call streams and the state of the system and allow us to determine the part of the incoming call stream λ_c to be transferred between the states $\{n\}$ and $\{n + t_c\}$ due to the specific structure of the limited-availability group. The parameter $\sigma_c(n)$ does not depend on the arrival process and can be calculated as follows [7]:

$$\sigma_c(n) = 1 - (F(V - n, \nu, t_c - 1)/F(V - n, \nu, f)) , \qquad (10)$$

where $F(x, \nu, f)$ is the number of arrangements of x free BBUs in ν links, the capacity of each link is equal to f BBUs:

$$F(x, \nu, f) = \sum_{i=0}^{\lfloor \frac{x}{f+1} \rfloor} (-1)^i \binom{\nu}{i} \binom{x + \nu - 1 - i(f + 1)}{\nu - 1} . \qquad (11)$$

To sum up, the algorithm of determination of the occupancy distribution and blocking probability (time congestion) in systems with multi-service Erlang, Engset and Pascal streams may be written as follows:

Algorithm 1. Blocking probability calculation in link groups with BPP Traffic

---

1. Determination of state-passage coefficients $\sigma_c(n)$, determining the dependency between the service process and the state of the system (Equation (10)).
2. Setting of the iteration number $l = 0$.
3. Determination of initial values of $n_j^{(l)}(n)$, $n_q^{(l)}(n)$:
   $$\forall_{1 \leq j \leq M_J} \forall_{0 \leq n \leq V} \; n_j^{(l)}(n) = 0, \; \forall_{1 \leq q \leq M_Q} \forall_{0 \leq n \leq V} \; n_q^{(l)}(n) = 0.$$
4. Increase of the iteration number: $l = l + 1$.
5. Determination of state probabilities $[Q_n^{(l)}]_V$ (Equation (6)).
6. Calculation of reverse transition rates $n_j^{(l)}(n)$ and $n_q^{(l)}(n)$ (Equation (8)).
7. Repetition of Steps No. 4–6 until the assumed accuracy of the iterative process is obtained:
   $$\forall_{n \in \langle 0, V \rangle} \left(\left| \frac{(n_j^{(l-1)}(n) - n_j^{(l)}(n))}{n_j^{(l)}(n)} \right| \leq \xi , \; \left| \frac{n_q^{(l-1)}(n) - n_q^{(l)}(n)}{n_q^{(l)}(n)} \right| \leq \xi \right) . \qquad (12)$$
8. Determination of blocking probabilities $e(c)$ for calls of particular traffic classes:
   $$e(c) = \sum_{n=0}^{V-t_c} [Q_n]_V [1 - \sigma_c(n)] + \sum_{n=V-t_c+1}^{V} [Q_n]_V . \qquad (13)$$

Observe that the conditional transition coefficients σ_c that determine the dependency between the service process and the state of the system are determined once and do not change during successive iterations.

Full-Availability Group Model. The full-availability group (FAG) is a discrete model of a single link that uses complete sharing policy [2]. This system is an example of a state-independent system in which the passage between two adjacent states of the process associated with a given class stream does not depend on the number of busy BBUs in the system. Therefore, the conditional state-passage probability $\sigma_c(n)$ in FAG is equal to 1 for all states and for each traffic class. Consequently, the occupancy distribution and blocking probabilities in the groups with an infinite and a finite source population can be calculated by the equations (6) and (13), taking into consideration the fact that: $\forall_c \forall_n \sigma_c(n) = 1$.

2.3   Effective Availability Parameter

The basis of the proposed recurrent method of blocking probability calculation in multi-stage switching networks is the method proposed by Ershov in [14] and, subsequently, modified in [15]. These methods exploit the parameter of effective availability, the calculation of which is based on the parameter π determining the probability of non-availability of a last-stage outgoing link in the required direction for the selected first-stage switch. The proposed original approach [14] of calculating the parameter π by the channel graph method can lead to increase in complexity of the process of blocking probability calculation in multi-stage switching networks. Consequently, in this section the recurrent method is applied for switching networks with BPP traffic, in which the parameter π in l-stage subsystem of the switching network is determined on the basis of blocking probability in the $(l-1)$-stage subsystem of the switching network. Such an approach allows us to omit the process of channel graph determination and start the calculation process from one-stage subsystem of the switching network.

In order to determine the blocking probability in multi-stage switching networks let us consider a z-stage multi-service switching network with point-to-group selection. Now, for class-c calls we can determine the so-called equivalent switching network. The concept of the equivalent switching network [7] is the base for effective availability calculation for a class-c traffic stream. Following this concept, the network with multi-rate traffic is reduced to an equivalent network carrying a single-rate traffic. Each link of the equivalent network is treated as a single-channel link with a fictitious load $e_l(c)$ equal to the blocking probability for the class-c stream in a link of a real switching network between section l and $l + 1$. This probability can be calculated on the basis of the occupancy distribution in the full-availability group with BPP traffic streams (Sect. 2.2).

The effective availability in a real z-stage switching network is equal to the effective availability in an equivalent switching network. According to recent work [7], it can be determined by the following formula:

$$d_{e,c,z} = [1 - \pi_z(c)]V_r + \pi_z(c)\eta_r Y_1(c) + \pi_z(c)[V_r - \eta_r Y_1(c)]y_{z,r}(c)\theta_z(c) \ , \quad (14)$$

where:

- $d_{e,c,z}$ – the effective availability for the class-c stream in an equivalent z-stage switching network;
- $\pi_l(c)$ – the probability of non-availability of a stage l switch for the class-c call; $\pi_l(c)$ is the probability of an event where a class-c connection path cannot be set up between a given first-stage switch and a given stage l switch. Evaluation of this parameter is traditionally based on the channel graph of the equivalent switching network. For example, on the basis of channel graph of 3-stage network presented in Fig. 1, we obtain:

$$\pi_3(i) = \{1 - [1 - e_1(i)][1 - e_2(i)]\}^\nu \; ; \tag{15}$$

- V_r – the number of links in direction r of the considered switching network;
- $Y_l(c)$ – the average value of the fictitious traffic served by the switch of the stage l, $Y_l(c) = m_l e_l(c)$, where m_l is the number of the outgoing links of the stage l switch;
- η_r – a portion of the average fictitious traffic from the switch of the first stage which is carried by the direction r. If the traffic is uniformly distributed between all h directions, we obtain: $\eta_r = 1/h$;
- $\theta_z(c)$ – the so-called *secondary availability coefficient* [7] which is the probability of an event in which the connection path of the class-c connection passes through directly available switches of intermediate stages.
- $y_{z,r}(c)$ – the fictitious load carried by one outgoing link in the direction r of the equivalent switching network, in most switching networks $y_{z,r}(c) = e(c)$.

In Equation (14), the first element ($[1 - \pi_z(c)]V_r$) determines the average number of last-stage switches directly available for a first-stage switch, the second element ($\pi_z(c)\eta_r Y_1(c)$) determines the average number of last-stage switches available by direct occupancy, and the last element ($\pi_z(c)[V_r - \eta_r Y_1(c)]y_{z,r}(c)\theta_z(c)$) determines the average number of last-stage switches available by the secondary availability [7].

Analysing Equation (14) we can notice that the main problem is caused by the determination of channel graphs for equivalent switching networks, and by calculation of secondary availability coefficient. Consequently, in this paper (Sect. 2.4) the recurrent method of parameter $\pi(c)$ calculation (the probability of direct non-availability of the last-stage switch for the first-stage switch for a class-c call) is applied. Additionally, it is proposed in the paper that the effective availability method, in conjunction with the recurrent method for switching networks with BPP traffic, can be calculated by the following simplified formula:

$$d_{e,c,z} = [1 - \pi_z(c)]V_r + \pi_z(c)\eta_r Y_1(c) \; . \tag{16}$$

Equation (16) allows us to eliminate the determination of the secondary availability in the process of the effective availability estimation.

2.4   Recurrent Method of Blocking Probability Calculation in Switching Networks

Having determined the effective availability parameter in an equivalent switching network we can explain the basic assumptions of the proposed recurrent method of blocking probability calculation in multi-service switching networks.

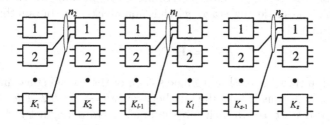

Fig. 3. A diagram of multi-stage switching network

Let us consider a diagram of multi-stage switching network presented in Fig. 3. We can notice that the probability $\pi_l(c)$ of non-availability of stage-l switch for class-c calls is equal to the blocking probability in the group of n_l links entering this switch, i.e. is equal to the point-to-group blocking probability E_{l-1} of the switching network consisting of $(l-1)$ stages (Fig. 3):

$$\pi_l(c) = E_{l-1}(c). \tag{17}$$

Consequently, the effective availability parameter $d_{e,c,l}$ for class-c calls in the subsystem consisting of l stages of the z-stage switching network depends on the point-to-group blocking probability in the subsystem consisting of $(l-1)$ stages:

$$d_{e,c,l} = f(E_{l-1}(c)) = d_{e,c,l}(E_{l-1}(c)). \tag{18}$$

In the paper, it is assumed that the internal point-to-group blocking probability E^{in} in an equivalent switching network (calculated for a given class of multi-rate traffic) can be approximated by the formula proposed by Ershova and Ershov for switching networks with single-rate traffic [14]:

$$E^{in} = \mathbf{EIF}(A_r, V_r, d), \tag{19}$$

where A_r is the traffic offered in direction r of the equivalent switching network, V_r is the number of links in direction r of the equivalent switching network and EIF means Erlang's Interconnection Formula:

$$EIF(A, V, d) = \sum_{l=d}^{V} \frac{\binom{l}{d}}{\binom{V}{d}} \frac{A^l}{l!} \prod_{k=d}^{l-1}\left[1 - \frac{\binom{k}{d}}{\binom{V}{d}}\right] \bigg/ \sum_{j=0}^{V} \frac{A^j}{j!} \prod_{k=d}^{j-1}\left[1 - \frac{\binom{k}{d}}{\binom{V}{d}}\right]. \tag{20}$$

Taking the notation used in Fig. 3 into account we can rewrite (19) as follows:

$$E_l^{in}(c) = \mathbf{EIF}\left(A_{l+1}(c), n_{l+1}, d_{e,c,l}(E_{l-1}(c))\right), \tag{21}$$

where A_{l+1} is the traffic offered to a single switch of stage $l + 1$ and n_{l+1} is the number of links between stage l switches and a single switch of stage $l + 1$. The values of the parameters V and d, inserted into binomial coefficients in (20), for real switching networks are usually not greater than twenty.

On the basis of (17), (18) and (21) we can perceive that the internal blocking probability in multi-stage switching networks can be calculated recurrently. The calculation process can begin from determining the blocking probability $E_1(c)$. Assuming that the single first-stage switch is non blocking we obtain that $d_e(c) = 1$, and, consequently:

$$E_1(c) = \mathbf{EIF}(A_2, 1, 1),\tag{22}$$

where A_2 is the traffic offered to a single switch of the second stage and is equal to the value of fictitious load of the link between stages 1 and 2. The calculation process can also start from a such subsystem of the switching network for which the calculation of the parameter $\pi(c)$ is not complicated.

The final internal blocking probability $E^{in}(c)$, according to the proposed calculation method, is equal to the blocking probability $E_z^{in}(c)$, i.e.:

$$E^{in}(c) = E_z^{in}(c) = \mathbf{EIF}(A_r(c), V_r, d_{e,c,z}(E_{z-1}(c))),\tag{23}$$

where $A_r(c)$ is the total traffic of the class-c stream offered to the outgoing direction with the capacity equal to V_r links.

The phenomenon of the external blocking occurs when none of the outgoing links of the demanded direction of the switching network can service the class-c call (i.e. does not have t_c free BBUs). The occupancy distribution of the outgoing direction can be approximated by the distribution of available links in LAG with BPP traffic. Thus, the external blocking probability can be calculated by (13), i.e.:

$$E_c^{ex} = e(c).\tag{24}$$

The total blocking probability E_c for a class-c call is a sum of external and internal blocking probabilities. Assuming the independence of internal and external blocking events, we obtain:

$$E_c = E_c^{ex} + E_c^{in}[1 - E_c^{ex}].\tag{25}$$

The proposed recurrent method allows us to determine the point-to-group blocking probability. However, this method may be also directly used for point-to-point blocking probability calculation in accordance with Lotze's remark [25] that point-to-point blocking in z-stage switching network is equal to point-to-group blocking in a $(z - 1)$-stage switching network. In such a system the incoming links to the switch of the last z-stage are considered to be an outgoing group (direction).

To sum up, the algorithm of determination of the occupancy distribution in systems with multi-service BPP traffic streams is presented as Algorithm 2.

Algorithm 2. Blocking probability calculation in multi-service switching networks with BPP Traffic

1. Determination of fictitious load $y(c) = e(c)$ for class-c calls in interstage links (full-availability groups) between stage 1 and 2 on the basis of Algorithm 1.
2. Calculation of the offered traffic $A(c)$ (the input parameter in **EIF**) on the basis of fictitious load $e(c)$ and Erlang-B formula:

$$A(c)\{1 - E_f[A(c)]\} = e(c) \ , \tag{26}$$

   where $A(c)$ is the traffic offered to a single input of the considered switching network and $E_f[A(c)]$ is the blocking probability in an interstage-link (between stages 1 and 2) with capacity equal to f BBUs, calculated according to Erlang-B formula.
3. Calculation of internal blocking probability in the switching network according to (23).
4. Calculation of external blocking probability on the basis of the limited-availability group modelling outgoing directions (Algorithm 1).
5. Calculation of total blocking probability on the basis of (25).

3   Calculation and Simulation Results

In order to confirm the adopted assumptions in the proposed method for switching networks with BPP traffic, the results of the analytical calculations were compared with the simulation results of multi-stage switching networks. The results presented in the paper were obtained for 3- and 5-stage switching networks consisting of the switches of $\nu \times \nu$ links. The results presented in the paper (Figs. 4–5) were obtained for the switching network with the parameters: $\nu = 4$, $f = 30$ BBUs. The switching networks were offered three traffic classes in the following proportions: $A_1 t_1 : N_2 \alpha_2 t_2 : S_3 \beta_3 t_3 = 1 : 1 : 1$, where $t_1 = 1$ BBU (Erlang traffic class), $t_2 = 2$ BBUs (Engset traffic class), $t_3 = 6$ BBUs (Pascal traffic class). The research was carried out for $N_2 = S_3 = 320$ sources for Pascal and Engset traffic streams. The results of the simulation (implemented in C++) are shown in the charts in the form of marks with 95% confidence intervals that have been calculated according to the Student-t distribution for the five series with 100,000,000 calls of this traffic class that generates the lowest number of calls. For each of the points of the simulation, the value of the confidence interval is at least one order lower than the mean value of the results of the simulation. In many a case, the value of the confidence interval is lower than the height of the symbol used to indicate the value of the simulation experiment. All the results are expressed in relation to the value of total traffic a offered to a single BBU at the entry to the network:

$$a = (A_1 t_1 + N_2 \alpha_2 t_2 + S_3 \beta_3 t_3)/V,$$

where $V = \nu \times \nu \times f$ is the total capacity of the considered switching networks, expressed in BBUs.

Figures 4 and 5 show the results of point-to-point and point-to-group blocking probability in the 3-stage and 5-stage switching network with Erlang, Engset

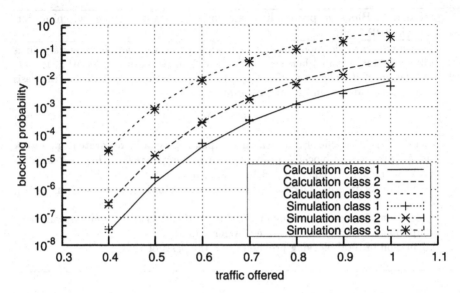

Fig. 4. Point-to-point blocking probability in 3-stage switching network with BPP traffic, $\nu = 4$, $f = 30$, $V = 120$; Three traffic classes; Class 1: Erlang traffic stream, $t_1 = 1$ BBU, $\mu_{1,0}^{-1} = 1$; Class 2: Engset traffic stream, $t_2 = 2$ BBUs, $\mu_{1,0}^{-1} = 1$, $N_2 = 320$, Class 3: Pascal traffic stream, $t_3 = 6$ BBUs, $\mu_{1,0}^{-1} = 1$, $S_3 = 320$

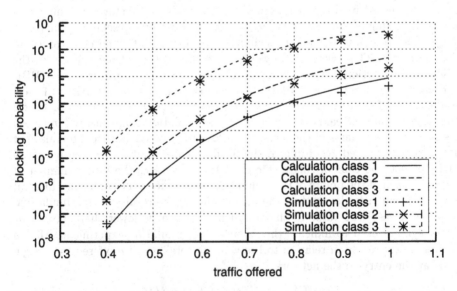

Fig. 5. Point-to-group blocking probability in 5-stage switching network with BPP traffic, $\nu = 4$, $f = 30$, $V = 120$; Three traffic classes; Class 1: Erlang traffic stream, $t_1 = 1$ BBU, $\mu_{1,0}^{-1} = 1$; Class 2: Engset traffic stream, $t_2 = 2$ BBUs, $\mu_{1,0}^{-1} = 1$, $N_2 = 320$, Class 3: Pascal traffic stream, $t_3 = 6$ BBUs, $\mu_{1,0}^{-1} = 1$, $S_3 = 320$

and Pascal sources, respectively. We can notice that the proposed methods of blocking probability calculation in switching networks with BPP traffic ensures high accuracy.

4 Conclusions

The paper presents the approximate recurrent method of point-to-group and point-to-point blocking probability calculation in switching networks with multirate traffic generated by a finite and an infinite source population (BPP traffic). The method is based on the concept of effective availability. The proposed method introduced two simplifications which can be applied for the effective availability methods. The first simplification results from the calculation of the probability of non-availability $\pi(c)$ on the basis of blocking probability in subsequent stages of the switching networks (without prior determination of a channel graph) while the second simplification allows us to calculate the effective availability parameter without determination of the so-called *secondary availability*.

The analytical results of blocking probability in multi-stage switching networks, obtained on the basis of the proposed methods, are compared with the simulation results. It should be emphasized that this paper presents for the first time the results obtained in the multi-service switching network servicing a mixture of BPP streams. The simulation results confirm high accuracy of the proposed analytical models. A lot of simulation experiments carried out by the author so far indicate that similar accuracy can be obtained for greater capacity of switching networks and greater number of offered traffic streams.

The method proposed in the paper can be applied for traffic engineering of multi-rate networks as well as the networks with switched virtual circuits.

References

1. Zhou, Y., Poo, G.S.: Optical multicast over wavelength-routed WDM networks: A survey. Optical Switching and Networking 2(3), 176–197 (2005)
2. Roberts, J., Mocci, V., Virtamo, I. (eds.): Broadband Network Teletraffic, Final Report of Action COST 242. Commission of the European Communities. Springer, Berlin (1996)
3. Roberts, J.: Teletraffic models for the Telcom 1 integrated services network. In: Proceedings of 10th International Teletraffic Congress, Montreal, Canada (1983) 1.1.2
4. Sanso', B., Girard, A., Mobiot, F.: Integrating reliability and quality of service in networks with switched virtual circuits. Computers and Operations Research 32(1), 35–58 (January 2005)
5. Conradt, J., Buchheister, A.: Considerations on loss probability of multi-slot connections. In: Proceedings of 11th International Teletraffic Congress, Kyoto, Japan, 4.4B–2.1 (1985)

6. Beshai, M., Manfield, D.: Multichannel services performance of switching networks. In: Proceedings of 12th International Teletraffic Congress, Torino, Italy, pp. 857–864. Elsevier, Amsterdam (1988)

7. Stasiak, M.: Combinatorial considerations for switching systems carrying multichannel traffic streams. Annales des Télécommunications 51(11–12), 611–625 (1996)

8. Głąbowski, M., Stasiak, M.: Point-to-point blocking probability in switching networks with reservation. Annales des Télécommunications 57(7–8), 798–831 (2002)

9. Fortet, R., Grandjean, C.: Congestion in a loss system when some calls want several devices simultaneously. Electrical Communication 39(4), 513–526 (1964)

10. Iversen, V.: The exact evaluation of multi-service loss systems with access control. In: Seventh Nordic Teletraffic Seminar (NTS-7), Lund, Sweden, August 1987, pp. 56–61 (1987)

11. Kaufman, J.: Blocking in a shared resource environment. IEEE Transactions on Communications 29(10), 1474–1481 (1981)

12. Roberts, J.: A service system with heterogeneous user requirements—application to multi-service telecommunications systems. In: Pujolle, G. (ed.) Proceedings of Performance of Data Communications Systems and their Applications, pp. 423–431. North Holland, Amsterdam (1981)

13. Lotze, A., Roder, A., Thierer, G.: PPL — a reliable method for the calculation of point-to-point loss in link systems. In: Proceedings of 8th International Teletraffic Congress, Melbourne, Australia, 547/1–44 (1976)

14. Ershov, V.A.: Some further studies on effective accessibility: Fundamentals of teletraffic theory. In: Proceedings of 3rd International Seminar on Teletraffic Theory, Moscow, pp. 193–196 (1984)

15. Stasiak, M.: Blocage interne point a point dans les reseaux de connexion. Annales des Télécommunications 43(9-10), 561–575 (1988)

16. Głąbowski, M.: Blocking probability in multi-service switching networks with finite source population. In: Proceedings of The 14th IEEE International Conference On Telecommunications, Penang, Malaysia (May 2007)

17. Głąbowski, M.: Point-to-point blocking probability calculation in multi-service switching networks with BPP traffic. In: Czachórski, T. (ed.) Proceedings of The 14th Polish Teletraffic Symposium, Zakopane, September 2007, pp. 65–76 (2007)

18. Głąbowski, M.: Point-to-point and point-to-group blocking probability in multiservice switching networks with BPP traffic. Electronics and Telecommunications Quarterly 53(4), 339–360 (2007)

19. Głąbowski, M.: Recurrent calculation of blocking probability in multiservice switching networks. In: Proceedings of the Asia-Pacific Conference on Communications (2006), doi:10.1109/APCC.2006.255964

20. Kogan, Y., Shenfild, M.: Asymptotic solution of generalized multiclass Engset model. In: Labetoulle, J., Roberts, J. (eds.) Proceedings of 14th International Teletraffic Congress, Antibes Juan-les-Pins, France, vol. 1b, pp. 1239–1249. Elsevier, Amsterdam (1994)

21. Delbrouck, L.: On the steady-state distribution in a service facility carrying mixtures of traffic with different peakedness factors and capacity requirements. IEEE Transactions on Communications 31(11), 1209–1211 (1983)

22. Stasiak, M., Głąbowski, M.: A simple approximation of the link model with reservation by a one-dimensional Markov chain. Journal of Performance Evaluation 41(2-3), 195–208 (2000)

23. Głąbowski, M., Stasiak, M.: An approximate model of the full-availability group with multi-rate traffic and a finite source population. In: Buchholtz, P., Lehnert, R., Pióro, M. (eds.) Proceedings of 3rd Polish-German Teletraffic Symposium, Dresden, Germany, September 2004, pp. 195–204. VDE Verlag (2004)
24. Głąbowski, M.: Modelling of state-dependent multi-rate systems carrying BPP traffic. Annals of Telecommunications (2007), doi:10.1007/s12243-008-0034-5
25. Lotze, A., Roder, A., Thierer, G.: Point-to-point selection versus point-to-group selection in link systems. In: Proceedings of 8th International Teletraffic Congress, Melbourne, Australia, 541/1–5 (1976)

An Approximate Model of the WCDMA Interface Servicing a Mixture of Multi-rate Traffic Streams with Priorities

Damian Parniewicz, Maciej Stasiak,
Janusz Wiewióra, and Piotr Zwierzykowski

Poznan University of Technology
Chair of Communications and Computer Networks
ul. Polanka 3, Poznań 60965, Poland
piotr.zwierzykowski@put.poznan.pl

Abstract. The paper presents an approximate method for blocking probability determination in the WCDMA interface of the UMTS network with priorities. In our considerations we use a new model of the full-availability group servicing multi-rate traffic with priorities. In the proposed model we assume that a new call with a higher priority can terminate connections already in service if they are characterized by a lower priority than a new call. The proposed scheme is applicable for cost-effective WCDMA resource management in 3G mobile networks and can be easily applied to network capacity calculations.

Keywords: WCDMA, full-availability group, priorities.

1 Introduction

Universal Mobile Telecommunication System (UMTS) using the Wideband Code Division Multiple Access (WCDMA) radio interface is one of the standards proposed for third generation cellular technologies (3G). According to the 3rd Generation Partnership Project (3GPP) recommendations, 3G systems should include services with circuit switching and packet switching, transmit data at a speed of up to 2 Mbit/s, and ensure access to multimedia services [1]. The dimensioning process for the UMTS system should make it possible to determine such a capacity of individual elements of the system that will secure - with the assumed load of the system - a pre-defined level of the Grade of Service (GoS). Due to the possibility of resource allocation for different traffic classes, the capacity determination of the WCDMA radio interface is much more complex than in the case of Global Systems for Mobile Communications (GSM). The capacity of the WCDMA interface is limited by the increase in interference caused by the users serviced by other cells of the system who make use of the same frequency channel as well as by the users making use of the adjacent radio channels and by the multipath propagation occurring in the radio channel. To ensure an appropriate level of service in UMTS it is thus necessary to limit the interference by decreasing the number of active users or the allocated resources employed

N. Thomas and C. Juiz (Eds.): EPEW 2008, LNCS 5261, pp. 168–180, 2008.

to service them. A number of papers have been devoted to traffic modelling in cellular systems with the WCDMA radio interface, i.e. [2, 3, 4, 5, 6, 7, 8, 9, 10]. The works [2, 4, 5, 3, 6, 7, 10] proposed models of the WCDMA interface without priorities. In [8, 9], the authors used the multi-rate Erlang-B loss formula for evaluation of the blocking probabilities in a single cell servicing three multi-rate traffic classes with priorities.

This paper presents a new effective blocking probability determination method for a cellular system with the WCDMA interface with priorities. The proposed method can be used for the uplink and downlink directions. The paper has been divided into five sections. Section 2 discusses basic dependencies describing the WCDMA interface in the UMTS network. Section 3 presents an analytical model applied to blocking probability determination for different traffic classes with priorities. The following section includes the results obtained in the study of the system. The final section sums up the discussion.

2   WCDMA Interface in the UMTS Network

In a UMTS network it is possible to determine priorities for particular services. The priorities define the sequence of resource allocations that can result in a decrease in resources or the termination of a connection with a lower priority, if the resources are insufficient. A decision on the priority of a given service is made by the operator of the network, who defines its importance in the core network (Fig. 1). UTRAN (*UMTS Terrestrial Radio Access Network*) identifies the priority values of particular classes and, employing appropriate mechanisms (admission/congestion control or scheduling [11]), manages traffic accordingly. In general, this management is related to decreasing the flow capability or terminating connections at the point when a new call with a higher priority arrives.

An important element of the UTRAN is the WCDMA radio interface (Fig. 1). The capacity of the WCDMA radio interface in cellular systems is seriously limited due to the occurrence of some types of interference [1], namely: co-channel

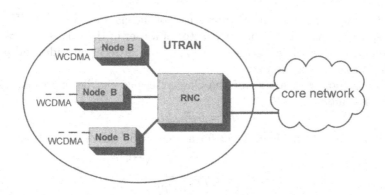

Fig. 1. Elements of the UMTS network structure

interference within a cell – from concurrent users of a frequency channel within the area of a given cell; outer co-channel interference – from concurrent users of the frequency channel working within the area of adjacent cells; adjacent channels interference – from the adjacent frequency channels of the same operator or other cellular telecommunication carriers; and all possible noise and interference coming from other systems and sources, both broadband and narrowband.

Before admitting a new connection in systems with the WCDMA radio interface, admission control needs to check whether the admittance will not sacrifice the quality of the existing connections. The admission control functionality is located in RNC (*Radio Network Controller*), where the load information from the surrounding cells can be obtained. The admission control algorithm estimates the load increase that would be caused in the radio network by setting up a new connection [1]. This is done not only in the access cell[1] but also in the adjacent cells, in order to take the inter-cell interference effect into account. A new call is rejected if the predicted load exceeds particular thresholds set by the radio network planning [12].

Summing up, in the WCDMA radio interface a growth in the load is accompanied by a simultaneous growth in interference generated by other users serviced by the same cell or other cells. Thus, to secure an appropriate level of service, it is necessary to limit the number of allocated resources by active traffic sources. It is estimated that the maximum usage of the resources of the radio interface without lowering the quality of service will be equal to about 50-80% [1]. For the same reason, one can talk about the so-called *soft capacity* of the WCDMA radio interface, which is also described as the noise limited capacity.

Accurate signal reception is possible only when the relation of energy per bit E_b to noise spectral density N_0 is appropriate. A too low value of E_b/N_0 will cause the receiver to be unable to decode the received signal, while a too high value of the energy per bit in relation to noise will be perceived as interference for other users of the same radio channel. The relation E_b/N_0 for a user of the class i service can be calculated as follows [1]:

$$\left(\frac{E_b}{N_0}\right)_i = \frac{W}{\nu_i R_i} \frac{P_i}{I_{total} - P_i},$$ (1)

where: P_i – signal power received from a user of the class i connection, W – chip rate of spreading signal, ν_i – activity factor of a user of the class i service, R_i – bit rate of a user of the class i service, I_{total} – total received wideband power, including thermal noise power.

The mean power of a user of the class i service can be expressed by the following formula:

$$P_i = L_i I_{total},$$ (2)

where L_i is the so-called load factor for a user of the class i connection:

$$L_i = \left(1 + \frac{W}{\left(\frac{E_b}{N_0}\right)_i R_i \nu_i}\right)^{-1}.$$ (3)

---

[1] The access cell is the cell to which a new call is offered.

Table 1. Examples of E_b/N_0, ν_i and L_i for different service classes [4]

Class of service (i)	Emergency call	Voice	Video call	Data
W [Mchipps]	3.84			
R_i [kbps]	12.2	12.2	64	144
ν_i	0.67	0.67	1	1
$(E_b/N_0)_i$ [dB]	4	4	2	1.5
L_i	0.0053	0.0053	0.0257	0.0503

Sample values E_b/N_0 for different traffic classes and corresponding values of the load factor L_i, with the dependency (3) taken into account, are shown in Table 1.

In the case of perfect power control, the condition E_b/N_0 is always fulfilled. In real systems, E_b/N_0 for a given service can sometimes differ from the target value. However, the system will work properly only if the mean value oscillates around the target value. We can use this requirement to determine the total load for the uplink connection, which should be lower than the assumed capacity η_{UL} of the radio interface in the uplink direction:

$$\eta_{UL} \geq \left(1 + \bar{\delta}\right) \sum_{i=1}^{M} L_i n_i, \tag{4}$$

where M is the number of services, n_i is the number of users of i service, L_i is the load factor of a user of i service, parameter $\bar{\delta}$ is defined as the mean value of other cell interference over proper cell interference and conventionally is between 0.2 and 0.8 [1].

The bigger the load of a radio link, the higher level of the noise generated. When the load of the uplink direction approaches unity, the corresponding increase in noise tends towards infinity. Therefore, it is assumed that the actual maximum use of the resources of a radio interface without lowering the level of the quality of service, will amount to about 50-80% [1].

The calculation of possible load in the downlink direction is similar to that of the uplink direction with the addition of the orthogonality factor ξ, due to the orthogonality provided by the OVSF (*Orthogonal Variable Spreading Factor*) codes. In the WCDMA interface, OVSF codes are used to separate the downlink direction channels transmitted from a single Node B. Thus, the capacity is expressed in the percentage usage of the radio interface and can be calculated as follows [1]:

$$\eta_{DL} \geq \left(1 + \bar{\delta} - \xi\right) \sum_{i=1}^{M} L_i n_i. \tag{5}$$

Conventionally, the orthogonality factor is between 0.4 and 0.9 [1].

In the considerations presented in the paper we have assumed that the influence of interference on the flow capacity of the WCDMA radio interface can be determined by the pair of the parameters $\bar{\delta}$ and ξ.

3   Model of the System

The WCDMA interface in an UMTS network can be treated as the full-availability group (FAG) with multi-rate traffic. Let us assume that the total capacity of the group is equal to V Basic Bandwidth Units (BBUs) [13]. The group is offered M independent classes of Poisson traffic streams, having the intensities: $\lambda_1, \lambda_2, ..., \lambda_M$. The class i call requires t_i BBUs to set up a connection. The holding time for calls of particular classes has an exponential distribution with the parameters: $\mu_1, \mu_2, ..., \mu_M$. Thus, the mean traffic offered to the system by the class i traffic stream is equal to:

$$a_i = \frac{\lambda_i}{\mu_i}. \tag{6}$$

The demanded resources in the group for servicing particular classes can be treated as a call demanding an integer number of BBUs. The value of BBU, i.e. t_{BBU}, is calculated as the greatest common divisor (GCD) of all resources demanded by traffic classes offered to the system:

$$L_{BBU} = GCD(L_1, ..., L_M), \tag{7}$$

where L_i is load factor for a user of the class i call (Tab.1), defined in Eq. (3).

The multi-dimensional Markov process in the FAG can be approximated by the one-dimensional Markov chain which can be described by Kaufman-Roberts recursion [14, 15]:

$$nP(n) = \sum_{i=1}^{M} a_i t_i P(n - t_i), \tag{8}$$

where $P(n)$ is the probability of state of n BBUs being busy, and t_i is the number of BBUs required by a class i call:

$$t_i = \left\lfloor \frac{L_i}{L_{BBU}} \right\rfloor. \tag{9}$$

On the basis of Formula (8), the blocking probability B_i for the class i stream can be expressed in the following form:

$$B_i = \sum_{n=V-t_i+1}^{V} P(n), \tag{10}$$

where V is defined as follows:

$$V = \begin{cases} \frac{\eta_{DL}}{1+\bar{\delta}-\xi} & \text{for} \quad \text{downlink} \quad \text{direction,} \\ \frac{\eta_{UL}}{1+\delta} & \text{for} \quad \text{uplink} \quad \text{direction.} \end{cases} \tag{11}$$

In Eq. (11) η_{DL} and η_{UL} are the physical capacity of the WCDMA interface in the downlink and in the uplink direction, respectively [4].

In the proposed analytical model we assume that the arrival of a new call with a higher priority can, in the case of the lack of free resources, terminate the currently serviced connections with a lower priority. Additionally, we assume in the model:

- all classes offered to the system are designated by priorities,
- each of the classes is characterized by a different priority,
- the first class (class 1) is characterized by the highest priority, whereas the last class (class M) has the lowest priority,
- traffic from the lower priority class does not have any influence on the blocking probability of the higher priority class (i.e. separation of the classes).

The blocking probability for class i in the FAG which services j traffic classes can be calculated as follows:

$$([B_1]_j, ..., [B_i]_j) = f((a_1, t_1), ..., (a_j, t_j)), \tag{12}$$

where $j \in \{1, .., M\}$. The function f can be determined on the basis of Eqs. (8) and (10).

The following notation has been adopted in the paper: $[x_i]_j$ in which the direct index to the parameter x, i.e. i, determines the traffic class, while the index j outside the brackets denotes the number of serviced classes in the system.

3.1   Systems with Two and Three Priorities

Assume that the FAG services three classes of calls, in which the first, in line with the adopted notation, has the highest priority and second and third class has the lower and the lowest priority, respectively.

Thus, in the system with two priorities the calls of the second class (with the lower priority) do not influence the service of the calls of the first class (with the higher priority). In the system with three priorities the calls of the third class (with the lowest priority) do not influence the service of the calls of the second class (with the lower priority) and the first class (with the highest priority), and the calls of the second class do not influence the service of the calls of the first class (with the highest priority).

Consider now five systems of the FAG. The first system is assumed to service only calls with the highest priority. In the second system, without priorities, the FAG services two parallel classes of calls and the third system services three parallel classes of calls, without priorities, while the forth and fifth systems carried two and three classes of calls with priorities, respectively.

System 1. The FAG Carrying Only One Traffic Class. The blocking probability in the first system can be described in the following way:

$$[B_1]_1 = f(a_1, t_1). \tag{13}$$

After determining the blocking probability, it is possible to define the total traffic carried, i.e. the carried traffic of the first class calls:

$$[Y]_1 = [Y_1]_1 = a_1 t_1 (1 - [B_1]_1). \tag{14}$$

System 2. The FAG without Priorities Carrying Two Traffic Classes.

The blocking probabilities in the system can be calculated in the following way:

$$([B_1]_2, [B_2]_2) = f((a_1, t_1), (a_2, t_2)), \tag{15}$$

and the total traffic carried by the system:

$$[Y]_2 = \sum_{k=1}^{2} [Y_k]_2 = \sum_{k=1}^{2} a_k t_k (1 - [B_k]_2). \tag{16}$$

System 3. The FAG without Priorities Carrying Three Traffic Classes.

The blocking probabilities in the system can be calculated in the following way:

$$([B_1]_3, [B_2]_3, [B_3]_3) = f((a_1, t_1), (a_2, t_2), (a_3, t_3)), \tag{17}$$

and the total traffic carried by the system:

$$[Y]_3 = \sum_{k=1}^{3} [Y_k]_3 = \sum_{k=1}^{3} a_k t_k (1 - [B_k]_3). \tag{18}$$

In Formulas (14), (16) and (18), the parameter $[Y]_j$ determines the total traffic carried in a system servicing j classes of calls, while $[Y_i]_j$ defines the carried traffic of class i in a system servicing j classes of calls.

System 4. The FAG with Priorities Carrying Two Traffic Classes.

As it was mentioned earlier in the description of the FAG with two classes of calls and with priorities, the service of calls with the lower priority, i.e. the second class, does not influence the service of calls with the higher priority, i.e. the first class. Thus, the blocking probability and carried traffic of the first class will always be the same as in System 1, carrying one class of calls:

$$[B_1]_2^P = [B_1]_1, \tag{19}$$

and

$$[Y_1]_2^P = [Y_1]_1. \tag{20}$$

The upper index P outside the brackets in Formulas (19) and (20) indicates a system with priorities.

The operation of the system with priorities is based on the fact that calls with a higher priority, in the case of the lack of free resources, push out the calls with a lower priority, i.e. force the termination of service with a lower priority, and then occupy the resources released by the calls of a lower class. In such a mode of operation, it can be assumed that the total traffic carried in a system without priorities (System 2) is identical to the traffic carried in a system with priorities (the traffic conservation law). Thus, we can write:

$$[Y]_2^P = [Y]_2, \tag{21}$$

or

$$[Y_1]_2^P + [Y_2]_2^P = [Y]_2. \tag{22}$$

In Formula (22), the total traffic carried $[Y]_2$ in the system without priorities is known (Eq. (16)). The characteristics for the traffic of the first class with the higher priority are also known (Eqs. (19) and (20)). Hence, on the basis of Eqs. (20) and (22), traffic $[Y_2]_2^P$ can be determined in the following way:

$$[Y_2]_2^P = [Y]_2 - [Y]_1. \tag{23}$$

Let us notice that the traffic of the second class in the system with priorities is determined by the difference between the total traffic carried in the system without priorities (System 2) and the total traffic carried in the system with one class of calls (System 1). Taking into consideration the following dependency:

$$[Y_2]_2^P = a_2 t_2 (1 - [B_2]_2^P). \tag{24}$$

and substituting Eq. (24) to (23), we can determine the blocking probability for the second class of calls in the system with priorities:

$$[B_2]_2^P = \frac{a_2 t_2 - [Y_1]_2 + [Y_1]_1}{a_2 t_2}. \tag{25}$$

The formula, with Eqs. (14) and (16) taken into consideration, can be eventually written in the following form:

$$[B_2]_2^P = \frac{a_1 t_1 ([B_1]_2 - [B_1]_1) + a_2 t_2 [B_2]_2}{a_2 t_2}. \tag{26}$$

Thus, observe the fact that, similarly to the carried traffic of the second class (Eq. (23)), the blocking probability of calls of the second class (with the lower priority) can be determined on the basis of the blocking probabilities in System 1 and System 2.

System 5. The FAG with Priorities Carrying Three Traffic Classes. In the the FAG with three classes of calls and with priorities, the calls with the lowest priority, i.e. the third class, does not influence the service of calls with a higher priority, i.e. the first and the second class. The calls of the first class have the priority higher than the calls of the second class. So, the blocking probability and traffic carried for the first and the second class will always be the same as in the System 4, carrying two classes of calls with priorities:

$$[B_1]_3^P = [B_1]_2^P = [B_1]_1, \tag{27}$$

$$[Y_1]_3^P = [Y_1]_2^P = [Y_1]_1, \tag{28}$$

$$[B_2]_3^P = [B_2]_2^P. \tag{29}$$

$$[Y_2]_3^P = [Y_2]_2^P = [Y]_2 - [Y]_1. \tag{30}$$

The operation of the system with priorities is based on the fact that calls with a higher priority, in the case of the lack of free resources, push out the calls with a lower priority and it can be assumed that the total traffic carried in the system without priorities (System 3) is identical to the traffic carried in the system with priorities (the traffic conservation law). Thus, we can write:

$$[Y]_3^P = [Y]_3, \tag{31}$$

or

$$[Y_1]_3^P + [Y_2]_3^P + [Y_3]_3^P = [Y]_3. \tag{32}$$

In Formula (32), the total traffic $[Y]_3$ carried in the system without priorities is known (Eq. (18)). The characteristics for the traffic of the first and second class are also known (Eqs. (27), (28), (29) and (30)). Hence, on the basis of Eqs. (28), (30) and (32), traffic $[Y_3]_3^P$ can be determined in the following way:

$$[Y_3]_3^P = [Y]_3 - [Y]_2. \tag{33}$$

The traffic of the third class in the system with priorities is determined by the difference between the total traffic carried in the system with three classes of calls (System 3) and the total traffic carried in the system with two classes of calls (System 2). Taking into consideration the dependency:

$$[Y_3]_3^P = a_3 t_3 (1 - [B_3]_3^P). \tag{34}$$

and substituting Eq. (34) to Eq. (33), we can calculate $[B_3]_3^P$:

$$[B_3]_3^P = \frac{a_3 t_3 - [Y]_3 + [Y]_2}{a_3 t_3}. \tag{35}$$

The formula can be also written in the following form (Eqs. (16) and (18)):

$$[B_3]_3^P = \frac{a_1 t_1 ([B_1]_3 - [B_1]_2) + a_2 t_2 ([B_2]_3 - [B_2]_2) + a_3 t_3 [B_3]_3}{a_3 t_3}. \tag{36}$$

Thus, the blocking probability of calls of the third class (with the lowest priority) can be determined on the basis of the blocking probabilities in System 2 and 3.

3.2   System with n Priorities

Let us discuss FAG with priorities carrying M traffic classes. The system can be then presented as an $n-1$ step calculational algorithm, in each step, the system with two priorities is considered.

In the first step, the calls of the lowest priority (a_n), under the assumption that the remaining classes of calls $(a_1, ..., a_{n-1})$ have a higher priority and push out the calls of class n, are considered. In the successive steps, the traffic of class k (a_k) has the lowest priority, while the remaining traffic classes $(a_1, ..., a_{k-1})$ have a higher priority and can push out traffic of class k.

Hence, to facilitate similar considerations as with the case of the system with two priorities, we can determine the blocking probability for calls of class k with $M - k + 1$ priority on the basis of the following formula:

$$[B_k]_k^P = \frac{a_k t_k [B_k]_k + \sum_{i=1}^{k-1} a_i t_i \left([B_i]_k - [B_i]_{k-1}\right)}{a_k t_k}. \tag{37}$$

Following the above considerations, the algorithm for blocking probability calculations may be written as follows:

1. Calculation of offered traffic a_i of class i calls (Eq. (6)).
2. Determination of the value of L_{BBU} as the greatest common divisor (Eq. (7)).
3. Calculation of the value of t_i as the integer number of demanded resources for class i (Eq. (9)).
4. Setting up the initial value of j: $j = M$
5. Determination of the values of blocking probabilities in the FAG for j traffic classes (Eq. (12)).
6. Decreasing the value of j: $j = j - 1$, and if $j > 0$, return to step 5.
7. Determination of the values of the blocking probabilities for all traffic classes in the FAG with priorities based on (Eq. (37)).

4   Numerical Examples

The proposed analytical model of the WCDMA interface with priorities is an approximate model. Thus, the results of a analytical calculations of the WCDMA have been compared with the results of a simulation experiments.

The study was carried out for users demanding a set of services (Tab. 1) in the uplink direction and it was assumed that:

– a call of the particular services demanded $t_1 = 53$, $t_2 = 53$, $t_3 = 257$ and $t_4 = 503$ BBUs,
– the services were demanded in the following proportions:
  $a_1 t_1 : a_2 t_2 : a_3 t_3 : a_4 t_4 = 10 : 1 : 1 : 1$,
– the L_{BBU} was equal to 0.0001,
– the maximum uplink direction load were set to 50% of the theoretical capacity (Eq. (11)):

$$V_{UL} = \left\lfloor \frac{V}{L_{BBU}} \right\rfloor = \left\lfloor \frac{50\%}{0.0001} \right\rfloor = 5000 BBUs.$$

Figures 2 and 3 show the results obtained for the traffic classes presented in Tab. 1. Fig. 2 presents the results for the WCDMA radio interface which serviced a mixture of multi-rate traffic with priorities, whereas Fig. 3 shows the results for the WCDMA radio interface which serviced a mixture of the multi-rate traffic streams without priorities. The values of the blocking probabilities presented in Fig. 2 correspond to the priorities of particular classes, i.e. the higher priority, the lower value of the blocking probability. Comparing the results presented in

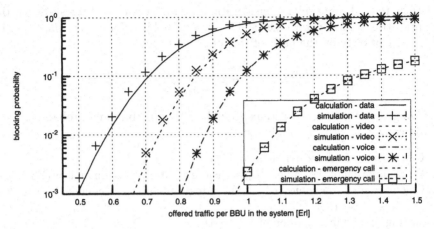

Fig. 2. Blocking probability for traffic classes presented in Tab. 1. with priorities

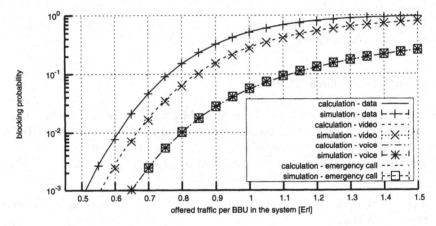

Fig. 3. Blocking probability for traffic classes presented in Tab. 1. without priorities

Figs. 2 and 3 makes it noticeable that the value of blocking probability is lower in the system with priority only for the class with the highest priority (emergency call) and the blocking probabilities for other traffic classes are higher.

The accuracy of the blocking probabilities for particular traffic classes obtained for the system with priorities is less than respective accuracy in the system without priorities. This difference results from the assumption taken on in the model with priorities, i.e. the traffic carried in the system with priorities is approximated by the traffic carried in the system without priorities. This assumption was adopted in many analytical models with priorities [16,8,9] and, as it was shown in numerous of simulation experiments, leads to acceptable, from the engineering point of view, inaccuracy. Thus, also all the results presented in Figs. 2 and 3 show the robustness of the proposed method for blocking probability calculation. The research study was carried out also for different capacities of the WCDMA interface and for different structures of the offered traffic. In each case, regardless of the offered traffic load, the results are characterized by fair accuracy.

For verification of the analytical results a simulation program based on the Monte Carlo method [17] was used. The simulator of the full-availability group servicing multi-rate traffic with and without priorities was implemented in C++ language. Each point of the plot shown in Figs. 2 and 3 is the average value of blocking probabilities obtained in 5 series. In particular simulation series 10^7 of the incomming calls of the "oldest"[2] class were offered. The results of the simulations are shown in the charts in the form of marks with 95% confidence intervals calculated after the t-Student distribution. 95% confidence intervals of the simulation are almost included within the marks plotted in the figures.

5   Conclusions

The dimensioning process for the UMTS system should aim at determining such a capacity of the elements of the system that will allow to, with the pre-defined load of the system, ensure the assumed level of the Grade of Service. In the dimensioning of the UMTS system, one of the most important characteristics is the radio interface which can use priorities for services. The importance of the implementation of priorities in the UMTS network, increases with the volume of the load carried by the network. The priorities in the UMTS system are used for determining the sequence in resource allocations. A decision on the priority of a given service is made by the operator of the UMTS network who defines its importance in the core network. Thus, the defined priority is carried out, by admission/congestion control for Relase 99 [1] and scheduling for High Speed Downlink Packet Access (HSDPA) [11] mechanisms, in the WCDMA interface.

The paper presents a new analytical model which allows blocking probability determination for different traffic classes with priorities offered to the WCDMA interface. In the proposed model we assume that the arrival of a new call with a higher priority can, in the case of the fully occupied resources, terminate the connections with a lower priority. In our considerations we use a new model of the full-availability group with priorities for multi-rate traffic as a model of the interface. The calculations are validated by simulation. The proposed method can be easily applied to 3G network capacity calculations for the uplink and the downlink directions.

References

1. Holma, H., Toskala, A.: WCDMA for UMTS. Radio Access For Third Generation Mobile Communications. John Wiley and Sons, Ltd., Chichester (2000)
2. Staehle, D., Mäder, A.: An analytic approximation of the uplink capacity in a UMTS network with heterogeneous traffic. In: Proccedings of 18th International Teletraffic Congress (ITC18), Berlin, pp. 81–91 (2003)

---

[2] The class which demands the highest number of BBUs.

3. Kwon, Y.S., Kim, N.: Capacity and cell coverage based on calculation of the erlang capacity in a WCDMA system with multi-rate traffic. IEICE Transactions on
   Communications E87-B(8), 2397–2400 (2004)
4. Stasiak, M., Wiśniewski, A., Zwierzykowski, P.: Blocking probability calculation in
   the uplink direction for cellular systems with WCDMA radio interface. In: Buchholtz, P., Lehnert, R., Pióro, M. (eds.) Proceedings of 3rd Polish-German Teletraffic
   Symposium, Dresden, Germany, pp. 65–74. VDE Verlag GMBH, Berlin (2004)
5. Głąbowski, M., Stasiak, M., Wiśniewski, A., Zwierzykowski, P.: Uplink blocking
   probability calculation for cellular systems with WCDMA radio interface and finite source population. In: Kouvatsos, D. (ed.) Proceedings of 2nd International
   Working Conference on Performance Modelling and Evaluation of Heterogeneous
   Networks (HET-NETs), Ilkley, Networks UK, pp. 80/1–80/10 (2004)
6. Głąbowski, M., Stasiak, M., Wiśniewski, A., Zwierzykowski, P.: Uplink blocking
   probability calculation for cellular systems with WCDMA radio interface, finite
   source population and differently loaded neighbouring cells. In: Proceedings of
   Asia-Pacific Conference on Communications, Perth, pp. 138–142 (2005)
7. Koo, I., Kim, K.: Erlang capacity of multi-service multi-access systems with a
   limited number of channel elements according to separate and common operations.
   IEICE Transactions on Communications E89-B(11), 3065–3074 (2006)
8. Subramaniam, K., Nilsson, A.A.: An analytical model for adaptive call admission
   control scheme in a heterogeneous UMTS-WCDMA system. In: Proceedings of
   International Conference on Communications, vol. 5, pp. 3334–3338 (2005)
9. Subramaniam, K., Nilsson, A.A.: Tier-based analytical model for adaptive call
   admission cntrol scheme in a UMTS-WCDMA system. In: Proceedings of Vehicular
   Technology Conference, vol. 4, pp. 2181–2185 (2005)
10. Stasiak, M., Wiśniewski, A., Zwierzykowski, P.: Uplink and downlink blocking
    probability calculation for cellular systems with WCDMA radio interface and finite
    source population. In: Proceedings of 14th Polish Teletraffic Symposium, Gliwice,
    Poland, pp. 99–110. Institute of Theoretical and Applied Informatics of the Polish
    Academy of Sciences (2007)
11. Holma, H., Toskala, A.: HSDPA/HSUPA for UMTS: High Speed Radio Access for
    Mobile Communications. Wiley and Sons, Chichester (2006)
12. Laiho, J., Wacker, A., Novosad, T.: Radio Network Planning and Optimization for
    UMTS, 2nd edn. John Wiley and Sons, Ltd., Chichester (2006)
13. Roberts, J., Mocci, V., Virtamo, I. (eds.): Broadband Network Teletraffic, Final
    Report of Action COST 242. Commission of the European Communities. Springer,
    Berlin (1996)
14. Kaufman, J.: Blocking in a shared resource environment. IEEE Transactions on
    Communications 29(10), 1474–1481 (1981)
15. Roberts, J.: A service system with heterogeneous user requirements—application
    to multi-service telecommunications systems. In: Pujolle, G. (ed.) Proceedings of
    Performance of Data Communications Systems and their Applications, pp. 423–
    431. North Holland, Amsterdam (1981)
16. Katzschner, L.: Loss sytstems with displacing priorities. In: Proccedings of 6th In-
    ternational Teletraffic Congress (ITC6), Munchen, Germany, pp. 224II–224 (1970)
17. Rubinstein, R.Y., Kroese, D.P.: Simulation and the Monte Carlo Method, 2nd edn.
    Wiley Series in Probability and Statistics. Wiley-Interscience, Chichester (2007)

Performance Analysis of Dynamic Priority Shifting

Philipp Reinecke, Katinka Wolter, and Johannes Zapotoczky

Humboldt-Universität zu Berlin
Institut für Informatik
Berlin, Germany
{preineck,wolter,jzapotoc}@informatik.hu-berlin.de

Abstract. We investigate the benefit of priority shifting for resource allocation in systems with a shared resource, where higher priority implies better service. Priority schemes where priority levels are assigned fixed shares of the resource experience underutilisation if there are only low-priority tasks present. In these situations, lower priority tasks can be 'shifted up' to higher priority. This increases overall system utilisation and improves the service experienced by low-priority tasks. We present a shifting framework, study its properties and develop a Petri net model for a shifting algorithm. We analyse the model in order to identify situations where shifting of priorities is beneficial.

1 Introduction

Dynamic priority assignment is a well-known concept from real-time systems where a schedule is defined according to the priorities of all jobs in the system. A job's priority typically is set to assure that the deadline is met [1]. In pursuit of this target task priorities may be modified during runtime of the task, shifting priorities up and down. A characteristic of real-time systems is that resources are used up to full capacity at all times and the resource share provided to an individual task is not constant over time.

The systems considered in this paper also employ dynamic priority assignment and dynamic resource allocation. However, they are different from real-time systems in several respects. Priorities implement differences in requirements of e.g. different applications, and may correlate with a difference in the price paid for a task's execution. Priority assignment typically is intended to be constant for each task, and no mechanisms for re-allocation of unused resources exist. As a consequence, the systems do not always fully utilise their available resources.

In such systems manipulation of priorities may be beneficial, as it not only can improve the service provided to individual tasks but may also prevent resource underutilisation.

Looking at different types of resource-sharing systems we want to identify those that are amenable to manipulation of priorities. Computer networks are an example as they share communication channels among several users. While in wired networks today the transmission capacity is no longer a scarce resource

N. Thomas and C. Juiz (Eds.): EPEW 2008, LNCS 5261, pp. 181–196, 2008.

that needs to be allocated carefully, in wireless networks this is still often the case. The different wireless technologies use different resource allocation mechanisms. While UMTS and Bluetooth always distribute all available transmission capacity [2,3], the Quality-of-Service (QoS) enabled extension of wireless LAN has a fixed, priority-based medium access mechanism that does not necessarily use all available channel capacity [4]. Another area where there may be interest in priority shifting could be computational grids, where tasks are assigned to nodes in the grid following some assignment scheme [5,6]. One may want to consider different priority classes of tasks that are assigned to nodes of different computational power. The bronze/silver/gold priority classes considered here present an example for adaptive, pricing-based task assignment in computational grids.

In general, we assume that agents execute jobs using a shared resource, such as a communication link. The agent's priority determines the access to the shared resource. A higher priority implies more aggressive access to the resource. Lower priorities do not make use of all available resource capacity, leaving room for higher priority access. If no high priority jobs are present in the system, some share of the resource remains unused and one may consider shifting all jobs up in priority. This indeed increases resource utilisation and in many cases service quality for the jobs [7,8]. We extend the work already presented in [7] by providing a general theoretical treatment of priority shifting and deriving a set of criteria for priority shifting. Furthermore, we present a Petri net model of a shifting algorithm. Although the IEEE 802.11e WLAN standard serves as an illustrating example for the application of the model, the Petri net is not limited to this protocol and may be employed in the evaluation of priority shifting algorithms in general.

This paper is structured as follows: In Section 2 we present a general definition of priority shifting in an arbitrary context, discuss limitations and derive a set of criteria for the applicability of priority shifting. We then review two instances where priorities are used to provide differing levels of service. In Section 3 we present a stochastic Petri net model for priority shifting. We employ this model in an analysis of priority shifting in the IEEE 802.11e WLAN standard [4] as an example. A summary and an outlook on future work conclude the paper.

2   Priority Shifting

Priority schemes are employed in many resource sharing scenarios. The schemes we consider aim to assure a certain QoS standard for tasks with higher priority by providing them with privileged access to the shared resource. Assigning a static quantum of the resource to higher priorities may in the absence of high priority tasks result in underutilisation of the resource. Then, better QoS may be provided to lower-priority tasks by shifting them into the vacant higher priorities. The approach we study here maintains the relative order of priorities, i.e. tasks can only be shifted to priorities not occupied by higher priority tasks, and tasks cannot overtake occupied higher priorities.

We formalise the problem as follows: Given $K+1$ priority classes $0, 1, \ldots, K$, the vector $M_N = (m_0, m_1, \ldots, m_K)$ represents the assignment of $N = \sum_{i=0}^{K} m_i$ tasks to the $K+1$ priority classes, and $\mathcal{M}_N$ is the set of all possible assignments for N tasks.

We use stochastic ordering [9] on the set of task–priority assignments $\mathcal{M}_N$ to define successful shifts:

$$M_N \leq_{\mathrm{st}} M_N' : \quad \Leftrightarrow \quad 1 - \Pr\{M_N \leq K - k\} \leq 1 - \Pr\{M_N' \leq K - k\}$$
$$\text{for } k = 0, \ldots, K,$$

where

$$\Pr\{M_N \leq K - k\} := \frac{\sum_{i=0}^{k} m_{K-i}}{N} .$$

Let $s_k(M_N)$ denote the level of service provided to each priority class k, given that the N tasks are assigned to priorities as specified by M_N. Priorities are strictly ordered by their level of service and listed in descending order, that is, $\forall k : \ s_{k+1}(M_N) < s_k(M_N)$. This implies that 0 and K are the highest and lowest priorities, respectively. The total service provided is denoted by $S := \sum_{k=0}^{K} m_k s_k(M_N)$. In the following we assume that all service functions s_k grow monotonously in M_N, i.e. that for all $M_N, M_N' \in \mathcal{M}_N$:

$$M_N \leq_{\mathrm{st}} M_N' \Rightarrow \forall k : \ s_k(M_N) \leq s_k(M_N') .$$

Furthermore, let $R(M_N)$ denote the total resource utilisation for N tasks allocated to priorities as given in M_N. The definition of R obviously depends on the scenario. In the following we consider R only in terms of some of its properties.

We discuss priority shifting in terms of a *shift* operator defined on the set of task allocations $\mathcal{M}_N$. We will start with the following abstract definition of a shifting operator:

$$\mathrm{shift}(M_N^1) \in \{M_N^2 \in \mathcal{M}_N \mid M_N^1 \leq_{\mathrm{st}} M_N^2\} ,$$

which denotes an operator returning a set of stochastically greater or equal task allocations for a given allocation M_N^1.

Example 1. Let us illustrate these concepts using a small example: For $K = 4$ (i.e. 5 priorities) and $N = 6$, $M_6^1 = (0, 2, 3, 0, 1)$, $M_6^2 = (2, 3, 0, 1, 0)$ and $M_6^3 = (3, 2, 0, 0, 1)$ are potential allocations. We observe that $M_6^1 \leq_{\mathrm{st}} M_6^2$, since:

$$1 - Pr\{M_6^1 \leq 0\} = 1 - 1/6 = 5/6 \qquad\qquad 1 - Pr\{M_6^2 \leq 0\} = 1$$
$$1 - Pr\{M_6^1 \leq 1\} = 1 - 1/6 = 5/6 \qquad 1 - Pr\{M_6^2 \leq 1\} = 1 - 1/6 = 5/6$$
$$1 - Pr\{M_6^1 \leq 2\} = 1 - 4/6 = 1/3 \qquad\qquad 1 - Pr\{M_6^2 \leq 2\} = 5/6$$
$$1 - Pr\{M_6^1 \leq 3\} = 1 - 6/6 = 0 \qquad 1 - Pr\{M_6^2 \leq 3\} = 1 - 4/6 = 1/3$$
$$1 - Pr\{M_6^1 \leq 4\} = 0 \qquad\qquad 1 - Pr\{M_6^2 \leq 4\} = 0 .$$

On the other hand, the stochastic order does not hold for M_6^2 and M_6^3:

$$1 - Pr\{M_6^3 \leq 0\} = \,^5\!/_6$$
$$1 - Pr\{M_6^3 \leq 1\} = \,^5\!/_6 \qquad 1 - Pr\{M_6^3 \leq 3\} = 1 - \,^3\!/_6 = \,^1\!/_2$$
$$1 - Pr\{M_6^3 \leq 2\} = \,^5\!/_6 \qquad 1 - Pr\{M_6^3 \leq 4\} = 0,$$

i.e. for $k = 4$, $1 - Pr\{M_6^2 \leq K - k\} > 1 - Pr\{M_6^3 \leq K - k\}$. Consequently, M_6^3 cannot be derived from M_6^2 in a regular shift, i.e. $M_6^3 \notin \text{shift}(M_6^2)$. Note that $M_6^1 \leq_{\text{st}} M_6^2$ and $M_6^1 \leq_{\text{st}} M_6^3$ but $M_6^2 \not\leq_{\text{st}} M_6^3$. □

2.1   Applicability Criteria

To ease the further discussion we stipulate a set of criteria for priority schemes in which priority shifting is applicable:

1. Several parties contend for access to a shared resource. Access is regulated by fixed priorities assigned to the parties.
2. There is no mechanism to redistribute unused service capacity to jobs from other priorities. Formally, this means that for a task allocation M_N there exists another allocation $M_N' \in \text{shift}(M_N)$, $M_N <_{\text{st}} M_N'$ that provides a higher total level of service $S(M_N') > S(M_N)$.
3. Resource use incurs no or only marginal external costs. This is required because usually resource utilisation grows monotonously in M_N. i.e. $M_N \leq_{\text{st}} M_N' \Rightarrow R(M_N) \leq R(M_N')$ and higher priority implies higher resource usage. Obviously, the increased resource utilisation that results from providing better service must not increase the costs of the service, otherwise cost would need to be an additional parameter in priority shifting algorithms.
4. The overhead of shifting is negligible. This is particularly important where tasks may enter or leave the system at any time, i.e. where shifting (to provide better service to low-priority tasks) and unshifting (to guarantee a high level of service to newly arriving high-priority tasks) may happen frequently.

2.2   Interesting Properties of Shift Operators

Before providing constructive definitions for two shift operators, we will first discuss a number of interesting properties of shift operators in general. First, we may be interested in whether the shifting operator preserves 'gaps' between occupied priorities. For an allocation M_N, let

$$Z_N := \{i \mid m_i = 0; i = 0, \dots, K\}$$

denote the set of priorities which are empty in M_N, i.e. those priorities at which no task is being served. In our running example $Z_6^1 = \{0, 3\}$. We call a shifting algorithm *gap-preserving*, if and only if it preserves the length of gaps between occupied priorities, that is, iff for all $M_N^2 \in \text{shift}(M_N^1)$

$$Z^2 = \{i + \sigma \mid i \in Z^1\}$$

holds (where σ is the number of steps of the shift).

The gap preservation property also touches upon the question whether tasks are shifted *'en bloc'* or *'one by one.'* With 'en bloc' shifting, all tasks from one priority are shifted up at once, whereas 'one by one' shifting is performed for one task at a time and only eventually results in all tasks at the higher priority.

Finally, an interesting property is the distance tasks jump up (or down) in the priorities. Shifting occurs in *one-step* fashion if tasks move by only one priority level at a time, and in *skip* (or n-step) fashion else ($\sigma = 1$ and $\sigma > 1$, respectively, for a gap-preserving operator).

2.3   Some Shift Operators

We will first define an atomic one-step shift operator. Atomic one-step shifting is the shifting of one task to the next higher free neighbouring priority. Atomic n-step shifting then consists in a sequence of several one-step shifts at once.

The atomic one-step shifting does not violate the stochastic order of the shifting procedure as we will briefly show. Let $M_N^1 = (m_0, \ldots, m_j, m_{j+1}, \ldots, m_K)$. Then the one-step shifted configuration is $M_N^2 = (m_0, \ldots, m_j + 1, m_{j+1} - 1, \ldots, m_K)$ and we have to show that $M^1 \leq_{\text{st}} M^2$. We do so by showing that

$$\Pr\left\{M_N^2 \leq K - k\right\} \leq \Pr\left\{M_N^1 \leq K - k\right\} .$$

For the unshifted and the shifted vector we need to compute

$$\left(\frac{\sum_{i=0}^k m_{K-i}}{N}\right)_{k=1,\ldots,K} .$$

For $k < K - j$ the two vectors are identical. The first term we consider is therefore m_{j+1}, where $k = K - (j+1)$ and

$$\Pr\left\{M_N^2 \leq (j+1)\right\} = \frac{\sum_{i=0}^{K-(j+1)} m_{K-i}^2}{N} =$$

$$\frac{\sum_{i=0}^{K-(j+1)} m_{K-i}^1 - 1}{N} \leq \Pr\left\{M_N^1 \leq (j+1)\right\} .$$

Similarly, for m_j, where $k = K - j$ we can easily see that

$$\Pr\left\{M_N^2 \leq j\right\} = \frac{\sum_{i=0}^{K-j} m_{K-i}^2}{N} =$$

$$\frac{\sum_{i=0}^{K-(j+2)} m_{K-i}^1 + (m_{j+1}^1 - 1) + (m_j^1 + 1)}{N} = \frac{\sum_{i=0}^{K-j} m_{K-i}^1}{N} = \Pr\left\{M_N^1 \leq j\right\} .$$

For all $k > K - j$ we have $m_k^1 = m_k^2$ again and thus the stochastic order holds. The atomic n-step shift can be defined as a sequence of atomic one-step shifts, which again does not violate the stochastic order.

Second, we define a gap-preserving, 'en-bloc', one-step shift operator: Let Z_N be defined as above. If $0 \in Z_N^1$ (i.e. the highest priority is empty), we can move

all tasks up by one priority, or, alternatively, shift all zeros in the index list down
by one:

$$Z_N^2 := \{i+1 \mid i \in Z_N^1, i < K\} \ .$$

The one-step shift-operator is thus defined as

$$M_N^2 = \text{shift}(M_N^1) := (m_0^2, m_1^2, \ldots, m_K^2),$$

where

$$m_i^2 = \begin{cases} m_{i+1}^1 & i < K \\ 0 & i = K \end{cases} \ .$$

It is obvious from this definition that $M_N^1 \leq_{\text{st}} M_N^2$:

$$1 - Pr\{M_N^1 \leq K - k\} = 1 - \frac{\sum_{i=0}^{k} m_{K-i}^1}{N} \leq 1 - \left[\frac{\sum_{i=0}^{k-1} m_{K-i}^1}{N} + 0\right] =$$

$$1 - \frac{\sum_{i=0}^{k} m_{K-i}^2}{N} = 1 - Pr\{M_N^2 \leq K - k\},$$

i.e. the before/after pairs M_N^1, M_N^2 generated by this operator can always be
ordered using stochastic ordering.

A skip-fashion operator can be constructed by repeated application of the
one-step operator and restricting the output to allocations M_N^l in which the
highest priority is occupied, i.e. $0 \notin Z_N^l$.

2.4   IEEE 802.11e WLAN Access Categories

The IEEE 802.11e standard [4] for quality of service enhanced wireless LAN
offers both contention-based and contention-free channel access strategies similar to the original standard IEEE 802.11 [10]. As it is more common, we will
only consider the contention-based enhanced distributed channel access (EDCA),
however, priority shifting may also be applied to the contention-free strategy.

IEEE 802.11e EDCA defines four access categories (for Voice, Video, Best
Effort and Background transmission). The standard implements the priorities
by a dedicated choice of parameter values for the different access categories.
Medium access is primarily determined by the values of the arbitration inter-
frame space (AIFS), the time a station needs to wait before transmitting to
a free channel, and the contention window size, from which the backoff timer,
used to avoid collisions, is randomly drawn. Those two parameters determine
the differing length of idle times for the different priorities, which is the cause
for varying throughput across priorities.

Priority-based medium access as defined in IEEE 802.11e corresponds nicely
to our set of criteria:

1. In a wireless LAN, typically several stations contend for access on the wireless
   medium. The parameters for QoS implementation on the CSMA-CA scheme
   are fixed and prescribed in the standard.

2. If the access category with highest priority (voice) is not used, this has no effect on the parameters or distribution of the other access categories.
3. Usage of WLAN resources, irrespective of possible costs on a backbone to other networks, typically incurs no external costs.
4. The overhead of shifting depends on the shifting strategy and on the number of participating stations. The non-invasive mechanism proposed in [7] uses the type-of-service (TOS) field in the IP header, which is interpreted by 802.11e-capable WLAN drivers. Setting the TOS field, however, involves only a negligible delay.

Without using the highest priority, not the full capacity will be utilised. Based on this observation, [11,7] propose approaches for dynamic priority shifting. The interesting question is, of course, whether priority shifting is beneficial to the service of individual stations and the network as a whole. Of course, this depends on the priorities used by stations in the network. It also depends on the number of stations in the network. Higher priorities have on the average less waiting times and therefore a higher probability of collision for the same number of active stations in the network. At some point more frequent collisions cancel out the benefit of lower waiting times.

The service capacity $\hat{S}$ has no proportional partitioning in 802.11e. The distribution of $\hat{S}$ among configurations M_N of N stations depends primarily on the access category-specific QoS parameters (AIFS and the backoff time).

In [12] an analytical model for the probability of successfully transmitting data is formulated for two priority classes. This model would have to be generalised to all four priority classes and could then be used to determine the channel throughput as service function s_k. However, combinatorial complexity makes this a challenging task which we leave for future work.

In this paper we adopt an empirical approach and approximate the service function for the IEEE 802.11e protocol by fitting a curve to simulation data (cf. (1) in Section 4).

2.5   Economic Feasibility of Priority Shifting

In some settings, providers offer higher priorities at a higher price. For instance, $2/3$ and $2/9$ of the available service capacity $\hat{S}$ may be reserved for gold and silver customers (priorities 0 and 1), respectively, while the rest ($1/9\hat{S}$) is available for bronze customers. All customers in one class share the capacity equally, e.g. a gold customer receives service $s_0 = 2/3m_0\hat{S}$. The provider prices services according to the allocated resources: Bronze service is provided free of charge, while silver and gold services are progressively more expensive.

Then, an interesting question is: Is it economically feasible for the provider to apply shifting to improve customer satisfaction? That is: Why should any customer pay for the service if (due to shifting) the same may be available for free? Let us consider the case that we have m_{00} gold customers that would pay, and m_{20} customers who enjoy gold service, but are not willing to pay. That is, the m_{20} customers are satisfied with whatever service they get. Then, the

potential gold customers have an incentive to pay for gold service if they receive
better service being served at gold priority, exclusively:

$$\frac{2}{3(m_{00} + m_{20})}\hat{S} < \frac{2}{3m_{00}}\hat{S},$$

which is obviously the case for $m_{20} > 0$, which implies that as soon as one
free-rider is present in the system, gold customers have an incentive to pay. In
contrast, consider silver customers (m_{11}) enjoying gold service together with a
number of non-paying customers (m_{20}):

$$\frac{2}{3(m_{11} + m_{20})}\hat{S} < \frac{2}{9m_{11}}\hat{S}.$$

Here, $m_{20} > 2m_{11}$, i.e. potential silver customers will prefer to pay for silver
service only if there are more than twice as many free-riders than potential
silver customers present.

3   The Petri Net Model

In order to analyse dynamic priority shifting we use a stochastic Petri net
model of a shifting algorithm for four priorities. We employ the Petri net tool
TimeNET [13] in the construction and analysis of the model. Since the full model
is too complex for inclusion here, we discuss its structure using a simplified two-
priority version and refer the reader to the appendix for the full model.

Figure 1 presents the simplified model. We model tasks as tokens and priority
levels as places. The parameter N gives the maximum number of tasks. There
are three kinds of places: waiting places (upper centre) model a waiting state
that tasks enter if they cannot be served at their nominal priority. This situation occurs when the nominal priority is occupied or blocked by a shifted lower
priority task. Tasks executed at their nominal priority are modelled as markings
on normal places. Shifted places (lower centre) model shifted tasks.

We distinguish transitions according to their function. First, the enter and
depart transitions (upper left and centre left, respectively) model tasks entering and leaving the system. There is one enter transition for each priority level.
Since tasks can depart if they are being served at their normal priorities and at
any of the shifted priorities, there is one depart transition assigned to each of
the places modelling task execution at a certain priority. The shift and unshift
transitions (lower left and upper right) model the shifting and unshifting of tasks.
Shifting transitions move tasks from lower to higher priorities whenever higher
priorities are not occupied. These transitions are connected to the respective
higher-priority places by inhibitor arcs, to ensure that tasks neither overtake
each other nor move to priorities occupied by higher-priority tasks. Unshifting
transitions move shifted lower-priority tasks down to their waiting priority level
if higher-priority tasks enter. The assign transitions (lower right) assign tasks
from the waiting state to their nominal priorities, as soon as the nominal priorities are available (again accomplished by inhibitor arcs).

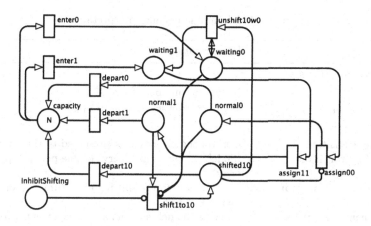

Fig. 1. Petri net model for priority shifting using two priorities

In the full model (see the appendix), places and transitions are grouped into separate blocks according to their function. Note that the lowest priority does not feature a waiting state.

3.1 Model Parameters

Table 1 presents an overview of the model parameters and their interpretation. We will discuss these parameters according to the model aspects they affect. We start with the parameters controlling the basic functionality of the system, i.e. the execution of tasks: The marking N on the `Capacity` place models the maximum number of tasks in the system. The firing delays of the entering transitions control the number of tasks in the system as well as the ratio between tasks of different priorities. Delays of the departing transitions model how fast tasks are completed at their nominal priority (i.e. without shifting).

All other parameters control the model of the shifting algorithm. Firing delays of the shifting and unshifting transitions and the assignment transitions model overhead during shifting and unshifting. The delay of the `depart10` transition models how fast tasks are executed when shifted to a higher priority (for instance, tasks of priority 1 may finish faster when shifted to priority 0). Finally, the marking on the `InhibitShifting` place controls whether the shifting algorithm is applied at all. The parameter values are discussed with the model analysis in Section 4.

3.2 Model Characteristics and Limitations

The Petri net employed here models a non-gap-preserving shifting algorithm with random atomic n-step shifting. That is, each individual task is shifted on its own and the target priority is selected randomly with uniform probability

Table 1. Model parameters and interpretation

Parameter	Interpretation
Markings and places	
N	Maximum number of tasks.
InhibitShifting	Controls whether shifting is applied.
Delays	
Entering transitions	Control the priority mix presented to the system.
Departing transitions	Model the job length (service time per task per priority).
Shifting/Unshifting transitions	Model delays in the shifting algorithm, e.g. management overhead.
Assignment transitions	Used to model additional management overhead during assignment of higher priority tasks.

from all available higher priorities. From there the task will eventually arrive at the highest free priority.

We chose a non-gap-preserving model since its structure is still relatively simple. Even for this model numerical complexity only allows for an analysis with up to 7 stations. We also constructed a version of the model wherein all lower-priority tasks are shifted at the same time (using marking-dependent arcs), i.e. an 'en bloc' shifting operator. Unfortunately, technical difficulties precluded an analysis of this model.

Job Length Distribution. The length of jobs presented to the system can be adjusted through the rates of the **depart** transitions. However, it should be noted that when using the shifting algorithm the actual job length in the model does not follow an exponential distribution, even though the **depart** transitions have exponentially distributed delays. This is a result of the shifting and unshifting, which results in the **depart** transitions losing their activation before expiry of the firing delay. While we cannot delve into a detailed examination of the phenomenon here, preliminary results suggest that job lengths are best described by cyclic continuous-time phase-type distributions (CPH) of increasing order for lower priorities. Analysis and parameter fitting of the CPHs would be necessary to determine (or set) the precise job length distribution.

4   Analysis

We employ the model in a case study of priority shifting in an IEEE 802.11e wireless LAN. In order to do so, we must determine values for each of the parameters listed in Table 1. We arbitrarily assume a delay of 1 s for all shifting/unshifting and assignment transitions. We consider transmissions with a mean length of 100 s in all access categories (i.e. transmissions do not finish faster

Table 2. Priority Mixes for IEEE 802.11e Priority Shifting Analysis

	λ_{enter0}	λ_{enter1}	λ_{enter2}	λ_{enter3}
P_1	$^{10}/_{16}$	$^{3}/_{16}$	$^{2}/_{16}$	$^{1}/_{16}$
P_2	$^{1}/_{4}$	$^{1}/_{4}$	$^{1}/_{4}$	$^{1}/_{4}$
P_3	$^{1}/_{16}$	$^{2}/_{16}$	$^{3}/_{16}$	$^{10}/_{16}$

when executed at higher priority, which is reasonable for e.g. video streams). Since the most powerful available machine (having 16 AMD64 CPUs and 32GB RAM) was only able to solve up to a few thousand states, we could only analyse the model for $N = 1, \ldots, 7$ stations.

We study three priority mixes, modelled by the rates of the entering transitions, as shown in Table 2. The first mix (P_1) is dominated by high-priority stations, while the third mix consists mostly of low-priority stations. The second mix represents an equal distribution of stations across priorities. Note that the nominal total arrival rate of all three mixes is equal to 1.

Reward Definition. Rewards in the model correspond to the service functions s_k in the WLAN scenario. These service functions measure the throughput achievable by a station in the kth category. As discussed in Subsection 2.4, the service functions depend on the contention window and the AIFS for each priority level k as well as on the number of stations using each priority.

We derived the service function in category k, s_k, as a function of the number of stations N, as follows: Using the ns-2 network simulator [14], we simulated one station sending at category k, and $N-1$ stations transmitting at the highest priority (Voice), for $N = 1, \ldots, 10$. This provides a lower bound for the throughput achievable by the station sending at category k. Figure 2 presents the throughput for the station sending at category k. Note that each of the throughput curves (one for each category k) in Figure 2 can be approximated by an exponential function of the number of stations, N. We thus define the service function for one station at priority k as

$$s_k(M_N) := \alpha e^{-\beta N}, \qquad (1)$$

where we fit the parameters α and β using curve fitting in Gnuplot [15]. Curve parameters are shown in Figure 2. The overall reward is then defined as the sum of the service obtained by all stations:

$$S := \sum_{i=0}^{K} \left[\sum_{j=i+1}^{K} E[\#\text{shifted}_{ji}]s_i(M_N) + E[\#\text{normal}_i]s_i(M_N) \right],$$

where $\#\text{shifted}_{ji}$ and $\#\text{normal}_i$ denote the number of tokens on the respective places in the model. Note that the service function is strictly monotonous in M_N.

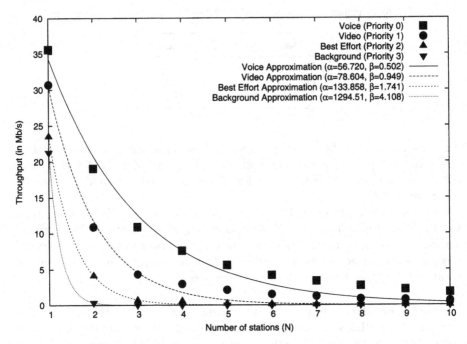

Fig. 2. Simulation throughput and approximating service functions

4.1   Results

Figure 3 shows accumulated throughput for the three priority mixes, with and without shifting. We observe that shifting increases the throughput for all priority mixes. The largest increase occurs with P_3, in which there are only a few stations in the voice category. The increase is considerably smaller with P_2, where stations are distributed evenly over the priority categories, and rather small with P_1, which contains mostly high-priority stations. The small benefit from shifting with P_1 is expected, since in P_1 most stations are already at the highest priority. In contrast, P_3 has most stations at the lowest priority. These stations may then be shifted up to priority 0, whereby their throughput increases significantly. Because of space limitations we omit detailed results for individual priorities here.

We also note that the accumulated throughput decreases with a growing number of stations. This is to be expected, since with an increase in the number of stations collisions become more likely, and thus throughput drops, as can be observed in the service functions (Figure 2). Furthermore, the benefit from shifting shrinks as well. This is due to the decreasing number of opportunities for shifting. That is, the more stations there are in the system, the less likely it becomes that higher priorities are empty and shifting can take place. In fact, for $N \to \infty$, we expect the curves for shifting to converge to those without shifting. As a rule of thumb, we conclude from our model that in a network with more than 5 stations

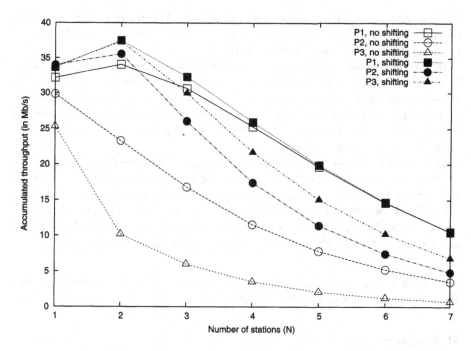

Fig. 3. Accumulated throughput without and with shifting

mainly using high priorities (such as configuration P_1) shifting is not beneficial, even if stations would have the opportunity to do so. For an evenly distributed priority mix (such as P_2) we can deduce that the limit where shifting does no longer pay off is at roughly 8 stations, and from the shape of the curves in Figure 3 we assume that in a network with predominantly low priorities shifting is useful for up to 10 stations at least.

5   Conclusion and Further Work

In this work we formalised priority shifting and presented criteria for its applicability. We illustrated the criteria on the IEEE 802.11e priority scheme. We then presented a stochastic Petri net model for the evaluation of a shifting operator. The model was parametrised for an analysis of the IEEE 802.11e priority scheme. Analysis results show that shifting is beneficial in this scenario, although the magnitude of the benefit depends on the priority mix present, and on the number of stations in the system. Both observations are not surprising as such, but our analysis provides concrete results. We can determine the number of stations up to which priority shifting is beneficial for a given priority mix. In a network with 10 or more stations shifting should only be applied if the network is used primarily by low priority stations, such as demonstrated in configuration P_3. With less than 5 stations shifting is beneficial even if high-priority stations are quite dominant, such as in our configuration P_1. When stations equally likely use any of the priorities a network with up to 7 stations, as we solved for in this analysis, still benefits from priority shifting.

In the future, we want to analyse models with a larger number of stations. In order to be able to do so we will either need a more powerful machine or an algorithm especially tailored for large Markov chains. As an interesting application domain we want to investigate whether the gold, silver, bronze categories for resource allocation with dynamic priority shifting can be applied to resource allocation in computational grids.

One important aspect of further work in the development of shifting algorithms is the monotonicity of the service functions: For simplicity, we assumed that service functions grow monotonously for stochastically larger task allocations M_N. However, in many scenarios this may not be the case, i.e. there may be stochastically larger task allocations that result in lower service. Appropriate shifting algorithms for these scenarios must avoid such allocations.

Acknowledgement. This work has been supported by the German Science Foundation (DFG) under grant Wo 898/1-2 and Wo 898/2-1.

References

1. Kopetz, H.: Real-Time Systems Design Principles for Distributed Embedded Applications. Springer, Heidelberg (1997)
2. Bhatia, R., Segall, A., Zussman, G.: Analysis of Bandwidth Allocation Algorithms for Wireless Personal Area Networks. ACM/Springer Wireless Networks (WINET) 12(5), 589–603 (2006)
3. Terré, M., Vivier, E., Fino, B.: Optimisation of Downlink Resource Allocation Algorithms for UMTS Networks. EURASIP Journal on Wireless Communication and Networking 5(4), 573–578 (2005)
4. IEEE 802.11 Working Group: Part 11: Wireless LAN Medium Access Control (MAC) and Physical Layer (PHY) specifications. Amendment 8: Medium Access Control (MAC) Quality of Service Enhancements (802.11e) (last seen June 6, 2008), http://www.ieee802.org/11/
5. Wolski, R., Brevik, J., Plank, J., Bryan, T.: Grid resource allocation and control using computational economies. In: Berman, F., Fox, G., Hey, T. (eds.) Grid Computing: Making the Global Infrastructure a Reality, pp. 747–772. Wiley and Sons, Chichester (2003)
6. Wolski, R., Obertelli, G., Allen, M., Nurmi, D., Brevik, J.: Predicting Grid Resource Performance On-line. In: Handbook of Innovative Computing: Models, Enabling Technologies, and Applications. Springer, Heidelberg (2005)
7. Zapotoczky, J., Wolter, K.: Increasing Performance of the 802.11e Protocol through Access Category Shifting. In: Proc. International Conference on Quantitative Evaluation of Systems (MMB 2008), Dortmund, Germany, pp. 195–204 (2008)
8. Zhao, Y., Tavares, C.: Network adaptive priority management in wireless local area networks, USPTO Application No. 20070258419, Palo Alto, CA, US (2007)
9. Szekli, R.: Stochastic Ordering and Dependence in Applied Probability. Springer, Heidelberg (1995)

10. IEEE 802.11 Working Group: Part 11: Wireless LAN Medium Access Control (MAC) and Physical Layer (PHY) specifications (last seen June 6, 2008), http://www.ieee802.org/11/
11. Iera, A., Ruggeri, G., Tripodi, D.: Providing Throughput Guarantees in 802.11e WLAN Through a Dynamic Priority Assignment Mechanism. Wireless Personal Communications 34, 109–125 (2005)
12. Ge, Y., Hou, J.C., Choi, S.: An analytic study of tuning systems parameters in IEEE 802.11e enhanced distributed channel access. Comput. Netw. 51(8), 1955–1980 (2007)
13. Zimmermann, A., German, R., Freiheit, J., Hommel, G.: Petri Net Modelling and Performability Evaluation with TimeNET 3.0. In: Haverkort, B.R., Bohnenkamp, H.C., Smith, C.U. (eds.) TOOLS 2000. LNCS, vol. 1786, pp. 188–202. Springer, Heidelberg (2000)
14. Various authors: The Network Simulator ns-2 (last seen June 6, 2008), http://www.isi.edu/nsnam/ns/
15. Janert, P.: Gnuplot in Action: Understanding Data with Graphs. Manning Publications (2008) ISBN 978-1933988399

Appendix: Complete Petri Net Model for Priority Shifting

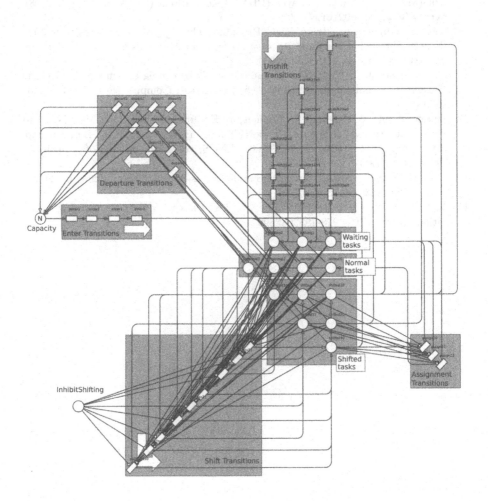

Performance Analysis of a Priority Queue with Place Reservation and General Transmission Times

Bart Feyaerts and Sabine Wittevrongel

SMACS Research Group, TELIN Department, Ghent University
Sint-Pietersnieuwstraat 41, 9000 Gent, Belgium
{bfeyaert,sw}@telin.ugent.be

Abstract. In this paper, we analyze a discrete-time single-server queue with two classes of packet arrivals and a reservation-based scheduling discipline. The objective of this discipline is to give a certain priority to (delay-sensitive) packets of class 1 and at the same time to avoid packet starvation for the (delay-tolerant) packets of class 2. This is achieved by the introduction of a reserved place in the queue that can be taken by a future arrival of class 1. Both classes contain packets with generally distributed transmission times.

By means of a probability generating functions approach, both the class-1 and the class-2 packet delay are studied. By some numerical examples, the delay performance of the Reservation discipline is compared to that of the classical Absolute Priority (AP) and First-In First-Out (FIFO) scheduling disciplines.

Keywords: Discrete-time queueing model, priority scheduling, place reservation, delay analysis.

1 Introduction

Modern packet-based communication networks have to support an increasingly diverse range of applications with different Quality of Service (QoS) requirements. Real-time applications (e.g. voice, video or audio streaming, gaming, ...) have strict delay-related requirements. For such applications, it is important that the mean delay and the delay jitter experienced by the data packets are minimal. Non-real-time applications (e.g. file transfer, email, ...) on the other hand, require low packet loss but can tolerate much larger delays. A method to guarantee acceptable delays to real-time applications is the use of priority scheduling in the network nodes, as opposed to the simple First-In First-Out (FIFO) scheduling where all packets are treated the same. Suppose we have a queue with two types of packet arrivals. We refer to packets from delay-sensitive and delay-tolerant applications as class-1 and class-2 packets respectively.

The most drastic way of priority scheduling is then Absolute Priority (AP), where transmission priority is always given to class-1 packets. This means that when the server becomes free, any available class-1 packet will always be scheduled next. Class-2 packets can thus only be transmitted when no class-1 packets

N. Thomas and C. Juiz (Eds.): EPEW 2008, LNCS 5261, pp. 197–211, 2008.

are present. This AP scheduling discipline has been analyzed extensively in the literature; for discrete-time studies (i.e. with slotted time), see e.g. [1,2,3,4] for the case of uncorrelated packet arrivals from slot to slot and [5,6,7] for the case of a correlated packet arrival process. It has been shown that AP indeed decreases the delay for class-1 packets. However, this comes at the cost of increasing the delay for the class-2 packets. Especially when the network load is high, this may lead to excessive delays for class-2 packets or so-called packet starvation.

In order to avoid such excessive class-2 delays, while still giving a certain priority to class-1 packets, a new reservation-based priority scheduling discipline has been proposed in [8]. This Reservation discipline introduces a reserved place (R) in the queue that can be taken by a future arrival of class 1. The specific operation of the queue under the Reservation discipline is as follows. There is always exactly one reserved place R in the queue. Of all the arriving packets during a certain slot, the class-1 packets are always inserted into the queue before the class-2 packets. When a class-1 packet is inserted, it takes the position of the reserved place R and makes a new reserved place R at the end of the queue. Afterwards, class-2 packets are inserted at the end of the queue in the classical FIFO way. Once packets are stored in the queue, all packets are treated independently from their class. As long as it is not taken by a class-1 packet, the reserved place R behaves like any other packet in the sense that it advances one place closer to the server whenever a packet leaves the server. The reserved place R can however not enter the server nor leave the system. So, whenever there are no packets in the queue, R is placed at the position closest to the server. Clearly, under the Reservation discipline, a class-1 packet may jump over some class-2 packets when it is stored in the queue; this reduces the class-1 delay.

In the literature, there is some previous work with respect to the analysis of the Reservation discipline. In [8], the mean delay of class-1 and class-2 packets is roughly estimated by means of a simple continuous-time model with Poisson arrivals. The distribution of the packet delay for both classes in a discrete-time queue with the Reservation discipline and general time-independent arrivals has been studied, both in the case of deterministic packet transmission times equal to exactly one slot [9,10] as in the case of geometrically distributed transmission times [11]. In the current paper, we further extend this work by allowing a general distribution for the transmission times of the packets. Our analysis is based on probability generating functions (pgf's) and leads to closed-form expressions for the distribution, the mean and the variance of the delay of both classes.

The rest of the paper is structured as follows. The mathematical model we use to study the Reservation discipline in case of general packet transmission times is described in Section 2. In Section 3, we identify an adequate Markovian description for the state of the system at an arbitrary slot and we establish a number of system equations that govern the evolution in time of the system state vector. The joint pgf of the system state in equilibrium is derived in Section 4. In Section 5, we then analyze the steady-state delay of both classes of packets. In Section 6, we present some numerical examples and we compare the performance of the Reservation discipline to that of the classical FIFO and AP disciplines.

2   Model Description

In this paper, we study a discrete-time single-server queueing system with infinite buffer capacity. The time axis is assumed to be divided into fixed-length intervals, referred to as slots and chronologically labeled.

There are two types of packets arriving to the system, namely high-priority (class-1) packets and low-priority (class-2) packets. In our model, we assume that the numbers of class-j packet arrivals during the consecutive slots are *iid* (independent and identically distributed) random variables. Let the random variable $a_{j,k}$ denote the number of packet arrivals of class j ($j = 1, 2$) during slot k. The joint pgf of $a_{1,k}$ and $a_{2,k}$ will be indicated as

$$A(z_1, z_2) \triangleq E\left[z_1^{a_{1,k}} z_2^{a_{2,k}}\right] = \sum_{\eta_1=0}^{\infty} \sum_{\eta_2=0}^{\infty} \mathrm{Prob}[a_{1,k} = \eta_1, a_{2,k} = \eta_2]\, z_1^{\eta_1} z_2^{\eta_2} \ , \quad (1)$$

where $E[.]$ denotes the expected value of the quantity between brackets. Note that the numbers of arrivals of both classes during the same slot may be correlated. For further use, we also define the marginal pgf's of the number of class-j packet arrivals during a slot:

$$A_1(z) \triangleq E[z^{a_{1,k}}] = A(z, 1) \ ; \quad (2)$$

$$A_2(z) \triangleq E[z^{a_{2,k}}] = A(1, z) \ . \quad (3)$$

The total number of packet arrivals during slot k is denoted by $a_{T,k} \triangleq a_{1,k} + a_{2,k}$ and has pgf $A_T(z) \triangleq E[z^{a_{1,k}+a_{2,k}}] = A(z, z)$. We denote the arrival rate of class-j packets ($j = 1, 2$) by $\lambda_j = A'_j(1)$ and the total arrival rate by $\lambda_T \triangleq \lambda_1 + \lambda_2$.

The service (or transmission) times of the packets belonging to both classes are assumed to be *iid* random variables and generally distributed. Their common pgf is denoted by $S(z)$ and the mean service time is denoted by $\mu = S'(1)$. The service times and the random variables related to the packet arrival process are assumed to be mutually independent.

Also, we assume a stable system. That is, the mean number of packet arrivals per slot is assumed to be strictly less than the mean number of packets that can be transmitted per slot:

$$\lambda_T < \frac{1}{\mu} \ . \quad (4)$$

Under the Reservation discipline, all the arriving packets during a certain slot are ordered before inserting them into the queue: the class-1 packets are always inserted before the class-2 packets. When a class-1 packet is stored in the queue, it takes the position of the reserved place R and makes a new reserved place R at the end of the queue, so that there is always exactly one reserved place. Afterwards, class-2 packets are inserted at the end of the queue in the classical FIFO way. Once inserted, all packets are treated independently from their class.

Note that due to the operation of the Reservation discipline, no class-1 packet will ever be behind the reserved place R (otherwise, that R would have been seized). Also note that no class-2 packet is ever inserted in front of R (the reserved place can only appear behind class-2 packets by inserting class-1 packets).

As long as it is not seized by a class-1 packet, the reserved place R behaves like any other packet, in the sense that it advances one place whenever a packet leaves the server. The reserved place R can however not enter the server, nor leave the system.

3 Markovian State Description and System Equations

Let us define the random variable u_k as the total system content (i.e., the total number of packets present in the system including all class-1 and class-2 packets, but excluding the reserved place R) at the beginning of slot k.

Because of the general packet transmission times, in order to obtain a Markovian description of the system state at the beginning of slot k, we also need information about the progress of the service process for the packet in service, if any, at the beginning of slot k. We therefore introduce the random variable h_k as the number of slots to service completion of the packet in the server at the beginning of slot k, if $u_k \geq 1$, and $h_k = 0$ if $u_k = 0$. Note that h_k takes integer values that can only be 0 if the system is empty.

In addition, for the delay analysis we moreover need to keep track of the position of R at slot boundaries. Thus, we define the random variable m_k as the position of R at the beginning of slot k. The position of a packet $\mathcal{P}$ in the queue is defined as a non-negative integer, equal to the number of queue positions to the server, including the position of $\mathcal{P}$ itself, with position 0 corresponding to the server. Since R can never enter the server, we find for m_k:

$$1 \leq m_k \leq u_k \text{ if } u_k > 0 , \qquad\qquad m_k = 1 \text{ if } u_k = 0 . \tag{5}$$

The vector (h_k, m_k, u_k) allows us to adequately monitor the entire system state and to derive the distributions of the delays of packets of any of the two classes. In the sequel, we will refer to it as the *system state vector*.

In order to express the evolution in time of the system state vector, we need to distinguish three separate cases. First, if the system is empty at the beginning of slot k, the system content at the beginning of slot $k + 1$ equals the number of packet arrivals during slot k. In this case, the remaining time until service completion of the packet in service at the beginning of slot $k + 1$ equals the full service time of the packet, unless there were no packet arrivals during slot k, in which case the system stays empty. Secondly, if the system is nonempty at the beginning of slot k and $h_k = 1$, there is a packet departure at the end of slot k and the system either becomes empty or the service of a new packet starts at the beginning of slot $k + 1$. Finally, in case $h_k > 1$, there is no packet departure and the remaining time until service completion is simply decreased by one slot.

With respect to the evolution of the position of the reserved place R, we note that when there are no class-1 arrivals during slot k, R advances one position closer to the server, except when it was already at position 1 or when there is no packet departure, in which case the position of R remains unchanged. On the other hand, if there is at least one class-1 arrival during slot k, R is seized and a new reservation is created at the end of the queue.

All these observations lead to the following set of system equations:

1. if $h_k = 0$ (hence, $u_k = 0$ and $m_k = 1$):

$$u_{k+1} = a_{T,k} \ ,$$

$$m_{k+1} = \begin{cases} 1 & , a_{1,k} = 0 \ , \\ a_{1,k} & , a_{1,k} > 0 \ , \end{cases}$$

$$h_{k+1} = \begin{cases} 0 & , a_{T,k} = 0 \ , \\ s^* & , a_{T,k} > 0 \ ; \end{cases} \tag{6}$$

2. if $h_k = 1$ (hence, $u_k > 0$ and $1 \le m_k \le u_k$):

$$u_{k+1} = u_k - 1 + a_{T,k} \ ,$$

$$m_{k+1} = \begin{cases} (m_k - 2)^+ + 1 & , a_{1,k} = 0 \ , \\ u_k - 1 + a_{1,k} & , a_{1,k} > 0 \ , \end{cases}$$

$$h_{k+1} = \begin{cases} 0 & , u_k = 1 \text{ and } a_{T,k} = 0 \ , \\ s^* & , u_k > 1 \text{ or } a_{T,k} > 0 \ ; \end{cases} \tag{7}$$

3. if $h_k > 1$ (hence, $u_k > 0$ and $1 \le m_k \le u_k$):

$$u_{k+1} = u_k + a_{T,k} \ ,$$

$$m_{k+1} = \begin{cases} m_k & , a_{1,k} = 0 \ , \\ u_k + a_{1,k} & , a_{1,k} > 0 \ , \end{cases}$$

$$h_{k+1} = h_k - 1 \ . \tag{8}$$

Here $(.)^+$ is the operator $\max(.,0)$ and s^* denotes the service time of the next packet to enter the server at the beginning of slot k, if any.

4 Equilibrium Distribution of the System State

The main goal of this section is to derive the steady-state distribution of the system state vector. This distribution will then be used in the next section to analyze the packet delays of both classes.

We define the joint pgf of the system state vector (h_k, m_k, u_k) at the beginning of slot k as

$$P_k(x, y, z) \triangleq E\left[x^{h_k} y^{m_k - 1} z^{u_k}\right] \ . \tag{9}$$

The next step is then to relate the system state pgf's at two successive slots k and $k + 1$ by means of the above system equations. As a result, we obtain:

$$P_{k+1}(x, y, z) = \frac{xS(x) - 1}{xy}\big((y - 1)A(0, z) + A(yz, z)\big)p_{0,k}$$

$$+ \big(1 - S(x)\big)A_T(0)\big(p_{0,k} + R_k(0, 0)\big) + \frac{y - 1}{y}S(x)A(0, z)R_k(0, z)$$

$$+ \frac{S(x) - yz}{y}\big[\big(A(yz, z) - A(0, z)\big)R_k(1, yz) + A(0, z)R_k(y, z)\big]$$

$$+ \frac{1}{x}A(0, z)P_k(x, y, z) + \frac{1}{xy}\big(A(yz, z) - A(0, z)\big)P_k(x, 1, yz) \ , (10)$$

where $p_{0,k}$ denotes the probability of an empty system at the beginning of slot k and where the function $R_k(y, z)$ is defined as

$$R_k(y, z) \triangleq E\big[y^{m_k - 1}z^{u_k - 1}\{h_k = 1\}\big]$$

$$= \sum_{i=1}^{\infty}\sum_{j=1}^{\infty}\text{Prob}[h_k = 1, m_k = i, u_k = j]\, y^{i-1}z^{j-1} \ , \quad (11)$$

with the notation $E[X\{Y\}] \triangleq \text{Prob}[Y]\, E[X|Y]$.

Note that since $u_k = 0$ implies that $h_k = 0$ and $m_k = 1$, the following equivalent expressions for $p_{0,k}$ hold:

$$p_{0,k} \triangleq \text{Prob}[u_k = 0] = \text{Prob}[h_k = 0, m_k = 1, u_k = 0]$$

$$= P_k(0, 0, 0) = P_k(x, y, 0), \ \forall x, y \ . \quad (12)$$

Similarly, since $u_k = 1$ implies that $m_k = 1$,

$$R_k(0, 0) = \text{Prob}[h_k = 1, m_k = 1, u_k = 1] = R_k(y, 0), \ \forall y \ . \quad (13)$$

These results will be useful further in our analysis.

We now assume that for $k \to \infty$, the system reaches a steady state, such that the functions $P_k(x, y, z)$ and $P_{k+1}(x, y, z)$ both converge to the same limiting function, indicated as $P(x, y, z)$. Similarly, we define (h, m, u) and a_j as the system variables and the number of class-j arrivals for an arbitrary slot during equilibrium. Remember that the condition for the system to reach such an equilibrium is given by $\lambda_T < \frac{1}{\mu}$.

We can then derive the limiting function $P(x, y, z)$ by taking the limit $k \to \infty$ in (10) and solving for $P(x, y, z)$. This yields:

$$P(x, y, z) = \frac{1}{y(x - A(0, z))}\bigg[xy\big(1 - S(x)\big)A_T(0)\big(p_0 + R(0, 0)\big)$$

$$+ \big(xS(x) - 1\big)\big((y - 1)A(0, z) + A(yz, z)\big)p_0$$

$$+ x\big(S(x) - yz\big)\big(\big(A(yz, z) - A(0, z)\big)R(1, yz) + A(0, z)R(y, z)\big)$$

$$+ x(y - 1)S(x)A(0, z)R(0, z) + \big(A(yz, z) - A(0, z)\big)P(x, 1, yz)\bigg] \ .$$

$$(14)$$

What remains in order to determine $P(x, y, z)$ completely is to obtain the unknown functions $P(x, 1, yz)$, $R(y, z) \triangleq \lim_{k \to \infty} R_k(y, z)$, $R(0, z)$, $R(1, yz)$ and the unknown probabilities $R(0, 0)$ and $p_0 \triangleq \lim_{k \to \infty} p_{0,k}$. These will be determined one by one in the remainder of this section.

First, we note from (12) that $p_0 = P(x, y, 0)$ for all x and y. From (14), it then follows that

$$p_0 = \frac{A_T(0)}{x - A_T(0)} \big((x - 1)p_0 + xR(0, 0) \big), \; \forall x \; , \tag{15}$$

and hence

$$\big(1 - A_T(0) \big) p_0 = A_T(0)R(0, 0) \; . \tag{16}$$

Another remarkable property comes forth when we derive an expression for $P(x, 1, z)$ from (14):

$$P(x, 1, z) = \frac{1}{x - A_T(z)} \Big(x \big(1 - S(x) \big) A_T(0) \big(p_0 + R(0, 0) \big)$$
$$+ \big(xS(x) - 1 \big) A_T(z)p_0 + x \big(S(x) - z \big) A_T(z)R(1, z) \Big) \; . \tag{17}$$

This equation exactly matches the one for the joint pgf of the remaining service time and system content of a simple GI-G-1 queue, as found in [12]. This could be expected, as the substitution of $y = 1$ in $P(x, y, z)$ results in the joint pgf of (h, u), not taking the Reservation discipline into account, which are exactly the same system variables as used in the analysis of the non-priority queue in [12]. Thus we can also derive an expression for p_0 and $R(1, z)$, based upon the corresponding expressions from previous research:

$$p_0 = 1 - A'_T(1)S'(1) = 1 - \lambda_T \mu \; , \tag{18}$$

$$R(1, z) = \frac{p_0 \big(A_T(z) - 1 \big) S \big(A_T(z) \big)}{A_T(z) \big(z - S \big(A_T(z) \big) \big)} \; . \tag{19}$$

Since $P(x, y, z)$ is a pgf, it must be bounded for all values of x, y and z such that $|x| \leq 1$, $|y| \leq 1$ and $|z| \leq 1$. In particular, this should be true for $x = A(0, z)$, $|y| \leq 1$ and $|z| \leq 1$, since $|A(0, z)| \leq 1$ for all such z, because $A(z_1, z_2)$ is a pgf. If we choose $x = A(0, z)$ in (14), where $|y| \leq 1$ and $|z| \leq 1$, the denominator $x - A(0, z)$ vanishes. The numerator in (14) therefore also has to vanish for the arguments. This leads to an additional relation, which allows us to determine $R(y, z)$ as

$$R(y, z) = \frac{S \big(A(0, z) \big)}{yz - S \big(A(0, z) \big)} \frac{A(0, z) - 1}{A(0, z)} \left[y + \frac{A(yz, z) - A(0, z)}{A(0, z) - A_T(yz)} \right] p_0$$
$$+ \frac{(y - 1)S \big(A(0, z) \big)}{yz - S \big(A(0, z) \big)} R(0, z) - \frac{A(yz, z) - A(0, z)}{A(0, z) - A_T(yz)} R(1, yz) \; . \tag{20}$$

The function $R(y, z)$ is a partial pgf. Just like a normal pgf, partial pgf's must be bounded for arguments on the unit disc, which implies that there must not be any singularities in the open unit disc. As in [11], it can be shown that there always exists a non-empty subset $\aleph$ of the open unit disc such that

$$z \in \aleph \Rightarrow \left| \frac{S\big(A(0, z)\big)}{z} \right| < 1 \ . \tag{21}$$

If we then were to choose for z^* a value in $\aleph$ and $y^* = \dfrac{S\big(A(0, z^*)\big)}{z^*}$, then the denominator $yz - S\big(A(0, z)\big)$ vanishes for $y = y^*$ and $z = z^*$, seemingly causing a singularity, which is impossible. The only remaining option is then dor the numerator in (20) to disappear for (y^*, z^*) as well. This provides us with a means to determine $R(0, z)$:

$$R(0, z) = \frac{1 - A(0, z)}{A(0, z)\big(z - S(A(0, z))\big)} \Big[-S\big(A(0, z)\big) + z\phi(z) \Big] p_0 \ , \tag{22}$$

where we have defined $\phi(z)$ as

$$\phi(z) \triangleq \frac{A(0, z) - A\Big(S\big(A(0, z)\big), z\Big)}{A(0, z) - A_T\Big(S\big(A(0, z)\big)\Big)} \ . \tag{23}$$

Joining the bits and pieces, we finally obtain the following closed-form expression for the joint pgf of the system state:

$$
\begin{aligned}
P(x, y, z) = {} & p_0 \left[1 - xz \frac{1 - A(0, z)}{x - A(0, z)} \frac{S(x) - S\big(A(0, z)\big)}{z - S\big(A(0, z)\big)} \right] \\
& + \frac{p_0}{yz - S\big(A(0, z)\big)} \left\{ \frac{xz\big(yz - S(x)\big)}{A(0, z) - A_T(yz)} \frac{A(yz, z) - A(0, z)}{yz - S\big(A_T(yz)\big)} \right. \\
& \qquad \left(S\big(A(0, z)\big) \frac{1 - A(0, z)}{x - A(0, z)} - S\big(A_T(yz)\big) \frac{1 - A_T(yz)}{x - A_T(yz)} \right) \\
& + xz^2(y - 1) \frac{1 - A(0, z)}{x - A(0, z)} \frac{S(x) - S\big(A(0, z)\big)}{z - S\big(A(0, z)\big)} \frac{A(0, z) - A\Big(S\big(A(0, z)\big), z\Big)}{A(0, z) - A_T\Big(S\big(A(0, z)\big)\Big)} \\
& + \frac{xz(1 - x)}{x - A(0, z)} \frac{A(yz, z) - A(0, z)}{x - A_T(yz)} \left. \left(S\big(A(0, z)\big) \frac{S(x) - S\big(A_T(yz)\big)}{yz - S\big(A_T(yz)\big)} - S(x) \right) \right\}.
\end{aligned}
\tag{24}
$$

5   Distribution of the Packet Delay

With the above results in hand, we are now able to analyze the packet delay for both packet classes. Therefore, we choose an arbitrary packet $\mathcal{P}$ from all class-j

packets arriving to the queue and we define I as the arrival slot of $\mathcal{P}$. The delay d_j of $\mathcal{P}$ is then given by the total number of slots from the end of slot I until $\mathcal{P}$ leaves the system. Thus, slot I itself does not contribute to the delay of $\mathcal{P}$. In general, the delay experienced by $\mathcal{P}$ consists of the time until service completion of the packet in service, if any, and the full service times of all packets served until $\mathcal{P}$ leaves the system. This results in

$$d_j = (h_I - 1)^+ + \sum_{i=1}^{n_j+1} s_i \ , \tag{25}$$

where h_I is the system state variable h at the beginning of slot I, n_j is the number of packets to be served before $\mathcal{P}$ (excluding the packet in service during slot I, if any) and the s_i's are the service times of those n_j packets. Note that we also have to take the service time of $\mathcal{P}$ itself into account.

The total number of packets to be served before $\mathcal{P}$, excluding the packet in service, denoted as n_j, not only depends on the system content at the start of slot I, but also on how many packets arrive during I that are inserted before $\mathcal{P}$. Therefore we introduce the random variable ℓ_j such that $\mathcal{P}$ is the ℓ_j-th class-j packet that is inserted during slot I. The pgf $L_j(z)$ of ℓ_j can be shown to be given by (see e.g. [12])

$$L_j(z) = \frac{z(1 - A_j(z))}{\lambda_j(1 - z)} \qquad , j = 1, 2 \ . \tag{26}$$

The derivation of expression (26) makes use of knowledge on the arrival process during slot I. Let a_1^I and a_2^I be the respective number of class-1 and class-2 arrivals during slot I. Note that slot I is *not* a randomly chosen slot, but the arrival slot of the randomly chosen class-j packet $\mathcal{P}$ so that $a_j^I > 0$. Therefore the vector (a_1^I, a_2^I) does not have the same distribution as the vector (a_1, a_2). The relation between the two distributions is given by the equation

$$\mathrm{Prob}\big[a_1^I = \alpha_1, a_2^I = \alpha_2\big] = \frac{\alpha_j}{\lambda_j} \mathrm{Prob}[a_1 = \alpha_1, a_2 = \alpha_2] \qquad , j = 1, 2 \ . \tag{27}$$

As the foregoing observations indicate, we also rely on the system state vector at the beginning of slot I, denoted by (h_I, m_I, u_I), with joint pgf $P_I(x, y, z)$. Due to the *iid* nature of the arrival process, the system state as observed by an arbitrary packet (just like $\mathcal{P}$), has the same distribution as the system state at the beginning of an arbitrary slot. Thus, we can state:

$$(h_I, m_I, u_I) \stackrel{d}{=} (h, m, u) \ , \qquad\qquad P_I(x, y, z) = P(x, y, z) \ . \tag{28}$$

5.1   The PGF of the Class-1 Packet Delay

If $\mathcal{P}$ is a class-1 packet, n_1 is equal to the number of packets in the queue, that are positioned between the reserved place and the server. If $\mathcal{P}$ is the first class-1 packet to be inserted during I, R still is at position m_I. If $\mathcal{P}$ is not the first class-1 packet, R will be at the end of the queue, at a position that depends on the system content u_I at the beginning of slot I and the number of preceding class-1 packet arrivals during I. Based on these considerations, n_1 can be expressed as follows:

$$\begin{cases} n_1 = m_I - 1 & , \ \ell_1 = 1 \ , \\ n_1 = (u_I - 1)^+ + \ell_1 - 1 & , \ \ell_1 > 1 \ . \end{cases} \tag{29}$$

The probability $\mathrm{Prob}[\ell_1 = 1]$ can be obtained from the pgf $L_1(z)$ given by (26). Specifically, we have that

$$\mathrm{Prob}[\ell_1 = 1] = \left.\frac{L_1(z)}{z}\right|_{z=0} = \frac{1-\alpha}{\lambda_1} \ , \tag{30}$$

where we have made use of de l'Hôpital's rule and where we have introduced the notation $\alpha \triangleq A_1(0)$ for convenience.

From (25) and (29), we can now determine $D_1(z)$, the pgf of d_1:

$$\begin{aligned} D_1(z) &\triangleq E\left[z^{d_1}\right] = p_0 L_1\big(S(z)\big) + \frac{S(z)}{z}\mathrm{Prob}[\ell_1 = 1]\Big(P\big(z, S(z), 1\big) - p_0\Big) \\ &\quad + \frac{1}{zS(z)}\Big(L_1\big(S(z)\big) - S(z)\mathrm{Prob}[\ell_1 = 1]\Big)\Big(P\big(z, 1, S(z)\big) - p_0\Big) \\ &= \frac{p_0}{\lambda_1}S(z)\bigg\{\frac{1 - A_1\big(S(z)\big)}{1 - S(z)} + (z-1)\frac{1-\alpha}{z-\alpha}\frac{A_1\big(S(z)\big) - \alpha}{z - A_T\big(S(z)\big)} \\ &\quad + \frac{A_T\big(S(z)\big) - 1}{z - A_T\big(S(z)\big)}\frac{S(z) - A_1\big(S(z)\big) + \big(1 - S(z)\big)\alpha}{1 - S(z)} \\ &\quad + \frac{(1-\alpha)^2}{(z-\alpha)\big(1 - S(\alpha)\big)}\big[S(\alpha) - S(z) + \big(S(z) - 1\big)\phi(1)\big]\bigg\} \ . \end{aligned} \tag{31}$$

5.2   The PGF of the Class-2 Packet Delay

If $\mathcal{P}$ is a class-2 packet, it will be inserted at the end of the queue, at a position somewhere behind the reserved place. Let n_2^* be the number of packets waiting in the queue - excluding the packet in service, if any - at the insertion of $\mathcal{P}$. Since all class-1 packets arriving in slot I are inserted first, we find that

$$n_2^* = (u_I - 1)^+ + a_1^I + \ell_2 - 1 \ . \tag{32}$$

These are the packets waiting in the queue at the end of slot I and to be served before $\mathcal{P}$. This number is equal to n_2 only if R is not seized by a class-1 packet (i.e., if there is no class-1 packet arrival) during the waiting time of $\mathcal{P}$. The waiting time of $\mathcal{P}$ is the number of slots from the end of $\mathcal{P}$'s arrival slot I, up to the end of the last slot $\mathcal{P}$ is waiting in the queue.

In case R is not seized before $\mathcal{P}$ reaches the server, the waiting time of $\mathcal{P}$, denoted by v, consists of the remaining number of slots to service completion of the packet in service, if any, and the sum of the service times of the n_2^* packets stored in front of $\mathcal{P}$:

$$v = (h_I - 1)^+ + \sum_{i=1}^{n_2^*} s_i \ . \tag{33}$$

Note that in general a_1^I and ℓ_2 are not independent when a_2^I is unknown. The joint pgf of a_1^I and ℓ_2 can easily be found from (27) as

$$F(x, y) \triangleq E\left[x^{a_1^I} y^{\ell_2}\right] = \frac{y}{1 - y} \frac{A_1(x) - A(x, y)}{\lambda_2} \ , \tag{34}$$

so that the pgf of $a_1^I + \ell_2$ is $F(z, z)$. From (32)–(34), we can then derive the pgf $V(z)$ of v as

$$V(z) \triangleq E[z^v] = \frac{F\big(S(z), S(z)\big)}{S(z)} \left(p_0 + \frac{P\big(z, 1, S(z)\big) - p_0}{z S(z)}\right)$$

$$= \frac{p_0}{\lambda_2} \frac{1 - z}{1 - S(z)} \frac{A_T\big(S(z)\big) - A_1\big(S(z)\big)}{z - A_T\big(S(z)\big)} \ . \tag{35}$$

In case R is seized before $\mathcal{P}$ reaches the server, the waiting time of $\mathcal{P}$ is increased with the service time of the class-1 packet seizing the reserved place. Let γ_n be a Bernoulli random variable with pgf $\Gamma_n(z) = \alpha^n + (1 - \alpha^n) z$, i.e., γ_n equals 1 if at least one class-1 packet arrives in n consecutive slots and γ_n equals 0 otherwise. Then the delay of $\mathcal{P}$ is expressed as

$$d_2 = v + \gamma_v \tilde{s} + s_{\mathcal{P}} \ , \tag{36}$$

where $\tilde{s}$ is the service time of the class-1 packet seizing R, if any, and $s_{\mathcal{P}}$ is the service time of $\mathcal{P}$. From this relation, the pgf $D_2(z)$ finally follows as

$$D_2(z) \triangleq E\left[z^{d_2}\right] = \frac{p_0}{\lambda_2} S(z) \left\{ S(z) \frac{1 - z}{1 - S(z)} \frac{A_T\big(S(z)\big) - A_1\big(S(z)\big)}{z - A_T\big(S(z)\big)} \right.$$

$$\left. + \big(1 - S(z)\big) \frac{1 - z\alpha}{1 - S(z\alpha)} \frac{A_T\big(S(z\alpha)\big) - A_1\big(S(z\alpha)\big)}{z\alpha - A_T\big(S(z\alpha)\big)} \right\} \ . \tag{37}$$

Note that the expressions (31) and (37) are completely in accordance with the results of [10] and [11], where similar queueing systems have been analyzed, but with service times of one slot and geometrically distributed service times instead of general service times.

5.3 Moments of the Packet Delay

Using the moment generating property of pgf's, we can now determine the moments of the class-j packet delay from the pgf $D_j(z)$ (e.g. $E[d_j] = D_j'(1)$). More specificaly we find

$$D_1'(1) = \mu\left(2 + \frac{\mu\lambda_T'}{2p_0} + \frac{\lambda_1'}{2\lambda_1} - \frac{p_0}{\lambda_1} \frac{1 - \alpha}{1 - S(\alpha)}\big(1 - \phi(1)\big)\right) + \frac{\mu'\lambda_T}{2p_0} - \frac{1 - p_0}{\lambda_1} \tag{38}$$

and

$$D_2'(1) = \mu\left(2 + \frac{\lambda_T' - \lambda_1'}{2\lambda_2} - V(\alpha)\right) + \frac{1}{2p_0}\left(\mu^2\lambda_T' + \mu'\lambda_T\right) , \qquad (39)$$

to respectively be the mean packet delay for packets of class 1 and class 2. Please note that we have defined $\mu' \triangleq S''(1)$, $\lambda_1' \triangleq A_1''(1)$ and likewise $\lambda_T' \triangleq A_T''(1)$. Similarly, the mean system content can be calculated from $U(z) \triangleq E[z^u] = P(1, 1, z)$ as found in (24). This way it can be verified that Little's law, which here takes the form $\lambda_1 E[d_1] + \lambda_2 E[d_2] = E[u]$ is satisfied by (38) and (39).

$D_j(z)$ can also be used to calculate higher-order moments, again by means of the moment generating property. Thus, one can calculate the class-j packet delay variance using

$$\mathrm{var}[d_j] = D_j''(1) + D_j'(1) - D_j'(1)^2 . \qquad (40)$$

6   Numerical Results and Discussion

In this section, we will investigate the delay performance of the Reservation discipline by means of a practical example, and compare the Reservation discipline with the First-In First-Out (FIFO) and Absolute Priority (AP) scheduling disciplines. Therefore we consider a practical situation of a non-blocking output buffering switch with N inlets and N outlets and each output buffer has one outlet. When a packet arrives on one of the switch's inlets, it is first routed and then stored into the output buffer corresponding to the packet's destination. This routing is done in an independent and uniform way. On each of the inlets of the switch, we assume *iid* Bernoulli arrivals, such that the joint pgf of the number of per-slot class-1 and class-2 arrivals in an output buffer is given by

$$A(z_1, z_2) = \left(1 - \frac{\lambda_1}{N}(1 - z_1) - \frac{\lambda_2}{N}(1 - z_2)\right)^N , \qquad (41)$$

where λ_j is the probability of a class-j arrival at an arbitrary switch inlet. We then define $\lambda_T \triangleq \lambda_1 + \lambda_2$ as the total arrival rate at an arbitrary switch inlet. Due to the Bernoulli nature of the arrivals on the switch inlets, at most N packet arrivals can occur per slot. This implies that the numbers of class-1 and class-2 packet arrivals are correlated. At any inlet at which there is a class-1 arrival, there cannot be a class-2 arrival. In this paper we consider $N = 16$.

In the example, both classes contain packets with Poisson distributed service times, such that $S(z)$ is given by

$$S(z) = ze^{(\mu-1)(z-1)}. \qquad (42)$$

In the remainder of this section, we will investigate the effects on the delay performance of three main parameters (the system load $\rho \triangleq \lambda_T\mu$, the traffic mix $\frac{\lambda_1}{\lambda_T}$ and the mean service speed $\frac{1}{\mu}$). The delay performance measures we consider are both the mean delay and the delay variance for both classes of packets. Note that the results for FIFO and AP are respectively drawn from [2] and [13].

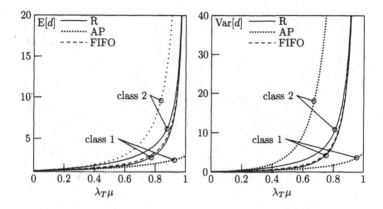

Fig. 1. Mean delay and delay variance for both packet classes as a function of ρ, for Reservation discipline (full), AP (dotted) and FIFO (dashed)

First of all, we study the effects of a varying load on the packet delay for both classes. We consider a traffic mix $\frac{\lambda_1}{\lambda_T}$ equal to 0.75 and a mean service speed $\frac{1}{\mu}$ of 0.9. The curves of the corresponding mean packet delay and the delay variance are shown in figure 1. Since for $\rho \to 1$ the system becomes unstable, we can observe a vertical asymptote. We also see that under heavy load, the class-2 delay performance for Absolute Priority becomes very bad, whereas it remains close to FIFO performance for the Reservation discipline: the class-2 curves for AP grow to infinite measures much faster than for the Reservation discipline.

Next, we investigate the effects of a varying traffic mix $\frac{\lambda_1}{\lambda_T}$ on the mean delay and the delay variance. To construct figure 2, we have chosen $\frac{1}{\mu} = 0.9$ and $\lambda_T = 0.8$. Due to the specific nature of the arrival process, we can observe that

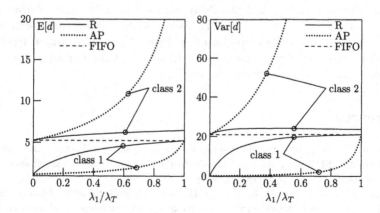

Fig. 2. Mean delay and delay variance for both packet classes as a function of $\frac{\lambda_1}{\lambda_T}$, for Reservation discipline (full), AP (dotted) and FIFO (dashed)

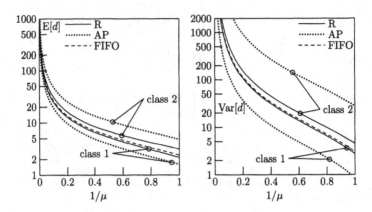

Fig. 3. Mean delay and delay variance for both packet classes as a function of $1/\mu$, for Reservation discipline (full), AP (dotted) and FIFO (dashed)

the FIFO curve is horizontal. Note that when all traffic is of class j ($\frac{\lambda_1}{\lambda_T} = 0$ or 1), the corresponding measures coincide with the FIFO curve. This is because the packets are then exclusively inserted in arrival order, as is the case in FIFO scheduling. We can also observe that for a low partial load of class 1, the delay measures for the Reservation discipline do not significantly differ from the AP delay measures. For an increased class-1 traffic fraction however, the differences between AP and the Reservation discipline are much more striking. At a high fraction of class-1 traffic, AP has the side-effect of class-2 packet starvation: class-2 packets seldomly reach the server, leading to an ever increasing delay. Under the Reservation discipline, any class-2 packet can only be passed by one class-1 packet, since there is only 1 reserved place, resulting in a delay performance that stays rather close to FIFO performance.

Finally, we take a look at the effect of different service speeds. In figure 3, we show the mean delay and the delay variance as a function of the service speed $\frac{1}{\mu}$, for $\lambda_T = 0.8$ and $\frac{\lambda_1}{\lambda_T} = 0.75$. We observe that all curves exhibit the same behaviour: low service speeds mean long transmission times, leading to long delay times, which is intuitively clear. Note that the impact of the service speed on the delay characteristics is very high.

References

1. Takine, T., Sengupta, B., Hasegawa, T.: An analysis of a discrete-time queue for broadband ISDN with priorities among traffic classes. IEEE Transactions on Communications 42(24), 1837–1845 (1994)
2. Walraevens, J., Steyaert, B., Bruneel, H.: Delay characteristics in discrete-time GI-G-1 queues with non-preemptive priority queueing discipline. Performance Evaluation 50(1), 53–75 (2002)
3. Mazzini, G., Rovatti, R., Setti, G.: A closed form solution of Bernoullian two-classes priority queue. IEEE Communications Letters 9(3), 264–266 (2005)

4. Ndreca, S., Scoppola, B.: Discrete time GI/Geom/1 queueing system with priority. European Journal of Operational Research 189(3), 1403–1408 (2008)
5. Ali, M.M., Song, X.: A performance analysis of a discrete-time priority queueing system with correlated arrivals. Performance Evaluation 57(3), 307–339 (2004)
6. Jin, X.L., Min, G.: Performance analysis of priority scheduling mechanisms under heterogeneous network traffic. Journal of Computer and System Sciences 73(8), 1207–1220 (2007)
7. Walraevens, J., Wittevrongel, S., Bruneel, H.: A discrete-time priority queue with train arrivals. Stochastic Models 23(3), 489–512 (2007)
8. Burakowski, W., Tarasiuk, H.: On new strategy for prioritising the selected flow in queuing system. In: Proceedings of the COST 257 11th Management Committee Meeting, Barcelona (January 2000) COST-257 TD(00)03
9. De Vuyst, S., Wittevrongel, S., Bruneel, H.: Delay differentiation by reserving space in queue. Electronics Letters 41(9), 564–565 (2005)
10. De Vuyst, S., Wittevrongel, S., Bruneel, H.: Place reservation: delay analysis of a novel scheduling mechanism. Computers & Operations Research 35(8), 2447–2462 (2008)
11. Feyaerts, B., De Vuyst, S., Wittevrongel, S., Bruneel, H.: Analysis of a discrete-time priority queue with place reservations and geometric service times. In: Proceedings of the Sixth Conference on Design, Analysis, and Simulation of Distributed Systems, DASD 2008, Edinburgh (June 2008)
12. Bruneel, H.: Performance of discrete-time queueing systems. Computers & Operations Research 20(3), 303–320 (1993)
13. Bruneel, H., Kim, B.G.: Discrete-Time Models for Communication Systems Including ATM. Kluwer Academic Publishers, Boston (1993)

Analysis of $BMAP/G/1$ Vacation Model of Non-$M/G/1$-Type*

Zsolt Saffer and Miklós Telek

Department of Telecommunications,
Technical University of Budapest,
1521 Budapest Hungary
{safferzs,telek}@hit.bme.hu

Abstract. In this paper we present the analysis of $BMAP/G/1$ vacation models of non-$M/G/1$-type in a general framework. We provide new service discipline independent formulas for the vector generating function (GF) of the stationary number of customers and for its mean, both in terms of quantities at the start of vacation.

We present new results for vacation models with gated and G-limited disciplines. For both models discipline specific systems of equations are setup. Their numerical solution are used to compute the required quantities at the start of vacation.

Keywords: queueing theory, vacation model, BMAP, M/G/1-type process.

1 Introduction

Queueing models with server vacation have been studied in the last decades due to their general modeling capability. In these models the server occasionally takes a vacation period, in which no customer is served. For details on vacation models and for their analysis with Poisson arrival process we refer to the comprehensive survey of Doshi [1] and to the excellent book of Takagi [2].

The batch Markovian arrival process ($BMAP$) introduced by Lucantoni [3] enables more realistic and more accurate traffic modeling than the (batch) Poisson process. Consequently analysis of queueing models with $BMAP$ attracted a great attention. The vast majority of the analyzed $BMAP/G/1$ queueing models exploit the underlying $M/G/1$-type structure of the model, i.e., that the embedded Markov chain at the customer departure epochs is of $M/G/1$-type [4] in which the block size in the transition probability matrix equals to the number of phases of the $BMAP$. Hence most of the analysis of $BMAP/G/1$ vacation models are based on the standard matrix analytic-method pioneered by Neuts [5] and further extended by many others (see e.g., [6]).

Chang and Takine [7] applied the factorization property (presented by Chang et al. [8]) to get analytical results for queueing models of $M/G/1$-type with or without vacations using exhaustive discipline. The factorization property states

---

* This work is supported by the NAPA-WINE FP7-ICT (http://www.napa-wine.eu) and the OTKA K61709 projects.

N. Thomas and C. Juiz (Eds.): EPEW 2008, LNCS 5261, pp. 212–226, 2008.

that the vector probability-generating function (vector PGF or vector GF) of the stationary queue length is factored into two PGFs of proper random variables. One of them is the vector PGF of the conditional stationary queue length given that the server is on vacation.

The class of $BMAP/G/1$ vacation models, for example with gated discipline can not be described by an $M/G/1$-type Markov chain embedded at the customer departure epochs, because at least one supplementary variable is required to describe the discipline. In case of gated discipline this variable is the number of customers not yet served from those present at the beginning of the vacation.

We define the $BMAP/G/1$ *vacation model of non-$M/G/1$-type* as the vacation model, which can not be described by an $M/G/1$-type Markov chain embedded at the customer departure epochs. Numerous disciplines fall into this category, like e.g. the gated, the E-limited or the G-limited ones, etc.

Very few literature is available on $BMAP/G/1$ vacation models of non-$M/G/1$-type. Ferrandiz [9] used Palm-martingale calculus to analyze a flexible vacation scheme. Shin and Pearce [10] studied queue-length dependent vacation schedules by using the semi-Markov process technique. Recently Banik et al. [11] studied the BMAP/G/1/N queue with vacations and E-limited service discipline. They applied supplementary variable technique to get the queue length distributions and several system performance measures.

The principal goal of this paper is to analyze $BMAP/G/1$ vacation models of non-$M/G/1$-type in a unified framework, which utilizes the advantages of separating the service discipline independent and dependent parts of the analysis.

The contributions of this paper are twofold. The main contribution is the new service discipline independent formulas for the vector GF of the stationary number of customers and for its mean, both in terms of the vector GF of the stationary number of customers at start of vacation, and its factorial moments, respectively.

The second contribution is the new results for the $BMAP/G/1$ vacation models with gated and G-limited disciplines. To the best knowledge of the authors, no results are available for these vacation models of non-$M/G/1$-type. For both models system equations are setup, which can be numerically solved by methods for systems of linear equations. Afterwards the required quantities at the start of the vacation can be computed.

The rest of this paper is organized as follows. In section II we introduce the model and the notations. The derivation of the stationary number of customers in vacation follows in Section III. The new formulas of the vector GF of the stationary number of customers at an arbitrary moment and its mean are derived in section IV. In section V we present the analysis of vacation models of non-M/G/1-type. Numerical example follows in section VI. We give final remarks in section VII.

2 Model and Notation

2.1 $BMAP$ Process

We give a brief summary on the $BMAP$ related definitions and notations. For more details we refer to [3].

$\Lambda(t)$ denotes the number of arrivals in $(0, t]$. $J(t)$ is the state of a background continuous-time Markov chain (CTMC) at time t, which is referred to as phase and phase process, respectively. The *BMAP* batch arrival process is characterized by $\{(\Lambda(t), J(t)) ; t \geq 0\}$ bivariate CTMC on the state space $(\Lambda(t), J(t))$; where $(\Lambda(t) \in \{0, 1, \ldots\}, J(t) \in \{1, 2, \ldots, L\})$. Its infinitesimal generator is:

$$
\begin{pmatrix}
\mathbf{D}_0 & \mathbf{D}_1 & \mathbf{D}_2 & \mathbf{D}_3 & \cdots \\
0 & \mathbf{D}_0 & \mathbf{D}_1 & \mathbf{D}_2 & \cdots \\
0 & 0 & \mathbf{D}_0 & \mathbf{D}_1 & \cdots \\
0 & 0 & 0 & \mathbf{D}_0 & \cdots \\
\vdots & \vdots & \vdots & \vdots & \ddots
\end{pmatrix},
$$

where $\mathbf{0}$ is an $L \times L$ matrix and $\{\mathbf{D}_k; k \geq 0\}$ is a set of $L \times L$ matrices.

$\mathbf{D}_0$ and $\{\mathbf{D}_k; k \geq 1\}$ govern the transitions corresponding to no arrivals and to batch arrivals with size k, respectively. The irreducible infinitesimal generator of the phase process is $\mathbf{D} = \sum_{k=0}^{\infty} \mathbf{D}_k$. Let $\boldsymbol{\pi}$ be the stationary probability vector of the phase process. Then $\boldsymbol{\pi}\mathbf{D} = \mathbf{0}$ and $\boldsymbol{\pi}\mathbf{e} = 1$ uniquely determine $\boldsymbol{\pi}$, where $\mathbf{e}$ is the column vector having all elements equal to one. $\hat{\mathbf{D}}(z)$, the matrix generating function of $\mathbf{D}_k$ is defined as

$$
\hat{\mathbf{D}}(z) = \sum_{k=0}^{\infty} \mathbf{D}_k z^k, \quad |z| \leq 1. \tag{1}
$$

The stationary arrival rate of the BMAP,

$$
\lambda = \boldsymbol{\pi} \left. \frac{d}{dz} \hat{\mathbf{D}}(z) \right|_{z=1} \mathbf{e} = \boldsymbol{\pi} \sum_{k=0}^{\infty} k \mathbf{D}_k \mathbf{e}, \tag{2}
$$

is supposed to be positive and finite.

2.2   The *BMAP/G/*1 Queue with Server Vacation

Batch of customers arrive to the infinite buffer queue according to a *BMAP* process defined by $\hat{\mathbf{D}}(z)$. The service times are independent and identically distributed. B, $B(t)$, b, $b^{(2)}$ denote the service time r.v., its cumulated distribution function and its first two moments, respectively. The mean service time is positive and finite, $0 < b < \infty$.

The server occasionally takes vacations, in which no customer is served. After finishing the vacation the server continues to serve the queue. The model with this strategy is called *queue with single vacation*. If no customer is present in the queue after finishing the vacation, the server immediately takes the next vacation. We define the *cycle time* as a service period and a vacation period together. The server utilization is $\rho = \lambda b$. On the vacation model we impose the following assumptions:

A.1 Independence property: The arrival process and the customer service times are mutually independent. In addition the customer service time is independent of the sequence of vacation periods that precede it.

A.2 Customer loss-free property: All customers arriving to the system will be served. Thus the system has infinite queue and $\rho < 1$.

A.3 Nonpreemtive service property: The service is nonpreemtive. Hence the service of the actual customer is finished before the server goes to vacation.

A.4 Phase independent vacation property: The length of the vacation period is independent of the arrival process and from the customer service times.

In the following $[Y]_{i,j}$ stands for the i,j-th element of matrix $\mathbf{Y}$. Similarly $[y]_j$ denotes the j-th element of vector $\mathbf{y}$.

We define matrix $\mathbf{A}_k$, whose (i,j)-th element denotes the conditional probability that during a customer service time the number of arrivals is k and the initial and final phases of the $BMAP$ are i and j, respectively. That is, for $k \geq 0$, $1 \leq i,j \leq L$,

$$[\mathbf{A}_k]_{i,j} = P\{\Lambda(B) = k, J(B) = j | J(0) = i\}.$$

The matrix GF $\widehat{\mathbf{A}}(z)$ is defined as $\widehat{\mathbf{A}}(z) = \sum_{k=1}^{\infty} \mathbf{A}_k z^k$. $\widehat{\mathbf{A}}(z)$ can be expressed explicitly as [3]

$$\widehat{\mathbf{A}}(z) = \int_{t=0}^{\infty} e^{\widehat{\mathbf{D}}(z)t} dB(t).$$

For later use we also express $\boldsymbol{\pi}\left(\mathbf{I} - \left.\frac{d\widehat{\mathbf{A}}(z)}{dz}\right|_{z=1}\right)\mathbf{e}$, where $\mathbf{I}$ denotes the unity matrix. To this end we rewrite the term $\boldsymbol{\pi} \left.\frac{d\widehat{\mathbf{A}}(z)}{dz}\right|_{z=1} \mathbf{e}$ as

$$\boldsymbol{\pi} \left.\frac{d\widehat{\mathbf{A}}(z)}{dz}\right|_{z=1} \mathbf{e} = \boldsymbol{\pi} \left.\frac{dE\left(e^{\widehat{\mathbf{D}}(z)B}\right)}{dz}\right|_{z=1} \mathbf{e} = \boldsymbol{\pi} E \left(\sum_{k=0}^{\infty} \left.\frac{d\left(\widehat{\mathbf{D}}(z)^k\right)}{dz}\right|_{z=1} \mathbf{e} \frac{B^k}{k!}\right) =$$

$$E\left(\sum_{k=1}^{\infty} \boldsymbol{\pi}\mathbf{D}^{k-1} \left.\frac{d\widehat{\mathbf{D}}(z)}{dz}\right|_{z=1} \mathbf{e} \frac{B^k}{k!}\right) = \boldsymbol{\pi} \left.\frac{d\widehat{\mathbf{D}}(z)}{dz}\right|_{z=1} \mathbf{e}\, E(B) = \lambda b = \rho,$$

where we used that $\boldsymbol{\pi}\mathbf{D} = 0$.

Now the term $\boldsymbol{\pi}\left(\mathbf{I} - \left.\frac{d\widehat{\mathbf{A}}(z)}{dz}\right|_{z=1}\right)\mathbf{e}$ can be given explicitly as

$$\boldsymbol{\pi}\left(\mathbf{I} - \left.\frac{d\widehat{\mathbf{A}}(z)}{dz}\right|_{z=1}\right)\mathbf{e} = 1 - \rho. \tag{3}$$

$V, V(t), v$ denote the vacation time r.v., its cumulated distribution function and its mean, respectively. The mean vacation time is positive and finite, $0 < v < \infty$. Similar to the quantities associated with the service period, we define matrix $\mathbf{U}_k$, whose elements, for $k \geq 0$, $1 \leq i,j \leq L$, are

$$[\mathbf{U}_k]_{i,j} = P\{\Lambda(V) = k, J(V) = j | J(0) = i\},$$

and the matrix GF $\widehat{\mathbf{U}}(z) = \sum_{k=1}^{\infty} \mathbf{U}_k z^k = \int_{t=0}^{\infty} e^{\widehat{\mathbf{D}}(z)t} dV(t)$.

Our vacation model is similar to the *generalized vacation model* for the $M/G/1$ queue defined in Fuhrmann and Cooper [12]. The phase independent vacation property **A.4** corresponds to the independence assumption 6. of [12].

Vacation models are distinguished by their (service) discipline that is the set of rules determining the beginning and the end of the vacation (service). Commonly applied service disciplines are, e.g., the exhaustive, the gated, the limited, etc. In case of exhaustive discipline, the server continues serving the customers until the queue is emptied. Under gated discipline only those customers are served, which are present at the beginning of the service period. In case of E-limited discipline either N customers are served in a service period or the queue becomes empty before and the service period ends. In case of G-limited discipline at most N customers are served among the customers, which are present at the beginning of the service period.

3   Stationary Number of Customers in the Vacation Period

We define $N(t)$ as the number of customers in the system at time t, and $\widehat{\mathbf{q}}(z)$ and $\widehat{\mathbf{q}}^v(z)$ as the vector GFs of the stationary number of customers and of the stationary number of customers during the vacation period, respectively. The elements of $\widehat{\mathbf{q}}(z)$ and $\widehat{\mathbf{q}}^v(z)$ are defined as

$$[\widehat{\mathbf{q}}(z)]_j = \lim_{t \to \infty} \sum_{n=0}^{\infty} P\{N(t) = n, J(t) = j\} z^n, \quad |z| \le 1, \text{ and}$$

$$[\widehat{\mathbf{q}}^v(z)]_j = \lim_{t \to \infty} \sum_{n=0}^{\infty} P\{N(t) = n, J(t) = j \mid t \in vacation\ period\} z^n, \quad |z| \le 1,$$

respectively.

Furthermore, t_k^m denotes the start of vacation (the instant just after the completion of service) in the k-th cycle. The vector GF, $\widehat{\mathbf{m}}(z)$, is defined by its elements as

$$[\widehat{\mathbf{m}}(z)]_j = \lim_{k \to \infty} \sum_{n=0}^{\infty} P\{N(t_k^m) = n, J(t_k^m) = j\} z^n, \quad |z| \le 1.$$

Theorem 1. *The following relation holds for the vector GF of the stationary number of customers in the vacation period:*

$$\widehat{\mathbf{q}}^v(z)\widehat{\mathbf{D}}(z) = \frac{\widehat{\mathbf{m}}(z)\left(\widehat{\mathbf{U}}(z) - \mathbf{I}\right)}{v}. \tag{4}$$

Proof. The matrix GF of the number of customers arriving during the vacation period is $E\left(e^{\hat{\mathbf{D}}(z)V}\right)$, from which

$$E\left(e^{\hat{\mathbf{D}}(z)V}\right) = \int_{t=0}^{\infty} e^{\hat{\mathbf{D}}(z)t}dV(t) = \hat{\mathbf{U}}(z). \tag{5}$$

The vector GF of the stationary number of customers in the system at instant τ in the vacation period is $\hat{\mathbf{m}}(z)\,e^{\hat{\mathbf{D}}(z)\tau}$, where the first term stands for the stationary number of customers in the system at the beginning of the vacation and the second term stands for the number of customers arriving in the $(0,\tau)$ interval of the vacation period. To obtain the stationary number of customers during the vacation period we need to average the number of customers in the system over the duration of the vacation period

$$\hat{\mathbf{q}}^v(z) = \frac{\hat{\mathbf{m}}(z)E\left(\int_{\tau=0}^{V} e^{\hat{\mathbf{D}}(z)\tau}d\tau\right)}{E(V)}. \tag{6}$$

Based on the definition of $\hat{\mathbf{q}}^v(z)$, we have $\hat{\mathbf{q}}^v(1)\,\mathbf{e} = 1$. Indeed the numerator of (6) at $z = 1$ multiplied by $\mathbf{e}$ can be written as

$$E\left(\int_{\tau=0}^{V} \hat{\mathbf{m}}(1)\left(e^{\mathbf{D}\tau}\,\mathbf{e}\right)\,d\tau\right) = E\left(\int_{\tau=0}^{V} \hat{\mathbf{m}}(1)\,\mathbf{e}\,d\tau\right) = E\left(\int_{\tau=0}^{V} 1\,d\tau\right) = E(V),\tag{7}$$

because $e^{\mathbf{D}\tau}$ is a stochastic matrix and consequently $e^{\mathbf{D}\tau}\,\mathbf{e} = \mathbf{e}$. Multiplying both sides of (6) by $\hat{\mathbf{D}}(z)$ and using $E(V) = v$ we have

$$\hat{\mathbf{q}}^v(z)\,\hat{\mathbf{D}}(z) = \frac{1}{v}\,\hat{\mathbf{m}}(z)E\left(\int_{\tau=0}^{V} e^{\hat{\mathbf{D}}(z)\tau}\,\hat{\mathbf{D}}(z)\,d\tau\right). \tag{8}$$

The integral term can be rewritten as

$$\int_{\tau=0}^{V} e^{\hat{\mathbf{D}}(z)\tau}\,\hat{\mathbf{D}}(z)\,d\tau = \int_{\tau=0}^{V} \sum_{k=0}^{\infty} \frac{\tau^k \hat{\mathbf{D}}(z)^k}{k!}\,\hat{\mathbf{D}}(z)\,d\tau =$$

$$\sum_{k=0}^{\infty} \int_{\tau=0}^{V} \tau^k\,d\tau\,\frac{\hat{\mathbf{D}}(z)^{k+1}}{k!} = \sum_{k=0}^{\infty} \frac{V^{k+1}}{k+1}\,\frac{\hat{\mathbf{D}}(z)^{k+1}}{k!} = e^{\hat{\mathbf{D}}(z)V} - \mathbf{I}. \tag{9}$$

Using (5) and (9) the theorem comes from (8).   Q.E.D.

4   Service Discipline Independent Stationary Relations

4.1   Vector GF of the Stationary Number of Customers

Theorem 2. *The following service discipline independent relation holds for the vector GF of the stationary number of customers at an arbitrary instant:*

$$\hat{\mathbf{q}}(z)\hat{\mathbf{D}}(z)\left(z\mathbf{I}-\hat{\mathbf{A}}(z)\right) = \frac{\hat{\mathbf{m}}(z)\left(\hat{\mathbf{U}}(z)-\mathbf{I}\right)}{v}(1-\rho)(z-1)\hat{\mathbf{A}}(z). \quad (10)$$

Proof. Chang et al. [8] provided a factorization formula for the $BMAP/G/1$ queue with generalized vacations:

$$\hat{\mathbf{q}}(z)\left(z\mathbf{I}-\hat{\mathbf{A}}(z)\right) = \hat{\mathbf{q}}^v(z)(1-\rho)(z-1)\hat{\mathbf{A}}(z). \quad (11)$$

The theorem can be obtained by multiplying both sides of (11) by $\hat{\mathbf{D}}(z)$ from the right and applying (4), because $\hat{\mathbf{A}}(z)$ and $\hat{\mathbf{D}}(z)$ commute, as can be seen from the Taylor expansion of $\hat{\mathbf{A}}(z)$. Q.E.D.

Note that the contribution of the concrete service discipline to the relation (10) is incorporated by the quantity $\hat{\mathbf{m}}(z)$.

4.2   The Mean of the Stationary Number of Customers

This subsection presents the service discipline independent solution for the mean of the stationary number of customers in the system based on its vector GF (10). To this end, we introduce the following notations. When $\hat{\mathbf{Y}}(z)$ is a GF, $\mathbf{Y}^{(i)}$ denotes it i-th ($i \geq 1$) factorial moment, i.e., $\mathbf{Y}^{(i)} = \frac{d^i}{dz^i}\hat{\mathbf{Y}}(z)|_{z=1}$, and $\mathbf{Y}$ denotes its value at $z = 1$, i.e., $\mathbf{Y} = \hat{\mathbf{Y}}(1)$. We apply these conventions for $\hat{\mathbf{D}}(z)$, $\hat{\mathbf{A}}(z)$, $\hat{\mathbf{U}}(z)$, $\hat{\mathbf{q}}(z)$, $\hat{\mathbf{m}}(z)$ and for the later defined $\hat{\mathbf{r}}(z)$ and $\hat{\mathbf{t}}(z)$.

Theorem 3. *The service discipline independent solution for the mean of the stationary number of customers at an arbitrary instant is given by:*

$$\mathbf{q}^{(1)} = \frac{\mathbf{m}^{(1)}}{\lambda v}\left(\mathbf{U}^{(1)}\mathbf{e}\pi + (\mathbf{U}-\mathbf{I})\left(\mathbf{A}^{(1)}-\mathbf{A}(\mathbf{D}+\mathbf{e}\pi)^{-1}\mathbf{D}^{(1)}\right)\mathbf{e}\pi\right) \quad (12)$$
$$+ \frac{\mathbf{m}}{\lambda v}\left(\frac{1}{2}\mathbf{U}^{(2)}\mathbf{e}\pi + \frac{1}{2}(\mathbf{U}-\mathbf{I})\mathbf{A}^{(2)}\mathbf{e}\pi + \mathbf{U}^{(1)}\mathbf{A}^{(1)}\mathbf{e}\pi\right)$$
$$- \frac{\mathbf{m}}{\lambda v}\left(\mathbf{U}^{(1)}\mathbf{A} + (\mathbf{U}-\mathbf{I})\mathbf{A}^{(1)}\right)(\mathbf{D}+\mathbf{e}\pi)^{-1}\mathbf{D}^{(1)}\mathbf{e}\pi$$
$$+ \frac{\mathbf{m}}{\lambda v}\left(\mathbf{U}^{(1)}\mathbf{A}\mathbf{e}\pi + (\mathbf{U}-\mathbf{I})\mathbf{A}^{(1)}\mathbf{e}\pi\right)\left(\frac{\mathbf{C}_2\mathbf{e}\pi}{\lambda} + (1-\rho)\mathbf{C}_1\right)$$
$$+ \frac{\mathbf{m}}{\lambda v}(\mathbf{U}-\mathbf{I})\mathbf{A}(\mathbf{D}+\mathbf{e}\pi)^{-1}\left(\lambda\mathbf{I}-\mathbf{D}^{(1)}\mathbf{e}\pi\right)\left(\frac{\mathbf{C}_2\mathbf{e}\pi}{\lambda} + (1-\rho)\mathbf{C}_1\right)$$
$$+ \pi\left(\frac{\mathbf{A}^{(2)}\mathbf{e}\pi}{2(1-\rho)} - \left(\mathbf{I}-\mathbf{A}^{(1)}\right)\mathbf{C}_1\right),$$

where matrices $\mathbf{C}_1$ *and* $\mathbf{C}_2$ *are defined as*

$$\mathbf{C}_1 = (\mathbf{I}-\mathbf{A}+\mathbf{e}\pi)^{-1}\left(\frac{\mathbf{A}^{(1)}\mathbf{e}\pi}{(1-\rho)} + \mathbf{I}\right), \quad \mathbf{C}_2 = \mathbf{D}^{(1)}(\mathbf{D}+\mathbf{e}\pi)^{-1}\mathbf{D}^{(1)} - \frac{1}{2}\mathbf{D}^{(2)}.$$

To prove the theorem we need the following lemmas.

Lemma 1. *The term* $\mathbf{q}^{(1)}$ *can be expressed from (14) in terms of* $\mathbf{r}^{(1)}$ *and* $\mathbf{r}^{(2)}\mathbf{e}$ *as follows:*

$$\mathbf{q}^{(1)} = \frac{\mathbf{r}^{(2)}\mathbf{e}\boldsymbol{\pi}}{2\left(1-\rho\right)} + \mathbf{r}^{(1)}\mathbf{C}_1 + \boldsymbol{\pi}\left(\frac{\mathbf{A}^{(2)}\mathbf{e}\boldsymbol{\pi}}{2\left(1-\rho\right)} - \left(\mathbf{I}-\mathbf{A}^{(1)}\right)\mathbf{C}_1\right), \qquad (13)$$

where vector $\widehat{\mathbf{r}}\left(z\right)$ *is defined as*

$$\widehat{\mathbf{r}}\left(z\right) = \widehat{\mathbf{q}}\left(z\right)\left(z\mathbf{I}-\widehat{\mathbf{A}}(z)\right). \qquad (14)$$

Proof. Starting from (14) we apply the method used by Lucantoni in [3] and Neuts in [4], which utilizes that $(\mathbf{I}-\mathbf{A}+\mathbf{e}\boldsymbol{\pi})$ is nonsingular. Taking the first two derivatives of (14) at $z=1$, we get:

$$\mathbf{q}^{(1)}\left(\mathbf{I}-\mathbf{A}\right) = \mathbf{r}^{(1)} - \boldsymbol{\pi}\left(\mathbf{I}-\mathbf{A}^{(1)}\right), \qquad (15)$$

$$\mathbf{q}^{(2)}\left(\mathbf{I}-\mathbf{A}\right) = \mathbf{r}^{(2)} - 2\mathbf{q}^{(1)}\left(\mathbf{I}-\mathbf{A}^{(1)}\right) + \boldsymbol{\pi}\mathbf{A}^{(2)}. \qquad (16)$$

Adding $\mathbf{q}^{(1)}\mathbf{e}\boldsymbol{\pi}$ to both sides of (15) and using $\boldsymbol{\pi}\left(\mathbf{I}-\mathbf{A}+\mathbf{e}\boldsymbol{\pi}\right)^{-1} = \boldsymbol{\pi}$ leads to

$$\mathbf{q}^{(1)} = \left(\mathbf{q}^{(1)}\mathbf{e}\right)\boldsymbol{\pi} + \left(\mathbf{r}^{(1)} - \boldsymbol{\pi}\left(\mathbf{I}-\mathbf{A}^{(1)}\right)\right)\left(\mathbf{I}-\mathbf{A}+\mathbf{e}\boldsymbol{\pi}\right)^{-1}. \qquad (17)$$

The next step is to get the unknown term $(\mathbf{q}^{(1)}\mathbf{e})$ in (17). Post-multiplying (16) by $\mathbf{e}$ and post-multiplying (17) by $\left(\mathbf{I}-\mathbf{A}^{(1)}\right)\mathbf{e}$ and rearranging gives

$$\mathbf{q}^{(1)}\left(\mathbf{I}-\mathbf{A}^{(1)}\right)\mathbf{e} = \frac{1}{2}\mathbf{r}^{(2)}\mathbf{e} + \frac{1}{2}\boldsymbol{\pi}\mathbf{A}^{(2)}\mathbf{e}, \qquad (18)$$

$$\mathbf{q}^{(1)}\left(\mathbf{I}-\mathbf{A}^{(1)}\right)\mathbf{e} = \left(\mathbf{q}^{(1)}\mathbf{e}\right)\boldsymbol{\pi}\left(\mathbf{I}-\mathbf{A}^{(1)}\right)\mathbf{e} \qquad (19)$$
$$+ \left(\mathbf{r}^{(1)} - \boldsymbol{\pi}\left(\mathbf{I}-\mathbf{A}^{(1)}\right)\right)\left(\mathbf{I}-\mathbf{A}+\mathbf{e}\boldsymbol{\pi}\right)^{-1}\left(\mathbf{I}-\mathbf{A}^{(1)}\right)\mathbf{e},$$

respectively. Combining (18) and (19) and applying $\boldsymbol{\pi}\left(\mathbf{I}-\mathbf{A}^{(1)}\right)\mathbf{e} = 1-\rho$ results in the expression of the required term:

$$\mathbf{q}^{(1)}\mathbf{e} = \frac{1}{2\left(1-\rho\right)}\left(\mathbf{r}^{(2)}\mathbf{e} + \boldsymbol{\pi}\mathbf{A}^{(2)}\mathbf{e}\right) + \qquad (20)$$
$$\frac{1}{\left(1-\rho\right)}\left(\boldsymbol{\pi}\left(\mathbf{I}-\mathbf{A}^{(1)}\right) - \mathbf{r}^{(1)}\right)\left(\mathbf{I}-\mathbf{A}+\mathbf{e}\boldsymbol{\pi}\right)^{-1}\left(\mathbf{I}-\mathbf{A}^{(1)}\right)\mathbf{e}.$$

We can simplify (20) by using $(I - A + e\pi)^{-1} e = e$ and $(r^{(1)} - \pi (I - A^{(1)})) e = 0$ from (15):

$$q^{(1)} e = \frac{1}{2(1-\rho)} \left(r^{(2)} e + \pi A^{(2)} e \right) \tag{21}$$

$$+ \frac{1}{(1-\rho)} \left(r^{(1)} - \pi \left(I - A^{(1)} \right) \right) (I - A + e\pi)^{-1} A^{(1)} e.$$

Substituting (21) into (17) leads to:

$$q^{(1)} = \frac{r^{(2)} e\pi}{2(1-\rho)} + r^{(1)} \left(\frac{1}{1-\rho} (I - A + e\pi)^{-1} A^{(1)} e\pi + (I - A + e\pi)^{-1} \right) \tag{22}$$

$$+ \pi \left(\frac{A^{(2)} e\pi}{2(1-\rho)} \right)$$

$$- \pi \left(\frac{1}{1-\rho} \left(I - A^{(1)} \right) (I - A + e\pi)^{-1} A^{(1)} e\pi + \left(I - A^{(1)} \right) (I - A + e\pi)^{-1} \right).$$

Substituting matrix C_1 into (22) results in the statement.   Q.E.D.

Lemma 2. *The terms* $r^{(1)}$ *and* $r^{(2)} e$ *can be expressed from (25) in terms of* $t^{(1)}$, $t^{(2)} e$, $t^{(2)}$ *and* $t^{(3)} e$ *as follows:*

$$r^{(1)} = \frac{t^{(2)} e\pi}{2\lambda} + t^{(1)} (D + e\pi)^{-1} \left(I - \frac{D^{(1)} e\pi}{\lambda} \right), \tag{23}$$

$$r^{(2)} e = \frac{t^{(3)} e}{3\lambda} - \frac{t^{(2)}}{\lambda} (D + e\pi)^{-1} D^{(1)} e + \frac{t^{(2)} e\pi}{2\lambda} \frac{2C_2 e}{\lambda} + \tag{24}$$

$$t^{(1)} (D + e\pi)^{-1} \left(I - \frac{D^{(1)} e\pi}{\lambda} \right) \frac{2C_2 e}{\lambda},$$

where vector $\hat{t}(z)$ *is defined as*

$$\hat{t}(z) = \hat{r}(z) \hat{D}(z). \tag{25}$$

Proof. We apply again the same method as in Lemma 1, but now utilizing that $(D + e\pi)$ is nonsingular. Setting $z = 1$ in (14) we get:

$$r = \pi (I - A) = 0. \tag{26}$$

Taking the first three derivatives of (25) and applying (26) results in

$$r^{(1)} D = t^{(1)}, \tag{27}$$

$$r^{(2)} D = t^{(2)} - 2r^{(1)} D^{(1)}, \tag{28}$$

$$r^{(3)} D = t^{(3)} - 3r^{(2)} D^{(1)} - 3r^{(1)} D^{(2)}. \tag{29}$$

Adding $r^{(1)} e\pi$ to both sides of (27) and using $\pi (D + e\pi)^{-1} = \pi$ we obtain

$$r^{(1)} = \left(r^{(1)} e \right) \pi + t^{(1)} (D + e\pi)^{-1}. \tag{30}$$

Post-multiplying (28) by $\mathbf{e}$ and (30) by $\mathbf{D}^{(1)}\mathbf{e}$ after rearranging yields

$$\mathbf{r}^{(1)}\mathbf{D}^{(1)}\mathbf{e} = \frac{1}{2}\mathbf{t}^{(2)}\mathbf{e}, \tag{31}$$

$$\mathbf{r}^{(1)}\mathbf{D}^{(1)}\mathbf{e} = \left(\mathbf{r}^{(1)}\mathbf{e}\right)\boldsymbol{\pi}\mathbf{D}^{(1)}\mathbf{e} + \mathbf{t}^{(1)}\left(\mathbf{D}+\mathbf{e}\boldsymbol{\pi}\right)^{-1}\mathbf{D}^{(1)}\mathbf{e}, \tag{32}$$

respectively. Combining (31) and (32) and applying $\boldsymbol{\pi}\mathbf{D}^{(1)}\mathbf{e} = \lambda$ results in:

$$\mathbf{r}^{(1)}\mathbf{e} = \frac{1}{2\lambda}\mathbf{t}^{(2)}\mathbf{e} - \frac{1}{\lambda}\mathbf{t}^{(1)}\left(\mathbf{D}+\mathbf{e}\boldsymbol{\pi}\right)^{-1}\mathbf{D}^{(1)}\mathbf{e}. \tag{33}$$

Substituting (33) into (30) results in the first statement.
    Adding $\mathbf{r}^{(2)}\mathbf{e}\boldsymbol{\pi}$ to both sides of (28) gives:

$$\mathbf{r}^{(2)} = \left(\mathbf{r}^{(2)}\mathbf{e}\right)\boldsymbol{\pi} + \left(\mathbf{t}^{(2)} - 2\mathbf{r}^{(1)}\mathbf{D}^{(1)}\right)\left(\mathbf{D}+\mathbf{e}\boldsymbol{\pi}\right)^{-1}. \tag{34}$$

Post-multiplying (29) by $\mathbf{e}$ and (34) by $\mathbf{D}^{(1)}\mathbf{e}$ after rearranging leads to

$$\mathbf{r}^{(2)}\mathbf{D}^{(1)}\mathbf{e} = \frac{1}{3}\mathbf{t}^{(3)}\mathbf{e} - \mathbf{r}^{(1)}\mathbf{D}^{(2)}\mathbf{e}, \tag{35}$$

$$\mathbf{r}^{(2)}\mathbf{D}^{(1)}\mathbf{e} = \left(\mathbf{r}^{(2)}\mathbf{e}\right)\boldsymbol{\pi}\mathbf{D}^{(1)}\mathbf{e} + \left(\mathbf{t}^{(2)} - 2\mathbf{r}^{(1)}\mathbf{D}^{(1)}\right)\left(\mathbf{D}+\mathbf{e}\boldsymbol{\pi}\right)^{-1}\mathbf{D}^{(1)}\mathbf{e}, \tag{36}$$

respectively. Combining (35) and (36) and applying $\boldsymbol{\pi}\mathbf{D}^{(1)}\mathbf{e} = \lambda$ results in:

$$\mathbf{r}^{(2)}\mathbf{e} = \frac{1}{3\lambda}\mathbf{t}^{(3)}\mathbf{e} - \frac{1}{\lambda}\mathbf{r}^{(1)}\mathbf{D}^{(2)}\mathbf{e} + \frac{1}{\lambda}\left(2\mathbf{r}^{(1)}\mathbf{D}^{(1)} - \mathbf{t}^{(2)}\right)\left(\mathbf{D}+\mathbf{e}\boldsymbol{\pi}\right)^{-1}\mathbf{D}^{(1)}\mathbf{e}. \tag{37}$$

Substituting (23) into (37) leads to:

$$\mathbf{r}^{(2)}\mathbf{e} = \frac{\mathbf{t}^{(3)}\mathbf{e}}{3\lambda} - \frac{\mathbf{t}^{(2)}}{\lambda}\left(\mathbf{D}+\mathbf{e}\boldsymbol{\pi}\right)^{-1}\mathbf{D}^{(1)}\mathbf{e} + \frac{\mathbf{t}^{(2)}\mathbf{e}\boldsymbol{\pi}}{2\lambda}\left(\frac{2\mathbf{D}^{(1)}}{\lambda}\left(\mathbf{D}+\mathbf{e}\boldsymbol{\pi}\right)^{-1}\mathbf{D}^{(1)}\mathbf{e} - \frac{\mathbf{D}^{(2)}\mathbf{e}}{\lambda}\right)$$
$$+ \mathbf{t}^{(1)}\left(\mathbf{D}+\mathbf{e}\boldsymbol{\pi}\right)^{-1}\left(\mathbf{I} - \frac{\mathbf{D}^{(1)}\mathbf{e}\boldsymbol{\pi}}{\lambda}\right)\left(\frac{2\mathbf{D}^{(1)}}{\lambda}\left(\mathbf{D}+\mathbf{e}\boldsymbol{\pi}\right)^{-1}\mathbf{D}^{(1)}\mathbf{e} - \frac{\mathbf{D}^{(2)}\mathbf{e}}{\lambda}\right). \tag{38}$$

Inserting matrix $\mathbf{C_2}$ into (38) results in the second statement.   Q.E.D.

Proof. PROOF OF THEOREM 3
    Due to the fact that $\widehat{\mathbf{D}}(z)$ and $\widehat{\mathbf{A}}(z)$ commute $\widehat{\mathbf{t}}(z)$ equals to the left hand size of (10)

$$\widehat{\mathbf{t}}(z) = \widehat{\mathbf{q}}(z)\widehat{\mathbf{D}}(z)\left(z\mathbf{I} - \widehat{\mathbf{A}}(z)\right). \tag{39}$$

We apply Lemma 1 and 2 to get $\mathbf{q}^{(1)}$ from (39). Substituting (23) and (24) into (13) gives the expression of $\mathbf{q}^{(1)}$ in terms of $\mathbf{t}^{(1)}$, $\mathbf{t}^{(2)}\mathbf{e}$, $\mathbf{t}^{(2)}$ and $\mathbf{t}^{(3)}\mathbf{e}$:

$$\mathbf{q}^{(1)} = \frac{\mathbf{t}^{(3)}\mathbf{e}\boldsymbol{\pi}}{6\lambda\left(1-\rho\right)} - \frac{\mathbf{t}^{(2)}}{2\lambda\left(1-\rho\right)}\left(\mathbf{D}+\mathbf{e}\boldsymbol{\pi}\right)^{-1}\mathbf{D}^{(1)}\mathbf{e}\boldsymbol{\pi} \tag{40}$$

$$+ \frac{\mathbf{t}^{(2)}\mathbf{e}\boldsymbol{\pi}}{2\lambda\left(1-\rho\right)}\left(\frac{\mathbf{C}_2\mathbf{e}\boldsymbol{\pi}}{\lambda}+\left(1-\rho\right)\mathbf{C}_1\right)$$

$$+ \frac{\mathbf{t}^{(1)}}{\left(1-\rho\right)}\left(\mathbf{D}+\mathbf{e}\boldsymbol{\pi}\right)^{-1}\left(\mathbf{I}-\frac{\mathbf{D}^{(1)}\mathbf{e}\boldsymbol{\pi}}{\lambda}\right)\left(\frac{\mathbf{C}_2\mathbf{e}\boldsymbol{\pi}}{\lambda}+\left(1-\rho\right)\mathbf{C}_1\right)$$

$$+ \boldsymbol{\pi}\left(\frac{\mathbf{A}^{(2)}\mathbf{e}\boldsymbol{\pi}}{2\left(1-\rho\right)}-\left(\mathbf{I}-\mathbf{A}^{(1)}\right)\mathbf{C}_1\right).$$

Substituting (10) into (39) yields:

$$\widehat{\mathbf{t}}\left(z\right) = \frac{\widehat{\mathbf{m}}\left(z\right)\left(\widehat{\mathbf{U}}\left(z\right)-\mathbf{I}\right)}{v}\left(1-\rho\right)\left(z-1\right)\widehat{\mathbf{A}}(z). \tag{41}$$

Taking the first three derivatives of $\widehat{\mathbf{t}}\left(z\right)$ at $z=1$:

$$\mathbf{t}^{(1)} = \left(1-\rho\right)\frac{\mathbf{m}}{v}\left(\mathbf{U}-\mathbf{I}\right)\mathbf{A}, \tag{42}$$

$$\mathbf{t}^{(2)} = 2\left(1-\rho\right)\frac{\mathbf{m}^{(1)}}{v}\left(\mathbf{U}-\mathbf{I}\right)\mathbf{A}+2\left(1-\rho\right)\frac{\mathbf{m}}{v}\left(\mathbf{U}^{(1)}\mathbf{A}+\left(\mathbf{U}-\mathbf{I}\right)\mathbf{A}^{(1)}\right), \tag{43}$$

$$\mathbf{t}^{(2)}\mathbf{e} = 2\left(1-\rho\right)\frac{\mathbf{m}}{v}\left(\mathbf{U}^{(1)}\mathbf{A}\mathbf{e}+\left(\mathbf{U}-\mathbf{I}\right)\mathbf{A}^{(1)}\mathbf{e}\right), \tag{44}$$

$$\mathbf{t}^{(3)}\mathbf{e} = 6\left(1-\rho\right)\frac{\mathbf{m}^{(1)}}{v}\left(\mathbf{U}^{(1)}\mathbf{e}+\left(\mathbf{U}-\mathbf{I}\right)\mathbf{A}^{(1)}\mathbf{e}\right)$$

$$+ 3\left(1-\rho\right)\frac{\mathbf{m}}{v}\left(\mathbf{U}^{(2)}\mathbf{e}+\left(\mathbf{U}-\mathbf{I}\right)\mathbf{A}^{(2)}\mathbf{e}+2\mathbf{U}^{(1)}\mathbf{A}^{(1)}\mathbf{e}\right). \tag{45}$$

Substituting (42), (43), (44) and (45) into (40) gives the theorem.   Q.E.D.

Note that in (12) the impact of the concrete service discipline on the mean of the stationary number of customers is expressed by the quantities $\mathbf{m}^{(1)}$ and $\mathbf{m}$.

5 Vacation Models of Non-M/G/1-Type

Let t_k^f denotes the end of vacation (the instant just before the start of service) in the k-th cycle. The vectors $\mathbf{f}_n$ and $\mathbf{m}_n$, $n \geq 0$, are defined by their elements as

$$[\mathbf{f}_n]_j = \lim_{k\to\infty} P\left\{N(t_k^f) = n, J(t_k^f) = j\right\},$$

$$[\mathbf{m}_n]_j = \lim_{k\to\infty} P\left\{N(t_k^m) = n, J(t_k^m) = j\right\},$$

To get the unknown quantities $\mathbf{m}$, $\mathbf{m}^{(1)}$ in (12), we compute the stationary probability vectors $\mathbf{m}_n$, $n \geq 0$. For doing that we setup a system of linear equations for each studied discipline.

5.1 Vacation Model with Gated Discipline

Theorem 4. *In the vacation model with gated discipline the probability vectors* $\mathbf{m}_n$, $n \geq 0$ *are determined by the following system equation:*

$$\sum_{n=0}^{\infty} \mathbf{m}_n \sum_{k=0}^{\infty} \mathbf{U}_k \left(\widehat{\mathbf{A}}(z)\right)^k \left(\widehat{\mathbf{A}}(z)\right)^n = \sum_{n=0}^{\infty} \mathbf{m}_n z^n. \tag{46}$$

Proof. Each customer, who is present at the end of the vacation, generates a random population of customers arriving during its service time. The GF of number of customers in this random population is $\widehat{\mathbf{A}}(z)$. Hence the governing relation for transition $f \to m$ of the vacation model with gated discipline is given by

$$\sum_{n=0}^{\infty} \mathbf{f}_n \left(\widehat{\mathbf{A}}(z)\right)^n = \sum_{n=0}^{\infty} \mathbf{m}_n z^n. \tag{47}$$

The number of customers at the end of the vacation equals the sum of those present at the beginning of the vacation and those who arrived during the vacation period. Applying the phase independent vacation property **A.4**, we get discipline independent governing relation for transition $m \to f$ of the vacation model

$$\sum_{k=0}^{n} \mathbf{m}_k \mathbf{U}_{n-k} = \mathbf{f}_n. \tag{48}$$

Combining (47) and (48) and rearranging results in the statement.   Q.E.D.

To compute the probability vectors $\mathbf{m}_n$ a numerical method can be developed by setting a ρ dependent upper limit X for n and k in (46). Taking the x-th derivatives of (46) at $z = 1$, where $x = 0, \ldots, X$, leads to a system of linear equations, in which the number of equations and the number of unknowns is $L(X+1)$:

$$\sum_{n=0}^{X} \mathbf{m}_n \sum_{k=0}^{X} \mathbf{U}_k \sum_{l=0}^{x} \binom{x}{l} \left. \frac{d^{(x-l)}\left(\left(\widehat{\mathbf{A}}(z)\right)^k\right)}{dz^{(x-l)}} \right|_{z=1} \left. \frac{d^l\left(\left(\widehat{\mathbf{A}}(z)\right)^n\right)}{dz^l} \right|_{z=1}$$

$$= \sum_{n=x}^{X} \mathbf{m}_n \frac{n!}{(n-x)!}, \quad x = 0, \ldots, X. \tag{49}$$

5.2 Vacation Model with G-Limited Discipline

Theorem 5. *In the vacation model with G-limited discipline the probability vectors* $\mathbf{m}_n$, $n \geq 0$ *are determined by the following system equation:*

$$\sum_{n=0}^{K} \sum_{k=0}^{n} \mathbf{m}_k \mathbf{U}_{n-k} \left(\widehat{\mathbf{A}}(z)\right)^n + \sum_{n=K+1}^{\infty} \sum_{k=0}^{n} \mathbf{m}_k \mathbf{U}_{n-k} \left(\widehat{\mathbf{A}}(z)\right)^K = \sum_{n=0}^{\infty} \mathbf{m}_n z^n. \tag{50}$$

Proof. According to the G-limited discipline, the service is gated up to a maximum number K of customers present at the beginning of service. Hence the governing relation for transition $f \to m$ of the vacation model with G-limited discipline is given by

$$\sum_{n=0}^{K} \mathbf{f}_n \left(\widehat{\mathbf{A}} (z) \right)^n + \sum_{n=K+1}^{\infty} \mathbf{f}_n \left(\widehat{\mathbf{A}} (z) \right)^K = \sum_{n=0}^{\infty} \mathbf{m}_n z^n. \tag{51}$$

Combining (51) with the discipline independent governing relation for transition $m \to f$ (48) and rearranging leads to the statement.   Q.E.D.

Again to compute the probability vectors $\mathbf{m}_n$ a numerical method can be developed by setting a ρ dependent upper limit X for n in (50). Taking the x-th derivatives of (50) at $z = 1$, where $x = 0, \ldots, X$, leads to a system of linear equations, in which the number of equations and the number of unknowns is $L(X+1)$:

$$\sum_{n=0}^{K} \sum_{k=0}^{n} \mathbf{m}_k \mathbf{U}_{n-k} \frac{d^x \left(\left(\widehat{\mathbf{A}}(z) \right)^n \right)}{dz^x} \Bigg|_{z=1} + \sum_{n=K+1}^{X} \sum_{k=0}^{n} \mathbf{m}_k \mathbf{U}_{n-k} \frac{d^x \left(\left(\widehat{\mathbf{A}}(z) \right)^K \right)}{dz^x} \Bigg|_{z=1}$$

$$= \sum_{n=x}^{X} \mathbf{m}_n \frac{n!}{(n-x)!}, \quad x = 0, \ldots, X. \tag{52}$$

6 Numerical Example

We provide a simple numerical example just with illustrative purpose for the case of vacation model with gated discipline.

The arrival process is given by

$$\widehat{\mathbf{D}}(z) = \mathbf{D}_0 + z\mathbf{D}_1,$$

$$\mathbf{D}_0 = \begin{pmatrix} -\lambda_1 - \beta_1 & \lambda_1 \\ 0 & -\lambda_2 - \beta_2 \end{pmatrix}, \quad \mathbf{D}_1 = \begin{pmatrix} 0 & \beta_1 \\ \lambda_2 & \beta_2 \end{pmatrix}.$$

The customer service time is constant with value $B = \tau$, and hence

$$\widehat{\mathbf{A}}(z) = \int_{t=0}^{\infty} e^{(\mathbf{D}_0 + z\mathbf{D}_1)t} dB(t) = e^{(\mathbf{D}_0 + z\mathbf{D}_1)\tau}.$$

The vacation time V is exponential with parameter γ. It follows

$$\mathbf{U}_k = \left((-\mathbf{D}_0 + \gamma\mathbf{I})^{-1} \mathbf{D}_1 \right)^k (-\mathbf{D}_0 + \gamma\mathbf{I})^{-1} \gamma\mathbf{I}, \quad k \geq 0.$$

We set $X = 3$ and the following parameter values:

$$\lambda_1 = 1, \quad \lambda_2 = 2, \quad \beta_1 = 3, \quad \beta_2 = 4, \quad \tau = 0.01, \quad \gamma = 10.$$

Based on (49) these results in $2(X+1) = 8$ equations, whose solution is

$$\mathbf{m}_0 = (0.3539940000, \quad 0.6233670000),$$
$$\mathbf{m}_1 = (0.0060541700, \quad 0.0156250000),$$
$$\mathbf{m}_2 = (0.0002602540, \quad 0.0006635270),$$
$$\mathbf{m}_3 = (0.0000101579, \quad 0.0000260429),$$

from which

$$\mathbf{m} = \sum_{n=0}^{3} \mathbf{m}_n = (0.360318, \quad 0.639682),$$

$$\mathbf{m}^{(1)} = \sum_{n=0}^{3} n\, \mathbf{m}_n = (0.00660515, \quad 0.0170302).$$

The following table illustrates the dependency of $\mathbf{m}$ and $\mathbf{m}^{(1)}$ on the parameter γ:

γ	$\mathbf{m}$	$\mathbf{m}^{(1)}$
5	(0.415355, 0.584645)	(0.00992439, 0.02573280)
10	(0.360318, 0.639682)	(0.00660515, 0.01703020)
20	(0.341865, 0.658135)	(0.00368462, 0.00944405)

7 Final Remarks

A simple numerical algorithm to solve (46) and (50) can be developed by means of consecutive manyfold solution of the corresponding system of linear equations. Starting with an initial X, X is doubled in each iteration until the absolute error becomes less than the prescribed limit.

It is a topic of future work to investigate the numerical solutions of the system equations (46) and (50) and to evaluate the complexity of the above mentioned numerical procedure.

The phase independent vacation property A.4 can be relaxed, and hence the presented analysis can be extended to the case, when the vacation period depends on at least the phase of the $BMAP$.

Moreover the model can be also extended by handling further quantities like the set-up time or repair time.

References

1. Doshi, B.T.: Queueing systems with vacations - a survey. Queueing Systems 1, 29–66 (1986)
2. Takagi, H.: Queueing Analysis - A Foundation of Performance Evaluation, Vacation and Prority Systems, vol. 1. North-Holland, New York (1991)

3. Lucantoni, D.L.: New results on the single server queue with a batch Markovian arrival process. Stochastic Models 7, 1–46 (1991)
4. Neuts, M.F.: Structured stochastic matrices of $M/G/1$ type and their applications. Marcel Dekker, New York (1989)
5. Neuts, M.F.: Matrix-Geometric Solutions in Stochastic Models: An Algorithmic Approach. John Hopkins University Press, Baltimore (1981)
6. Lucantoni, D.L.: The BMAP/G/1 queue: A tutorial. In: Donatiello, L., Nelson, R. (eds.) Models and Techniques for Performance Evaluation of Computer and Communications Systems. Springer Verlag, Heidelberg (1993)
7. Chang, S.H., Takine, T.: Factorization and Stochastic Decomposition Properties in Bulk Queues with Generalized Vacations. Queueing Systems 50, 165–183 (2005)
8. Chang, S.H., Takine, T., Chae, K.C., Lee, H.W.: A unified queue length formula for $BMAP/G/1$ queue with generalized vacations. Stochastic Models 18, 369–386 (2002)
9. Ferrandiz, J.M.: The BMAP/G/1 queue with server set-up times and server vacations. Adv. Appl. Prob. 25, 235–254 (1993)
10. Shin, Y.W., Pearce, C.E.M.: The BMAP/G/1 vacation queue with queue-length dependent vacation schedule. J. Austral. Math. Soc. Ser. B 40, 207–221 (1998)
11. Banik, A.D., Gupta, U.C., Pathak, S.S.: BMAP/G/1/N queue with vacations and limited service discipline. Applied Mathematics and Computation 180, 707–721 (2006)
12. Fuhrmann, S.W., Cooper, R.B.: Stochastic Decompositions in the M/G/1 Queue with Generalized Vacations. Operations Research 33, 1117–1129 (1985)

Stochastic Bounds for Partially Generated Markov Chains: An Algebraic Approach

Ana Bušić[1] and Jean-Michel Fourneau[1,2]

[1] INRIA Grenoble - Rhône-Alpes
51, Av. J. Kuntzmann, 38330 Montbonnot, France
[2] PRiSM, Université de Versailles-St-Quentin
45, Av. des Etats-Unis, 78035 Versailles, France

Abstract. We propose several algorithms to obtain bounds based on Censored Markov Chains to analyze partially generated discrete time Markov chains. The main idea is to avoid the generation of a huge (or even infinite) state space and to truncate the state space during the visit. The approach is purely algebraic and provides element-wise and stochastic bounds for the CMC.

1 Introduction

Even if it is simple to model systems with Markov chains, the analysis of such chains is still a hard problem when they do not exhibit some regularity or symmetry which allow analytical techniques or lumping. Furthermore, some transitions rates may be unknown. An alternative approach is to compute bounds on the rewards we need to check against requirements. We first bound the steady-state or transient distributions at time t. We define the elementary reward for all states and compute the expected reward by a simple summation of the product of the elementary rewards by the state probabilities. The main difficulty is to obtain a bound of the steady state or transient distributions. The key idea is to derive a smaller chain which provides a bound. Several algorithms have been proposed to obtain some stochastic bounds on Discrete Time Markov Chains (DTMC). Most of these algorithms have used the lumpability approach to reduce the size of the chain [1,6,7,16]. Stochastic comparison of DTMC can also be applied when some transition probabilities are unknown [2,10]. Recently a new approach based on Censored Markov Chain (CMC) have been proposed [4,8] to deal with large or infinite DTMC. Here we present new algorithms based on CMC when only some parts of the matrix are known. Indeed, when the state space is very large or infinite, we have to truncate the chain during the generation and only some parts of the matrix are computed [5]. CMCs provide an efficient way to describe such a truncated generation.

Consider a DTMC $\{X_t : t = 0, 1, \ldots\}$ with a finite state space S. Suppose that $S = A \cup A^c$, $A \cap A^c = \emptyset$. Suppose that the successive visits of X_t to A take place at time epochs $0 \leq t_0 < t_1 < \ldots$ Then the chain $\{X^A_u = X_{t_u}, u = 0, 1, \ldots\}$ is called the censored chain with censoring set A [17]. Let Q denote the transition

N. Thomas and C. Juiz (Eds.): EPEW 2008, LNCS 5261, pp. 227–241, 2008.
© Springer-Verlag Berlin Heidelberg 2008

probability matrix of chain X_t. Consider the partition of the state space to obtain a block description of Q:

$$Q = \begin{bmatrix} Q_{AA} & Q_{A*} \\ Q_{*A} & Q_{**} \end{bmatrix} \begin{matrix} A \\ A^c \end{matrix}$$

The censored chain only observes the states in A. Assume that the chain is ergodic (it may be finite or infinite). It can be proved [17] that the stochastic matrix of the censored chain is:

$$S_{AA} = Q_{AA} + Q_{A*}(I - Q_{**})^{-1}Q_{*A} = Q_{AA} + Q_{A*}\left(\sum_{i=0}^{\infty}(Q_{**})^i\right)Q_{*A}. \quad (1)$$

The second term of the right-hand side represents the probabilities of paths that return to set A through states in A^c.

Censored Markov chains have also been called restricted or watched Markov chains. They are also strongly related to the theory of stochastic complement [11]. Note that it is not necessary for censored Markov chains to be ergodic and we can study for instance the absorption time [8]. However, we assume in this paper that the chains are ergodic and that the CMC is finite.

In many problems, initial chain Q can be large or even infinite or some transition rates may be unknown. Therefore, it is difficult or even impossible to compute $(I - Q_{**})^{-1}$ to finally get S_{AA}. Deriving bounds of S_{AA} from Q_{AA} and from some information on the other blocks is thus an interesting alternative approach. Note that we may have various interesting cases:

– *Partial Generation:* Q_{**} and Q_{*A} are difficult to build or contain unknown rates while Q_{AA} is easy to compute from the specifications.
– *Complete Generation:* all the blocks are easy to compute but $(I - Q_{**})$ is difficult to invert because of its size.

Our major concern is the difficulty to obtain a complete description of the block Q_{*A} from a high-level specification framework such as a Stochastic Process Algebra model or a set of stochastic equations. They provide a continuous time Markov chain which can be uniformized to obtain a DTMC. All these formalisms are very efficient in describing forward transitions (i.e. transitions from state x to any state of the chain). Thus we can easily obtain the rows of matrix Q_{AA}. The first problem is to find the reachable state space to define A^c (the set of reachable states which are not censored). Remember that the reachability problem is a time consuming question in many high-level specification languages. Let us now turn to the block Q_{*A}. We have typically four problems :

– *Reachability.* Even with a tensor based approach it is hard to find the reachable state space. For a Stochastic Automata Network (SAN) we define a product space which contains the reachable state space [14]. It is simple to find the column of the matrix associated to a SAN or to any tensor based model with an algorithm developed by Sbeity in [9], but we build the column of the matrix for the product state space which is a superset of the reachable state space. We must remove the rows associated to non reachable states to obtain block Q_{*A} which is difficult because of the reachability problem.

- *Inversion of a stochastic equation.* For some high-level specification languages, transitions out of x are described by a stochastic recurrence equation $X_{n+1} = f(X_n, U)$, where U is a random variable. This is typically the case when one describes queues. But the transitions entering state x are described by function f^{-1}. This problem is very similar to the computation of the inverse function of a distribution. For some functions f, it is well known in simulation that the complexity of the computation of the inverse of function f is highly dependent on the state where we invert the function.
- *Infinite State Space.* When the chain is infinite, Q_{*A} has an infinite number of rows and it is not possible to generate all of them.
- *Unknown rates.* Assume that some rates of a transition from y to x in A are unknown. Assume that y is not a censored state. Then the transition from y to x is in column x of Q_{*A}. Here we consider that if a rate is missing in a column, the complete column of the block is unknown.

In [15], Truffet has proposed a two-level algorithm for Nearly Completely Decomposable (NCD) chains by using aggregation and stochastic ordering to compute bounding distributions. In [13], Truffet's approach has been combined with state reordering to improve the accuracy of a component-wise probability bounding algorithm. In these works, before employing the aggregation of blocks, the slack probabilities $\beta_i = 1 - \sum_{j \in A} Q[i, j]$, $i \in A$ (which are small due to the NCD structure) are included in the last column for the upper bound and in the first column for the lower bound. Clearly Truffet's approach is optimal when only the block Q_{AA} has been computed. Indeed the bound is tight in that case. For general Markov chains (i.e. not NCD), Dayar, Pekergin, and Younes proposed recently an algebraic approach to dispatch slack probabilities when blocks Q_{AA} and Q_{*A} are known [4]. In this paper, we will refer to their algorithm as DPY. DPY exhibits a desirable feature: under some algebraic conditions it provides the exact result (see [4] for a proof and some examples):

Property 1. If block Q_{*A} has rank 1, then the bound given by DPY is exact.

However, DPY needs both Q_{AA} and Q_{*A} to be known. Bounds of S_{AA} have also been derived in [8] in a completely different way by applying graph algorithms. This approach requires that Q_{AA} is computed and some parts (not necessary all elements) of Q_{*A}, Q_{**} and Q_{A*} are known. Here we propose a new approach and several algorithms which require less information on the blocks.

The paper is organized as follows. In Sect. 2 we present a brief introduction to stochastic bounds and CMC. Sect. 3 is devoted to the main concept and the first algorithm we obtained when Q_{*A} is known and satisfies some algebraic constraints. We also show that this first algorithm also gives exact result when Q_{*A} has rank 1. In Sect. 4, we present new algorithms when some columns of Q_{*A} are unknown, based on various assumptions on Q_{*A}. Due to the number of algorithms proposed, we do not have enough space to present a large example. Instead we show on small matrices how the algorithms perform.

2   Some Fundamental Results on Stochastic Bounds

We give first the definition of strong stochastic ordering of random variables on a finite state space $\{1,\ldots,n\}$. Let X and Y be two random variables with probability vectors p and q ($p_k = P(X = k), q_k = P(Y = k)$, $\forall k$). Throughout the paper, all the vectors are column vectors, v^t denotes a transposed vector, and $\preceq_{el}$ element-wise comparison of two vectors (or matrices).

Definition 1. $X \preceq_{st} Y$ if $\sum_{k=j}^n p_k \leq \sum_{k=j}^n q_k$, $\forall j$.

Let $\{X_t\}_{t \geq 0}$ and $\{Y_t\}_{t \geq 0}$ be two DTMC with transition probability matrices P and Q. Then we say that $\{X_t\}_{t \geq 0} \preceq_{st} \{Y_t\}_{t \geq 0}$ if $X_t \preceq_{st} Y_t$ for all $t \geq 0$. Sufficient conditions for comparison of two DTMC are given by the following classical theorem [12]:

Theorem 1. $\{X_t\}_{t \geq 0} \preceq_{st} \{Y_t\}_{t \geq 0}$ if $X_0 \preceq_{st} Y_0$ and there exists a transition probability matrix R such that:

- $P \preceq_{st} R \preceq_{st} Q$, i.e. $P[i, *] \preceq_{st} R[i, *] \preceq_{st} Q[i, *]$, $\forall i$ (comparison),
- $R[i-1, *] \preceq_{st} R[i, *]$, $\forall i > 1$ (monotonicity).

Furthermore, if both chains are ergodic, then $\pi_P \preceq_{st} \pi_Q$ (where π_P and π_Q are the steady-state distributions).

The above conditions can be easily checked algorithmically. Furthermore, it is also possible to construct a monotone upper bound for an arbitrary stochastic matrix P [3]. We define operators r and v as in [3]:

- $r(P)[i,j] = \sum_{k=j}^n P[i,k]$, $\forall i, j$,
- $v(P)[i,j] = \begin{cases} r(P)[1,j], & \text{if } i = 1 \\ \max\{v(P)[i-1,j], r(P)[i,j]\}, & \text{if } i > 1 \end{cases}$, $\forall j$.

Remark 1. It it worthy to remark that $P \preceq_{st} Q$ is equivalent to $r(P) \preceq_{el} r(Q)$.

Proposition 1. (Vincent's algorithm [3]) Let P be any stochastic matrix and $Q = r^{-1}v(P)$, where r^{-1} denotes the inverse of r. Then Q is $\preceq_{st}$-monotone et $P \preceq_{st} Q$, therefore (by Theorem 1) Q is a transition probability matrix of an upper bounding DTMC. Furthermore, if $P_1 \preceq_{st} P_2$, then $r^{-1}v(P_1) \preceq_{st} r^{-1}v(P_2)$.

2.1   CMC and Stochastic Bounds

Let us now consider CMC and it's transition probability matrix given by (1):

$$S_{AA} = Q_{AA} + \underbrace{Q_{A*}(I - Q_A)^{-1}Q_{*A}}_{Z}$$

Z is a sub-stochastic matrix which shows how the missing transition probability must be added to Q_{AA} to obtain S_{AA}. Truffet proposed in [15] an algorithm for the case when we know only the block Q_{AA}. An upper bound for S_{AA} can be obtained by adding first the slack of probability mass to the last column, and then applying operator $r^{-1}v$ to compute a monotone bound. More formally, let θ be the operator which transforms a sub-stochastic matrix M into a stochastic matrix by adding in the last column of M all the probability missing in M:

$$\theta(M)[i,j] = \begin{cases} M[i,j], & \text{if } j < n \\ M[i,j] + \beta_i, & \text{if } j = n \end{cases}, \ \forall i,$$

where $\beta_i = 1 - \sum_{j=1}^{n} M[i,j]$, $\forall i$. Of course, if M is stochastic, then $\theta(M) = M$. The upper bound for S_{AA} proposed in [15] is given by $r^{-1}v(\theta(Q_{AA}))$.

Remark 2. Similarly, a monotone lower bound for S_{AA} is given by $r^{-1}w(\phi(Q_{AA}))$, where operator ϕ adds the slack of probability mass to the first column and

$$w(P)[i,j] = \begin{cases} r(P)[n,j], & \text{if } i = n \\ \min\{w(P)[i+1,j], r(P)[i,j]\}, & \text{if } i < n \end{cases}, \ \forall j.$$

Notice that operator $r^{-1}w$ corresponds to the maximal st-monotone lower bound.

Suppose now that we have some partial information on Z, given by positive matrices L and U such that $L \preceq_{el} Z \preceq_{el} U$. Furthermore, we know that $Ze = \beta$, where e denotes a vector with all components equal to 1.

In the following we describe how we can use matrices L and U to construct an upper and a lower stochastic bound for S_{AA} that is more accurate than Truffet's bound (that uses only the information contained in Q_{AA}). Once we have obtained bounds on S_{AA}, we apply Vincent's algorithm to check the monotonicity and analyze the resulting chain to get steady-state or transient distributions (see [4,8] for more details). Here we only present the computations of the bounds of S_{AA} under various assumptions on the knowledge of Q_{*A}.

2.2   Bounds for a Family of Positive Matrices

In a recent paper [10], Haddad and Moreaux have proposed an algorithm to build a stochastic bound from two element-wise bounding matrices. More precisely, they are interested in absorption time and they only consider finite transient Markov chains. They assume that they do not know exactly the stochastic matrix P they need to analyze (because some terms are difficult to compute), but they know two positive matrices L and U such that $L \preceq_{el} P \preceq_{el} U$. In [10], matrix P is supposed transient (i.e. the last state is absorbing). Let $\mathcal{P}_{L,U}$ be the set of stochastic matrices which satisfy these constraints. They derived an algorithm to compute the smallest (in the st sense) transient matrix in $\mathcal{P}_{L,U}$. We give in Algorithm 1 a generalization of that algorithm: a) we don't need to have any absorbing state; b) we consider positive matrices (not necessarily stochastic). Let $\mathcal{M}_{L,U,\beta}$ be a family of positive matrices given by element-wise upper and lower bounds L and U, and a positive vector of normalization constants β:

$$\mathcal{M}_{L,U,\beta} = \{M \ : \ L \preceq_{el} M \preceq_{el} U \text{ and } Me = \beta\}.$$

We will use the following operator: $\ell(M)[i,j] = \sum_{k=1}^{j} M[i,k]$, $\forall i,j$.

Proposition 2. *Algorithm 1 computes matrices $\overline{M}$ and $\underline{M}$ in $\mathcal{M}_{L,U,\beta}$ such that:*

$$r(\underline{M}) \preceq_{el} r(M) \preceq_{el} r(\overline{M}), \ \forall M \in \mathcal{M}_{L,U,\beta}.$$

Proof. Notice that $L \preceq_{el} M \preceq_{el} U$ implies $r(L)[i,j] \leq r(M)[i,j] \leq r(U)[i,j]$ and $\ell(L)[i,j] \leq \ell(M)[i,j] \leq \ell(U)[i,j], \forall i,j$. The proof follows easily from the fact that $r(M)[i,j] = \beta_j - \ell(M)[i,j-1], \forall M \in \mathcal{M}_{L,U,\beta}$. We omit the technical details. $\qquad\square$

Algorithm 1. r-maximal $(\overline{M})$ and r-minimal $(\underline{M})$ elements for a family of positive matrices $\mathcal{M}_{L,U,\beta} = \{M : L \preceq_{el} M \preceq_{el} U \text{ and } Me = \beta\}$.

Input   : β - positive vector; L, U - positive matrices : $0 \preceq_{el} L \preceq_{el} U \preceq_{el} e\beta^t$
Notation : n - number of lines; m - number of columns
for $i = 1$ to n **do**
    for $j = m$ **downto** 2 **do**
        $\overline{H}[i,j] = \min\{r(U)[i,j], \beta_j - \ell(L)[i,j-1]\};$
        $\underline{H}[i,j] = \max\{r(L)[i,j], \beta_j - \ell(U)[i,j-1]\};$
    end
    $\overline{H}[i,1] = \beta_j; \underline{H}[i,1] = \beta_j;$
    $\overline{M} = r^{-1}(\overline{H}); \underline{M} = r^{-1}(\underline{H});$
end

Let us now go back to CMC problem. We assumed that we know matrix Q_{AA} and element-wise lower and upper bounds L and U for $Z = Q_{A*}(I - Q_A)^{-1}Q_{*A}$. Denote by $\beta = Q_{AA}e$. Algorithm 1 gives matrices $\overline{M}$ and $\underline{M}$ such that $r(\underline{M}) \preceq_{el} r(Z) \preceq_{el} r(\overline{M})$. Denote by $\underline{S} = Q_{AA} + \underline{M}$ and $\overline{S} = Q_{AA} + \overline{M}$.

Theorem 2. *Matrices $\underline{S}$ and $\overline{S}$ satisfy:*

$$\phi(Q_{AA}) \preceq_{st} \underline{S} \preceq_{st} S_{AA} \preceq_{st} \overline{S} \preceq_{st} \theta(Q_{AA}).$$

Proof. Follows directly from Remark 1. $\qquad\square$

Since operator $r^{-1}v$ (resp. $r^{-1}w$) preserves the $\preceq_{st}$-comparison, the upper (resp. lower) bound obtained by taking into account the partial information on Z is more accurate than the bounds proposed in [15]. In the following section we propose how to compute element-wise lower and upper bounds for Z.

3   Element-Wise Bounds for Matrix Z

First let us define the following binary relation on positive real vectors:

Definition 2. *Let x, y be two positive real vectors. Vector y supports x if there exist $\alpha > 0$ and $\gamma \geq 0$ such that $\alpha y \preceq_{el} x \preceq_{el} (\alpha + \gamma) y$.*

Remark 3. Vector y supports vector x if and only if they have the same support (the non zero elements have the same indices in both vectors). Note that if vectors x and y are colinear we have $\gamma = 0$.

Property 2. Relation "supports" is reflexive, symmetric and transitive. Thus the binary relation "supports" is an equivalence relation.

Suppose that vector $y \neq 0$ supports vector x and define $\alpha_{x,y}$ and $\gamma_{x,y}$ as follows:

$$\alpha_{x,y} = \min_{k \,:\, y_k > 0} \frac{x_k}{y_k}, \quad \gamma_{x,y} = \max_{k \,:\, y_k > 0} \frac{x_k}{y_k} - \alpha_{x,y}. \tag{2}$$

Lemma 1. *Constants $\alpha_{x,y}$ and $\gamma_{x,y}$ satisfy $\alpha_{x,y}\, y \preceq_{el} x \preceq_{el} (\alpha_{x,y} + \gamma_{x,y})\, y$. Furthermore, $\alpha_{x,y} = \frac{1}{\alpha_{y,x} + \gamma_{y,x}}$ and $\gamma_{x,y} = \frac{1}{\alpha_{y,x}} - \alpha_{x,y}$.*

Proof. Follows directly from (2). Note that if vector y supports vector x then $\alpha_{x,y} > 0$. By symmetry of relation "supports", we also have $\alpha_{y,x} > 0$. $\qquad \square$

3.1   Main Idea

We introduce here the main idea behind the algorithms for element-wise bounds for matrix Z on a very simple case. The following assumptions will be relaxed in Sect. 4.

Assumption 1. *We assume in this section that all columns of Q_{*A} are in the same class of equivalence for relation "supports" or are null. Furthermore, we suppose that there is at least one non null column.*

In the following, let us note by $C_i(M)$ the i-th column of a matrix M. Let v be any vector that belongs to the same equivalence class as the non null columns of matrix Q_{*A}. Thus, for all i, $C_i(Q_{*A})$ supports v or $C_i(Q_{*A}) = 0$.

For non null columns denote by $\alpha_i := \alpha_{C_i(Q_{*A}),v}$ and $\gamma_i := \gamma_{C_i(Q_{*A}),v}$. For columns i such that $C_i(Q_{*A}) = 0$ we will define $\alpha_i := 0$ and $\gamma_i := 0$ to simplify the formulas. Note that $\|\alpha\|_1 = \sum_i \alpha_i > 0$ and $\|\gamma\|_1 = \sum_i \gamma_i \geq 0$.

We will derive simple component-wise upper and lower bounds for columns of matrix Z in Algorithm 2. We use the following trivial property:

Property 3. $C_i(Z) = Q_{A*}(I - Q_{**})^{-1} C_i(Q_{*A})$.

Lemma 2. $\frac{\beta}{\|\alpha\|_1 + \|\gamma\|_1} \preceq_{el} Q_{A*}(I - Q_{**})^{-1} v \preceq_{el} \frac{\beta}{\|\alpha\|_1}$.

Proof. We have $\alpha_j v \preceq_{el} C_j(Q_{*A}) \preceq_{el} (\alpha_j + \gamma_j) v, \forall j$, which implies $\alpha_j Q_{A*}(I - Q_{**})^{-1} v \preceq_{el} C_j(Z) \preceq_{el} (\alpha_j + \gamma_j) Q_{A*}(I - Q_{**})^{-1} v$. Now by summation for all columns j we obtain $\|\alpha\|_1 Q_{A*}(I - Q_{**})^{-1} v \preceq_{el} \beta \preceq_{el} (\|\alpha\|_1 + \|\gamma\|_1) Q_{A*}(I - Q_{**})^{-1} v$. $\qquad \square$

Lemma 3. *Assume that vector v supports column i. Then:*

$$\beta \frac{\alpha_i}{\|\alpha\|_1 + \|\gamma\|_1} \preceq_{el} C_i(Z) \preceq_{el} \beta \frac{\alpha_i + \gamma_i}{\|\alpha\|_1}.$$

Proof. By definition of constants α_i and γ_i we have:

$$\alpha_i v \preceq_{el} C_i(Q_{*A}) \preceq_{el} (\alpha_i + \gamma_i) v.$$

By Property 3, $\alpha_i Q_{A*}(I - Q_{**})^{-1} v \preceq_{el} C_i(Z) \preceq_{el} (\alpha_i + \gamma_i) Q_{A*}(I - Q_{**})^{-1} v$, which together with Lemma 2 gives the result. $\qquad \square$

Algorithm 2. Element wise upper (U) and lower (L) bounds for matrix Z

Input   : $\beta = e - Q_{AA}e$; matrix Q_{*A}
Notation : m - right-most non null column of Q_{*A}
$v = C_m(Q_{*A})$;
$\alpha = 0;\ \gamma = 0$;
foreach *non null column j of Q_{*A}* **do**
$\quad \alpha_j = \min_{k\,:\,v_k>0} \frac{Q_{*A}[k,j]}{v_k};\ \gamma_j = \max_{k\,:\,v_k>0} \frac{Q_{*A}[k,j]}{v_k} - \alpha_j$;
end
$U = \frac{1}{||\alpha||_1}\beta(\alpha+\gamma)^t;\ L = \frac{1}{||\alpha||_1+||\gamma||_1}\beta\alpha^t$;

Remark 4. We can use Algorithm 1 to obtain matrices $\overline{M}$ and $\underline{M}$ such that $r(\underline{M}) \preceq_{el} r(M) \preceq_{el} r(\overline{M})$, $\forall M \in \mathcal{M}_{L,U,\beta}$. However, element-wise bounds L and U given by Algorithm 2 are rank 1 matrices. Therefore, it is sufficient to compute only two row vectors $\overline{w}$ and $\underline{w}$, the maximal and minimal elements of the family $\mathcal{M}_{U',L',\beta'}$ for $U' = \frac{1}{||\alpha||_1}(\alpha+\gamma)^t$, $L' = \frac{1}{||\alpha||_1+||\gamma||_1}\alpha^t$ and $\beta' = 1$. Vectors $\overline{w}$ and $\underline{w}$ can be computed by Algorithm 1 (as a special case of a matrix with only 1 row). Finally, matrices $\overline{M}$ and $\underline{M}$ are obtained as $\overline{M} = \beta\overline{w}$ and $\underline{M} = \beta\underline{w}$.

Example 1. Let us consider a matrix Q_{*A} given as follows:

$$Q_{*A} = \begin{bmatrix} 0.2 & 0.1 & 0.0 & 0.1 \\ 0.2 & 0.1 & 0.0 & 0.1 \\ 0.0 & 0.0 & 0.0 & 0.0 \\ 0.0 & 0.0 & 0.0 & 0.0 \\ 0.2 & 0.2 & 0.0 & 0.1 \end{bmatrix}$$

All the columns are null or support column 4. $\alpha^t = [2,1,0,1]$ and $\gamma^t = [0,1,0,0]$. Thus the upper bound is $(\alpha+\gamma)/4$ and the lower bound is $\alpha/5$. The st-upper bound is $\overline{w} = [0.4, 0.35, 0, 0.25]$ and the st-lower bound is $\underline{w} = [0.5, 0.3, 0, 0.2]$. It is interesting to remark that DPY [4] gives the same st-upper bound for this example.

Corollary 1. *If Q_{*A} is of rank 1, then Algorithm 2 gives the exact result.*

Proof. If Q_{*A} is of rank 1, then $\gamma_i = 0$, $\forall i$, so in Algorithm 2, $U = L = Z$.   □

4   Finding Bounds Using Incomplete Information

In this section we present different algorithms based on complete or partial information on the block Q_{*A}. Also, we consider here the general case where we can have more than one equivalence class (i.e. when Assumption 1 is not satisfied). In Algorithm 3 we assume less restrictive assumptions and in Algorithm 4 we iterate an approach based on Algorithm 3. In Algorithm 5 we apply Algorithm 2 on groups of columns.

These algorithms apply even if we do not know all the columns of matrix Q_{*A}. It is still possible to obtain in this case an element-wise and an st-upper bound. Lower bounds are much harder to obtain and only some methods will provide lower bounds under stronger assumptions. Finally, in the last two approaches we assume that the sum of the columns of Q_{*A} is known while some columns are unknown. Indeed, for some modeling frameworks it is possible to compute easily the sum of probabilities of a set of events even if the exact transitions are unknown.

Note that it may be possible to use more than one method for some problems and we can combine them to improve the accuracy using a very simple argument:

Lemma 4. *Let $\beta\lambda_1^t$ and $\beta\lambda_2^t$ be two element-wise upper bounds. Then $\beta(\min\{\lambda_1, \lambda_2\})^t$ is a more accurate upper bound (the min operator is element-wise).*

Finally, the preprocessing step of each algorithm is to compute $\beta = e - Q_{AA}e$.

4.1   Less Constrained Matrices

Denote by m the right-most non null column of Q_{*A} and let $v_m = C_m(Q_{*A})$.

Assumption 2. *We assume that some columns (not all of them) of Q_{*A} support v_m. We can decompose Q_{*A} as follows:*

$$C_i(Q_{*A}) = \alpha_i v_m + W_i, \tag{3}$$

with $0 \preceq_{el} W_i$ and $\alpha_i \geq 0$. This decomposition is always possible. If column $C_i(Q_{*A})$ supports column v_m we get $\alpha_i > 0$ as usual, otherwise we may have $\alpha_i = 0$ or a positive α_i if we are lucky. So we decompose Q_{*A} into a rank 1 matrix and a positive matrix W whose columns are W_i. The stochastic complement is:

$$Q_{AA} + Q_{A*}(I - Q_{**})^{-1}v_m\alpha^t + Q_{A*}(I - Q_{**})^{-1}W.$$

Let $Z_1 = Q_{A*}(I - Q_{**})^{-1}v_m\alpha^t$ and $Z_2 = Q_{A*}(I - Q_{**})^{-1}W$. Z_1 and Z_2 are positive matrices.

Some results obtained in the last section for more constrained matrices are still true.

Lemma 5. $C_m(Z) \preceq_{el} \beta\frac{1}{||\alpha||_1}$

Proof. The decomposition implies that: $Q_{A*}(I - Q_{**})^{-1}v_m||\alpha||_1 \preceq_{el} \beta$. In the decomposition $W_m = 0$. Thus: $C_m(Z) = Q_{A*}(I - Q_{**})^{-1}v_m$. Combining both relations, we get the result.   □

It is also possible to find an upper bound for all the columns which support column m.

Lemma 6. *Assume that column i supports column m. Then $C_i(Z) \preceq_{el} \beta\frac{\alpha_i+\gamma_i}{||\alpha||_1}$. But when the column does not support v_m, the upper bound is β.*

Proof. From Lemma 5, we get $C_m(Z) \preceq_{el} \beta \frac{1}{||\alpha||_1}$, and if column i supports column m we have $C_i(Z) \preceq_{el} C_m(Z)(\alpha_i + \gamma_i)$. Combining both inequalities we get the first result. Finally it is sufficient to remark that $C_i(Z) \preceq_{el} \beta$.   □

We introduce two operators, q (quotient) and R (reminder) defined as follows. Let x and $y \neq 0$ be two positive vectors:

$$q(x, y) = \min_{k:y_k>0} \left\{ \frac{x_k}{y_k} \right\}, \quad R(x, y) = x - q(x, y)y. \tag{4}$$

Algorithm 3. Upper bounds for Z when Assumption 1 is not satisfied

1. Consider the right-most non null column of Q_{*A}, say v_m. Set $\alpha_m = 1$, $\gamma_m = 0$ and $\alpha_i = 0$ for all index $i > m$.
2. For all columns i between 1 to m check if it supports v_m:
   (a) If YES compute α_i and γ_i.
   (b) If NO perform the decomposition described in (3) to obtain α_i:
      $\alpha_i = q(C_i(Q_{*A}), C_m(Q_{*A}))$ and $W = R(C_i(Q_{*A}), C_m(Q_{*A}))$.
3. The upper bound is $\frac{1}{||\alpha||_1} \beta(\alpha_i + \gamma_i)^t$ for columns i which support v_m, 0 for the null columns and β for the remaining ones.

Remark 5. All the columns where $\alpha_i > 0$ are used to bound column m. α_i is positive when column i supports column m but this is not necessary. For instance $[1, 1, 1]^t$ does not support $[1, 1, 0]^t$ but we obtain $\alpha_i = 1$. Note however we are only able to obtain a non trivial bound for columns which support column m.

Theorem 3. *Algorithm 3 provides an upper bound when we know all columns of Q_{*A}. If some columns of Q_{*A} are unknown, Algorithm 3 provides an upper bound based on known columns. The upper bound for unknown columns is β.*

Proof. Lemmas 5 and 6 give the answer for known columns. Unknown columns i do not support the column m (the last *known* non null column) so the corresponding $\alpha_i = 0$.   □

The following lemma gives a bound of all the colinear columns (it is a simple consequence of Lemma 3).

Lemma 7. *Let i be the index of a column of Q_{*A} which is colinear to v_m, then we have $C_i(Z) \preceq_{el} \beta \frac{\alpha_i}{||\alpha||_1}$*

Proof. For a column i colinear to column m, we have $\gamma_i = 0$.   □

4.2   Iteration

We decompose the columns according to their equivalence class and we perform a modified version of Algorithm 3 on each class. Then an upper bound for Z can be obtained by taking element-wise minimum of upper bounds obtained for each equivalence class (see Lemma 4).

Algorithm 4. Iteration

1. Decompose the columns of Q_{*A} according to the equivalence relation "support".
2. Upper bounds for columns which are equal to $\mathbf{0}$ are equal to $\mathbf{0}$.
3. For all (non null) equivalence classes:
   (a) Let Δ be the set of index of the columns that belong to that class.
   (b) Let v be the right-most non null vector in Δ.
   (c) For all i, $\alpha_i = q(C_i(Q_{*A}), v)$. (Note that for $i \in \Delta$, $\alpha_i = \alpha_{C_i(Q_{*A}), v}$.)
   (d) For all $i \in \Delta$, compute $\gamma_i = \gamma_{C_i(Q_{*A}), v}$.
   (e) Compute $\alpha = \sum_i \alpha_i$.
   (f) The upper bound for column $i \in \Delta$ is $\beta \frac{\alpha_i + \gamma_i}{\alpha}$.

Theorem 4. *When all columns of Q_{*A} are known, Algorithm 4 provides an upper bound. Assume now that some columns of Q_{*A} are unknown, Algorithm 4 provides an upper bound based on known columns. The upper bound for unknown columns is β. (Note that Algorithm 4 gives always better bounds than Algorithm 3.)*

Proof. The proof is similar to the proof of Algorithm 3. It is omitted here for the sake of conciseness. □

4.3 Partial Summations

Assumption 3. *Without loss of generality we assume that $C_n(Q_{*A}) \neq 0$. The main assumption is the following: we can find a partition of $\{1, \ldots, n\}$ into k subsets $\Gamma_1, \ldots, \Gamma_k$ such that for all set index j, $\sum_{i \in \Gamma_j} C_i(Q_{*A})$ supports $C_n(Q_{*A})$. Without loss of generality we assume that $\Gamma_k = \{n\}$. Let us denote by α_j and γ_j the coefficient of the support relation for set Γ_j. Clearly we have: $\alpha_k = 1$ and $\gamma_k = 0$.*

Algorithm 5 consists in building a new matrix where the columns are summed up for all index in the same subset in the partition. This new matrix satisfies the assumptions of Algorithm 2.

Algorithm 5. Partial summations

1. Find a partition satisfying the constraints.
2. Sum up the columns of Q_{*A} according to the partition to obtain a new matrix with k columns.
3. Apply Algorithm 2 on this matrix to obtain some α_j and γ_j for all set index j.
4. The element-wise upper bound for an arbitrary column i is $\beta \frac{\alpha_j + \gamma_j}{||\alpha||_1}$ where j in the index of the set which contains i.
5. The st-upper bound for an arbitrary column i is $\beta \frac{\alpha_j + \gamma_j}{||\alpha||_1}$ if i is the largest element of set Γ_j and 0 otherwise.

Theorem 5. *Algorithm 5 provides an upper bound when all columns are known. Assume now that some columns of Q_{*A} are unknown, Algorithm 5 provides an upper bound based on the known columns. The upper bound for the unknown column is β.*

Proof. Step 3 and the bound computed for the sum are exactly the same as in Algorithm 2 and we can apply the results we have already proved. Thus $\sum_{i \in \Gamma_j} C_i(Z) \preceq_{el} \beta \frac{\alpha_j + \gamma_j}{||\alpha||_1}$. Step 4 simply states that each element has the same upper bound than the sum. In Step 5 the st-bound is computed from the element-wise upper bound with Algorithm 1. □

4.4   If the Sum of Columns is Known

Assumption 4. *We assume that $\sum_{i=1}^{n} C_i(Q_{*A}) = \sigma$ is known. Only some columns are known. For all the known columns (say with index i) that are not equal to $\mathbf{0}$, we use operators q and R in (4) to get $\sigma = q_i C_i(Q_{*A}) + W_i$, where W_i is non negative.*

Note that it is not necessary to know matrix Q_{*A} to compute σ, it can be obtained from a high-level specification of the model.

Lemma 8. *As all the columns are non negative (even if they are unknown...) we clearly have $q_i \geq 1$.*

Theorem 6. *Consider σ and an arbitrary column index k. Use operators q and R in (4) with input arguments σ and $C_k(Q_{*A})$ to obtain q_k and W_k. $C_k(Z)$ is element-wise upper bounded by $\frac{\beta}{q_k}$.*

Proof. We clearly have:

$$\beta = \sum_i C_i(Z) = Q_{A*}(I - Q_{**})^{-1} \sum_i C_i(Q_{*A}) = Q_{A*}(I - Q_{**})^{-1}\sigma. \quad (5)$$

As $\sigma = q_k C_k(Q_{*A}) + W_k$, and as W_k, Q_{A*}, and $(I - Q_{**})^{-1}$ are non negative, we get: $Q_{A*}(I - Q_{**})^{-1}C_k(Q_{*A}) \preceq_{el} \frac{\beta}{q_k}$. As $Q_{A*}(I - Q_{**})^{-1}C_k(Q_{*A}) = C_k(Z)$ we prove the theorem. □

It is even possible to find a bound if we are not able to compute exactly σ. Assume that we are able to compute δ such that $\delta \preceq_{el} \sigma$. This is typically the case when we have a high level description of the chain and we are able to classify the transitions according to their destination set.

Theorem 7. *Consider δ and an arbitrary column index k. Use operators q and R in (4) with parameters δ and $C_k(Q_{*A})$ to obtain q'_k and W'_k. If $q'_k \geq 1$, column k of Z is element-wise upper bounded by $\frac{\beta}{q'_k}$.*

Proof. As $\delta \preceq_{el} \sigma$, we have $q'_k \leq q_k$ and we apply the former theorem. □

4.5   Examples

We illustrate algorithms proposed in this section on small numerical examples.
Algorithm 3. Let

$$
Q_{AA} = \begin{bmatrix} 0.1\ 0.3\ 0.2\ 0.1 \\ 0.1\ 0.4\ 0.2\ 0.0 \\ 0.2\ 0.1\ 0.5\ 0.2 \\ 0.2\ 0.0\ 0.4\ 0.0 \end{bmatrix} \quad \beta = \begin{bmatrix} 0.3 \\ 0.3 \\ 0.0 \\ 0.4 \end{bmatrix} \quad Q_{*A} = \begin{bmatrix} 0.1\ 0.0\ 0.1\ 0.2 \\ 0.0\ 0.1\ 0.0\ 0.0 \\ 0.2\ 0.2\ 0.1\ 0.1 \\ 0.0\ 0.0\ 0.0\ 0.0 \\ 0.0\ 0.1\ 0.0\ 0.0 \\ 0.1\ 0.1\ 0.1\ 0.1 \end{bmatrix}
$$

Let us consider the columns of Q_{*A}. Clearly, column 3 supports column 4 and $\alpha_3 = 0.5$, $\gamma_3 = 0.5$. Column 2 does not support column 4 and α_2 in the decomposition is 0. Finally column 1 supports column 4 and $\alpha_1 = 0.5$ $\gamma_i = 1.5$. So $\|\alpha\|_1 = 2$. We find upper bounds for columns 1, 3 and 4 which are respectively $2\beta/2$, $\beta/2$ and $\beta/2$. The upper bound for Z is thus $\beta[1, 1, 1/2, 1/2]$. A strong stochastic bound for Z is $\beta[0, 0, 1/2, 1/2]$ (see Remark 4). The bound provided by DPY is $\beta[0, 1/4, 1/4, 1/2]$, so DPY is better for this example.

Now assume that we are not able to compute column 2.

$$
Q_{*A} = \begin{bmatrix} 0.1\ *\ 0.1\ 0.2 \\ 0.0\ *\ 0.0\ 0.0 \\ 0.2\ *\ 0.1\ 0.1 \\ 0.0\ *\ 0.0\ 0.0 \\ 0.0\ *\ 0.0\ 0.0 \\ 0.1\ *\ 0.1\ 0.1 \end{bmatrix}
$$

where $*$ denotes that the value is unknown. We are not able to use DPY because the matrix is unknown. But the st-bound with Algorithm 2 is still $\beta[0, 0, 1/2, 1/2]$.

Now assume that we are not able to compute columns 1 and 2. Again it is not possible to use DPY. We still have a support for column 4 from column 3. But as α_1 is unknown, $\|\alpha\|_1 = 1.5$. The element-wise upper bound is now $\beta[1, 1, 2/3, 2/3]$ and the st-upper bound is $\beta[0, 0, 1/3, 2/3]$.

Algorithm 4. Let

$$
\beta = \begin{bmatrix} 0.3 \\ 0.3 \\ 0.0 \\ 0.4 \end{bmatrix} \quad Q_{*A} = \begin{bmatrix} 0.4\ 0.1\ 0.1\ 0.2 \\ 0.0\ 0.1\ 0.1\ 0.0 \\ 0.2\ 0.15\ 0.1\ 0.1 \\ 0.0\ 0.0\ 0.0\ 0.0 \\ 0.0\ 0.1\ 0.1\ 0.0 \\ 0.2\ 0.1\ 0.1\ 0.1 \end{bmatrix} \quad H14 = \begin{bmatrix} 0.4\ 0.2 \\ 0.0\ 0.0 \\ 0.2\ 0.1 \\ 0.0\ 0.0 \\ 0.0\ 0.0 \\ 0.2\ 0.1 \end{bmatrix} \quad H23 = \begin{bmatrix} 0.1\ 0.1 \\ 0.1\ 0.1 \\ 0.15\ 0.1 \\ 0.0\ 0.0 \\ 0.1\ 0.1 \\ 0.1\ 0.1 \end{bmatrix}
$$

We have two classes of equivalence in this example, corresponding to matrices $H14$ (columns 1 and 4) and $H23$. For the first class ($H14$), $v = C_4(Q_{*A})$ and the values of α_i are $[2, 0.5, 0.5, 1]$, so $\alpha = 4$. Since columns 1 and 4 are colinear,

$\gamma_1 = \gamma_4 = 0$. The corresponding upper bounds for columns 1 and 4 are: $\beta/2$ and $\beta/4$. Thus the upper bound for Z for this class is $\beta[1/2, 1, 1, 1/4]$. For the second class $(H23)$, $v = C_3(Q_{*A})$, the values of α_i are $[0, 1, 0, 1]$, $\alpha = 2$, and $\gamma_2 = 0.5$, $\gamma_3 = 0$. The corresponding upper bound for Z is $\beta[1, 3/4, 1/2, 1]$. The final upper bound for Z is then $\beta[1/2, 3/4, 1/2, 1/4]$ and the corresponding strong stochastic bound is $\beta[0, 1/4, 1/2, 1/4]$. For the sake of comparison, the st bound provided by DPY is $\beta[0, 1/2, 1/4, 1/4]$.

Known sum. Let

$$\beta = \begin{bmatrix} 0.3 \\ 0.3 \\ 0.0 \\ 0.4 \end{bmatrix} \quad Q_{*A} = \begin{bmatrix} 0.1 & 0.0 & 0.1 & 0.2 \\ 0.0 & 0.1 & 0.0 & 0.0 \\ 0.2 & 0.2 & 0.1 & 0.1 \\ 0.0 & 0.0 & 0.0 & 0.0 \\ 0.0 & 0.1 & 0.0 & 0.0 \\ 0.1 & 0.1 & 0.1 & 0.1 \end{bmatrix} \quad \sigma = \begin{bmatrix} 0.4 \\ 0.1 \\ 0.6 \\ 0.0 \\ 0.1 \\ 0.4 \end{bmatrix}$$

Then we use operators q and R in (4) to obtain the ratios q_i. Some values of the rests W_i are omitted for the sake of conciseness. We have: $q_1 = 3$, $W_1^t = [0.1, 0.1, 0, 0, 0.1, 0.1]$, $q_2 = 1$, $q_3 = 4$, and $q_4 = 2$. And finally the bounding matrix is $\beta[1/3, 1, 1/4, 1/2]$ and the st bound is $\beta[0, 1/4, 1/4, 1/2]$.

Assume now that we are not able to compute the second column of Q_{*A}. We have: $\delta^t = [0.4, 0, 0.4, 0, 0, 0.3]$. Then $q_1 = 2$, $W_1^t = [0.2, 0, 0, 0, 0, 0.1]$, $q_3 = 3$ and $q_4 = 2$. As we cannot compute another bound for the second column, we keep the simplest one (i.e. 1), so the element-wise bound is $\beta[1/2, 1, 1/3, 1/2]$ and the st bound is $\beta[0, 1/6, 1/3, 1/2]$.

5 Concluding Remarks

In this paper we have presented several algorithms to obtain bounds of the transition probability matrix S_{AA} of a CMC. These methods apply even if the initial chain is infinite. The CMC is obtained after a partial generation of the state space. More precisely, we only know Q_{AA} and some columns of Q_{*A}. When the whole block Q_{*A} is known, it is possible to use both DPY and the algorithms presented here. On many examples DPY and Algorithm 2 provide the same result for the upper bound and lower bound. We have also proved that they give an exact result if matrix Q_{*A} has rank 1. Note however that in general Algorithm 2 requires strong assumptions on the matrix and we have also found some matrices where the bound is worse than the bound provided by DPY even if we have no proof that DPY is always better. However, the aim of our algorithms is to find bounds of S_{AA} when Q_{*A} is only partially known or when Q_{*A} is infinite. In both cases we cannot apply DPY. The algorithms presented here (except Algorithm 2) still apply if some columns of matrix Q_{*A} are unknown. Thus they may be used even when some part of the matrix (or the models) are difficult to compute. We do not have comparison of results for these algorithms (except Algorithm 4 which is always better than Algorithm 3). Indeed, they are not based on the same assumptions. When several algorithms can be applied, the best solution is to use all of them and combine the element-wise upper bounds.

Acknowledgments. This work was partially supported by ANR-05-BLAN-0009-02 SMS and ANR-06-SETIN-002 Checkbound.

References

1. Busic, A., Fourneau, J.-M.: Bounds for point and steady-state availability: An algorithmic approach based on lumpability and stochastic ordering. In: Bravetti, M., Kloul, L., Zavattaro, G. (eds.) EPEW/WS-EM 2005. LNCS, vol. 3670, pp. 94–108. Springer, Heidelberg (2005)

2. Busic, A., Fourneau, J.-M., Pekergin, N.: Worst case analysis of batch arrivals with the increasing convex ordering. In: Horváth, A., Telek, M. (eds.) EPEW 2006. LNCS, vol. 4054, pp. 196–210. Springer, Heidelberg (2006)

3. Dayar, T., Fourneau, J.-M., Pekergin, N.: Transforming stochastic matrices for stochastic comparison with the st-order. RAIRO-RO 37, 85–97 (2003)

4. Dayar, T., Pekergin, N., Younes, S.: Conditional steady-state bounds for a subset of states in Markov chains. In: SMCtools 2006. ACM Press, New York (2006)

5. de Souza e Silva, E., Ochoa, P.M., Mejiá Ochoa, P.: State space exploration in Markov models. ACM SIGMETRICS Perform. Eval. Rev. 20(1), 152–166 (1992)

6. Fourneau, J.-M., Lecoz, M., Quessette, F.: Algorithms for an irreducible and lumpable strong stochastic bound. Linear Algebra and its Applications 386(1), 167–185 (2004)

7. Fourneau, J.-M., Pekergin, N.: An algorithmic approach to stochastic bounds. In: Calzarossa, M.C., Tucci, S. (eds.) Performance 2002. LNCS, vol. 2459, pp. 64–88. Springer, Heidelberg (2002)

8. Fourneau, J.-M., Pekergin, N., Younes, S.: Censoring Markov chains and stochastic bounds. In: Wolter, K. (ed.) EPEW 2007. LNCS, vol. 4748, pp. 213–227. Springer, Heidelberg (2007)

9. Fourneau, J.-M., Plateau, B., Sbeity, I., Stewart, W.J.: SANs and lumpable stochastic bounds: Bounding availability. In: Computer System, Network Performance and Quality of Service, Imperial College Press (2006)

10. Haddad, S., Moreaux, P.: Sub-stochastic matrix analysis for bounds computation - theoretical results. Eur. Jour. of Op. Res. 176(2), 999–1015 (2007)

11. Meyer, C.D.: Stochastic complementation, uncoupling Markov chains and the theory of nearly reducible systems. SIAM Review 31(2), 240–272 (1989)

12. Muller, A., Stoyan, D.: Comparison Methods for Stochastic Models and Risks. Wiley, New York (2002)

13. Pekergin, N., Dayar, T., Alparslan, D.: Compenent-wise bounds for nearly completely decomposable Markov chains using stochastic comparison and reordering. Eur. Jour. of Op. Res. 165, 810–825 (2005)

14. Plateau, B., Fourneau, J.M., Lee, K.H.: PEPS: a package for solving complex Markov models of parallel systems. In: Proceedings of the 4th Int. Conf. on Modelling Techniques and Tools for Computer Performance Evaluation, Spain (1988)

15. Truffet, L.: Near complete decomposability: Bounding the error by a stochastic comparison method. Ad. in App. Prob. 29, 830–855 (1997)

16. Truffet, L.: Reduction technique for discrete time Markov chains on totally ordered state space using stochastic comparisons. Jour. of App. Prob. 37(3), 795–806 (2000)

17. Zhao, Y.Q., Liu, D.: The censored Markov chain and the best augmentation. Jour. of App. Prob. 33, 623–629 (1996)

Evaluation of P2P Algorithms for Probabilistic Trust Inference in a Web of Trust

Huqiu Zhang and Aad van Moorsel*

School of Computing Science
Newcastle University
Newcastle upon Tyne, UK
{huqiu.zhang, aad.vanmoorsel}@newcastle.ac.uk

Abstract. The problem of finding trust paths and estimating the trust one can place in a partner arises in various application areas, including virtual organisations, authentication systems and reputation systems. We study the use of peer-to-peer algorithms for finding trust paths and probabilistically assessing trust values in systems where trust is organised similar to the 'web of trust'. We do this through discrete event simulation of random as well as scale free trust networks based on flooding as well as selective search algorithms. Our main conclusion is that in many situations these algorithms can be seen as belonging to a single class of algorithms that perform equally, and only differ through (and are sensitive to) parameter choices. We will also see that flooding is the only applicable method if one stresses the requirement for finding all trust paths, and if networks are less connected.

Keywords: Peer-to-Peer, Web of Trust, Trust Paths, Trust Inference.

1   Introduction

To motivate our study, consider a possibly large number of people or businesses that want to collaborate, and not all players know each other. Internet and B2B technologies promise a world in which such collaborations can be created almost instantly (called virtual organisations). One of the challenges in creating such dynamic business interactions is the establishment of trust, and assume therefore that each party maintains a list of trusted parties, including a probability quantifying the amount of trust place in a party. In that situation, parties may decide to trust each other and initiate business if a path of trust relations exists between them (in both directions), and they may calculate risks and decide about their actions depending on the trust values associated with these paths. In this paper, therefore, we analyse how peer-to-peer algorithms perform when applied to finding trust paths and calculating trust values.

---

* The authors are supported in part by: EU coordination action 216295 ('AMBER: Assessing, Measuring, and Benchmarking Resilience') and UK Department of Trade and Industry, grant nr. P0007E ('Trust Economics').

N. Thomas and C. Juiz (Eds.): EPEW 2008, LNCS 5261, pp. 242–256, 2008.

Our trust model views the system as Web of Trust, a network or graph where nodes are linked if they have a trust relation. We assume links are directed, that is, a link or arc from A to B implies that A trusts B, but not B does not necessarily trust A. The problem we address is if, for a given pair of request node and target node, a trust path exists in the trust network. We associate a probability with each link to represent the trust value associated to the trust relation (either specified by the requester or by the trusting party associated with an arc). The overall trust value of a trust path is the product of the probabilities on the links. Moreover, when multiple trust paths exist between requester and target, the problem of computing the overall trust value translates to the network reliability problem, as pointed out in [1].

Given the above trust model, we are interested in evaluating how peer-to-peer algorithms perform when used for identifying trust paths. We quantify their performance by comparing the overhead (in number of messages used) with the achieved success rate (in fraction of paths found). We then also compare the achieved trust value with to the trust value obtained if all trust paths are considered. In all steps of this study we use Monte Carlo and discrete-event simulation: for generating the networks, executing the peer-to-peer algorithms, and sampling the resulting paths to obtain the trust value. This paper builds on our earlier work in the same area [2], but that work was limited to the question if at least one trust path could be found, thus not including the overall success rates, nor introducing trust values and trust value computation.

The network we consider is an unstructured peer-to-peer network for which we consider flooding and selective algorithms. Perhaps surprising (since it contradicts a possible tendency to think that flooding is expensive), our results show that these algorithms are largely equivalent when considering the overhead versus the success rate, provided one sets the configuration parameters optimally. This holds true if the fraction of trust paths one wants to find is not too high. However, if a high success rate is required, flooding becomes superior, simply because it covers more paths. Selective algorithms do not find all trust paths, and the resulting computed trust value is therefore lower than for pure flooding.

Several reputation-based trust systems for peer-to-peer system have been proposed in the literature, such as CORE [3], EigenTrust [4], TrustGuard [5], Scrivener [6], P2PRep [7], Credence [8]. In [9], the authors present an analysis framework for reputation systems, classify the known and potential attacks and describe defense strategies. Our work differs from existing research, in that we do not consider attacks, but discuss the performance of P2P algorithms for trust inference. Moreover, compared with existing research on performance evaluation of P2P algorithms (e.g. [10]), our work differs by considering trust values and multiple paths to the target.

The rest of the paper is organized as follows. Section 2 provides a overview of the problems and analysis and explore the potential solutions. The analytical search algorithm technique are presented in Section 3. Numerical experiments are detailed in Section 4. The performance and cost comparison among various

P2P algorithms to obtain probabilistic trust inference in Section 5. Section 6 concludes the paper and presents some possible direction for further study.

2   Problem Definition

2.1   Trust Path Discovery Problem

In abstract terms, one can model a web of trust as a directed graph $G = (V, E)$, in which the set of vertices V represent the nodes and the set of directed edges E represent trust relations. A directed edge from i to j corresponds to i's trust in j. In terms of this trust relation, i is the truster [11], and j is the trustee [11]. As an example, in the PGP trust model [1], vertices are public keys and edges are certificates. A directed edge from i to j represents i signing a certificate which binds j to a key.

Assume trust relations exist between some of the nodes of a network, and based on direct interactions between them, direct trust [12] is created. But since not all nodes of a network have direct interactions, direct trust links do not exist between all pairs. Nodes without direct interactions, however, can estimate trust depending on its trustees and so on. For instance, as in [2], assume there is no directed edge from A to C, A can still trust C if there exists at least one path from A to C in the graph. That is, it is accepted that trust is transitive in the trust model: if A trusts B, and B trusts C, then A trusts C. The trust A places on C is viewed as indirect trust [12], which is derived from the beliefs of others. As pointed out in [12], trust relations usually are one-way: A trusts B does not mean B trusts A.

In our model, every node maintains its trust relations associated with other nodes. If a node (called the requester) wants to establish the trustworthiness of another node (called the target) with which he has had no direct interactions before, the trust path discovery problem is to find one or more trust path to the target. In [2], the authors indicate that P2P search algorithms can be applied to discover trust paths, due to the similarity of the structure of a web of trust network and an unstructured P2P network. In what follows, the process of finding trust paths is called a search phase. After the search phase, and if such trust path exists, the requester requires some mathematical method to estimate the trustworthiness of the target. How to develop a reasonable trust measure is presented in the following subsection. On the other hand, if no such trust path exists, the trustworthiness of a target cannot be established from the requester's point of view.

2.2   Trust Inference Problem

How to define a reasonable trust metric to estimate the trust placed on the target? Our work follows the approach in [1], which shows that the trust inference problem can be translated into the two-terminal network reliability problem.

Network reliability concerns the performance study of computer networks, in which components are subject to random failures. In network reliability analysis, it is assumed that edges have probabilities of failure [13]. That is, at a particular time, an edge can take one of the two states, operative or failed. The two-terminal network reliability is computed as a probability of establishing at least one operating network path from s to t. Mapping the (s, t) network reliability problem to web of trust context, requester-target trust inference is viewed as determining the probability of establishing at least one trust path from the requester to the target.

To solve the network reliability problem, exact methods and approximate methods have been developed. In general, exact methods first calculate minimal operating states, path sets or cut sets, and then apply inclusion-exclusion principle to compute the result [13]. However, exact methods suffer from an exponential worst-case complicity [13]. That is caused by the computation of path sets or cut sets, which is an NP-hard problem [13]. A Monte-Carlo technique belonging to approximate methods is commonly proposed and employed in network reliability computation [14]. This method is implemented in our experiments to compute the trust value.

3   Methodology

3.1   Topologies

The topology of a P2P network may influence the effectiveness of various search algorithms. We focus on two network topologies in our study: random graph and scale-free graph. Both are generated by the approaches provided by Peersim [15].

Random Graph. Given the network size S (the number of nodes) and an integer value d, PeerSim generates randomly d directed links out of each node. The neighbours are chosen randomly without replacement from the nodes of the network except the source node. We modified the basic algorithm in Peersim so that the out-degree follows a truncated standard normal distribution around d.

Scale-free Graph. Given the network (S, d and network seed), Peersim provides the Barabasi-Albert approach [16] to generate a directed graph with a power law in-degree distribution and for each node the out-degree value zero or d. We modified the generation of outgoing links to follow a more reasonable distribution, namely a standard normal distribution around d. A power law in-degree distribution reflects that most of the nodes can be trusted by a few nodes and a few nodes can be trusted by most of the nodes, which can be said to match our experience in the real world.

3.2   P2P Search Algorithms

The trust path discovery algorithms considered in this paper all are variations of flooding in unstructured P2P networks. More specifically, they are controlled flooding algorithms. For these approaches in the context of file sharing, we refer to [10].

Flooding. "Pure" Flooding has been mainly used in Gnutella networks [17]. In this approach, a requester sends query messages to every node to which it directly connects. Receiving a query message, if a node does not find information being searched, it will forward this query message to all of its connected neighbour nodes. To avoid unlimitedly propagating messages, every query message is fixed with a time-to-live (TTL) parameter, which takes a positive integer value. Each time the query is forwarded by a node, the TTL value is decremented by 1. When the TTL value reaches zero, the query message will stop to be forwarded. We will see later that setting the TTL value is a critical aspect for the performance of the algorithm.

Random querying. In comparsion with Flooding, in Random querying, a requester sends query messages to a subset of its neighbour nodes, which is set to K percent of its neighbour nodes rounded below or rounded above. Upon receiving the incoming query, a node then continues forwarding the messages to its K percent randomly selected neighbour nodes. This method also relies on TTL parameter to limit the search.

Selective querying. Rather than forwarding incoming queries to randomly chosen neighbours, the Selective querying approach [18] intelligently selects a subset of neighbours according to some specific criterion, for instance, the latency of connection, number of results for past queries, location and message queue capacity, etc. In the trust path searching, best neighbours are nodes with the most trust relations.

3.3   Metrics

To measure the efficiency of these algorithms, we considered three aspects reflecting the fundamental characteristics of the algorithms.

Success rate: the fraction of for which an algorithm successfully locates the target.

Number of messages: overhead of an algorithm is measured as the total number of search messages passed over the network during the search.

Trust inference value: A probability within a range $[0, 1]$, where 0 denotes no trust, and 1 denotes full trust. If no trust path exists, the trust value is 0, otherwise, the probabilistic trust value is computed as the solution of the network reliability problem as discussed in Section 4.3.

4   Simulation Methodology

In this section, we explain details of our simulations.

4.1   Peersim

We use PeerSim for our simulations. PeerSim is a Peer-to-Peer simulation framework, which is implemented in JAVA. It can be used to model any kind of P2P search algorithms. PeerSim simulator consists of several different components which can be easily plugged together by using an ASCII configuration file. It can work in two different modes: cycle-based or event-based. The cycle-based engine is a sequential simulation, in each cycle every node executes its own protocol's actions in a global sequential order. In the event-based mode, events are scheduled in different simulation time and nodes execute protocols according to message delivery times [15]. A very detailed account of performance and scalability comparison between these two modes is studied in [19]. As recommended in [19], cycle-based mode of the PeerSim simulator is used in our study.

4.2 Sampling Method

As a network topology consists of an infinite number of possible network instances, it is impossible to survey all its members to obtain the characteristics of a network topology. But a small cautiously chosen sample can be used to achieve the same aim.

In sampling technologies [20], the term population denotes the complete set of observations that one wants information about, while the term sample stands for a subset of the population that we actually examine. In an experiment, a sample is selected from the population and statistic is collected from experimental samples in order to draw the conclusion about some properties of the population. In our simulation, a particular network topology (e.g. random network) is viewed as a population.

To simulate P2P search algorithms, the process of obtaining a sample is as follows: at first draw particular networks; then, within networks, select search queries (requester-target pairs). This way of selecting sample is called the Subsampling approach [20]. Sample selection is done in two steps: first select a sample of units from the population, named the primary units, and for each chosen primary unit, a sample of subunits are selected.

In the experiment, a particular network structure related to a specific network is viewed as a primary unit; one specific query inside is treated as a subunit. We use the symbol N to denote the population size, then a network topology consists of N primary units. Within a particular network (size S), if every node looks up all the other nodes, there will be a total of $S(S-1)$ query subunits constituting a particular network unit.

The following notation is used for obtaining estimate sample means and variances in Subsampling [20]:

n : number of primary unit samples
N : the total number of primary units
m : number of subunit samples per unit
M : the total number of subunits
$y_{i,j}$: value obtained for the jth subunit in the ith primary unit

$\bar{y}_i = \frac{1}{m} \sum_{j=1}^{m} y_{i,j} =$ sample mean per subunit in the ith primary unit

$\bar{\bar{y}} = \frac{1}{n} \sum_{i=1}^{n} \bar{y}_i =$ over-all sample mean per subunit

$f_1 = \frac{n}{N}$ = ratio of the size of the sample to the total of the primary units

$f_2 = \frac{m}{M}$ = ratio of the size of the sample to the total of the subunits

$s_1^2 = \frac{\sum_{i=1}^n (\bar{y}_i - \bar{\bar{y}})^2}{n-1}$ = variance among primary unit means

$s_2^2 = \frac{\sum_{i=1}^n \sum_{j=1}^m (y_{i,j} - \bar{y}_i)^2}{n(m-1)}$ = variance among subunits within primary units

$v(\bar{\bar{y}}) = \frac{1-f_1}{n} s_1^2 + \frac{f_1(1-f_2)}{mn} s_2^2$ = sampling variance

In sampling, sampling variance can be calculated to show the degree to which a sample may differ from the population. As the total number of members in the population N is infinite in our experiments, $f_1 = \frac{n}{N}$ is negligible, and then we obtain that the estimated variance can be computed as:

$$v(\bar{\bar{y}}) = \frac{s_1^2}{n} = \frac{\sum_{i=1}^n (\bar{y}_i - \bar{\bar{y}})^2}{n(n-1)} \quad ,$$

and the estimated sample standard deviation is $s(\bar{\bar{y}}) = \sqrt{v(\bar{\bar{y}})}$.

Given the estimated sample mean and sample standard deviation, if t_c is the t value associated with $c\%$, then a $c\%$ confidence interval for the mean is equal to $y \pm t_c s(\bar{y})$. For instance, if the desired confidence probability is 95%, the t_c value is 1.96. Then we say that a 95% chance that the population mean is within a range of $[\bar{y} - t_c s(\bar{y}), \bar{y} + t_c s(\bar{y})]$.

Statistics are collected from the n (number of primary unit samples) $\times$ m (number of subunit samples) queries. For the result we present in the paper, $n=50$ and $m=50$, which turns out to ensure small standard deviation in our results.

4.3   Trust Computation

As explained in Section 2.2, in our experiments, we implement the Monte-Carlo method. The Monte-Carlo method is a computation which performs statistical sampling to obtain the result [14]. As a consequence, the trust computation effictively becomes 'three-level-unit' samples. The primary units are the drawn particular networks, the secondary units are chosen random queries, and finally the tertiary units are generated trust graph samples. As a consequence, trust mean is:

$$\bar{\bar{y}} = \frac{1}{n} \sum_{i=1}^n \left\{ \frac{1}{m} \sum_{j=1}^m \left(\frac{1}{l} \sum_{k=1}^l y_{i,j,k} \right) \right\}.$$

For simplify, it is assumed that each edge has the same trust reliable value. In the experiment, the value was set to 0.8. Experiment results and discussions on interesting finding are presented in the following section.

5   Results

In this section, we start with the overview of the network topologies generated by the simulator, and then discuss performance results in random and scale-free networks, respectively. We assume that the trust network graph does not change during the simulation of the algorithms. Effectively, this implies that the time to complete a search enough so that no nodes leave or enter the network.

Parameters Values. Our simulations were carried out in a network of size $S=10000$. P2P search algorithms applications are tested on two types of network topology: random and scale-free topology. In the random networks, the average out-degree value is 5. The scale-free networks are drawn with three different average out-degree values (5, 10, 20). For Random and Selective querying algorithms, we chose three different values (10%, 50%, 70%) for the fraction of neighbours to which each query will be forwarded.

Network Characteristics. Before discussing the algorithm performance, we have a look at the networks on which the simulations perform. Figure 1 shows the distributions of links per node for random and scale-free networks (average out-degree=5). As we see from Figure 1(a), in scale-free network, the incoming links of each node follow a power law distribution. One can be interested in how the nodes link to each other. If there is at least one path leading to node j from node i, then we say this node pair $<i,j>$ is connected. We use the term node pair connection ratio (connection ratio for short) to present the fraction of node pairs being connected in a network. The node pair connection ratio is strongly influenced by network topology and the average out-degree value, which can be seen from Table 1. The query samples are the secondary units, and the network samples are the primary units. In the random networks, both in the query samples and network samples, the node pair connection ratio is over 99%, which implies nearly every node is connected to all the others. On the other hand, in the scale-free networks, the connection ratio is much smaller, although it increases with the average out-degree value. The reason why the connection ratio is smaller is that the number of nodes with zero in-degree value is large (see Figure 1(a)). That means many nodes are not reachable from other nodes, resulting in a low success rate. To obtain a higher success rate, we look at more possible higher connection ratios by given higher out-degree values. For random networks, the connection ratio is satisfactory. It can also be seen from Table 1, that the connection ratio in the query samples is similar to that in the network samples, which means the query samples basically reflect the feature of the node pair connection in the network samples.

Table 1. Node pair connection ratio in random and scale-free networks

Topology	Average out-degree	Node Pair Connection Ratio	
		query samples	network samples
Random	5	99.28%	99.12%
Scale-free	5	3.72%	3.88%
	10	13.12%	13.28%
	20	24.84%	26.32%

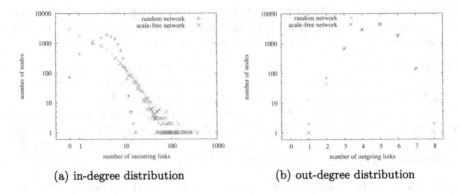

(a) in-degree distribution   (b) out-degree distribution

Fig. 1. Links distributions in random and scale-free networks (average out-degree=5)

5.1   Results in Random Networks

Figure 2 presents messages overhead and probability of success as TTL increases in random network. The shown lines are in the order they appear in the graphs. It can be observed that Flooding always has higher overhead and higher success rate than all the others, for identical TTL values. Random querying (70%) and Selective querying (70%) achieve similar success rate, quite a bit smaller than flooding until TTL reaches 6. From TTL=7 onwards, both algorithms obtain similar success rate close to that of Flooding.

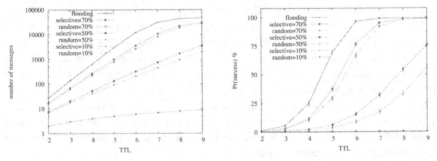

(a) message overhead under various TTLs (b) success probability under various TTLs

Fig. 2. Message overhead versus Pr(success) for different TTL values in random network (lines are in the order they appear in the graphs)

The key insight gained from our study is given in Figure 3, which combines the results of the two subfigures in Figure 2. It shows for each algorithm the message overhead versus the success rate, and each curve consists of eight points, with the results for TTL=2 until 9. It can be seen from Figure 3, that it does not matter if one uses Flooding or Random querying/Selective querying. For any success rate, the message overhead of the algorithms is similar. This implies that for a given

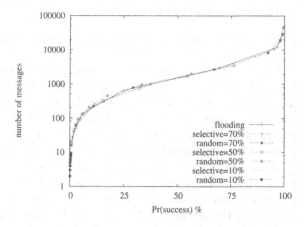

Fig. 3. Message overhead versus success rate in random network

algorithm, if one knows the TTL value that achieves the desired success rate on message overhead, this algorithm will be close to optimal. The problem is, of course, that the correct TTL value is not known beforehand. Note furthermore that Flooding achieves the highest success rate (as one would expect), but that the Selective/Random algorithm is competitive if the percentage is set high enough (70% in our case). For lower percentage, even very large TTL values may not provide the success rate achievable with Flooding. This indicates a second complication in Selective/Random querying: the percentage must be set, and the optimal value is (like in the case of the TTL value) not known.

The exact trust value would be obtained if all trust paths would be considered. As a consequence, all results in Table 2 are lower bounds for the trust value. Since Flooding has the highest success probability, it is not surprising that it also obtains the highest trust values. In particular, we see that the trust value of random networks is at least 0.974. One also see from Table 2 that a TTL value of at least 8 is needed for Selection/Random querying to give satisfactory results, and that the percentage must be set to 70%.

Table 2. Probabilistic trust inference values in random networks

Algorithm		Trust Inference			
		TTL=6	TTL=7	TTL=8	TTL=9
Flooding		0.871	0.968	0.974	0.974
Random	10%	0.001	0.001	0.002	0.002
	50%	0.025	0.043	0.078	0.156
	70%	0.305	0.742	0.929	0.958
Selective	10%	0.002	0.002	0.002	0.002
	50%	0.043	0.088	0.190	0.430
	70%	0.432	0.845	0.940	0.957

5.2   Results in Scale-free Networks

We consider scale-free networks with three different average out-degree value (5, 10, 20).

Figures 4(a), 5(a), 6(a) show the number of messages propagated through scale-free networks with different average out-degree values (5, 10, 20), for different values of TTL. Figures 4(b), 5(b), 6(b) present the success rate of searches. The y-axis of these figures gives the success probability as well as a normalised success probability between brackets. Since each algorithm finds only a subset of all trust paths, the success probability of an algorithm is bounded by the percentage of node pairs in a network for which a trust path exists. That maximum value is given on the y-axis with 100 between brackets. The percentage between brackets is thus a normalised success probability. For instance, in Figure 4(b) the success probability of the network is 4%, and the flooding algorithm finds almost all existing trust paths for high values of TTL. The shown lines are in the order they appear in the graphs. Similar to random networks, for each TTL value Flooding has the highest overhead and highest success rate. As we can see

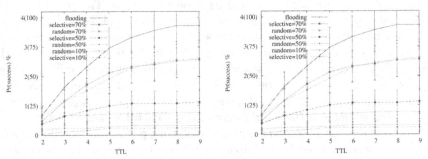

(a) message overhead under various TTLs (b) success probability under various TTLs

Fig. 4. Message overhead and Pr(success) for different TTL values in scale-free network(average out-degree=5)

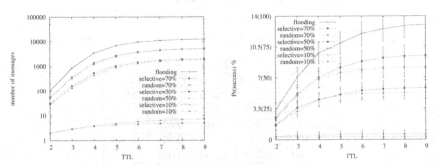

(a) message overhead under various TTLs (b) success probability under various TTLs

Fig. 5. Message overhead and Pr(success) for different TTL values in scale-free network(average out-degree=10)

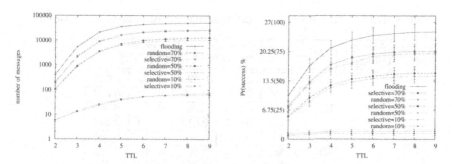

(a) message overhead under various TTLs (b) success probability under various TTLs

Fig. 6. Message overhead and Pr(success) for different TTL values in scale-free network(average out-degree=20)

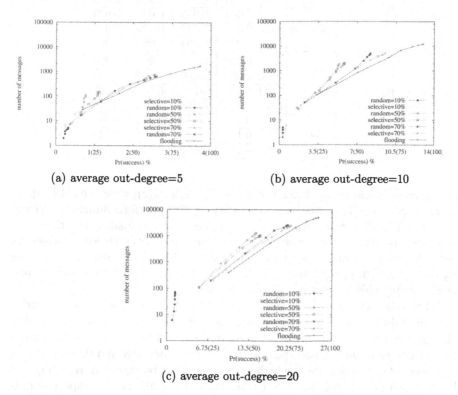

(a) average out-degree=5

(b) average out-degree=10

(c) average out-degree=20

Fig. 7. Message overhead versus success rate in scale-free networks

from figures 4(b), 5(b), 6(b), Selective querying achieves a little higher success rate than Random querying with the same K percent value with some exceptions, for instance, in Figure 4(b), when TTL=2, 7, 8, 9 and K=70%. This may be explained by targets with few incoming links, which will be ignored by the Selective querying algorithm. As for random networks, we plotted success prob-

Table 3. Trust inference values for different algorithms in scale-free networks

Average Out-dgree	Algorithm		Trust Inference			
			TTL=6	TTL=7	TTL=8	TTL=9
5	Flooding		0.020	0.022	0.023	0.023
	Random	10%	0.002	0.002	0.002	0.002
		50%	0.004	0.004	0.005	0.005
		70%	0.012	0.013	0.013	0.014
	Selective	10%	0.001	0.001	0.001	0.001
		50%	0.006	0.006	0.006	0.006
		70%	0.013	0.014	0.014	0.014
10	Flooding		0.088	0.091	0.093	0.094
	Random	10%	0.002	0.002	0.002	0.002
		50%	0.034	0.036	0.036	0.036
		70%	0.056	0.058	0.058	0.059
	Selective	10%	0.003	0.003	0.003	0.003
		50%	0.038	0.039	0.039	0.040
		70%	0.061	0.064	0.065	0.066
20	Flooding		0.200	0.204	0.206	0.206
	Random	10%	0.008	0.009	0.009	0.009
		50%	0.103	0105	0.107	0.107
		70%	0.145	0.153	0.154	0.155
	Selective	10%	0.012	0.012	0.012	0.012
		50%	0.110	0.113	0.114	0.114
		70%	0.156	0.160	0.161	0.161

ability versus message overhead in Figures 7(a), 7(b), 7(c), we see that Flooding, Random querying(70%) and Selective querying(70%) perform similarly, but importantly Flooding can obtain a higher success rate. Arguably, the difference between Flooding and other algorithms is even more pronounced in scale-free networks than in random networks. Note again that in the Selective/Random algorithms a high enough value for K (the percentage of selected nodes) must be chosen to achieve a reasonable success rate.

Table 3 shows the computed trust values. As we can see, in scale-free networks, the trust value is very low for all the search algorithms. This is caused by the low node pair connection ratio of scale-free networks, see Table 1. With the increase of the out-degree value, the node pair connection ratio increases and therefore, trust increases. Flooding obtains the highest values, as can be expected, resulting in a lower bound of the trust value of 0.023, 0.094 and 0.206 for the respective out-degrees. Selective querying slightly outperforms Random querying, even for the case of out-degree = 5, in which Random querying achieved higher success rate.

5.3 Discussion

For both network topologies, we notice the amount of messages to obtain a high success rate is very sensitive to the value of K, the number of nodes to which a query is forwarded.

The main challenge in using any of the studied algorithms is to set the value of TTL. To improve the performance, we need to consider how to assign the TTL value when a search algorithm is initialized, and how to efficiently control or avoid unnecessary messages being forwarded when the target has been located.

To avoid excessive messages being forwarded, adaptive termination can be considered. When a trust path is located, the requester broadcasts "stop searching" messages to other nodes to terminate the search process by dropping query messages whose TTL does not reach 0 yet. In terms of message overhead, the Expanding Ring search algorithm [10] can be a potential solution. The Expanding Ring algorithm starts searching with a small TTL value. When TTL reaches 0 and the search is not completed, the TTL value is incremented by 1 and the search is continued.

6 Conclusion

In this paper, we used discrete event simulation and Monte Carlo techniques to evaluate the suitability of using peer-to-peer algorithms for discovering trust paths and infering the trust value of a set of trust paths. This paper distinguishes itself from earlier work by considering the effort needed to find multiple paths, and by the computation of the overall trust value of a set of paths. We studied variations of the flooding search algorithm, in random as well as scale-free networks. The main conclusion is that all the variants of flooding perform almost equal when considering the message overhead for a certain probability of finding paths. When close to all paths need to be found, flooding outperforms selective flooding alternatives, since these alternatives miss out on certain paths.

Acknowledgements

We thank Emerson Ribeiro de Mello for the earlier PeerSim implementation [2], and for discussions on the current paper.

References

1. Jonczy, J., Wüthrich, M., Haenni, R.: A probabilistic trust model for GnuPG. In: 23C3, 23rd Chaos Communication Congress, Berlin, Germany, pp. 61–66 (2006)
2. Ribeiro de Mello, E., van Moorsel, A.P.A., da Silva Fraga, J.: Evaluation of P2P search algorithms for discovering trust paths. In: Wolter, K. (ed.) EPEW 2007. LNCS, vol. 4748, pp. 112–124. Springer, Heidelberg (2007)
3. Michiardi, P., Molva, R.: Core: a collaborative reputation mechanism to enforce node coopeation in mobile ad hoc networks. In: Proceedings of the IFIP TC6/TC11 Sixth Joint Working Conference on Communications and Multimedia Security, pp. 107–121. Kluwer, B. V, Dordrecht (2002)
4. Kamvar, S.D., Schlosser, M.T., Garcia-Molina, H.: The eigentrust algorithm for reputation management in P2P networks. In: WWW 2003: Proceedings of the 12th International Conference on World Wide Web, pp. 640–651. ACM, New York (2003)

 5. Srivatsa, M., Xiong, L., Liu, L.: Trustguard: countering vulnerabilities in reputation management for decentralized overlay networks. In: WWW 2005: Proceeding of the 14th international conference on World Wide Web, pp. 422–431. ACM, New York (2005)
 6. Nandi, A., Ngan, T.W., Singh, A., Druschel, P., Wallach, D.S.: Scrivener: Providing incentives in cooperative content distribution systems. In: Alonso, G. (ed.) Middleware 2005. LNCS, vol. 3790, pp. 270–291. Springer, Heidelberg (2005)
 7. Aringhieri, R., Damiani, E., Vimercati, S.D.C.D., Paraboschi, S., Samarati, P.: Fuzzy techniques for trust and reputation management in anonymous peer-to-peer systems. J. Am. Soc. Inf. Sci. Technol. 57(4), 528–537 (2006)
 8. Walsh, K., Sirer, E.G.: Experience with an object reputation system for peer-to-peer filesharing. In: NSDI 2006: Proceedings of the 3rd conference on 3rd Symposium on Networked Systems Design & Implementation. USENIX Association (2006)
 9. Hoffman, K., Zage, D., Nita-Rotaru, C.: A survey of attack and defense techniques for reputation systems. Technical report, Purdue University (2007)
10. Lv, Q., Cao, P., Cohen, E., Li, K., Shenker, S.: Search and replication in unstructured peer-to-peer networks. In: ICS 2002: Proceedings of the 16th international conference on Supercomputing, pp. 84–95. ACM, New York (2002)
11. Jøsang, A., Gray, E., Kinateder, M.: Simplification and analysis of transitive trust networks. Web Intelligence and Agent Systems 4(2), 139–161 (2006)
12. Mahoney, G., Myrvold, W., Shoja, G.C.: Generic reliability trust model. In: Third Annual Conference on Privacy, Security and Trust (2005)
13. Ball, M.O., Magnanti, T.L., Monma, C.L., Nmehauser, G.L.: Network Models. North Holland, Amsterdam (1995)
14. Fishman, G.S.: Monte Carlo: concepts, algorithms, and applications. Springer, Heidelberg (1995)
15. Jesi, G.P.: Peersim: A peer-to-peer simulator (2004), http://peersim.sourceforge.net
16. Albert, R., Barabási, A.: Statistical mechanics of complex networks. Reviews of Modern Physics 74 (2002)
17. Gnutella: The Gnutella Protocol Specification v0.4 (2001)
18. Yang, B., Garcia-Molina, H.: Improving search in peer-to-peer networks. In: ICDCS 2002: Proceedings of the 22nd International Conference on Distributed Computing Systems, pp. 5–14. IEEE Computer Society, Los Alamitos (2002)
19. Defude, B.: P2P simulation with peersim (January 2007), http://stromboli3.int-edu.eu/ bernard/ASR/projets/soutenances/ Ranaivo-Sabourin/rapport-Simulation_P2P.pdf
20. Cochran, W.: Sampling Techniques, 3rd edn. Wiley and Sons, Chichester (1977)

Approximation for Multi-service Systems with Reservation by Systems with Limited-Availability

Maciej Stasiak and Sławomir Hanczewski

Chair of Telecommunication and Computer Networks,
Poznań University of Technology,
Piotrowo 3A, 60-965 Poznań, Poland
Tel.: +48 61 6653905, Fax: +48 61 6653922
{stasiak,shancz}@et.put.poznan.pl
http://www.et.put.poznan.pl

Abstract. The paper presents a new method for modeling systems with reservation. The method is based on the generalized ideal grading model servicing multi-rate traffic. The paper proposes an algorithm for determining such an availability value in the ideal grading that causes blocking equalization of different classes of calls. The proposed method was worked out for integer and non-integer values of the availability parameters. A comparison of the analytical results with the simulation data proves high accuracy of the proposed method.

Keywords: Markov Processes, reservation, Erlang's ideal grading, availability.

1 Introduction

The ideal grading model with single-service traffic is one of the oldest traffic engineering models. The appropriate formula to determine the blocking probability in the group was worked out by A. K. Erlang as early as 1917 [1]. The formula is called Erlang's interconnection formula. Even though the ideal grading did not find any practical applications in the past due to a large number of load groups, the system was used for many years for approximate modeling of other telecommunications systems [2]. As it turned out that the characteristics and properties of the majority of homogenous grading were similar to those of ideal limited-availability groups. For example, the Erlang's ideal grading was used for modeling outgoing groups in single-service and multi-service switching networks [3], [4]. The ideal grading was also used to model switching networks with multicast connections [5]. In [8], an approximate ideal grading model servicing multi-rate traffic, which assumes identical availability value for all classes of calls, is proposed. The present paper proposes a generalized model of the ideal grading servicing multi-rate traffic in which each call class is characterized by a different availability. Such an approach has made it possible to model the values of the blocking probabilities of particular classes depending on the changes in

N. Thomas and C. Juiz (Eds.): EPEW 2008, LNCS 5261, pp. 257–267, 2008.

the value of the availability parameter. The paper shows that with appropriately matched availability parameters in the ideal grading it is possible to equalize all blocking probabilities, which is, in fact, equivalent to the operation of the reservation mechanism in the full-availability group with multi-rate traffic. The paper also proposes an appropriate algorithm for determining such an availability value that effects in the blocking equalization in different classes of calls.

The obtained results are promising and indicate further possibilities in implementing the generalized formula of the ideal grading model in determining characteristics and properties of other systems. This approach can also be very effective in modeling systems for 3G mobile networks.

2   State-Dependent Multi-rate System

Let us consider a multi-rate system with a capacity of V basic bandwidth units (BBU)[1]. The system services M independent classes of Poisson traffic streams having the intensities: $\lambda_1, \lambda_2, \ldots, \lambda_M$. A class i call requires t_i basic bandwidth units to set up a connection. The holding time for the calls of particular classes has an exponential distribution with the parameters: $\mu_1, \mu_2, \ldots, \mu_M$. Thus the mean traffic offered to the system by the class i traffic stream is equal to:

$$a_i = \lambda_i / \mu_i. \tag{1}$$

The multi-rate systems can be determined by the multi-dimensional Markov process. This process cannot be used for practical calculations because of an excessive number of states in which the process can be found. However, in many cases the multi-dimensional process can be approximated by the one-dimensional Markov chain, which can be described by the so-called generalised Kaufman-Roberts recursion[9], [10]:

$$nP(n) = \sum_{i=1}^{M} a_i t_i \sigma_i \left(n - t_i \right) P \left(n - t_i \right), \tag{2}$$

where:
$P(n)$ – the state probability, i.e. the probability of an event that there are n busy BBUs in the system,
$\sigma_i(n)$ – the conditional probability of passing between the adjacent states of the process associated with the class i call stream. The way of determining the value of this parameter depends on the kind of a considered state-dependent system. If the probabilities of passing are equal to one for all states, the equation (2) is reduced to the Kaufman-Roberts recursion [6], [7]:

$$nP(n) = \sum_{i=1}^{M} a_i t_i P \left(n - t_i \right), \tag{3}$$

---

[1] The BBU is defined as the greatest common divisor of equivalent bandwidths of all call streams offered to the system [12].

Formula (3) determines the occupancy distribution in the state independent system i.e. full-availability group with multi-rate traffic streams.

The conditional probability of passing $(\sigma_i(n))$ in the state-dependent system (equation (2)) can be written as follows:

$$\sigma_i(n) = 1 - \gamma_i(n), \tag{4}$$

where $\gamma_i(n)$ is the blocking probability for class i calls in a considered system, calculated on the assumption that in this system n BBUs are busy. Therefore, the total blocking probability in the state-dependent multi-rate system for class i calls can be expressed by the following formula:

$$E_i = \sum_{n=0}^{V} \gamma_i(n)P(n), \tag{5}$$

Figure 1 shows a graphic interpretation of the process represented by the equation (2) for two class calls ($t_1 = 1$, $t_2 = 2$). The symbol $y_i(n)$ denotes the reverse transition rates of a class i service stream outgoing from state n [11]. The values of the parameters, however, are not needed for a determination of the occupancy distribution in a state-dependent system (equations (2)).

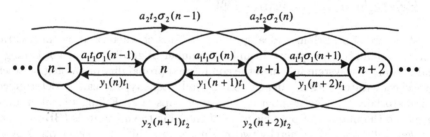

Fig. 1. A fragment of one-dimensional Markov chain in the state-dependent multi-rate system ($t_1 = 1$, $t_2 = 2$)

3   Full-Availability Group with Reservation (FAGR)

The aim of the introduction of the reservation mechanism in telecommunications systems is to ensure similar values of the parameters of the quality of servicing for calls of different classes. For this purpose, the reservation threshold Q_i for each traffic class is designated. The parameter Q_i determines the borderline state of a system, in which servicing class i calls is still possible. All states higher than Q_i belong to the so called reservation space R_i, in which class i calls will be blocked:

$$R_i = V - Q_i. \tag{6}$$

According to the equalisation rule [13], [14], [15], the blocking probability in the full-availability group will be the same for all call stream classes if the reservation threshold for all traffic classes is identical and equal to the difference between the total capacity of a group and the value of resources required by the call of maximum demands $(t_M = t_{max})$:

$$Q = V - t_M. \tag{7}$$

The occupancy distribution in the full-availability group with reservation (FAGR) can be calculated on the basis of equation (2) in which conditional probabilities of passing are determined in the following way:

$$\sigma_i(n) = \{ \begin{matrix} 0 \text{ for } n > Q \\ 1 \text{ for } n \leq Q \end{matrix} \tag{8}$$

Such a definition of the parameter $\sigma_i(n)$ means that in states higher than Q (reservation space), calls of all traffic classes will be blocked.

The equalized blocking probability for all traffic classes in the FAGR can be determined as follows:

$$E_i = \sum_{n=Q+1}^{V} P(n). \tag{9}$$

4   Erlang's Ideal Grading (EIG)

The structure of an Erlang's ideal grading (EIG) is characterized by three parameters: availability d, capacity V and the number of grading groups g. Erlang's ideal grading is a system in which the conditional probability of passing between the adjacent states does not depend on the call intensity, and can be determined combinatorially [1]. The number of grading groups of an Erlang's ideal grading is equal to the number of possible ways of choosing the d channels (BBUs) from their general number V, whereby two grading groups differ from each other by at least one channel. This means that, a separate grading group is intended for each possible combination of d channels. With the same traffic offered to all grading groups and the random hunting strategy, the load of each channel of an Erlang's ideal grading is identical. Moreover, for each combination of busy channels, the occupancy distribution in each grading group is the same. This means, that for an arbitrary "busy" state in n channels $(0 \leq n \leq V)$ in the considered grading, no matter how many n channels from among the possible V channels are busy, the probability of busy j channels of a given grading group $(0 \leq n \leq V)$ is equal to the probability of busy j channels in each other grading group.

4.1   Generalized Model of Erlang's Ideal Grading

In [8], a model of the ideal grading with multi-rate traffic is proposed. The model assumes that the availability for all classes of calls is the same.

Let us consider now the generalized model in which each call class is characterized by a different availability. This means that a different number of grading

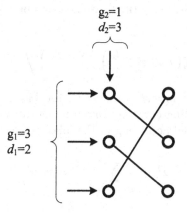

Fig. 2. Model of the ideal grading with different availabilities

groups is related to each of the call class. Figure 2 shows a simple model of the ideal grading with the capacity $V = 3$ BBU's. The group services two classes of calls with the availability $d_1 = 2$, $d_2 = 3$. Hence, the number of load groups for relevant call classes is equal to:

$$g_1 = \binom{V}{d_1} = \binom{3}{2} = 3, \ g_2 = \binom{V}{d_2} = \binom{3}{3} = 1$$

The occupancy distribution in an Erlang's ideal grading with multi-rate traffic can be determined on the basis of the recursive formula (2). To determine conditional blocking probabilities in the ideal grading with different availabilities for different call classes, model [8] is used, in which the parameters related to a given call of class i are made dependent on the availability d_i attributed to this class (in model [8] these parameters were dependent on the shared availability d). Due to ideal grading definition, the distribution of busy outgoing BBU's is identical in each group and the conditional probability of blocking of class i calls is equal to the blocking probability in one (given) grading group:

$$\gamma_i(n) = P_{i,n} = \sum_{x=d_i-t_i+1}^{k_i} P_{V,d_i}(n,x), \tag{10}$$

where:
$k_i = n$, if $(d_i - t_i + 1) \leq (n) < d_i$,
$k_i = d_i$, if $n \geq d$.

The parameter $P_{V,d_i}(n,x)$, is the conditional probability of x busy BBU's in one grading group, when the total number of busy BBU's in the system is equal to n. The probability $P_{V,d_i}(n, x)$ can be described by the hypergeometrical distribution [8]:

$$P_{V,d_i}(n, x) = \binom{d_i}{x} \binom{V - d_i}{n - x} \Big/ \binom{V}{n}. \tag{11}$$

After determining all probabilities $\gamma_i(n)$, the blocking probability for class i calls in the ideal grading carrying a mixture of different multichannel traffic streams can be calculated according to the following formula:

$$E_i = \sum_{n=d_i-t_i+1}^{V} P(n)\gamma_i(n). \tag{12}$$

4.2 Generalized Model of Erlang's Ideal Grading for Non-integer Availability

Formulae (10)–(12) enable to determine the values of blocking probabilities in the ideal grading only for integer values of the parameter d_i. Therefore, a special method for determining the values of the blocking probability in the ideal grading for non-integer value of the availability parameter has been worked out. In the proposed method (when the value of the parameter d_i takes on non-integer values), a given call of class i is replaced by two fictitious classes with appropriately attributed integer availability values (d_{i1}, d_{i2}) and the offered traffic (A_{i1}, A_{i2}). The values of these parameters are defined in the following way:

$$d_{i1} = \lfloor d_i \rfloor, \tag{13}$$

$$d_{i2} = \lceil d_i \rceil. \tag{14}$$

The traffic offered by the new fictitious call classes is respectively equal to:

$$A_{i1} = A_i[1 - (d_i - d_{i1})], \tag{15}$$

$$A_{i2} = A_i(d_i - d_{i1}), \tag{16}$$

where the difference $(d_i - d_{i1})$ determines the fractional part of the parameter d_i. Such a definition of the parameters A_{i1}, A_{i2}, d_{i1}, d_{i2} means that the values of the fictitious traffic A_{i2} is directly proportional to the fractional part of the availability parameter, i.e. to $\Delta_i = d_i - d_{i1}$, while the value of the fictitious traffic A_{i1} is directly proportional to the complement Δ_i , i.e. to the value $1 - \Delta_i = 1 - (d_i - d_{i1})$.

Let us consider an ideal grading with the capacity V and the number of serviced traffic classes equal to M. To simplify the description, let us assume that only the availability parameter of one class, i.e. of class i, takes on non-integer values. After replacing class i with two fictitious classes: $i1$ and $i2$, with the attributed availability values d_{i1}, d_{i2} and the traffic intensity A_{i1}, A_{i2} (formulae

(13)–(16)), it is possible, on the basis of (10)–(12), to determine blocking probabilities of all call classes, including the blocking probabilities of new classes of calls E_{i1} and E_{i2} . Now the blocking probability of calls of class i for non-integer availability d_i can be determined (estimated) in the following way:

$$ E_i = \frac{A_{i1}E_{i1} + A_{i2}E_{i2}}{A_i}. \tag{17} $$

In the case of a greater number of classes with non-integer availability, each call class is replaced with two fictitious classes with the parameters determined by formulae (13)–(16). Further calculations are performed in the same way as in the case of two call classes. The results of the simulation experiments carried out by the authors of the article have entirely confirmed high accuracy of the proposed solution.

5 Blocking Probability Equalization in Erlang's Ideal Grading with Multi-rate Traffic

Let us consider an ideal grading servicing two classes of calls. The calls of particular classes require respectively t_1 and t_2 BBUs ($t_1 < t_2$). The capacity of the group is equal to V, while the availability for each of the classes varies and equals respectively d_1 and d_2. In the considered group, changes in the value of the parameters d_1 and d_2 will result in changes in respective values of blocking probabilities of individual classes. In a particular case, it is possible to equalize the blocking probability of all serviced classes of calls. The study carried out by the authors has proved that the lowest value of the equalized blocking probability is obtained under the assumption that the availability of the second class of calls is constant and is equal to the capacity of the system, i.e. $d_2 = V$. Additionally, it turned out that the defined equalized blocking probability in the ideal grading following the above assumption is the same as the equalized blocking probability in the full-availability group with reservation (assuming the same capacity of the systems and the identical structure of the offered traffic). In order to determine the value of the parameter d_1 that effects in the equalization of blocking probabilities of serviced calls, the following iterative algorithm can be employed. In the first step of the algorithm, the initial value of the parameter d_1 is assumed (for example, $d_1^{(0)} = t_1$) and the blocking probability $E_1^{(1)}$ and $E_2^{(1)}$ is determined:

$$ (E_1^{(1)}, E_2^{(1)}) = F(A_1, t_1, d_1^{(0)}, A_2, t_2, d_2 = V), \tag{18} $$

where the function F determines blocking probabilities of calls in the ideal grading on the basis of formulae (10)–(12).

Each step of the iteration determines the successive values of the blocking probability on the basis of the value of the parameter d_1, determined in the previous step of the iteration, while the remaining parameters of the function F

do not change:

$$(E_1^{(n)}, E_2^{(n)}) = F(A_1, t_1, d_1^{(n-1)}, A_2, t_2, d_2 = V). \qquad (19)$$

The iterative process terminates when the following condition is met:

$$\frac{\left| |E_1^{(n-1)} - E_2^{(n-1)}| - |E_1^{(n)} - E_2^{(n)}| \right|}{|E_1^{(n)} - E_2^{(n)}|} < \epsilon \qquad (20)$$

where ϵ is the relative error assumed in the calculation. The availability parameter in each of the steps of the process is determined in the following way:

$$d_1^{(n)} = d_1^{(n-1)} + \Delta d^{(n)} \qquad (21)$$

where $\Delta d^{(0)} = 1$. The values of the successive increments of the availability depend on the mutual relationships of blocking probabilities. Therefore, before the determination of the increment $\Delta d^{(n)}$, the following additional condition is checked in each of the steps of the iterative process:

$$E_1^{(n)} > E_2^{(n)} \qquad (22)$$

If the condition (22) is fulfilled, i.e. the blocking probability $E_1^{(n)}$ is greater than $E_2^{(n)}$, then the value of the parameter $d_1^{(n)}$ is increased by the adopted value $\Delta d^{(n)} = \Delta d^{(n-1)}$. Otherwise, the availability value for the next step will be determined on the basis of the following formula:

$$d_1^{(n)} = d_1^{(n-1)} - \Delta d^{(n-1)} + \Delta d^{(n)} \qquad (23)$$

where a new value of the increment $\Delta d^{(n)}$ is appropriately decreased in relation to $\Delta d^{(n-1)}$ (for example, it is assumed in the article that: $\Delta d^{(n)} = \Delta d^{(n-1)}/10$. Such an approach means that when the value $E_1^{(n)} < E_2^{(n)}$, i.e. when the blocking probability of the second class "exceeds" the value of the blocking probability for the first class, then the algorithm will "retract" to the previous step (in which $E_1^{(n)} > E_2^{(n)}$), and, in the next step, the probability E_1 starts to approach the probability E_2 with lower availability increments.

6   Numerical Examples

To prove the accuracy and correctness of the proposed analytical model, the results of the analytical calculations were compared with the results of the simulation experiments with sample groups. The operation of the proposed model is presented with the example of the Erlang's ideal grading with the capacity of

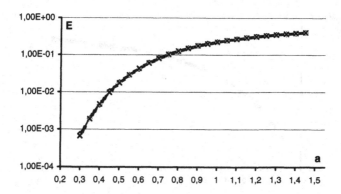

Fig. 3. Blocking probability in Erlang's ideal grading ($V = 30$ BBUs). Simulations: EIG ◇ $t_1 = 1$; × $t_2 = 3$; Calculations: EIG —— $t_1 = 1$; – – – $t_2 = 3$; Calculations: FAGR – · — $t_1 = 1$; – – – – $t_2 = 3$.

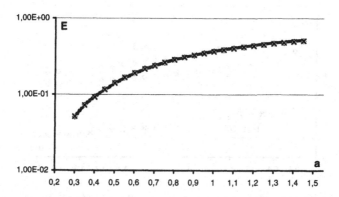

Fig. 4. Blocking probability in Erlang's ideal grading. Simulations: EIG ◇ $t_1 = 1$; × $t_2 = 9$; Calculations: EIG —— $t_1 = 1$; – – – $t_2 = 9$; Calculations: FAGR – · — $t_1 = 1$; – – – – $t_2 = 9$.

$V = 30$ BBU's servicing two classes of calls. Further diagrams show the results for the following mixture of classes: $t_1 = 1$, $t_2 = 3$, $a_1 : a_2 = 1 : 1$ (Figure 3), $t_1 = 1$, $t_2 = 9$, $a_1 : a_2 = 1 : 1$ (Figure 4), $t_1 = 2$, $t_2 = 5$, $a_1 : a_2 = 1 : 1$ (Figure 5) in relation to the offered to one BBU: $a = \sum_{i=1}^{M} \frac{a_i t_i}{V}$. The diagrams also show the results of the calculations obtained for the full-availability group with multi-rate traffic and reservation that equalize losses, i.e. the reservation space $R = t_2$. A comparison of the results for the Erlang's ideal grading and the full-availability group with reservation shows that the blocking probability equalization in both systems takes on identical values. Thus, systems with reservation can be modeled by the Erlang's ideal grading. Diagram 6 presents the changes in the parameter d_1 (in the function of traffic offered to one BBU of the group) that effect in the equalization of the blocking probability in the ideal grading. It is noticeable that

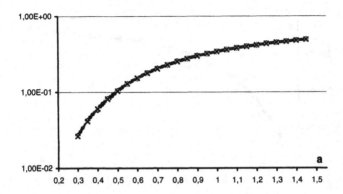

Fig. 5. Blocking probability in Erlang's ideal grading. Simulations: EIG ◇ $t_1 = 2$; ✕ $t_2 = 7$; Calculations: EIG ——— $t_1 = 2$; − − − $t_2 = 7$; Calculations: FAGR − · — $t_1 = 2$; − · · − $t_2 = 7$.

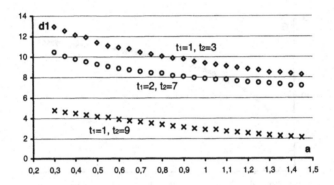

Fig. 6. Changes in parameter d_1 in relation to offered traffic

the value of the parameter d_1, with which the equalization of losses ensues, is not constant and decreases with the increase of the offered traffic. All the results presented in the diagrams confirm the accuracy of the adopted assumptions for the analytical model.

7   Conclusions

The article presents a method for modeling systems with reservation by limited-availability systems. The operation of the method is based on a generalized Erlang's ideal grading servicing multi-rate traffic. In order to increase the accuracy of the model, a special algorithm for determining all parameters of a limited-availability system has been worked out under the assumption that availabilities of individual classes of calls can take on non-integer values. A comparison of the analytical results with the simulation numerical results proves high accuracy of the proposed method. The obtained results indicate a possibility of implementing the generalized model of Erlang's ideal grading in determining characteristics of other systems. Such an approach can prove very beneficial in the case of modeling systems in 3G mobile networks.

References

1. Brockmeyer, E., Halstrom, H., Jensen, A.: The life and works of A. K. Erlang. Acta Polytechnica Scandinavica 287 (1960)
2. Lotze, A.: History and development of grading theory. In: 5th International Teletraffic Congress, New York, pp. 148–161 (1967)
3. Ershova, E.B., Ershov, V.A.: Cifrowyje sistiemy raspriedielenia informacji. Radio i swiaz, Moscow (1983) (in Russian)
4. Stasiak, M.: Blocage interne point a point dans les reseaux de connexion. Ann. Telecommun. 43, 561–575 (1988)
5. Hanczewski, S., Stasiak, M.: Point-to-group blocking in 3-stage switching networks with multicast traffic streams. In: Dini, P., Lorenz, P., de Souza, J.N. (eds.) SAPIR 2004. LNCS, vol. 3126, pp. 219–230. Springer, Heidelberg (2004)
6. Kaufman, J.S.: Blocking in shared resource environment. IEEE Transactions on Communications 29, 1474–1481 (1981)
7. Roberts, J.W.: A service system with heterogeneous user requirements. Performance of data communications systems and their applications. Nort Holland Pub. Co., Amsterdam (1981)
8. Stasiak, M.: An approximate model of a switching network carrying mixture of different multichannel traffic streams. IEEE Transactions on Communications 41, 836–840 (1993)
9. Beshai, M., Manfield, D.: Multichannel services performance of switching networks. In: 12th International Teletraffic Congress, Torino, Italy, pp. 857–864 (1988)
10. Stasiak, M.: Blocking probability in a limited-availability group carrying mixture of different multichannel traffic streams. Annals of Telecommunications 48, 71–76 (1993)
11. Stasiak, M., Glabowski, M.: A simple approximation of the link model with reservation by a one-dimensional Markov chain. Journal of Performance Evaluation 41, 195–208 (2000)
12. Roberts, J.W., Mocci, V., Virtamo, I. (eds.): Broadband Network Teletraffic. Final Report of Action COST 242. Commission of the European Communities. Springer, Heidelberg (1996)
13. Roberts, J.W. (ed.): Performance Evaluation and Design of Multiservice Networks. Final Report COST 224. Commission of the European Communities (1992)
14. Roberts, J.W.: Teletraffic models for the Telcom 1 integrated services network. In: 10th International Teletraffic Congress, Montreal, Canada, p. 1.1.2 (1983)
15. Tran-Gia, P., Hubner, F.: An analysis of trunk reservation and grade of service balancing mechanisms in multiservice broadband networks. In: International Teletraffic Congress Seminar: Modeling and Performance evaluation of ATM technology, La Martynique, pp. 83–97 (1993)

Author Index

Lecture Notes in Computer Science

Sublibrary 2: Programming and Software Engineering

For information about Vols. 1– 4589
please contact your bookseller or Springer

Vol. 4949: R.M. Hierons, J.P. Bowen, M. Harman (Eds.), Formal Methods and Testing. XIII, 367 pages. 2008.

Vol. 4937: M. Dumas, R. Heckel (Eds.), Web Services and Formal Methods. IX, 169 pages. 2008.

Vol. 4922: M. Broy, I.H. Krüger, M. Meisinger (Eds.), Model-Driven Development of Reliable Automotive Services. XVIII, 183 pages. 2008.

Vol. 4916: S. Leue, P. Merino (Eds.), Formal Methods for Industrial Critical Systems. X, 251 pages. 2008.

Vol. 4909: I. Eusgeld, F.C. Freiling, R. Reussner (Eds.), Dependability Metrics. XI, 305 pages. 2008.

Vol. 4906: M. Cebulla (Ed.), Object-Oriented Technology. VIII, 204 pages. 2008.

Vol. 4902: P. Hudak, D.S. Warren (Eds.), Practical Aspects of Declarative Languages. X, 333 pages. 2007.

Vol. 4899: K. Yorav (Ed.), Hardware and Software: Verification and Testing. XII, 267 pages. 2008.

Vol. 4895: J.J. Cuadrado-Gallego, R. Braungarten, R.R. Dumke, A. Abran (Eds.), Software Process and Product Measurement. X, 203 pages. 2008.

Vol. 4888: F. Kordon, O. Sokolsky (Eds.), Composition of Embedded Systems. XII, 221 pages. 2007.

Vol. 4880: S. Overhage, C.A. Szyperski, R. Reussner, J.A. Stafford (Eds.), Software Architectures, Components, and Applications. X, 249 pages. 2008.

Vol. 4849: M. Winckler, H. Johnson, P. Palanque (Eds.), Task Models and Diagrams for User Interface Design. XIII, 299 pages. 2007.

Vol. 4839: O. Sokolsky, S. Taşıran (Eds.), Runtime Verification. VI, 215 pages. 2007.

Vol. 4834: R. Cerqueira, R.H. Campbell (Eds.), Middleware 2007. XIII, 451 pages. 2007.

Vol. 4829: M. Lumpe, W. Vanderperren (Eds.), Software Composition. VIII, 281 pages. 2007.

Vol. 4824: A. Paschke, Y. Biletskiy (Eds.), Advances in Rule Interchange and Applications. XIII, 243 pages. 2007.

Vol. 4821: J. Bennedsen, M.E. Caspersen, M. Kölling (Eds.), Reflections on the Teaching of Programming. X, 261 pages. 2008.

Vol. 4807: Z. Shao (Ed.), Programming Languages and Systems. XI, 431 pages. 2007.

Vol. 4799: A. Holzinger (Ed.), HCI and Usability for Medicine and Health Care. XVI, 458 pages. 2007.

Vol. 4789: M. Butler, M.G. Hinchey, M.M. Larrondo-Petrie (Eds.), Formal Methods and Software Engineering. VIII, 387 pages. 2007.

Vol. 4767: F. Arbab, M. Sirjani (Eds.), International Symposium on Fundamentals of Software Engineering. XIII, 450 pages. 2007.

Vol. 4765: A. Moreira, J. Grundy (Eds.), Early Aspects: Current Challenges and Future Directions. X, 199 pages. 2007.

Vol. 4764: P. Abrahamsson, N. Baddoo, T. Margaria, R. Messnarz (Eds.), Software Process Improvement. XI, 225 pages. 2007.

Vol. 4762: K.S. Namjoshi, T. Yoneda, T. Higashino, Y. Okamura (Eds.), Automated Technology for Verification and Analysis. XIV, 566 pages. 2007.

Vol. 4758: F. Oquendo (Ed.), Software Architecture. XVI, 340 pages. 2007.

Vol. 4757: F. Cappello, T. Herault, J. Dongarra (Eds.), Recent Advances in Parallel Virtual Machine and Message Passing Interface. XVI, 396 pages. 2007.

Vol. 4753: E. Duval, R. Klamma, M. Wolpers (Eds.), Creating New Learning Experiences on a Global Scale. XII, 518 pages. 2007.

Vol. 4749: B.J. Krämer, K.-J. Lin, P. Narasimhan (Eds.), Service-Oriented Computing – ICSOC 2007. XIX, 629 pages. 2007.

Vol. 4748: K. Wolter (Ed.), Formal Methods and Stochastic Models for Performance Evaluation. X, 301 pages. 2007.

Vol. 4741: C. Bessière (Ed.), Principles and Practice of Constraint Programming – CP 2007. XV, 890 pages. 2007.

Vol. 4735: G. Engels, B. Opdyke, D.C. Schmidt, F. Weil (Eds.), Model Driven Engineering Languages and Systems. XV, 698 pages. 2007.

Vol. 4716: B. Meyer, M. Joseph (Eds.), Software Engineering Approaches for Offshore and Outsourced Development. X, 201 pages. 2007.

Vol. 4709: F.S. de Boer, M.M. Bonsangue, S. Graf, W.-P. de Roever (Eds.), Formal Methods for Components and Objects. VIII, 297 pages. 2007.

Vol. 4680: F. Saglietti, N. Oster (Eds.), Computer Safety, Reliability, and Security. XV, 548 pages. 2007.

Vol. 4670: V. Dahl, I. Niemelä (Eds.), Logic Programming. XII, 470 pages. 2007.

Vol. 4652: D. Georgakopoulos, N. Ritter, B. Benatallah, C. Zirpins, G. Feuerlicht, M. Schoenherr, H.R. Motahari-Nezhad (Eds.), Service-Oriented Computing ICSOC 2006. XVI, 201 pages. 2007.

Vol. 4640: A. Rashid, M. Aksit (Eds.), Transactions on Aspect-Oriented Software Development IV. IX, 191 pages. 2007.

Vol. 4634: H. Riis Nielson, G. Filé (Eds.), Static Analysis. XI, 469 pages. 2007.

Vol. 4620: A. Rashid, M. Aksit (Eds.), Transactions on Aspect-Oriented Software Development III. IX, 201 pages. 2007.

Vol. 4615: R. de Lemos, C. Gacek, A. Romanovsky (Eds.), Architecting Dependable Systems IV. XIV, 435 pages. 2007.

Vol. 4610: B. Xiao, L.T. Yang, J. Ma, C. Muller-Schloer, Y. Hua (Eds.), Autonomic and Trusted Computing. XVIII, 571 pages. 2007.

Vol. 4609: E. Ernst (Ed.), ECOOP 2007 – Object-Oriented Programming. XIII, 625 pages. 2007.

Vol. 4608: H.W. Schmidt, I. Crnković, G.T. Heineman, J.A. Stafford (Eds.), Component-Based Software Engineering. XII, 283 pages. 2007.

Vol. 4591: J. Davies, J. Gibbons (Eds.), Integrated Formal Methods. IX, 660 pages. 2007.